Disputing Disaster

BY THE SAME AUTHOR

Passages from Antiquity to Feudalism
Lineages of the Absolutist State

Considerations on Western Marxism
Arguments within English Marxism
In the Tracks of Historical Materialism
The Antinomies of Antonio Gramsci

English Questions
A Zone of Engagement
The Origins of Postmodernity
Spectrum
The H-Word

The New Old World
Ever Closer Union?
American Foreign Policy and Its Thinkers
The Indian Ideology
Brazil Apart

Different Speeds, Same Furies

Disputing Disaster

A Sextet on the Great War

PERRY ANDERSON

VERSO
London • New York

First published by Verso 2024
© Perry Anderson 2024

All rights reserved

The moral rights of the author have been asserted

1 3 5 7 9 10 8 6 4 2

Verso
UK: 6 Meard Street, London W1F 0EG
US: 388 Atlantic Avenue, Brooklyn, NY 11217
versobooks.com

Verso is the imprint of New Left Books

ISBN-13: 978-1-80429-767-4
ISBN-13: 978-1-80429-770-4 (UK EBK)
ISBN-13: 978-1-80429-771-1 (US EBK)

British Library Cataloguing in Publication Data
A catalogue record for this book is available from the British Library

Library of Congress Cataloging-in-Publication Data

Names: Anderson, Perry, author.
Title: Disputing disaster : a sextet on the Great War / Perry Anderson.
Other titles: Sextet on the Great War
Description: London ; New York : Verso Books, 2024. | Includes bibliographical references and index.
Identifiers: LCCN 2024023480 (print) | LCCN 2024023481 (ebook) | ISBN 9781804297674 (hardback) | ISBN 9781804297711 (ebk)
Subjects: LCSH: World War, 1914–1918 – Historiography. | World War, 1914–1918 – Origins. | Military historians – Biography.
Classification: LCC D522.42 .A524 2024 (print) | LCC D522.42 (ebook) | DDC 940.40072/2 – dc23/eng/20240604
LC record available at https://lccn.loc.gov/2024023480
LC ebook record available at https://lccn.loc.gov/2024023481

Typeset in Fournier MT by Hewer Text UK Ltd, Edinburgh
Printed and bound by CPI Group (UK) Ltd, Croydon CR0 4YY

CONTENTS

Foreword vii

1. Pierre Renouvin 1
2. Luigi Albertini 49
3. Fritz Fischer 91
4. Keith Wilson 139
5. Christopher Clark 181
6. Paul Schroeder 263

Acknowledgements 359

Index 361

FOREWORD

Some seventy years after the end of the First World War, argument over it had by one estimate already generated some 25,000 books and articles. Today, after over a century, the figure would be far higher. There is no way the Great War can be considered without some reference to this literature, and respect for the accumulated research and scholarship to which so many historians have devoted their lives. Respect is such only if it is critical, in the lucid – clear-eyed, rather than carping – sense of the term, as a normal practice of the profession. Less normal, but in this field more necessary than elsewhere, is contextualization: that is, attention not just to the quality of a body of work, but to the background informing it. In the case of the First World War, about which strong feelings and incompatible opinions have lasted longer than any comparable event in history, there are two obvious coordinates of the relevant background. The first is simply national: the war pitted six major states in Europe, and seven lesser ones, against each other, all in the name of patriotic defence of the homeland, and drew in two further major states, one in Asia and the other in America. Inevitably, historians of the war were never likely to be indifferent to the traditions and passions of their country; many, though over time not all, were dominated by them. The Great War, however, was not just a conflict between nations, but also one which catalysed a wide gamut of ideological reactions to it, within and across nations, during the fighting and after it. From the start the historiography of the disaster was thus highly charged – overdetermined – by politics, as it has remained.

The lines of division within it were also to be, from the outset too, intellectual. Where should causation start? Ought it to focus on the summer of 1914, when the assassination of the Archduke Franz Ferdinand caught all Europe by surprise, and in short order – scarcely more than a month later – unleashed the Great War? Or on the prior polarization of the continent into rival alliances? Alternatively, should its seeds be sought further back in time? By and large, the historical literature has elected one of two options, either focussing on short-term processes whose connexion with the outbreak of hostilities is plain and direct, or longer-term shifts of more tectonic and less immediately visible effect – one viewpoint principally concerned with events, the other with structures. Within each rough category, there was always room for differences: which period of events to take as critical, which kind of structures to identify as fundamental. If national and ideological leanings have often been markers in the field, which do not necessarily coincide, epistemological preferences offer another, at an angle to them.

Massive though the historiography of the First World War has long been, scrutiny of it remains far less; indeed surprisingly modest. Book-length treatments of the debates it has occasioned appear to have been thus far just three in number.[1] That this disproportion

---

1. One is John Langdon, *July 1914: The Long Debate, 1918–1990*, New York-Oxford 1991; another is Annika Mombauer, *The Origins of the First World War: Controversies and Consensus*, London-New York 2002. Both are heavily weighted towards German debates on the subject. The first has for many years been out of

should be so extreme is in some ways understandable. Not just because historians naturally prefer first-order investigations to second-order ones about them, but in this case also for more specific reasons. Though disagreements are bread and butter among them, professional etiquette in general restrains these from taking too personal or political a form, breaching the value of a shared community of scholars. Since, famously, the First World War has always aroused political passions, treatments of it from a standpoint at variance with them risk becoming particularly delicate, discouraging the kind of contextualization they might otherwise suggest. Philological attention to texts, a requirement for thinking about the pattern of scholarship on the war, is in any case foreign to many practising historians, while those for whom it is a necessity – essentially, intellectual historians – are typically attracted to bodies of work of a theoretical bent, in the fields of political or scientific thought, rather than of empirical research into events of the past. Such may be some of the reasons for the relative paucity of analytic considerations about so vast a literature as that to which the Great War continues to give rise.

In adding to the limited stock of reflections on the historiography of what George Kennan termed 'the seminal disaster of the twentieth century', I have thought it more productive to take a few exemplary cases than to attempt an overall survey of the boundless expanse of literature about it. What principles of selection govern those examined

---

print; the second has been replaced by an expanded and updated new edition this year, *The Causes of the First World War: The Long Blame Game*; a third, antithetical in stance, came out a little earlier: Troy Paddock, *Contesting the Origins of the First World War*, New York 2021. Of articles dealing with the same subject the most substantial is Gordon Martel's 'Explaining World War One: debating the causes', in Nicholas Atkin and Michael Biddiss (eds), *Themes in Modern European History, 1890–1945*, London–New York 2009, pp. 117–45.

here? One that is straightforward, and two that are questions of judgment, which do not necessarily coincide. The war in Europe was eventually fought between seven major powers, and accounts of its outbreak were subsequently generated in each of those that survived it – England, France, Germany, Italy and the United States. Imperial Russia and Austro-Hungary, which did not, were succeeded by states that lacked ideological or territorial continuity with their previous incarnations. They therefore did not possess the same need for an ensuing justification (or eventual rejection) of their actions before or during the war, so did not produce a comparable body of historical work about it. Choice has therefore fallen on a leading historian from each of the other five major countries involved in the European conflict, together with one of its minor belligerents. By what criteria have I picked the individual writers within this set of states? My selection has been governed by two: impact – inside or outside their own country – and originality. Of these, originality is certainly the more important, and at the limit suffices, as impact alone does not, though in all but one of the cases studied here, the two have gone together. The range of figures discussed in these pages is a subjective choice, not an objective elite; it implies no derogation of alternatives.

As a contribution to the field of second-order reflection on the First World War, the studies which follow may be of interest – though there can be no certainty of this – by reason either of the length at which they consider each of their subjects, greater than previously conceded them, or the relative novelty of the discoveries they offer about them.[2] The order in which the six historians I consider appear

---

2. There is some relationship between the two. Mombauer's massive reworking of her study of 2002 suggests why. Encompassing a bibliography that lists close to a thousand titles, its scale necessarily precludes extended treatment of any of the writers it covers, while containing much else of interest as a conscientious

is chronological, not by birth but by composition of their work on the First World War. First comes Pierre Renouvin (1893–1974), a *mutilé de guerre* who produced at the age of thirty-two the first scholarly study of the origins of the war to be published in any country: sober, careful and loyal to the cause of his country and the Entente. By then, close to Poincaré who had taken the country into the war, and ruled it as prime minister in the twenties, Renouvin was already lecturing at the Sorbonne, where he rose to become not only the leading authority on the conflict in France, and holder of its first chair in contemporary history, but an academic eminence of legendary power, who after 1945 introduced the study of international relations as a discipline to the country. During the Second World War, it has recently been revealed, he kept a Parisian journal under the German occupation recording his assessment of the course of the struggle, probably intended as material for a book on the war after it was over, in which he expressed approval of the conduct of Pétain, up to the moment when Anglo-American forces landed in North Africa. The diary, which he never mentioned and alters our understanding of Renouvin, remains under lock and key. But what it contains has been described with care by a good historian given access to it.

The next figure discussed is Luigi Albertini (1871–1941), the Italian newspaper editor, proprietor, and politician whose monumental trilogy on the origins of the First World War was published in Milan in 1943. When it appeared, Allied landings in Sicily were only two months away, and once Italy became a war-zone, notice taken of the book naturally ceased. After the war it had to wait seventy-five years to be republished in the country where it was written. Neglect at home, however, was

---

adjustment of convictions formed in the nineties to arguments and evidence that have emerged in the course of this century, without abandoning them.

overshadowed by success abroad. Translated into English in the 1950s, it was soon recognized as by far the fullest and most balanced work ever to have been written on the subject, establishing itself as the gold standard for scholarship on the outbreak of the Great War, a position it would retain for half a century. But though the book came to acquire such widespread authority, its author has remained little known outside Italy, and – more surprisingly – little studied even in Italy, although he was a central figure in the political and cultural landscape of the country across the first quarter of the twentieth century. The reason, I suggest, lies in the ambivalence felt by the generations since 1945 towards Albertini's record as a politician – one who actively assisted Mussolini's rise to power, praising or defending fascism until he broke with the regime in 1925, for which he was evicted from his newspaper, and retired to write his histories. Unlike any other scholar of the First World War, however, he was himself a leading actor in pitching his country into it, as a politician and propagandist for Italian intervention in a conflict he envisaged as cleansing the country of corruption and mediocrity, to release the nation for its true vocation as a Great Power. In disappointment at the outcome, he achieved an equanimity of judgment about the First World War, before Italy joined the slaughter, belied by his ardour for its entry into the struggle.

Attention then turns to Fritz Fischer (1908–99), the German historian of greatest international fame during the Cold War, who owed his reputation to two major books, published respectively in 1961 and 1969. In these he argued that the Second Reich was responsible for launching the First World War as a bid for German domination of Europe and a sizeable overseas empire, after planning for its aggression years in advance of unleashing it. The impact of this body of work in the *Bundesrepublik*, overturning a national consensus dating back to the Weimar period that the charge of war guilt levelled against

Germany in the Treaty of Versailles lacked any historical foundation, was enormous. At first fiercely resisted by the historical profession and political authorities of the day alike, Fischer's findings received growing media support, eventual public and professional acceptance, and ultimately decoration by the state, becoming integral to a new West German identity cleansed of its past. After Fischer's death, archival research began to modify his image, as evidence emerged of youthful connexions to the far right after 1918, and a record of collusion with Nazi ideas and institutions under Hitler, casting doubt on his self-descriptions in the post-war period. Further archival evidence presented here, tending to deepen Fischer's implication with the Third Reich, raises questions about the general record of the profession in Germany during those years, as too about his career as a scholar and consecration as a national icon after the war.

Keith Wilson (1944–2018), two generations younger than Fischer, and nearly four distant from Albertini, is the exception to one of the criteria for the selection of scholars in this book. He had no public reception of any kind, and his professional impact, though not zero, was marginal. He belongs in the company discussed in this book by force of originality alone. For in Britain he was the one radical deviant from a patriotic consensus about the country's role in the outbreak of the First World War. A student at Oxford in the sixties, Wilson seems not to have been affected by the campus unrest of the period. Unremarked, he worked for six years on a doctorate about the complexion of policy-advisory personnel in the Foreign Office during the Liberal regime 1906–14: a text longer than any book he ever wrote, which never saw publication. On display in it was a mind that could not only assemble and master a mass of primary materials empirically, but organize and analyze them sharply and conceptually in ways unfamiliar in Britain. It would be another twelve years before he produced his first book, a collection of essays setting out a stringent overall critique of the orthodox English view of the country's foreign policy in the years leading up to 1914, as rightly vigilant about the menace of Germany to peace in Europe, and innocent of any responsibility for war when the threat from Berlin materialized. Wilson's dissent was more slighted than rebutted; his subsequent developments of it, not infrequently bringing new evidence to light, were ignored completely. Towards the end of his career, Wilson departed from the otherwise Anglocentric focus of his work with a distinctive synoptic account of major cruces and crises in European statecraft from the Congress of Vienna to the Conference at Versailles, ending with the inability in 1914–18 of all the leading powers to curb their imperial drives, as he had previously demonstrated in the case of Britain. Complete silence met this work too.

A generation further on, Christopher Clark (1960–) comes from Australia, a country automatically brigaded as a British dominion into the First World War, where it suffered proportionately higher casualties than Britain itself. *The Sleepwalkers*, a meticulous examination of the way Europe capsized into war, which he published in 2012 and became an international best-seller, exceeded the impact of all its predecessors put together. Surpassing Albertini in the balance of judgment and scope of analysis accorded each of the belligerents, in a work at once more precise and more succinct than the Italian trilogy of the forties, Clark set aside the verdicts of Fischer and his school in Germany, and the traditions descending from Renouvin in France and England, without polemically engaging with either. Retorts from adherents to these in some cases followed, but no sustained engagement with *The Sleepwalkers*, perhaps deterred by its redoubtable authority and success. I suggest a sketch for one that would bring out the critical thrust of Clark's version of the origins of the war more sharply than his book does itself; but at the same time the limitations of the framework in which it sets out its case, and possible conceptual reasons for these. Since the publication of his *magnum opus* on the First World War, Clark has produced another on the European revolutions of 1848–49, comparable in virtuoso compass and fluency to *The Sleepwalkers*, if quite different in object and optic. Yet despite the marked contrasts in period, focus, and timbre between the two books, the new one may throw some light on the older one relevant to it, and in doing so earns inclusion in this one. That, at all events, is the premise of its treatment here, whose good sense or lack of it readers can decide for themselves.

Disputing Disaster ends with an American historian, Paul Schroeder (1927–2020). Since the book begins by pointing out the primacy of the United States in producing the first two large, thoroughly researched interpretations of the causes of the First World War, before any European country could match such an enterprise, it might seem that one or other of their authors – Sidney Bradshaw Fay or Bernadotte Schmitt – would have been the logical candidate for this position, rather than Schroeder, who never published a book, as distinct from essays, on the war at all. The impact of the latter's historical output – essentially, just of his commanding work *The Transformation of European Politics 1763–1848*, which came out in 1994 – was confined to specialists of the period. His texts on the First World War were little known and rarely cited even among those professionally concerned with it, comprising moreover only a tithe of his writing as a whole. Why then Schroeder to conclude this enterprise?

The simple answer is that among American historians he was the greatest mind of his generation or its predecessor. That was so because he combined qualities rarely found together in any scholar: a formidable empirical grasp of events, persons, processes and details across a continent and three centuries, which set a unique benchmark for international history as a modern discipline; a powerful conceptual intelligence and theoretical imagination that gave him an ability to think both systemically about the logic of interstate relations, and longitudinally about their continuities over very extended stretches of time. In bringing these gifts to bear on the question of why the First World War broke out, he arrived at better answers than any of his peers. If he winds up the sequence of historians considered here, however, it is also because his final project, left unfinished at his death, was a book on the war whose composition postdates *The Sleepwalkers*, to which it refers.

In Schroeder's case, it is clear that it makes no sense to detach his formidable bloc of writing on the First World War from all that he wrote about Europe before the final collapse of the Concert of Powers whose construction was the central theme of *The Transformation of European Politics*. Nor, for that matter, to separate his account of the reasons for the war from what followed it: the disintegration of the order of Versailles; the peace of the Cold War built on the defeat of the Third Reich; the end of the Cold War, dissolution of the USSR and proclamation of a New World Order; the descent of America into successive wars in the Middle East, whose fate he predicted before they started, and were still being waged when he died. No other scholar covered the arc of history from the Treaty of Paris in 1763 to the War on Terror of 2001–08, in which the downward spiral towards the Great War came at midpoint in its course, with comparable fluency and assurance. In tracing it, he left not a few hostages to fortune, as any continuum of retrospect and prospect across such a span of time is liable to do, some of which are indicated here. But if any lessons are to be drawn from the fate of Europe's Concert of Powers for our own time, as mechanized war is waged once more across the plains of Ukraine, this is the historian from which to start.

1

PIERRE RENOUVIN

The Treaty of Versailles, which consecrated the victory of the Entente in 1919 by officially assigning guilt for the war to Germany, precipitated the first wave of history on its origins. In response, the Weimar Republic published some fifty volumes of documents from its archives to disprove the charge, followed in due course by documentation upholding it released by Britain and France. Though they recruited historians to help assemble them, the governments that generated these collections carefully vetted them, weeding out material that might damage their respective cases in the service of versions of the past convenient to them. Propaganda of this kind did, however, in due course stimulate and, within limits, enable scholars of more independent mind to produce the beginnings of history proper of the First World War. Unsurprisingly, the country where antithetical versions of it first appeared was not any of the European participants, where patriotic sentiments about the conflict continued to hold sway. It was the United States, a late entrant to the war on the side of the Entente without ever fully assimilating its outlook, where opinion reacted strongly against its participation in the conflict in the aftermath. There elections in 1920 delivered a landslide victory to the Republican Party, whose opposition to Wilson's conduct of the peace had killed US participation in the League of Nations, ushering in a decade of control of the White House under Harding, Coolidge and Hoover. In this climate the ball was set rolling in 1926 by a furious broadside against the Treaty from a sociologist, Harry Elmer Barnes, *The Genesis of the World War: An Introduction to the Problem of War Guilt*, claiming that a Franco-Russian conspiracy had stoked the conflict. A prolific journalist, as well as teacher at Smith College, his book was a popular success, but too overtly polemical to win much professional respect. In 1928, however, a historian at the same institution, Sidney Bradshaw Fay, published the first landmark of serious American scholarship on the conflict, a massive two-volume study entitled *The Origins of the World War*, becoming in due course the authority on the subject at Harvard. Within another two years, a historian at the University of Chicago, Bernadotte Everly Schmitt, produced a work on the same question of comparable size and standing, but opposite standpoint. Both authors came from academic families. Internationally, their two books commanded the field in the United States in the interwar period.

Fay — the older of the pair by a decade (b. 1876) — had spent a year at the Sorbonne and another at the university in Berlin before completing his doctorate at Harvard in 1900. Meticulous in research and mild in disposition, while from time to time he wrote articles on contemporary affairs he remained a scholar of independent mind throughout his life, whose magnum opus on the First World War was marked by two features. Noting at the outset that in writing of the Peloponnesian conflict, Thucydides had taken care to distinguish between 'the more remote or underlying, and the immediate causes of the war', he observed that confusion of thought had often arisen over the Great War from a failure to understand that responsibility for the one did not always coincide with responsibility for the other. 'One country may for years have been much to blame for creating a general situation dangerous to peace, but may have had relatively little to do with the final outbreak of war – or *vice versa*.'[1] In the case of the First World War, 'all the powers were more or less responsible', without any of them bearing sole 'guilt' for it, since they were each caught within the nexus of its underlying causes: first and foremost 'the system of secret alliances that developed after the Franco-Prussian War'; followed by the forces of militarism ('great standing armies and large navies, with the attendant evils of espionage', and a powerful officer class capable of prevailing over civilian politicians in situations of crisis); of nationalism (nourishing enmity between neighbours); of imperialism ('by 1914 all the Great European Powers had secured slices of Africa', though in the scramble for them economic motives had less weight than considerations of prestige, borders, and the balance of power); and a jingoistic press poisoning public attitudes.[2]

In keeping with this analytic framework, Fay devoted his first volume to a longitudinal study of the underlying pattern of international tensions across the four decades separating the end of the Franco-Prussian War from the onset of the Great War, before proceeding in his second volume to the assassination of the Archduke of Austria and his wife in 1914, and so to the immediate causes of the descent of Europe into industrialized slaughter six weeks later. His examination of these exonerated neither Austria for attacking Serbia nor Germany for having initially offered a blank cheque to it. But nor did it offer any exculpation of Russia for proceeding to a mobilization against the Central Powers that the two architects of its alliance with France – a Russian and a French general – had both defined *ab initio*

---

1. *Origins*, Vol. I, second revised edition, New York 1932, p. 1.
2. *Origins*, Vol. I, pp. 34, 39, 44, 46.

as meaning a declaration of war; of the role of Paris in instigating the Tsarist rush to arms; not to speak of the duplicity of England in failing to warn Europe of a military bond with France concealed from the British public and most of the Cabinet itself. As for upshot, Fay ended his work by calmly concluding that 'the verdict of the Versailles Treaty that Germany and her allies were responsible for the War, in view of the evidence now available, is historically unsound. It should therefore be revised.'[3]

Schmitt's riposte, *The Coming of the War*, two volumes of comparable length, moved – procedurally and substantively – in a diametrically opposite direction. As he wrote, the book 'deals primarily with the crisis of July 1914'. The purpose of the two opening chapters, on the 'European System' and the 'Near East', was 'merely to analyse the international situation in Europe at the moment when Archduke Francis Ferdinand was assassinated'. The remaining twenty-two chapters were devoted to the hectic drama that followed. In effect, where Fay had paid equal attention to underlying and immediate causes of the war, Schmitt dedicated over four-fifths of his to immediate causes, after brisk mention of democracy, nationality, industry, and 'so-called imperialism', in his eyes an 'ineluctable necessity of modern industrialism', as a background to these, before explaining that the reason why a quarrel between Austria-Hungary and Serbia could have produced a European conflagration lay in 'the tradition of the balance of power' which had generated the conflict of the Central Powers and the Triple Entente.[4] The United States had offered mediation for over two years of the fighting between them, 'only to discover that

---

3. *Origins*, Vol. II, p. 558.
4. *The Coming of the War*, Vol. I, New York–London 1930, pp. vii, 3–6, 8–12 ff.

there was but one kind of effective mediation: armed intervention', on the side of the Entente.[5] For its cause was just. All the Great Powers had made diplomatic mistakes in 1914, but France, England and Russia were innocent of any part in setting off the war, for which Germany and Austria alone bore the blame, Berlin yet more than Vienna. 'The primary responsibility of Germany for the fatal ending of the crisis is clear and overwhelming,' Schmitt would reiterate.[6] The Allied condemnation of 1919 was right. Versailles was 'a good treaty', if alas not enforced.[7]

Like Fay, Schmitt was an accomplished professional scholar, but quite unlike him in background, temperament and career. He enjoyed recalling that he was named Bernadotte after the name chosen for his son by the Swiss immigrant who started the family in America, selecting it out of hatred for Napoleon, in honour of the general who betrayed him as king of Sweden. Equation of Wilhelm II with Napoleon, in despotic ambition if not in military talent, was a popular trope in England at the turn of the century, where Schmitt acquired his political outlook. Arriving at the age of eighteen as a Rhodes Scholar at Oxford, he made friends with patriots of the Navy League, detesters of the Second Reich, and formed a deep emotional attachment to Britain. On returning home, he began in his mid-twenties to compose a work tracing the 'bitter animus' of Germany against England since the turn of the century, and its roots in Prussian vainglory and militarism, writing about half of it before the War broke out. Finished in the autumn of 1915, it was published

---

5. *Coming*, Vol. II, p. 480.
6. 'July 1914: Thirty Years After', *Journal of Modern History*, September 1944, p. 204.
7. 'Valedictory', *Journal of Modern History*, September 1946, p. 194.

six months later as *England and Germany 1740–1914*.[8] There were no half-tones in its conclusion. Though there might be a few minor spots on England's record, 'compared with the crimson offenses of Germany, her peccadilloes are insignificant'. Schmitt ended with a rousing peroration:

> To the lover of liberty and the opponent of forceful domination, the situation need not seem more hopeless than was the state of affairs in 1811, when the whole of Europe, except England, lay prostrate at the feet of Napoleon. The Napoleonic Empire collapsed with nerve-racking suddenness. We are permitted to hope that British stubbornness, British credit, British valor will yet, with the assistance of its allies, prevail against the forces of militarism and absolutism, and that the German *débacle*, far off as it may be, is as inevitable as the fall of the first French empire.[9]

The two volumes that appeared fifteen years later were fruit of the same passion, ideas conceived before their author had set foot in any archive of the conflict.

Such predispositions were no impediment to professional success. Possessed of notable administrative skills and entrepreneurial energy, two years after arriving at Chicago, Schmitt had founded America's flagship *Journal of Modern History*, which he would edit for twenty years. In 1931 his magnum opus, *The Coming of the War, 1914*, for which he had interviewed leading statesmen involved in it,[10] was

---

8. *England and Germany*, Princeton 1916, pp. vii–viii. Happy memories of Oxford contrasted with painful impressions of Berlin, where arrogant junkers had swept the young American off a pavement.

9. *England and Germany*, pp. 497–8.

10. Poincaré: 'The moment he began to speak, one was instantly aware of a remarkable intelligence, which commanded all the pertinent facts and reached conclusions intuitively and instantly'; Grey: 'Of all my interviews that with Lord

awarded the Pulitzer Prize. Making no secret of his ideological bent, he informed his compatriots during the Second World War that 'the Germans are not like Frenchmen or Britishers or Americans but possess certain national traits which make them impervious to reason, generosity, or even fair play. The one argument the Germans understand is force' and 'these things being so, the only sensible course is to give the Germans a strong dose of their own medicine. Let us make life difficult and unpleasant for them', forcing them to 'suffer so much that of their own initiative they ask themselves why they are treated in this fashion'.[11] In 1944 he joined the OSS intelligence service in Washington and thereafter the State Department, where he served as a political consultant for seven years, as hot war against the Axis segued into cold war against Communism. No inmate of an ivory tower, in a subsequent presidential address to the American Historical Association, he would declare on the eve of its escalation in Vietnam, that this was a time when 'the United States has worked zealously for peace'.[12]

In Europe, the first serious historical writing on the outbreak of the Great War had begun earlier than in America, if in different conditions – in each of the belligerents, consensus rather than dispute prevailed – and to different effects. France led the way. There a young scholar,

---

Grey was the most agreeable ... His handsome, clear-cut face, a rich voice, fine command of language and perfect courtesy are perhaps only outward symbols of character. Yet one did not have to speak long with him to be aware that here was a deeply sensitive person devoted to the finer things of life', etc. *Interviewing the Authors of the War*, Chicago Literary Club 1930.

11. *What Shall We Do with Germany?*, Public Policy Pamphlet no. 38, Chicago 1943, pp. 220–1.

12. 'With How Little Wisdom', *American Historical Review*, January 1961, p. 322. In the struggle with Russia, the free world was not willing to admit that capitalism was doomed.

Pierre Renouvin, published an earlier and much shorter study, *Les Origines immédiates de la première guerre mondiale*, in 1925. Its author was one of the most remarkable figures of the period. Born in 1893 into a comfortable Parisian family (his father was an interior decorator), an outstanding pupil at the elite Lycée Louis-le-Grand, after passing the *agrégation* in history at the age of nineteen, he began research on the provincial assemblies of 1787 under Alphonse Aulard, the first professional historian of the French Revolution; and travelled early to Russia and Germany. Twenty-one when the war broke out in 1914, he was sent to the front, where he has twice severely wounded, losing his right thumb and then his left arm before being invalided out in 1916. Recovering, by 1920 he had completed his dissertation and was teaching at a lycée in Orléans. There he was chosen by the Minister of Education, André Honnorat, probably on the recommendation of Aulard, to run the documentation section of the newly created Library and Museum of the War in Vincennes.[13] By 1922, at the age of twenty-seven, he was already giving a course at the Sorbonne on the history of the war, out of which came the book he produced three years later. In 1928, he became secretary of the commission charged with publishing French Diplomatic Documents (1871–1914), and later its president. By 1934 he had published a more wide-ranging study on the genesis and course of Great War, *La Crise Européenne et la grande guerre (1904–1918)*, and at the age of forty-four was awarded the first French chair in contemporary history. It was a meteoric career.

Like most of his contemporaries, Renouvin believed that the cause of the Entente was just and its victory well deserved. Concentrating

---

13. See Guillaume Tronchet, *André Honnorat. Un visionnaire en politique*, Paris 2020, p. 225. The Bibliothèque et Musée de la Guerre (BMG) was given scholarly backing by the creation of the Société d'histoire de la guerre (SHG) the following year, among whose moving spirits was Aulard, an administrator of the former.

more exclusively on the immediate origins of the war even than Schmitt – everything that happened prior to 28 June 1914 was dispatched in two pages, on the grounds that preceding years had seen a number of crises in Europe, yet each had ended in a compromise, so why not this time too? – Renouvin exonerated the Serbian government of any foreknowledge of the killings in Sarajevo, and France of any aggressive designs in the Balkans or elsewhere. Nor had Russian mobilization any malign intent. He broke, nevertheless, with two standard claims of Entente self-justification. It was not the case that the Central Powers had deliberately planned a European war, nor that Wilhelm II had determined their acts of aggression. But that did not mean they were innocent of these. They had stumbled by miscalculation into conflict with the Entente by refusing any solution to Austria's conflict with Serbia other than force. There lay their undivided responsibility for what ensued. They *alone* had willed the provocation of war on Belgrade.[14] In the same year, he ended another text with an affirmation, no less categorical, of France's unique fidelity, once the war had broken out, to its traditions and constitutional principles.[15]

Careful, logical and sober by the standards of the time, Renouvin's book – composed while he was still in his twenties – was a scholarly feat, respected even by those who differed with its standpoint. It was the work of a patriot who had suffered for the French Republic, and embodied its values. Perhaps more striking still, in writing on the war he refused to make not only any appeal, but any reference whatever to his own traumatic time in it – indeed to the subjective testimonies of any combatant, of which others might make what they would,

---

14. *Les Origines immédiates de la guerre*, Paris 1925, p. 268 – Renouvin's italics.
15. *Les Formes du gouvernement de guerre*, Paris 1925, p. 147.

but by which the historian should not be misled, trusting critical examination of documents alone.[16] The precondition of scholarship was an austere objectivity. Not only personal memories, but political conclusions were foreign to it.[17] Throughout his life, Renouvin's authority owed much to that reserve. In his teaching and writing on the war, he never spoke of his own experience of it. Though never free of the pain left by his mutilation, he was a model of self-control, handling his condition with a deft aplomb, haunting the memory of his students with the authority of his swift gesture in donning his coat with a single arm.[18] He was a commanding presence.

In the United States, Fay responded warmly to Renouvin's *Origines immédiates* on its appearance in 1925, saluting its author as the best type of French scholar, and when its revised second edition appeared in English in the same year as his own *Origins*, reiterated his praise of the 'clarity, grasp and judiciousness with which M. Renouvin has sifted the mass of documentary evidence, punctured and discarded untenable legends'; it was the 'best comprehensive treatment in any language' he had read of 'this difficult and thorny subject'.[19] In his own work, whose direction so clearly differed, Fay nevertheless pointed out how untenable was Renouvin's claim, designed to absolve Russia

---

16. For particulars, see the fine article 'Pierre Renouvin', by Jacques and Annette Becker, in Veronique Sales (ed.), *Les Historiens*, Paris 2004, pp. 106–18, who speak of the general paradox of 'silence about the war' among many scholars and intellectuals who fought in it, by contrast with subsequent historians of it as a collective experience.

17. 'Not the business of a historian': *Les Cahiers des Droits de l'Homme*, no. 11, 1923, p. 249.

18. Jean-Baptiste Duroselle, 'Pierre Renouvin (1893–1974)', *Revue d'histoire moderne et contemporaine*, October–December 1975, p. 498.

19. See *Political Science Quarterly*, December 1925, pp. 637–9, and *The American Historical Review*, July 1928, pp. 877–8.

from any blame for mobilizing before any other power in 1914, that declarations by both Russian and French chiefs of staff in the 1890s to the effect that 'mobilization means war', applied only to Austria and Germany, not to their own countries, so acquitting France from any blame in failing to restrain Russia from its mobilization.[20] For his part, Renouvin had from the start been attentive to America, whose Carnegie Endowment for International Peace was in touch with the BMG in Vincennes already in 1921, in the person of James Shotwell, a Canadian with a long-term post in the history department at Columbia who had been so ardent an advocate of US intervention in the Great War that he was recruited by Wilson's *homme de confiance* Colonel House to the brains trust he had organized in 1917 to work out US designs for post-war Europe.[21] Now director of historical and economic research for the Endowment, Shotwell contracted Renouvin to write a *Forms of Government* book for Carnegie, publishing the result in the United States. Collaboration between the two continued in the interwar years, Renouvin teaching at the Carnegie centre in Paris from 1926 onwards, and editing the Endowment's European quarterly *L'Esprit international* from 1927 to 1940. So it is not surprising that – perhaps provoked by the favourable reception of Fay's book in the US – Renouvin published in 1931 an extended essay in the *Revue des deux mondes* on American historians and the war, in which he contrasted the accounts of 1914 proposed by Fay and Schmitt, understandably to the advantage of the latter, whose 'sound displays of evidence' were to be preferred to the 'sometimes tendentious interpretations' of the

---

20. *The Origins of the World War*, II, pp. 477–81.
21. Herbert Croly of the *New Republic* was the linkman in the arrangement, which made Shotwell the highest-paid member of the inquiry: Harold Josephson, *James T. Shotwell and the Rise of Internationalism in America*, Rutherford NJ–London, 1975, pp. 71–2.

former.[22] Still, he observed, if Schmitt's contentions – among them, that Austria-Hungary had declared war on Serbia to please Germany – were convincing, they were not new. Judgments like these had been made several years earlier by historians in France. As for the question of who was to blame for the war, it was one – Renouvin opened his essay by explaining – that 'for the majority of Frenchmen, does not even merit discussion. That the will of France in 1914 was to avoid an international conflict in which its existence would be at stake, if it could do so without sacrificing its position in Europe and its future as a Great Power, is our intimate conviction. To us it seems unnecessary to prove a commitment to peace that is part of ourselves.' That attitude on the part of French public opinion had, admittedly, some drawbacks, since according to a recent questionnaire, far from sharing it, in America a majority not only of businessmen, functionaries and journalists, but even historians apparently believed that Germany bore neither sole nor even main responsibility for the war. Such ignorance should be remedied, Renouvin ended firmly. 'Did the Central Powers "impose war" on Europe in 1914?' he asked. 'Historical research says: yes.'[23]

In reality, there was by then in France neither the unanimity of opinion about the war nor the indifference to it as an issue suggested by Renouvin. In no other belligerent power, in fact, was there such vehement debate over the conflict. Apparent unanimity during the war ceased quite soon once it was over. There were at least three reasons for that. France had suffered more than double the number of deaths endured by Britain or Italy in the First World War. By reason of its alliance with Russia, France had played a far larger role

---

22. 'Les Historiens Américains et les responsabilités de la guerre', *Revue des deux Mondes*, 15 April 1931, pp. 902–3.
23. Ibid., pp. 886–7, 903.

in the onset of the conflict than Britain, which had stayed aloof till the last minute, let alone Italy, which had not joined it till the spring of 1915. After the war, France was the only Great Power where the politician who took the country into battle continued to dominate it for a decade after fighting had ended. By the end of 1922, Nicholas II and Sazonov, Asquith and Lloyd George, Salandra and Orlando, Bethmann Hollweg and the Kaiser were all gone, never to take the stage again. In France alone, Raymond Poincaré – president of the Republic from 1913 to 1920 – returned as prime minister from 1922 to 1924, recovering the post again from 1926 to 1929. Though successful enough in rallying the nation in 1914 with his call for a *union sacrée* against Germany, Poincaré saw his popularity drop as the fighting wore on and disillusionment with it grew; by 1916 mutinies were spreading at the front, and to his resentment, in the last year of the war he found himself displaced in public esteem by Clemenceau. Returning to power as prime minister in January 1922 after Clemenceau retired from public life, he had become a polarizing figure, incarnation of the conservative wing of the bourgeoisie in a political system divided for over a century between Right and Left. At the hustings and in the Chamber he was denounced for collusion with Russia in precipitating the war by the Communist writer and deputy Paul Vaillant-Couturier; the sobriquet *Poincaré-la-guerre* caught on. Some months later the former civil servant Georges Demartial – who would become the leading critic of Poincaré's performance in 1914 – published his first major attack on the *union sacrée*.[24]

In Britain, where radical opposition to the war had started much earlier and been more outspoken than in France, it had found expression in a public figure of greater impact and standing than any counterpart

---

24. *La Guerre de 1914. Comment on mobilise les consciences*, Paris 1922.

across the Channel, the fearless anti-imperialist campaigner Edmund Morel. French by birth and background, but schooled in England and naturalized a British subject in his twenties, after discovering the complicity of the shipping company for which he worked in Leopold II's reign in the Congo, Morel quit his job, campaigning with Roger Casement to expose Belgian atrocities in Africa until international pressure brought them to an end, and in 1911 denouncing British complicity with the French seizure of Morocco.[25] When the Great War broke out in 1914, he was instrumental in creating the Union of Democratic Control as a movement of resistance to the practices of secret diplomacy, which he held had brought the war about, and the official propaganda promoting it — an organization that came to number some 10,000 individuals, together with associations numbering 600,000. Imprisoned in 1917, Morel joined the Labour Party after the war, twice ran for Parliament, defeating Churchill himself at the polls, and before he died in 1924, his health ruined by his time in jail, was foreign policy adviser to the first Labour government, and a major influence on dissenters from official chauvinism in France.

There, a small group within the broad Ligue des Droits de l'Homme, whose membership included along with Demartial, a civil servant, two prominent scholars, the historian Charles Seignobos and economist Charles Gide, began in 1915 to discuss the causes of the war among themselves. The following year the authorities, treating the group as seditious, closed it down. The war over and censorship lifted, criticism in this milieu of how the war had begun extended to how it had ended too: could the Treaty of Versailles be regarded as

---

25. *Morocco in Diplomacy*, London 1912, justly recalled by Geoffrey Barraclough in his trenchant last book, *From Agadir to Armageddon*, London 1982, a work of modern scholarship on the same crisis, written in the same intransigent spirit.

a just peace? In 1919 Demartial published his first article on the war in *l'Humanité*, the paper Jaurès had founded; in 1920 he was openly attacking the claim that Germany bore sole responsibility for the war earning a riposte from Victor Basch, future president of the Ligue. It was the inception of a public split in the League which would deepen across the inter-war years. In 1922 Demartial published his first book on the issue dividing it, revealing his gifts as a mordant polemicist. *Comment on mobilisa les consciences* took as its target the renowned historian Ernest Lavisse. This academic pontiff, whose textbooks exalting France were mandatory instruction in its schools, and whose Teutophobe propaganda during the war had been a major service to the government, was subjected to a caustic demolition. Four years later, Demartial repeated the exercise to still more devastating effect with *L'Évangile du Quai d'Orsay*, this time on the Yellow Book that the French government had published at the outset of the war, purporting to be a collection of documents demonstrating the complete innocence of France and the utter iniquity of Germany in its outbreak. All the belligerents had produced a careful selection of official papers designed to put themselves in the best possible light, and their adversaries in the worst. But the Yellow Book exceeded all others in not just suppressing documents which had to be hidden, but forging documents which had never existed, becoming in due course an embarrassment even to apologists of the regime of the time. Demartial was the first to expose the falsifications which it contained. Drawing an analogy with the suicide of Dreyfus's accuser, which had made even those inclined to credit the accusations against Dreyfus ask why evidence had to be forged against him, Demartial asked: if the French government was innocent of any responsibility for the war, why did it have to falsify the record of its diplomacy preceding it?

Demartial, a functionary trained in law, was the most incisive and effective of the critics of the official version of the Great War from the Ligue des Droits de l'Homme, but by no means the only one. After 1918 a growing literature contended that France had been propelled into the conflict on false pretences, among its authors more than one decorated veteran of the battlefield, a *mutilé de guerre* like Renouvin himself, and several *normaliens*. Though this front of opinion never enjoyed a majority in the Ligue, it was a distinguished and vocal minority in an organization of great weight in French public life. possessing at its peak over 180,000 members, more than all parties to the left of centre combined, numbering among them ministers galore. When elections were held in 1924, it played a leading role in the campaign that toppled the *bloc national*, bringing the Cartel des Gauches for a time to power.[26] Passionate argument about the Great War, in which the role of Poincaré was repeatedly questioned or attacked, rolled on for another decade. Poincaré himself, his reputation under increasing threat from critics of the war, was forced to respond. Addressed directly by René Gérin, a young *normalien* with an outstanding record on the battlefield as an officer wounded three times and awarded the Legion d'Honneur for his service, in 1929 Poincaré granted him a lengthy interview, emboldening his interlocutor to put fourteen highly critical questions about France's part in the coming of the war to him on paper. To these Poincaré replied at book length, the exchange between the two appearing under the title *Les Responsabilités de la guerre* in 1930. Asserting the sincerity of his belief that Austria mobilized before Russia, even if

---

26. See the very careful, deeply researched study by the Canadian scholar Norman Ingram, *The War Guilt Problem and the Ligue des droits de l'homme*, Oxford 2018, pp. 3–4.

it later transpired that the opposite was true, he claimed that he had no idea what was going on in Russia in the days before the war, and defended his immaculate conduct of relations with France's ally in the East: imputations to the contrary were baseless. Repeatedly, the authority to which Poincaré appealed for confirmation of his version of recent history was 'the very remarkable and very impartial work' of Renouvin.[27] If there were imperfections in the Yellow Book of 1914 published by France to demonstrate the justice of its cause, he himself could not be blamed for them, as he had played no role whatever in its production.

Renouvin himself did not engage in the polemical exchanges of the period about the events of 1914 and the peace of 1919. Demartial and critics like him held no positions in the academic or established literary world; privately deplored, publicly they could be ignored.[28] The same was not possible with a work whose origin and scope were quite different. About a month before the elections of 1924, there appeared a historical reconstruction of the genesis of the First World War comparable in length to Renouvin's own study of it (which had yet to appear) combined with a political analysis of its outcome in the peace of Versailles, down to France's occupation of the Ruhr in 1923. *La Victoire* by Alfred Fabre-Luce, then just twenty-five years old, was a glittering performance – carefully researched, stylishly written, incisively argued throughout. Neither an indictment of France as architect of the war, nor an exoneration of Germany as guiltless of it, this was the first sustained work in any belligerent to hold all the major powers of 1914 implicated in the cataclysm that followed.

---

27. *Les Responsabilités de la guerre*, pp. 79–85, 102, 111, 117, 126, 154, 170.

28. Approached around 1930 to give a lecture in Berlin, Renouvin stipulated that for him a condition was that Demartial be 'dropped' in Germany.

The war had not been inevitable, Fabre-Luce argued, but if there was any element of fatality in it, the impossibility of maintaining the status quo in the East would have to be it. In the Balkans, two empires in dissolution confronted each other, Habsburg and Ottoman, while Russia was torn between Westernizing and Slavophile ambitions. For its part, Germany had lost the diplomatic moderation of Bismarck, when the rest of Europe put up with its domination, and had as the most powerful state a particular responsibility in giving way to arrogance and bluster; it could not gainsay the kernel of truth in the judgment of Versailles. What of France? Its alliance with Russia was an unequal relationship, since Russia was under no obligation to help it in a colonial conflict with Germany, as in Morocco. Yet France was obliged to help Russia in a conflict with Germany if it came to blows with Austria in the Balkans. Its own rulers, however, had scarcely wanted for arrogance themselves: first the reckless Delcassé, provoking Germany over Morocco, then Poincaré addressing Nicholas II in St Petersburg as if he, not the Tsar, were the emperor. Thereafter, 'the Republic waged war, but it had ceased to be altogether a Republic': a devastating portrait of its vainglorious ruler followed.[29]

The antagonism between France and Germany was the pivot of European politics, and an underlying reason for its slide towards war. England, after tying itself to France in the Entente Cordiale, was 'chained' to the same logic. Suffusing all the powers was the hold of the *moeurs politiques* of the time, lack of sufficient fear of war to avoid it generating the sophism that bellicose stances, by intimidating the enemy, were a way of preserving peace. 'Mars is a wily tempter, coaxing the authorities to catastrophe by insensible degrees.' Who then was responsible for the final fall over the precipice? 'By their

---

29. *La Victoire*, Paris 1924, pp. 90–3, 241–3, 146–7, 208–9, 266, 336–7.

gestures, Germany and Austria made the war possible; by theirs, the Triple Entente made it certain'.[30] The victory of the latter over the former was no guarantee of a better future: potentially, the Treaty of Versailles contained the seeds of another war. *La Victoire* was not a philippic against the powers that won the war, in the fashion of firebrands in the Ligue. Warning against post-war threats from the extreme left, Fabre-Luce indicated his own preference for the kind of mainstream politics represented by Joseph Caillaux, who had sought détente with Germany before the war, was accused of treason in 1917, and rehabilitated by the Cartel des Gauches.

The appearance of *La Victoire* was a sensation. Though denounced by the nationalist right, it garnered a laudatory to enthusiastic reception across a wide selection of the French press and Parisian culture at large. There were a number of reasons for its success. The book was an impressive feat for so young a writer; it chimed with the shift in political mood evident in the election of 1925; and its author had every credential to excite *la bonne société* of the time. He came from a family of great wealth – his grandfather was a founder of the Crédit Lyonnais, still one of France's major banks – and had been a brilliant *normalien*, served in the French Embassy in London, published his first novel, and contributed to the *Nouvelle revue française*. It was difficult for Renouvin to ignore it. All the more so, perhaps, since he figured in the first footnote to *La Victoire*, in which Fabre-Luce commended his scrupulous scholarship and praiseworthy efforts to square it with official doctrine about the war, 'while remaining much further from that than he seems to believe'.[31] In return, Renouvin would offer Fabre-Luce his own double-edged compliments. *La Victoire* was a

---

30. Ibid., pp. 109, 173, 248–53, 232.
31. Ibid., pp. 22–3.

book full of talent, subtle analysis and original views, if lacking half-tones and liable to be carried away by passion. Despite an intention to shock, it merited attention, which Renouvin gave it in the form of a summary of the book, without proceeding to the critical examination it was going to need. 'I do not share M. Fabre-Luce's conclusions and believe he has involuntarily omitted certain documents disproving this or that part of his argument, and sometimes let himself formulate his thought in terms that exceed it', was his feline conclusion, promising that his journal would return to the charge in due course.[32]

By the end of the twenties critics of the conventional narrative of the war tended to regard Renouvin as an official historian. In retrospect, there were reasons for doing so they did not know at the time. The Bibliothèque et Musée de la Guerre for which he worked was initially funded by money assigned to the secret service, and supplied with information by the Quai d'Orsay and the Deuxième Bureau, furnishing in exchange reports on German atrocities and estimates of reparations for the government and the legislature. Today, it has been described by historians with no hostility to Renouvin as an 'intellectual ammunitions depot' of the Foreign Office, integrating him into 'the politico-diplomatic apparatus' of the French state.[33] Over this, Poincaré presided at intervals for many years. Object of successive admiring biographies, he has often been represented – whatever other limitations are conceded – as the soul of probity, a misleading characterization. For among his traits was an addiction to stealth, illustrated by two features of his career as a politician: his corruption of the press before the war, employing secret funds

---

32. Compte-rendu in *Revue d'histoire de la guerre mondiale*, 1925, pp. 259–61.

33. See Laurence Badel, 'Introduction', and Benjamin Gilles and Anne Joly, 'La pérennisation de la collecte de la documentation sur la Grande Guerre, 1919–1925', in Badel (ed.), *Histoire et relations internationales*, Paris 2020, pp. 27, 30–1, 91–2.

supplied him by Russia to bend it to his will, amply documented in the thirties;[34] and his suppression of all trace of his conversations with the Tsar and his ministers during his state visit to St Petersburg on the eve of the war, in which it would later become obvious he urged them to stand firm, and then went to some lengths to conceal his part in bringing on the war. How far Renouvin was aware of imbrication with this side of Poincaré's *modus operandi* is uncertain. But that he enjoyed close relations with Poincaré from early on is plain. For in 1923 – two years before the publication of *Origines immédiates*, he co-authored a refutation of the chronology of events from 1871 to 1914 put together by Wilhelm II in his Dutch exile for propagandist purposes: a work introduced – and probably commissioned – by Poincaré, expressing his indignation at the 'clumsy and impotent lies' directed by the fallen kaiser at himself and 'Lord Grey'.[35] If the speed of Renouvin's arrival at the Sorbonne came at Honnorat's behest, his subsequent promotion there is likely to have enjoyed Poincaré's favour, and certainly his appointment five years later as secretary to the commission tasked with selecting French diplomatic documents for publication was Poincaré's doing.

The precise nature of the relations between the two remains a matter for conjecture, on which Renouvin's as yet unpublished papers may throw some light. But however similar their outlook on the war itself, they were not made of the same cloth. Renouvin could publicly

---

34. For which see Arthur Raffalovitch, *'L'abominable vénalité de la presse . . .' d'après les documents des archives russes (1897–1917)*, Paris 1931, pp. 332–3, 336–7, 346–7, 350–1, 366–7. Raffalovitch was a Russian economist seconded as clandestine counsellor to the Tsarist embassy in Paris, whose files were brought to France after the October Revolution by Boris Souvarine, and published there by *Critique Sociale*, the journal he founded in 1931, which lasted till 1934.

35. See 'Avant-Propos de Raymond Poincaré', in Charles Appuhn and Pierre Renouvin, *Introduction au Tableaux d'histoire de Guillaume II*, Paris 1923, p. ii.

regret Article 231 of the Treaty of Versailles assigning guilt for the war to Germany, not to speak of the Allied letter accompanying it that charged Berlin with a premeditated decision to launch a European war, as political declarations that were not based on any examination of archival evidence, about which the judgment of historians themselves would, as was customary, long remain contestable – though that did not, of course, mean that they should abstain from judgment of the issue meanwhile.[36] Without directly criticizing the manipulations of the diplomatic record under Poincaré's presidency – the Yellow Book which France released during the fighting contained outright forgeries, exceeding anything in Germany's prior White Book – Renouvin took his distance from them. By his own lights he remained a scrupulous historian. When many years later he wrote about the commission he had ended up heading, he did not conceal its failure to find any trace of Poincaré's conversations in St Petersburg.[37]

Two years after his essay on US historiography and the war was published in the *Revue des deux mondes*, a further contribution to the literature on its causes appeared in Paris, engaging with both Renouvin and American historians, and setting the stage for the most significant confrontation between contrasted scholarly standpoints on the Great War of the inter-war years. Jules Isaac, from a military family of Jewish descent originating in Alsace, was fifteen years older than Renouvin, receiving his *agrégation* a decade earlier, after which

---

36. In other words, what was inappropriate in a document of statecraft was perfectly in order in any other context: 'Le Problème des responsabilités de la guerre dans la politique internationale contemporaine', *L'Esprit international*, April 1929, pp. 228–43.

37. If without expressing any view as to what might explain such an 'exceptional' blank in the archives: see 'Les documents diplomatiques français 1871–1914', *Revue historique*, January 1961, p. 143.

he became a teacher in a lycée. Politically more radical and active than the younger man, in the pre-war years he had befriended Péguy and admired Jaurès, then fought and was wounded in the war. Resuming his career on his return, he updated or authored the most widely used textbooks on the history of France for use in secondary education. His intervention of 1933 – *Un Débat historique. Le problème des origins de la guerre* – was quite unlike the book that had made Renouvin's name, in both style and upshot: personally franker, theoretically sharper, and substantively more critical in its conclusions. It opened with a confession: writing an account of the war, after having served in it, for the textbook series once it was over, and relying on a pamphlet co-authored by Durkheim, he had repeated an assertion that was untrue, that Austria had mobilized before Russia in 1914. Soon, every day revealed a new fissure in official claims about the conflict, and now after seven years of full-time work in secondary education, he could for the first time approach the subject with a complete independence of mind, resolved to clear away such earlier lapses.

Historians, he observed, now confronted a mass of documentation on the origins of the war such as no previous hostilities had ever afforded, though it was early days yet and the record was still far from complete. In three countries, Germany, the United States and France, historians had been particularly active. However, only in America was historical work on the problem truly free – in Germany and France, political controversy over Article 231, the war-guilt clause of the Treaty of Versailles, still made that impossible. In the US alone had three important syntheses on the origins of the war appeared, each reaching a different verdict on them: Barnes assigning responsibility to France and Russia, Fay to both sides, Schmitt principally to Germany and Austria. All three had also considered the 'deeper causes' of the war, beyond the particular roles played by each of the powers in triggering it. But of the long-term forces enumerated for example by Fay, neither alliances, nor militarism, nor the press could really be regarded as decisive. Crucial in his listing were just two: nationalism and imperialism, though the former was better described by Schmitt as 'nationality', if the latter less well as 'mercantilism'. But it was still necessary to specify the concrete manifestations of each that were most combustible in 1914. These lay, respectively, in the volcanic energy of German imperialism – in itself neither worse nor better than the other imperialisms of the time, and not different in kind, but because less satisfied, more feverish and active; and in the decomposition of conflicting nationalities in the Austro-Hungarian Empire.[38]

There remained the critical question, however, of what temporal delimitation to assign to the operation of such causes – where to draw the chronological line at which attribution of them as causes should start. Fay began his account in 1871, after the Franco-Prussian War, but when asked by Isaac why, had replied only that American readers could not be assumed to know the history of the decades preceding the war; Barnes began in 1912, the better to substantiate his claim that the Franco-Russian alliance was to blame for the war; Schmitt, from the time when conflict developed between the Central Powers and the Entente, the most rational solution of the three. But for anyone like Isaac living in France, it was the Moroccan crisis of 1905 that set the slide towards war in motion, as the moment when Germany had tried to split the newly formed Anglo-French Entente apart, and psychological symptoms of a growing impatience with peace were noted by Péguy, in a

---

38. *Un débat historique*, Paris 1933, pp. 11–17.

change of atmosphere he himself could well remember.³⁹ By 1914, Germany was promising support for Austria in case of war with Russia, France support for Russia in case of war with Germany; the Germans with fewer illusions about Austrian performance than the French about Russian performance on the battlefield. As to which side actually detonated the war, Isaac found Schmitt's position more solidly based in the texts and facts of the final crisis of that year than Fay's, without entirely agreeing with it. Allocation of a unilateral responsibility for the war to either side was untenable. Yet most historians accepted the idea that responsibility for it was unequal, the greater part falling on the Central Powers. That said, there was small sign of any miraculous will to peace on the other side. In Renouvin's judgment, the Central Powers had imposed war on Europe. 'Strict equity obliges us to acknowledge that "Europe" did not seem very recalcitrant. The Central Powers deliberately offered it war (if not imposed it); it deliberately accepted the offer, with a promptness that surprised even its adversary.'⁴⁰

Isaac's book was put out by Éditions Rieder, whose directors had been close to Péguy, publishers of a list featuring socialist and anti-bellicist writers, from Jaurès and Rolland to Nizan, making his selection of the house itself a statement. Its original manuscript ended on an even more radical note, withheld in the printed version.⁴¹

---

39. Ibid., pp. 18–24.
40. Ibid., p. 228.
41. Which read: 'Each of these governments acted according to what it judged to be the main interest of its country, for the safety, profit, glory of its homeland. No profound feeling of a European community, no regret in breaking it. August 1914 was the triumph of national egoisms, each piously baptised "sacred", or what comes to the same, a "sacred union": every people responded to the summons of their chiefs and marched into battle with equal pride and confidence, equally sure they were right, equally ignorant of the truth – the truth of this war, the truth of its

Angry reaction to the book nevertheless followed. Renouvin's superior Camille Bloch, Poincaré's ambassador in Russia Maurice Paléologue, and Julien Benda all assailed it. Since Benda had been a fellow Dreyfusard, Isaac took most trouble in replying to him.[42] A little later, Renouvin took him to task for suggesting that discussion of the Great War in France was not as free as in America, and for conveying insufficient trust in the Quai d'Orsay. In July 1914 Russia had not, contrary to Isaac, violated a long-standing agreement with France for joint mobilization of their armed forces in case of war. Even if it had acted hastily in issuing orders for mobilization without consulting France and the French ambassador in St Petersburg had kept Paris in the dark about them (Isaac was right about that), there could be no doubt that it was the Central Powers who unleashed the war. Isaac himself had declared that a 'miracle' would have been needed to stay their aggression – why then reproach the Entente with not producing one?[43]

By this time Renouvin held a position of unrivalled influence in his field, at the crossroads of three major institutional networks – the library-museum at Vincennes, of which he would shortly become head, the Sorbonne, where he had become a full professor, and the Carnegie Endowment, of whose journal he was editor. Moreover, soon after his rejoinder to Isaac, he had published a new book, *La Crise européenne et la Grande Guerre*, a larger and more ambitious work than his first. Three times longer, its narrative began with the birth

---

genesis – that truth which History has such great difficulty, even today, in excavating from the depths in which it has been buried': see André Kaspi's biography, *Jules Isaac*, Paris 2002, p. 121.

42. 'Réponse provisoire à quelques critiques', *Europe*, 15 February 1935.

43. Compte rendu of Isaac's book in *Revue historique*, January–February 1934, pp. 190–3.

of the Entente Cordiale between France and England in 1904 and ended with the armistices of 1918. Conceding more weight to socio-economic developments and moral passions in the background to the war, and giving more attention to its global scope with the entry of America, Japan and China into the conflict, it covered the four years of the fighting itself in twice the number of pages given the ten years preceding its outbreak. So momentous in its effects had been the conflict that he decided it could well be described as a revolution.

Renouvin's standpoint on the war, however, had not changed. At the outset of his account, Europe was divided between three great democratic states, France, England and Italy, and three imperial monarchies, Germany, Austro-Hungary and Russia. By the end of it, America had joined the former, and Russia been knocked out of the ranks of the latter. What had caused the conflict? Certainly, nationalist sentiment had become increasingly inflamed, an arms race had accelerated, economic competition had intensified. But these were not the forces that unleashed the war. Those had to be sought in the actions of governments. The two Moroccan crises, thought by some to have sown the seeds of the war, were not primarily responsible for the drift towards it. More important were Anglo-German naval rivalry and Austro-Russian territorial rivalry in the Balkans. Responsibility for these two fatal tensions and their outcome was not, however, shared. True, Serb nationalism was often dangerously turbulent, and Russian policy sometimes disquietingly imprudent. But it was the Central Powers that took the decisions which led to disaster in 1914. 'Without the will to it of Germany and of Austria-Hungary the war would not have occurred.'[44] France could not be charged with any part in it. If *Origines immédiates* had been tight-lipped about Poincaré's visit to St

---

44. *La crise européenne et la Grande Guerre*, Paris 1934.

Petersburg in the week before the outbreak, dispatched in three brief pages, a decade later Renouvin's treatment of the president was still more taciturn, his name avoided wherever possible in favour of his function, about which too, at least it would seem for the purposes of the book, the less said the better.[45]

Unruffled by their differences, Renouvin asked Isaac to review his new work. Isaac obliged with a major essay in the *Revue Historique* in

---

45. That by this time a discomfort he may always to some extent have felt about Poincaré's persona had increased is suggested by the progression of the *comptes rendus* of Poincaré's memoirs – six in all – that Renouvin produced in the journal of the institution that launched his post-war career. The first two volumes, elevated in style and classical in form – which the world had 'awaited with impatience' – were not just 'solid and vigorous defences' of Poincaré's record in public affairs, but 'essential for an understanding of our diplomatic history' (1926). The next notice, lauding the 'meticulous, day-by-day account of the author's trip to Russia on the eve of the war, 'perfect in the precision of its details', saluted the 'lasting impression' left by a 'work of history in the full sense of the word' (1928). By the time of the next, 'it should be a matter of astonishment' that, with Poincaré prime minister once again, the burdens of office had not prevented a continuation of 'this great work' (1929). The next made clear the importance of his role as head of state in 1915, so different from that of George V across the water, and even if some readers might feel too much space was given to 'quarrels with other politicians, the pages devoted to these were of great psychological value.' (1931). By the time of the next, dealing with the year 1917, some disappointment could not be concealed: interesting enough as to domestic politics, this volume had virtually nothing to say about the great international events which changed the course of the war. Were the number of stars on the epaulettes of General Y or the bad temper of Senator Z really more important than the revolutions in Russia, or the entry of the United States into the battle (1932)? By the time of the last, covering the year 1918, Renouvin could no longer contain himself: Was it really necessary for Poincaré to pursue his personal grievances against Clemenceau and injuries to his amour-propre at the expense of any attention to the Treaty of Brest-Litovsk or other great happenings of that year? (1935 – Poincaré was now safely dead): *Revue d'histoire de la guerre mondiale*, July 1926, pp. 241–3; January 1927, pp. 57–9; July 1929, pp. 247–9; April 1931, pp. 173–6; January 1933, pp. 55–6; January 1935, pp. 57–8.

1935. After terming the book the first synthesis of the period which could be described as scientific, and a model of the kind of history held in honour by the French university system, he proceeded to a courteous but devastating critique of it. Renouvin had once told him that objectivity seemed easy and came naturally to him, of which he had given evidence in his writing.

> Perhaps, however, to attain, or at least approach it (as an inaccessible ideal), one must not trust oneself too much, impose on oneself too violent and permanent a constraint. Let us risk this paradox: it is better (perhaps) that a work of history not seem too objective, since it never is. If the historian appears in his work, why complain? It is franker. I begin to worry when a historical exposition, by its even, bare, 'scientific' tone, gives the reader the illusion of certainty: I ask myself where the author is hiding, for that he certainly has to do, and by looking carefully one always finds him, as in those picture-riddles where a sheep's fleece, insidiously drawn, contains the silhouette of a shepherd.[46]

---

46. 'La Crise européenne et la Grande Guerre: À l'occasion d'un livre récent', *Revue Historique*, July–December 1935, p. 413. In 1919 Isaac had himself written one of the most powerful evocations of experience in the trenches to come from the war, contrasting in pages of oneiric intensity memories of its deadly darkness with the oblivious illuminations of the Champs Elysées in its aftermath: 'Nous, Les Revenants', collected in *Paradoxe sur la Science homicide et autres hérésies*, Paris 1935, pp. 1–25. For the attitude of the two men to the value of personal testimonies as a historical source, see their differing reactions to accounts by survivors of the war collected by Norton Cru, an expatriate whose book about them, *Témoins* (1929) – supported as a project by Shotwell at Carnegie, though the Endowment eventually rejected it – was controversial in France, where it was initially shunned by publishers, among whose anonymous readers seems to have been Renouvin, as lacking in patriotism: see Frédéric Rousseau, *Le Procès des témoins de la grande guerre: L'affaire Norton Cru*, Paris 2003, pp. 22–37, 248–9. When it finally came out, however, both historians praised it: Renouvin more coolly, ending on a critical note, in the *Revue d'histoire de la guerre mondiale*, January 1930, pp. 76–7; Isaac more warmly and extensively in the *Revue historique* of January 1931, pp. 93–100.

Revealing, in this case, was the treatment accorded to persons featuring in Renouvin's book. Three pages on literature contained no mention of Gide, Claudel or Péguy. Much more significantly, of the leading political figures of the period, Lloyd George earned eighteen lines in the index, Wilson a disobliging fifteen, Nicholas II twelve, whereas a 'discreet veil' covered the figure of Poincaré, awarded just two. There was no reference to the expansion of the Franco-Russian alliance after 1912, nor mention even of Poincaré's election to the presidency of the Republic in 1913; silence as to the assassination of Jaurès. Missing, above all, and most surprising in a history of the war was the figure of the *poilu*, the ordinary French soldier, or the people in arms, the veritable human rampart whose unforeseeable resistance was the only moving revelation of a monstrous war. The German part in provoking and conducting the war was rightly recorded and condemned by Renouvin; less so the Russian, from the Bosnian crisis of 1907, in which Izvolsky's role was infinitely more dangerous than Aehrenthal's, to St Petersburg's suborning of the Parisian press and fomenting of Serb designs on Habsburg territory.

Beyond the assorted misdeeds or miscalculations of the various powers in 1914, moreover, the underlying forces of material interest and national emotion driving Europe into the world war were not registered with sufficient force. Anglo-German naval rivalry could not be isolated from the dynamics of the two rival imperialisms behind it, each with their own economic dimension; nor could the destructive collision of national passions in the Balkans be underplayed. It was true that the Central Powers weighed and accepted the risks of war in 1914. But had the Franco-Russian alliance countered them with an ardent or vigilant defence of peace? That could be doubted; less ardent and vigilant in any case than their resolve to prepare themselves for war. The complex reality of the disaster could not be reduced to Renouvin's simplistic formula that but for the actions of the Central Powers there would have been no war. Of course. 'But what do we reply to those who say: "without the attentat of Sarajevo and the activity of Yugoslav terrorism aiming to kill off the ancient Habsburg Empire, there would have been no war", or "without the will of Russia, the question of Serbia would not have become the seed of war"?' It would be easy, Isaac observed, to find many formulae of this kind, each with its part of truth, and Renouvin's was no doubt the best, the worst being Germany's 'without Russian mobilization there would have been no war'. Nevertheless, he went on:

> Would it not be better to renounce such summary formulas once and for all, and try to raise the level of debate? The unleashing of the Great War was a paroxysmic expression of the disequilibrium of old Europe, labouring under a weighty past that forged and hardened, along with the frontiers of states, the national egoism of each of them. In a world renewed, where forces liberated by science mocked frontiers and traditional measures of space and time evaporated, as the interdependence of nations – in Europe especially – became closer every day and the more absolute their need to agree or perish, each government continued down traditional paths, according to rules of the game that for France went back to Richelieu, for Prussia to Frederick II and to Bismarck. Each sensed that time-worn road was dangerous, and each persisted in taking it.[47]

Isaac ended his review by saying that if this was not 'the explanation of the war', it was at least the lesson of it.

Renouvin thanked Isaac for his criticisms, which were 'always interesting', saying he agreed with quite a few, while of course his

---

47. 'À l'occasion d'un livre rècent', p. 447.

interpretation of other questions differed. When Isaac asked him to direct the dissertation he planned to write at the Sorbonne on French foreign policy under Poincaré, Renouvin answered urbanely that it was the dean who decided whether or not to accept a subject for a thesis. The dean declined to let the name of Poincaré appear in one, and it was never written.[48]

In the same year, the two men worked together in an unexpected venture, which brought historians of France and Germany together in Paris to discuss the idea of textbook reforms to moderate nationalist feelings about the war in both countries. On the French side, Isaac organized the meeting, broached with a German counterpart in the spring, in which Renouvin was another participant. Obviously at variance with the Nazi regime in Berlin, a common resolution accompanied by differing national standpoints was agreed for publication in both countries, before contacts were suspended by the German side, briefly and inexplicably renewed in 1937, then shut down completely in 1938. By that time Isaac had been promoted to the powerful position of inspector-general of public education covering all secondary schools in France, and would head the jury for the *agrégation* in history, while at the Sorbonne Renouvin had acquired the first chair in contemporary history to be created in France.

With the outbreak of the Second World War, the pack of all those who had disputed the origins of the First was drastically shuffled. Blind to the contrast between the two conflicts, the dissidents of the Ligue, who quit its leadership in 1937, projected fixation on the events of 1914 onto those of 1939, as if there were no difference between Hitler and the Kaiser, and when Germany overpowered France, made their

---

48. Kaspi, *Jules Isaac*, pp. 126–7.

peace with the Occupation and the Vichy regime, playing no role in the Resistance.[49] Fabre-Luce, who had moved far to the right in the thirties, consorting with French fascists, went further, collaborating with the Nazi propaganda machine in Paris, and assimilating much of its ideology; changing his tune only when the tides of war turned against the Third Reich. Younger than the former troublemakers of the League, he alone —wealth, connexions and a fluent pen aiding – resurfaced from Swiss exile as a public figure in the fifties.[50]

With the fall of France in the spring of 1940, the fates of the two historians whose works survived the Second World War diverged sharply. His name alone enough for dismissal, Isaac was removed from his post by Pétain's regime, taking refuge in the south. From Aix he moved to the small town of Riom, between Clermont-Ferrand and Vichy, to be close to his daughter and son-in-law, working there in the Havas news agency. In October 1943 the two were arrested

---

49. There is a fine – humane, but stringent – critical analysis of the trajectory of this cohort, from the Popular Front to the Liberation, in *The War Guilt Problem*, pp. 204–64. For biographical particulars of two of its most significant members, see Guy Thuillier, *Bureaucratie et bureaucrates en France aux XIX siècle*, Paris 1980, pp. 134–53 (Georges Demartial) and 'Le Pacifisme avant 1939: René Gérin', *La Revue administrative*, September–October 1984, pp. 454–9. Demartial died in 1945; Gérin was a victim of the purges after the war, released after numerous protests from other writers.

50. For damning accounts of Fabre-Luce's record during the war, see Frederic Spotts, *The Shameful Peace: How French Artists and Intellectuals Survived the Nazi Occupation*, New Haven–London 2008, pp. 120–7 and Zev Sternhell, 'Entre le tragique et l'imposture: Raymond Aron, Carl Schmitt et Alfred Fabre-Luce', *Les Temps modernes*, January–March 2012, pp. 98–118. The only biography, Daniel Garbe's *Alfred Fabre-Luce: Un non-conformiste dans le tumulte du XXeme siècle*, Paris 2009, is an apologia, but one with access to his papers, informative of Fabre-Luce's recovery of literary standing among his peers in the sixties, by which time he was on terms again with Aron (who denounced him from London during the war), Renouvin, Furet and others.

by the Gestapo for links to the Resistance and deported to Germany, along with Isaac's wife and one of his sons. There all except his son perished. Isaac devoted the rest of the war and of his life to scholarly study of the Christian roots of anti-Semitism, on which he produced two major histories. In Paris, Renouvin kept his chair, unmolested by the Gestapo, became editor of the *Revue Historique* and composed his third book, on a century of interstate relations (1840–1940) in the Far East.[51] Unknown to any colleagues or friends in his lifetime, he also recorded his impressions and reflections on the Second World War – some three hundred pages of handwritten notes, tied in even bundles, donated by his heirs to the institute founded in his name, only recently revealed and discussed by Robert Frank, a historian of Polish-Scottish descent born half a century later. [52] Starting on 29 January 1938 and ending on 7 May 1945, they plainly form a remarkable document. Numerous on the Sudeten crisis and the talks in Munich, the notes after the war broke out contain two large blanks – September 1939 to May 1940 (very little on the Phoney War and virtually nothing on the defeat of France), and June to November 1941 (nothing on the German invasion of Russia); otherwise following and commenting on the course of the conflict in Europe.

To Munich, Renouvin reacted with a mixture of mortification and relief. It was a heavy setback and nothing to be proud of, but Czechoslovakia was an artificial state and France not ready for

---

51. Which appeared after the war: *La Question d'Extrême-Orient (1840–1940)*, Paris 1946.

52. 'Pierre Renouvin e la Second Guerre mondiale: Impressions au jour le jour, ou presque', in Badel (ed.), *Histoire et relations internationales*, pp. 161–86 – an admirably balanced analysis, which conjectures that the notes were written with a view to a subsequent work on the Second World War which Renouvin renounced. The manuscript has yet to be published. Frank held Renouvin's chair at the Sorbonne from 1994 to 2012.

war. When war came and France fell, he decided it was no time for sentimentalism. The French had to be realistic – they could not fight Germany, with its larger population, every twenty years; it was better to come to an agreement with the victor, inevitably leaving the country subordinate in the relationship, but hopefully preserving the freedom of its political and intellectual life, and without lessening English chances of resisting Germany. When Pétain announced formal collaboration with Berlin, and acceptance of the loss of Alsace-Lorraine, Renouvin approved his decision. Like most of the French, in Frank's view, he became not a Vichyist as such, but a *maréchaliste*, in the belief that a distinction could be made between Pétain and the regime over which he presided, an illusion comforted by the dismissal of Laval in December 1940. Ambivalent in his attitude to England, like many of his compatriots, Renouvin expressed at once pro-British attitudes in military matters, and Anglophobe sentiments in other ways, and in the spring of 1941 could strike anti-Semitic notes in recalling a pre-war meeting with Jules Isaac.

At the end of 1941, American entry into the war necessarily altered the realistic calculus of the balance of forces on which Renouvin's assessment of the options for France had rested in 1940. But his fear of communism, given free rein in the notes he wrote during the war, was such that he still speculated on divisions within the forces now arrayed against Germany. Could Britain or the US really want to see a victory of the USSR in Europe, given the Soviet 'desire to destroy the capitalist regimes'?[53] What suddenly changed his outlook were the Anglo-American landings in North Africa in November 1942, moving Renouvin to exclaim: 'a series of prodigious events!' The failure of Vichy to put up any resistance to Germany's riposte

---

53. Written October 1942, cited by Frank, p. 174.

in occupying the Free Zone and destroying its fleet in Toulon came as a disenchantment. Why did Pétain not resign? he asked himself; and, with one exception in 1944, Renouvin never mentioned his name again for the rest of the war. Yet he also scarcely ever spoke of the Resistance, and when he did, rarely in a positive sense; likewise of De Gaulle. In 1943 he continued to overestimate Allied difficulties in Italy and speculated on a second Soviet pact with Hitler. By early 1944, with the Red Army advancing into Poland, he noted that while many around him did not want a Russian victory, they preferred the risk of Bolshevism to the current situation in France, a view he shared.

In the summer, however, once the Allies had landed in Normandy and broken through German defences there, his notes multiplied with the relief he now felt, covering the liberation of Paris in late August in vivid, precisely observed detail, down to the sniper fire from which he and his wife sought shelter after joining the march behind De Gaulle from the Étoile to Notre Dame. His references to the General now became more positive, as a shield against unsettling threats from the Resistance. But he was soon sceptical of what he saw as his merely gestural politics, foreseeing a return of the old parties of the Third Republic, with their submission to American designs for making France an economic colony, not to speak of their inveterate anti-clericalism, and he continued above all to fear communism. The notes end with the formal surrender of the Third Reich by Dönitz in May 1945, and the lack of any explosion of popular enthusiasm at the news comparable to November 1918. That, Renouvin thought, could be explained by its gradual and predictable arrival, by the fact that it was not really a victory of France, and by awareness of the international difficulties to come – whereas 'in November 1918 there were illusions'.

Throughout these years, in Frank's estimate, Renouvin was

reacting out of his experience of that earlier time, articulating the pessimism of the generation of survivors to which he belonged. Had he learnt any lessons from the second war? Two, Frank thought: his subsequent writing about De Gaulle and the Resistance corrected his miscalculations of them during the conflict; and among the spiritual forces to be reckoned along with the material forces as the underlying drivers of modern warfare he would henceforward include moral principles that had once been neglected in his realism. To this judgment perhaps two considerations could be added. The hostility to communism so explicit in Renouvin's notes on the Second World War, largely absent in anything he had previously published, was common enough at the time in the class from which he came in France, though in his case clearly reflecting a Catholicism of which he never spoke even to his intimates. Unquestionably, it was a Catholicism of the Right, but what kind of Right – what variety of conservatism – was it? His discretion, imposing abstention from public commentary on domestic politics, precludes any too confident surmise. An analogous question is posed by the sequences of the notes themselves. What explains the two signal gaps in them? Mere circumstance? Given Renouvin's extremely disciplined and orderly ways, methodical to a fault in everything he did, it might seem unlikely. Certainly, the similarity of the events on which his notes left no trace is quite pointed: the fall of France and the invasion of Russia, the most spectacular triumphs of German arms in the Second World War; contemporary reactions to which could have been embarrassing once the direction of the war changed. But any surmise that he did away with what he wrote in those intervals can be no more than speculation.

The posture Renouvin adopted during the Second World War was not shared by his brother. Twelve years his junior, Jacques Renouvin differed from him in both character and opinion. An outspoken royalist, who studied and practised law, he became a militant of Action française, but broke with it over its role in the right-wing riots of February 1934. In November 1938 he made national headlines when he slapped the prominent conservative politician Pierre-Étienne Flandin twice in the face for laying a wreath on the tomb of the unknown soldier under the Arc de Triomphe after sending a fulsome telegram to Hitler and Mussolini congratulating them on Munich. A large man full of joie de vivre, after fighting with distinction during the fall of France he organized and led commando units in the Resistance until he was arrested by the Gestapo in 1943, tortured and deported to Mauthausen, where he died of exhaustion in 1944. Today streets in France are named after him. Renouvin's son Michel, who worked with his uncle in the Resistance and was caught and imprisoned in the summer of 1942, was released before the landings in Normandy.[54]

Hidden from view, the notes Renouvin wrote on the war during the occupation had no bearing on his fortunes after the war, which only prospered as his diligence and ascent continued. His *Crise* went through six editions, selling 50,000 copies. After the publication of his subsequent book on the Far East, he set to work editing the first four (Middle Ages to 1815) and writing the last four (1815 to 1945) of a massive eight-volume history of international relations, subsequently followed by an analytic overview of the most recent century co-authored with his pupil Duroselle, which appeared in the year of his retirement from the Sorbonne.[55] In these, he adjusted his outlook

---

54. For particulars of the incident in 1939, and Jacques Renouvin's record during the war, see François-Marin Fleutot, *Des royalistes dans la Résistance*, Paris 2000, pp. 30–4, 295–313, 367–70.

55. *Histoire des relations internationales*, Vols 1–8, Paris, 1953–58, and (with Jean-Baptiste Duroselle) *Introduction à l'histoire des relations internationales*, Paris, 1964.

to the altered historiographic climate of post-war France, dominated by the Annales school pioneered by Lucien Febvre and Marc Bloch before the war, and now led by Fernand Braudel, which tended to dismiss traditional diplomatic history as a superficial chronicle of events, in favour of the study of geography, demography and economy as the long-term determinants of any civilization and its alterations. Braudel and Renouvin disliked one another personally, and institutionally were rivals – the newly created École Pratique des Hautes Etudes, funded by the Rockefeller and Ford Foundations, fortress of the former; the Sorbonne and École des Sciences Politiques (by delegation) of the latter. Acknowledging the examples of Febvre and the Italian historian Federico Chabod, Renouvin now extended the range of his work to the *forces profondes* underlying the political story of interstate relations, of which the two most important were cultural and economic, the passions of nationalism and the drivers of industrialism.

The re-angling of his output was not just to the ascent of the Annales. It was also to the emergence of international relations as a very different kind of enterprise across the Atlantic, intellectually antithetical in its tendency to an abstract formalism. The study of IR which Renouvin now established as a discipline in France acknowledged American developments, but gave them a less conceptual, more empirical and historical turn. His one contribution to the journal directed by Braudel was a reflection on Raymond Aron's *Paix et Guerre entre Nations*, at the juncture between the two traditions to which he sought in his own way to adapt.[56] Today, the antagonists of the fifties are

---

56. The symposium, 'Pour ou contre une politocologie scientifique', was introduced by Braudel, noting the lack of enthusiasm of the school which he headed for standard diplomatic history, and featured inter alia François Chatelet, Bertrand de Jouvenel and Alain Touraine: *Annales*, January–February and March–April 1963, pp. 119–32 and 475–98; Renouvin at 475–8.

sometimes seen as more similar than either imagined, affected without being converted by the widespread influence of Marxism in post-war France, Renouvin's conception of *forces profondes* sharing its stress on the economy with Braudel's concern with capitalism and material civilization, and his allowance of the ideational component of these with the other pole of the Annales tradition, descending from Febvre, the importance it accorded to mentalities. Yet as a young scholar would later note, Renouvin did not succeed in truly articulating his *forces profondes* – which included demography and social change – with the realist primacy that in practice he tended to give to the plane of politics proper in the determination of international, still treated as strictly interstate, relations.[57]

Under the Fourth Republic he returned to the origins of the First World War, in the sixth volume of the octet over which he presided, covering the years 1871 to 1914. The 'most pressing question' posed by them was still 'why after forty-three years in which Europe knew only local wars, did the great powers come to blows?' Despite the abundant documentation that had become available, explanations beyond the realm of diplomatic history still lacked adequate empirical footholds in the economic, intellectual and psychological landscapes of the time. Historical research oscillated between 'sticking too closely to documents that seem solid and incontestable, at the risk of missing

---

57. See Ludovic Tournès, 'Relire Pierre Renouvin', in Jean-Michel Guieu and Claire Sanderson, eds, *L'historien et les relations internationales*, Paris 2012, pp. 169–78. Theoretically, Renouvin always insisted that what forces – demographic, economic, social, ideological, political – were causally decisive in any major historical development varied according to the epoch and the conjuncture, and could only be established empirically, not according to any a priori axiom, a view anticipating the position taken by the contemporary historical sociologist Michael Mann, with his IEMP model of the four sources (ideological, economic, military and political) of social power.

the essential, or looking beyond them at weak evidence, whose interpretation gives too free rein to seductive hypotheses'. Rather than recounting once again, as he had in some measure done in the past, the course of events leading to the Great War, he now preferred to 'stress only its most important moments, sacrificing a narrative of the conflicts of the time to a search for their explanation'.[58]

In practice, the end result did not differ greatly from that of 1925. Though proportionate space was now accorded to the economic and colonial expansion of Europe in the pre-war period, and collective psychologies preceded governmental intentions in the outbreak of the war – the arms race and bellicose nationalism holding pride of place in Renouvin's exposition – Germany remains the culprit in setting off the first and exhibiting the worst of the second of these dynamics, inciting Austria to a major war that Russia and France had to accept, on pain of 'a failure of nerve dangerous to their prestige as states and to the future of their national interests'.[59] Poincaré? More glowingly than ever, a patriot possessed of a sense of his country's 'national grandeur', who did not want war – for which there was no credible evidence – but a leader 'firmly determined to defend the rights of France', who knew that conflict with Germany was 'more or less inevitable'. After Bismarck, Europe had generally lacked statesmen of his calibre, but in a panorama of otherwise grey mediocrities, two figures stood out as exceptions: Salisbury and Poincaré – the first by virtue of his subtlety, the second for his resolve.[60] Nor, he would later go on to argue, were the Allies who rightly won the war much at

---

58. *Histoire des Relations Internationales, VI – Le XIXe Siècle: II De 1871 à 1914: L'apogée de l'Europ*e, Paris 1955, pp. 2–3.

59. Ibid., pp 351–2, 354–5, 371.

60. *Histoire des Relations Internationales, V*, pp. 360, 377–8. Outside Europe, Theodore Roosevelt and the Meiji *genro* were politicians of a different order.

fault in the peace they imposed after it. True, the war-guilt clause of Versailles could have been avoided, but not the general provisions of the treaty, many of them necessarily retributive. Its flaw as a settlement lay not in its content, but in the inadequacy of the means to enforce it, which the Allies failed to institute, condemning it to decay once they fell out, as they soon did.[61]

That Renouvin could nevertheless give original form to his dichotomy between *forces profondes* and *causes politiques* he showed in the book that he did, in the event, write about the Second World War, the last volume of the *Histoire des relations internationals* he brought out in the fifties, with which his war-time folders, when they are published, will repay comparison. In this, he applied his theoretical grid to the combined European and Asian, Atlantic and Pacific, theatres of the war with meticulous economy and consistency. On the one hand, both of the *forces profondes*, material and spiritual, singled out as most salient receive due coverage: the relative weight – numerical size and technical modernity – of the war-machines of each major belligerent, and the particular temper and morale of the population in each state engaged in hostilities. On the other hand, the political decisions of the leadership at the helm of each combatant state determine the dynamic of the narrative from the outset, in Europe Hitler's will to war leaving no room for ambiguity. A consequence of this way of construing the conflict was that the military history of the fighting, which occupies the larger part of standard accounts, scarcely figures at all in Renouvin's version of the war, whose outcome hinges on the alliances pitted against each other, rather than the battles they waged.

---

61. *Le traité de Versailles*, Paris 1966, pp. 115–17. After changing their conflicting positions on how to deal with Bolshevism, the Allies did eventually all agree on a military intervention in Russia, but by then it was too late. The peoples of Europe were exhausted, unwilling to embark on another war: pp. 104–13.

'The centre of interest, for a history of international relations, is the study of the interventions and defections, and the brusque changes they entrained, in the balance of military, naval and aerial forces.'[62]

What was the effect of this optic on the narrative, at the two junctures where Renouvin's war-time reflections broke off – the fall of France in the spring of 1940 and the invasion of Russia in the summer of 1941? Three pages consider the Nazi motivations for Operation Barbarossa; three sentences, its advance to the gates of Moscow. A page on the reasons why it was checked there; twenty pages later, a sentence on the Russian counter-attack at Stalingrad.[63] The fall of France is another matter, occupying a full chapter and a half, a difference due to the much better information about it at Renouvin's disposal, and his naturally greater interest in the fate of his own country.[64] Here too the fighting is dispatched in a few terse lines, but the subsequent story of the division of France into an occupied and an unoccupied zone, the formation of Free France abroad under De Gaulle, establishment of the Vichy regime under Pétain, the conflicts within it, popular attitudes and German policies towards Vichy, the fate of the French fleet in the Mediterranean and of its colonies in North Africa, are all covered in some detail, for the most part cogently and lucidly; the reasons why Hitler initially refrained from occupying the whole country, and Franco from keeping his initial pledge to bring Spain into the war on the Axis side, are well set out. The tone of the account is even and

---

62. *Histoire des relations internationales*, Vol. 8, *Les crises du XXe siècle – II: de 1929 à 1945*, Paris 1958, p. 204. The story ends on the same note: 'It sufficed for the coalition against it to hold fast, to settle the fate of Germany and its associates. Their arms and they alone ensured its defeat. The history of international relations has to limit itself to examining when and how the governments and peoples of the defeated states became aware of this and drew the consequences': p. 331.

63. Ibid., pp. 298, 320.

64. Ibid., pp. 252–82.

unemotional throughout. Pétain's regime, though collaborating with Germany, did not yield to pressures that would have led it to war with Britain, but it 'dangerously neglected moral values and deeply offended national feelings'. The marshal himself was too attached to power, in 'the dryness of his heart and his love of secrecy' playing a double game under the illusion that he could eventually mediate between Berlin and London, when in fact it was the existence of Free France alone that gave him what margin of autonomy he possessed, Hitler fearing that Algiers and the fleet would defect to De Gaulle if he ruled the whole country directly.[65] The distance of this verdict from the standpoint of his notebooks during the war bears out Frank's judgment that Renouvin had learnt post-war to leaven his realism with more ethical considerations. But it was a limited strand. Nowhere to be found is any mention of the fate of the Jews or the exactions of the *milices* under Vichy. Renouvin's retrospect of the Second World War had no words for its atrocities, the slaughter of populations by the Axis, the destruction of cities by the Allies. Diplomatic history, as in keeping with tradition as he practised it, could not but suffer from its own dryness of heart.

Institutionally, as his former assistant become colleague, Duroselle, noted on his death in 1974, Renouvin accumulated enormous power. President of the Academy of Social and Moral Sciences; of the historical section of the Consultative Commission of French Universities; of the Committee on History of the CNRS; of the National Foundation of Political Sciences (succeeding André Siegfried); of all juries for the award of doctorates in contemporary history, he eliminated competition for teaching posts in his field by ensuring there was only one candidate, selected by himself without ministerial interference,

---

65. Ibid., p. 282.

for each. After his death, those formed by him would constitute a posthumous bodyguard of his reputation, its latest celebration dating to 2020. In the 1980s Bourdieu could take him as the classic example of the 'great monarchs of the university' in France, citing Duroselle's *laudatio* of his person and his works: 'He seemed to accede to key positions as if by a natural necessity, without intriguing or pursuing them.' Indifferent to honours, Renouvin was nevertheless showered with them – Grand Cross of the Legion of Honour; membership in the academies of Belgium, Britain and Argentina; honorary doctorates from Cambridge, Liège, Padua, Rome – 'simply accepting them, in the quasi-obscurity of a life devoid of worldly distractions'. Yet he liked authority, which he considered a personal, not an institutional quality: to possess it was the highest compliment for him. In sum, he was 'a truly great man'.[66]

That was written nearly fifty years ago. Less reverent glimpses of Renouvin can be found in the first volume of Pierre Nora's memoirs of his youth, published in 2021. There, in pages describing Nora's early hopes, fresh from his national service in Oran in the early sixties, of becoming a historian in the established French mould, Renouvin appears more than once in the plenitude of his power. After the *succès de scandale* in 1961 of Nora's disobliging book on the French colons in Algeria, based on his experience there, when he had to choose between Braudel and Renouvin as director of his thesis, a sine qua non for a university career, and suspecting the former of a streak of anti-Semitic prejudice, he opted for the latter – in his eyes, 'the image of a mandarin dedicated to his teaching, to his students and to administration, solemn and liberal, born a dean as Dreyfus

---

66. Duroselle, 'Pierre Renouvin (1893-1974)', *Revue d'histoire moderne et contemporaine*, October–December 1975, pp. 499–500, 506–7.

was a captain', or more caustically in the eighties, 'Renouvin, the Just, the Majestic, the All-Powerful'.[67] Aware that Nora's book on Algeria, although or because it had sold well, could be viewed as a misstep for a scholar, Renouvin had written to him: 'Thank you for sending me your essay on *Les Français d'Algérie*. It comes at the right time and will, I am sure, occasion quite a few reflections. Remaining at your disposal to discuss your thesis . . .'[68] Nora decided to write an essay on Ernest Lavisse, with whose role in French higher education Renouvin's was often compared, as a reliable way of doing what was expected of him. Sure enough, the latter was delighted, telling his colleagues at the *Revue historique* that it should be the lead article in the next issue. His choice of subject for the thesis was thereafter obvious: an enlargement of his essay on Lavisse.[69]

Such a prospect, however, filled him with apprehension. Was

---

67. *Jeunesse*, Paris 2021, p. 189.

68. *Essais d'ego-histoire*, Paris 1985, p. 354, where Nora says he sent the book to Renouvin, 'trembling' with apprehension at his probable reaction. His account in *Jeunesse* curtails the letter and omits his tremors. The contribution to the same volume by the military historian Raoul Girardet, in his youth arrested and jailed for his role in the far-right paramilitary OAS, offers a very different image of Renouvin, who got him, like Nora, a job at Sciences Po. 'Behind an appearance of cold majesty lay in fact a strange shyness. Behind this shyness were soon to be found an attention to others, a concern to understand them, a generosity always circumspect in its expression but reliable in practical effect. A man who was said to be prudent (and was, perhaps to excess, for himself), he never discouraged audacity: more often and more efficaciously even than many others celebrated for their boldness, he knew how to protect and to help it. M. Renouvin or the spirit of equity': *Essais d'ego-histoire*, pp. 149–50. Nora reports that when Renouvin learnt of Girardet's imprisonment for his activities in the OAS, he lifted his one arm to the sky and 'seeking a precedent for the incendiary declarations of his protégé in the polemics of Aulard and Mathiez, remarked: "it's excessive, but after all it's always been like that, and it's certainly sincere."'

69. *Jeunesse*, pp. 197–8.

he to spend thirty years in some provincial outpost sweating in the straitjacket of a topic that had no real attraction for him, to be able to get back to Paris when he was fifty? 'Few people today have any idea of how hierarchical life in the universities was then – I never, in particular, allowed myself to sit down in the presence of Renouvin, who besides never suggested I do so.'[70] Not long afterwards, however, the Dean of Letters at the Sorbonne, a close friend of Renouvin's, asked him at a cocktail party whether he wouldn't like to travel round the world for nine months on a scholarship that could be arranged for him. But Nora, he confessed, was planning to get married, and this treat was only for bachelors. No problem: he could take his fiancée with him for the first part of the tour, bring her back for nuptials in Paris, and leave for the second part without her.

So he set off to see the world – USA, Mexico, Cuba, China – and on getting back was commissioned by Duroselle to contribute an essay to the *Festschrift* he was preparing for Renouvin on the occasion of his retirement, learning that Renouvin had actually vetted the list of contributors and, to Duroselle's astonishment, amidst the luminaries specifically included Nora. Overcome with gratitude for the benefits he received from a man whose disappointment and indifference he had feared, Nora produced an essay for the collection on 'The Burden of History' in the United States, of which Duroselle told him he understood not a word. It was a flying start to the polychromatic career that would make Nora arbiter of intellectual life in Paris for many years. His final vision of Renouvin? 'My statue of the *commendatore*.'[71]

---

70. Ibid., p. 198
71. Ibid., p. 201.

2

LUIGI ALBERTINI

Across the border meanwhile, an enterprise of an altogether larger order was under way in Italy. Its author, Luigi Albertini, remains to this day the most remarkable figure in the historiography of the First World War. Holding no academic position, often inadequately termed a journalist, he played a more significant role in the war itself than any other scholar, and left a lasting monument of research on the conflict, unfinished at his death. Born in 1871, the year Rome became the capital of a united Italy, he came from a wealthy family in Ancona, whose banking and real estate empire collapsed when he was in his late teens. Moving to Turin, where he took a law degree, the young Albertini was early drawn to political economy. At the age of twenty-three, in 1894 he spent eight months in London studying at the British Museum and acquainting himself with the workings of *The Times* in the Salisbury era. Returning to Italy, within little more than a year he was hired by the *Corriere della Sera*, the most respected though not the largest daily in Milan, as editorial secretary of the paper. Four years later, still in his twenties, he had become its director and managing editor. Purchasing the latest foreign printing press, hiring talented writers and reporters, expanding its international coverage, adding a cultural supplement, developing features for women, within a decade he had trebled its circulation. His modernization of the daily made it the most profitable and influential newspaper in the country, and he acquired in due course two-fifths of its shares.

Albertini's combination of organizational, financial and journalistic gifts made him a formidable figure at the *Corriere*. In all cultural matters, literary, theatrical, artistic or cinematic – his brother would remark in an admiring biography – he held 'clear, firm, absolute opinions: the damned on one side, the chosen on the other. Sure of his own judgments and that anyone who differed from them was wrong, so too about persons, politics, everything – he was intransigent.'[1] Under this 'tall, square man, heavy in foot and impassive in expression', wrote a young employee at the paper, later a well-known writer and critic, 'work at the *Corriere* is from the first day there an exercise in adaptation and submission'.[2] Yet though autocratic in manner, Albertini was also a magnetic entrepreneur and editorialist, who commanded considerable loyalty from his staff – a figure unique in the media landscape of the belle epoque, neither a crude tycoon like Northcliffe, nor a mandarin insider like Dawson. Architect of a lucrative high-quality daily, combining intellectual distinction with a mass circulation, he looked down on his English counterpart, who was enormously richer and more successful as an empire-builder but the ill-educated progenitor of a vulgarian *Daily Mail* and largely *fainéant* owner of *The Times*: 'Northcliffe has never been the real director of his political papers. I am.'[3]

---

1. Possessing 'a good dose of intolerance and a limited amount of patience', he 'could pass for a bad character; and perhaps he did not, in reality, have an easy character; but his very angularities imposed respect for him, and won over others': Alberto Albertini, *Vita di Luigi Albertini*, Rome 1945, pp. 275–6.

2. Corrado Alvaro, *Luigi Albertini*, Rome 1923, pp. 26, 40: the most perceptive, if often caustic, account of the ethos and atmosphere of the paper.

3. Luigi Albertini, *Epistolario*, Vol. II, Milan 1968, p. 733.

After 1860, parliamentary life in Italy – the electorate was 2 per cent of the population, of whom a third cast no ballot – was from the outset polarized between the heirs of Cavour, the moderates who presided over the country's unification, and the followers of Garibaldi or Mazzini who opposed them, the former becoming the Historic Right, the latter the Historic Left of the political system. For some fifteen years, the descendants of Cavour ruled the country, until in early 1876 divisions among them brought the opposition to power. Both sides proclaimed themselves liberals, as Cavour himself had done: in the Italian parlance of the time, a thin term denoting little more than loyalty to the Piedmontese monarchy and its constitution, adhesion to a laissez-faire economy, and vigilance against clericalism – since the papacy had pronounced excommunication on any Catholic who cast a vote or took office in the new order.[4] Within this common framework, the Right stood for strict budgetary economy and no electoral concessions, the Left for less rigorous control of expenditure and a modest broadening of the suffrage. Both repressed, regularly and ruthlessly, any popular protest against the oligarchic system they upheld. From 1876 till 1887, the Left was led by Agostino Depretis, who increased the number of voters to 6 per cent, but *pari passu* manipulation and corruption of elections and of parliament. After Depretis died, power passed to Francesco Crispi, a politician who had once been an insurgent with Garibaldi, but since become an authoritarian exponent of Italian imperialism in Africa, who after evading culpability in a financial

---

4. 'The liberals had no permanent organization, no party newspaper, no central funds, no party whip. In the words of one contemporary, the Liberal party was the "great absentee" of Italian political life. The terms "liberal" and "party" were indeed antipathetic': Christopher Seton-Watson, *Italy from Liberalism to Fascism 1870–1925*, London 1967, p. 246.

scandal came to grief with the defeat of an expedition in Ethiopia in 1896.

By this time, the mass of the population, excluded from the political life of the country since unification, could no longer be held down so easily. Before his fall, Crispi had declared martial law to crush a major peasant rising in Sicily, and after his departure workers in Milan, where the recently founded Socialist Party had won a following, rose in three days of riots in 1898, put down at royal command with heavy bloodshed and mass arrests by the army. When the Historic Right proved unable to stamp out the spread of social unrest to any effect, the Left took over once again, this time led by Giovanni Giolitti, who reiterated and radicalized the tactics of Depretis. His rule sought to neutralize the Socialists by absorbing them into his coalition with concessions to labour and eventually universal male suffrage, while rigging elections and buying parliamentary support more systematically than ever before, backed with the customary mailed fist if any serious trouble threatened from below.

Such was the regime that took over just as Albertini was remodelling the *Corriere*, and it was against its more centrist brand of liberal politics that he pitted the paper. Giolitti might talk of progress towards democracy, but Albertini denounced his reign as a venal dictatorship, subverting the constitution and demoralizing the nation. Certain reforms were no doubt needed: Cavour himself had introduced some. But not at the expense of the essential values of the Historic Right – austerity and probity. It was urgent to make these, rather than profligate spending, shady transactions and demagogic sops to the masses, the guiding principles of public life once again. Albertini hammered these motifs home with such style and brio that he would eventually be viewed by many as the 'real leader' of national opposition to the government, which faced no comparable adversary in parliament.⁵ Not that he was a political leader in any conventional sense, his character was too rigid for that. 'He was born to command and loved to command,' observed his brother, but the inflexibility of his principles – his absolute commitment to his own ideas – was ill-suited to the manoeuvres and compromises of government.⁶ His 'mentality was military' rather than parliamentary. As a result, though ideologically very influential, he was personally rather isolated, a combination that would define his public career.⁷

Fortified by rapid economic growth, in the summer of 1911 Giolitti passed a bill for universal male suffrage – which he had earlier dismissed as the 'apotheosis of ignorance', and which Albertini utterly rejected, later blaming it for the success of fascism⁸ – and another for national insurance, in a bid to integrate the right wing of the socialist party into his government and their voters into

---

5. 'Il vero capo dell'opposizione al regime "giolittiano" ', in the judgment of his biographer Ottavio Barié; see his preface to the edition of Albertini's correspondence he edited, Luigi Albertini, *Epistolario 1911–1926*, I, Milan 1968 p. viii. Though this life of Albertini now dates back half a century, it remains the only such work produced since the Second World War. For Richard Bosworth too, 'In the decade before 1914, Albertini was arguably the conservative leader of the opposition to *giolittismo*': *Italy and the Approach of the First World War*, London and Basingstoke, 1983, pp. 31–2.

6. Alberto Albertini, *Vita di Luigi Albertini*, p. 293. In the transformation of the *Corriere*, the role of the two brothers bears some resemblance to the relationship between Arthur and Harold Harmsworth in the Northcliffe empire, with the difference that Alberto was not the financial mind of the pair, but a talented writer and lucid sibling in his own right, who could claim that 'being so different from my brother, I could in a certain sense see him extraneously, knowing what were his qualities and what were his defects, however difficult it may be to decide at what point a good quality becomes a defect': p. 293.

7. 'Militare per mentalità': Glauco Licata, *Storia del Corriere della Sera*, Milan 1976, pp. 146, 164.

8. 'Universal suffrage gave us disastrous legislatures, which were not the last reason for the state of things that brought the arrival of fascism': *Venti Anni di Vita Politica*, I/II, Bologna 1951, p. 72.

his electorate. In much the same spirit, seeking to satisfy national aspirations to the standing of a great European power by emulating French colonial acquisition of Morocco, Giolitti took Italy into a war to seize Libya – represented as the breadbasket of the Roman Empire – from Ottoman control. Albertini's close friend Luigi Einaudi – another staunch pillar of the Historic Right, later president of Italy – had, like not a few of his associates, no time for these or other fantasies about the barren territory across the water. Albertini himself was a disciplinarian liberal of the same rigid stamp. In that he was quite unlike Northcliffe, who mostly just backed whatever would sell his products. But he had one streak in common with Northcliffe, whose only political belief was in the belligerent cult of the British Empire. Less fervent in Albertini's case, a similar outlook was nevertheless quite sufficient to propel him and his paper into imperialist transports over the adventure in Libya, vital not only for the prosperity, but the honour and the glory of Italy. Throwing any regard for truth – not to speak of taste – to the winds, the *Corriere* deluged the public with exultant chauvinist lies about the Libyan campaign, a debacle which ran into stiff Arab resistance that was not finally erased, after many an Italian atrocity, till the early thirties. Not only were the paper's reporters reduced to the bombast of official propaganda, but Albertini now touted D'Annunzio, whom he had long helped financially and published in his pages, as the great bard of the nation, giving lofty voice in the pages of the *Corriere* to the war as Italy's resplendent Mediterranean destiny.[9]

---

9. 'Why not an ode' – Albertini asked D'Annunzio before Italian troops had even landed in Tripoli – to this 'magnificent recovery of our national feeling?': *Epistolario* I, p. 14. Alvaro was not wrong to see what such indulgence implied, 'a discreet antipathy towards every form of intellectualism', the *Corriere* 'supplying the garb of its vestments to lend a decent appearance to many of the basest things

Giolitti brought the war to a formal end with the ostensible victory of an Ottoman cession of its province to Rome, for which King Victor Emmanuel III offered to make him a duke, while in Libya itself fighting against its inhabitants still raged and would worsen. Reaping the benefit of his expansion of the suffrage, Giolitti won another handsome majority when elections were held in 1913. But he could not shake off what had by now become 'the immense aura of opprobrium that surrounded the liberal state'.[10] The country was slipping out of his control. To his right, the first Nationalist Congress was held the year before the invasion of Libya, the second soon after it, signalling the rise of a militant expansionism that viewed Giolitti with contempt as a paltering time-server. To his left, social discontent intensified, scaring the property-owners behind him. His new majority, moreover, depended on a pact he had made with Catholics hitherto excluded from the political system, scandalizing the anti-clerical traditions of the Historic Right. Alarmed by the menace of Socialist–Catholic collusion in parliament, Albertini redoubled his attacks on the regime. When the bill for the Libyan war, which the government had sought to conceal, came due in early 1914 and required higher taxes, its Radical sector quit. Whereupon Giolitti, still in control of a majority and confident he could return when he wished, resigned, letting one of his most conservative ministers, Antonio Salandra, a professorial landowner from the South devoted to the canon of the Historic Right, take over. In June the police shot another trio of demonstrators against war and capitalism in Ancona,

---

in our country, much as 'Giolitti succeeded in giving the Italy of our time the semblance of a great nation among great nations'; *Luigi Albertini*, pp. 26, 34.

10. Disgust with which was 'shared by nearly all the most influential intellectuals of the day': Christopher Duggan, *The Force of Destiny: A History of Italy since 1796*, London, 2007, p. 369.

where the Socialist Party, now in full revolutionary spate had expelled its reformists that spring. The killings provoked a local insurrection that set off a wave of popular riots and attacks across Italy – a 'Red Week' terrifying bourgeois society at large. Without hesitation, Salandra mobilized 100,000 troops to crush the protests.

A month later the heir to the Habsburg throne was assassinated in Sarajevo, and Europe entered the countdown to the First World War. Technically, Italy was a member of the Triple Alliance with Germany and Austria it had signed in 1882 out of mortification that Tunisia had just been taken over by France, rather than by itself. But all three powers had long regarded the treaty as a malleable or temporary arrangement, to be dispensed with if it suited them to do so. Italy, at loggerheads with Austria not only because Vienna controlled pockets of territory inhabited by Italians in the Trentino and Trieste, but also harbouring ambitions of its own for an advance into the Balkans, had already violated the Alliance by annexing Libya without consulting its partners, just as Austria had done in delivering its ultimatum to Serbia. In 1914 there was no support in public opinion for joining the Central Powers in war against the Entente. Once the fighting started, in which neither Germany nor Austria attacked Italy, an overwhelming majority favoured staying out of the conflict. Yet ten months later, Italy plunged into the killing with a declaration of war on Austria. What had happened in the interim? A small minority in the country had unleashed a clamorous campaign for it to abandon neutrality and join the Entente, in the name either of the transfiguring virtues of heroic war as such (Futurists), or completion of the preordained mission of the Risorgimento to expel Austria from its last footholds on Italian soil (Nationalists), or the moral duty of standing by the Western democracies in their battle with Teutonic autocracy (Radicals and Republicans). But though the Nationalist component of this front, much the largest, had powers of physical and rhetorical intimidation (D'Annunzio to the fore), it was too limited a force to be decisive in the change of the country's direction, which came from the summit of the political system, not its *bas-fonds*.

Parliament was in recess when the war broke out, and Salandra – installed as a provisional locum for Giolitti, without a majority of his own in the Chamber – had no intention of recalling it. Initially himself inclined to neutrality, he was soon subject to rival inducements from the belligerents to take their side, and by the autumn was leaning towards intervention on the side of the Entente, for which Albertini – privately interventionist from the start, vociferously public soon afterwards – was openly campaigning. In October 1914 Salandra announced that he would consult only Italy's national interests – '*sacro egoismo*' – in deciding its policy. In December he rewarded Albertini for his support during Red Week and his attacks on neutrality by elevating him to the Senate, a life-appointment. By the spring, Salandra and his foreign minister, Sidney Sonnino, a still harder devotee of the Historic Right, had two sets of proposals before them. Germany, knowing that if Italy entered the war on the side of the Entente, Austria would have to divert troops which were needed against Russia in Galicia to the Alps, forced Vienna to promise Rome that if it remained neutral, the Trentino and Trieste would be ceded to Italy. The Entente was prepared to offer more, in exchange for more. If Italy engaged in the war on its side, it would receive not just the Trentino and Trieste, but South Tyrol too, and on the other side of the Adriatic the whole Istrian Peninsula, plus a substantial slice of Dalmatia and most of the islands along its coast, a fortified port in Albania, and the Dodecanese. In great secrecy, on 26 April 1915 Salandra signed the Treaty of London incorporating these provisions. The treaty committed Italy to opening hostilities against the Central

Powers within a month. Neither the cabinet, nor the general staff, nor the country were informed.[11]

Giolitti, who had been biding his time on his country estate in the expectation of resuming his post as premier, arrived in Rome on 9 May to learn that Salandra had privately notified the Central Powers that the Triple Alliance was terminated. He told both Salandra and the king that he was opposed to the war, for which Italy had neither need nor resources to fight, and for which there was no majority in parliament. Salandra admitted that by a wide margin most Italians were opposed to the war, and knowing how few were those in the chamber who favoured it, resolved to quit — confident that the king, who had approved the Treaty of London, would reappoint him. In an unprecedented move, he announced his resignation not to parliament, which had still not been recalled, but in the *Corriere*, which broke the news to the country that Italy had abrogated the Triple Alliance. Two days later the king refused to accept Salandra's resignation. Giolitti, unwilling to risk the monarchy, fell silent. D'Annunzio, discreetly summoned back to Rome by Albertini, mobilized mobs to swarm the streets and harass deputies, and when parliament finally assembled on 2 May, a cowed chamber reversed course and voted by a huge majority for war. The *Corriere* hailed the decision with the jubilant headline *Italy Awakens!*

In the panorama of powers that precipitated Europe into the catastrophe of the First World War, the case of Italy was unique. All the states that declared war in 1914 claimed that they had acted only defensively: Austria against a criminal *attentat* by

---

11. For this sequence of events, see Dennis Mack Smith's acerbic account, *Italy: A Modern History*, Ann Arbor 1969, pp. 289–305.

Serbia, Russia to thwart Austrian aggression, Germany to ward off Russian invasion, France to resist German assault, Britain to come to the rescue of Belgium. Italy alone could allege no such rationale. To all appearances, its rulers went to war purely and simply for territorial gain. That each side had no compunction in offering it to them is commentary enough on the truth of their own part in the slaughter. For the Italians who willingly rallied to the fight – once hostilities were engaged, the majority of those who were literate – their cause was just because it was the last war of the Risorgimento, fought to liberate the remainder of the country which, after the incomplete victories of 1860, 1866 and 1870, was still occupied by Austria. They were not to know of the terms of the Treaty of London, which went well beyond the aims of literal irredentism, until these were revealed by the Bolsheviks in 1918. But as an Italian scholar, Federico Curato, would point out much later, while it was true that Mazzini had distinguished between the principles of nationality and nationalism, upholding the first and reproving the second, it was a general rule that perfectly justified demands for national self-determination, once realized in a sovereign nation-state, usually tended to overflow into ambitions of a nationalist type for further territory lacking any such justification.[12] So it was with the Risorgimento too, breeding dreams of a Greater Italy of indefinite contours. In the event, though Italy ended up on the winning side of the war that it entered, the gains it achieved were not those promised by the Treaty of London. They were those it could have secured without the million Italian casualties of the First World War had

---

12. 'Aspetti nazionalistici della politica estera italiana 1870–1914', *Il Politico*, 47, 2, 1982, pp. 253–80.

it accepted the terms – which in a famous phrase Giolitti reckoned as *parecchio*, 'quite a lot' – offered by the Central Powers in 1915 and remained neutral.[13]

It would be a mistake, however, to think calculations of territorial swag were decisive in the option for war. They mattered to politically conscious Italians for whom memories of the Risorgimento were still active. But they were never the prime motivation of the tiny group who took the country into the abyss that awaited it. For them the prize lay elsewhere. For Salandra, Sonnino and Albertini, war was the way to achieve the overriding goal of their political careers: to put paid to Giolitti and his system.[14] Their calculation was not wrong, though it was not they who would be the beneficiaries of their decision. Nor was it actuated simply by detestation of Giolitti as the living negation of the ideals of the *Destra* to which they

---

13. All it gained was the pittance of German-speaking South Tyrol.
14. On this, the consensus of historians is overwhelming. Ricard Bosworth: 'What was becoming really important to Salandra, Sonnino and Albertini and their colleagues was the chance to dismantle Giolitti's political system, and bring Italy a more austere domestic order, which would avoid intellectually and socially dangerous compromises with Catholics and Socialists': *Italy: The Least of the Great Power*s, Cambridge 1979, p. 406; Adrian Lyttleton: 'War came to be identified in Salandra's eyes with the aim of destroying the Giolittian system in all its manifestations. War, Salandra believed, while making it possible to repress revolutionary demonstrations and limit criticism, would restore the prestige of the monarchy, the army and conservative liberalism': *The Seizure of Power: Fascism in Italy 1919–1928*, London 2004, p. 24. Mark Thompson: 'Salandra was not obsessed by territory. He later denied having ever believed that Italy would benefit from gaining Dalmatia or the Tyrol north of Bolzano; they were to be bargaining chips after the war. His project was something else. He wanted to move Italian politics permanently to the right by building a new anti-Socialist bloc of northern industrialists and Southern landowners, who both wanted markets abroad and civic discipline at home': *The White War: Life and Death on the Italian Front 1915–1919*, London 2008, p. 36.

clung. Their belief was that the purgative experience of war would transform the country, lifting Italy out of the slough of mediocrity, dishonesty and irresponsibility into which forty years of selfish *trasformismo* had sunk it, and making it at last a true Great Power, standing honourably erect among its peers. Of the trio who cast the die, Albertini was the most clear-sighted and resolute, plumping for war well before the other two and articulating more clearly what became their common vision of why it was needed. Salandra later confessed that without the campaign the *Corriere* led, he could not have gotten Italy into the field.[15]

In the event, Italy declared war – contrary to its pledge in London – in May 1915 not against the German, Austrian and Ottoman empires, but against Austria alone. With months of secret preparations for doing so, by the time it launched its assault on Habsburg lines it had an overwhelming superiority in numbers, a ratio of 4:1 for its attack. But most of its troops were peasant conscripts with little aptitude or enthusiasm for the harsh ordeal they faced; supplies were poor; and the high command was brutal and incompetent to a degree without equal in the Great War. The general who was appointed chief of staff in July 1914, Luigi Cadorna, was known for his 'irascibility and absolute refusal to accept any criticism'. The trademark of his command was the practice, unique in the First World War, of official decimation: orders to execute without trial enough men, picked at random from any unit deemed guilty of protest, desertion, or retreat, to instil

---

15. By the time he did so, Salandra was no longer on good terms with Albertini, and couched his admission in vague terms: 'I have to acknowledge that, without the newspapers, the intervention of Italy would not have been possible': *La Neutralità Italiana* [1914], Milan 1928, p. 228. Everyone with a memory of the time knew what lay behind the reference.

discipline in the rest.[16] Under such a regime, he sent troops into battle at a grindingly slow pace of advance, with heavy casualties, against a smaller but better trained and motivated enemy. In May 1916 a swift *Strafexpedition* through mountain valleys by Habsburg units inflicted 150,000 losses on Italian forces, a setback so sharp that it toppled Salandra in Rome. The following year another sudden Austrian counter-offensive again caught Cadorna by surprise, routing the Italians at Caporetto – the most ignominious single defeat of any belligerent in the First World War. Retreating 150 kilometres, close to half his effectives and equipment were lost, amid scenes of panic, chaos and plunder on jam-packed roads to the rear.[17] Cadorna's reaction was to blame the disaster on the soldiers he commanded, 'traitors, cowards and slackers' responsible for a 'moral crisis' in the army. He himself was blameless. This time it was not enough to save him. Dismissed, he was nevertheless given the honourable exit of a liaison post in Paris. Eventually, under a Neapolitan commander, Italy was able to claim a postiche victory over Austria in late October 1918, when the Central Powers were already beaten and suing for peace.

After the fighting ended a fortnight later, Italy's new prime minister, Vittorio Orlando, a Sicilian jurist and ardent interventionist, told the nation: 'This war is the greatest political and social revolution recorded by history, surpassing even the French Revolution.' Even

---

16. More soldiers were executed with or without trial in Italy than in any other belligerent for which there are figures: Marco Pluviano and Irene Guerrini, *Le Fucilazioni sommarie nella prima guerra mondiale*, Udine 2004, pp. 246–7. For cases, see Thompson, *The Winter War*, pp. 263–7; and for data, John Gooch, *The Italian Army and the First World War*, Cambridge 2014, pp. 123–39, 363.

17. For Caporetto, see Gooch's account in *The Italian Army in the First World War*, pp. 226–46.

decades later, Albertini could applaud this 'lofty discourse', expressing particular pleasure at its celebration of the ideal motives that 'attested to the nobility and grandeur' of Italy's role in the war.[18] From the outset, he had been an indefatigable crier for its cause, identifying personally with Cadorna as a fellow martinet, and turning the *Corriere* into an organ of official propaganda that deliberately suppressed or embellished the realities of the front, beyond even its performance in the Libyan War. So fervent was Albertini in his bellicism that he spent three to four days every month at the HQ of the high command in Udine, directing his paper in syncopation with Cadorna's direction of his troops, his reporters ghosting official communiqués and himself helping to compose the bulletin for which Cadorna became notorious after Caporetto.[19] Anything else was *lèse patria*, that could only encourage neutralism of a Giolittian ilk. Trumpeting final victory in November 1918, Albertini looked forward to a country that would show the world a unity and greatness of reconstruction in peace equal to its heroism in war.

---

18. Albertini, *Venti anni di vita politica*, Vols II/ III, Bologna 1953, pp. 748–9.

19. For the intimacy between the two men during and after the war, see Andrea Guiso, *Il direttore e il generale: Carteggio Albertini-Cadorna 1915–1928*, Milan 2014; and on Caporetto pp. 38, 60–1, 78. Giancarlo Finizio has now established just how closely involved Albertini was in the agitated circumstances at Treviso in which Cadorna's infamous communiqué was composed, and how he would later deny his part in them. See the intricate recent scholarship of Finizio's reconstruction of these in his study of *Il Bollettino Cadorna su Caporetto (28 Ottobre 1917)*, Lecce 2023, pp. 240–88. Albertini upheld a veritable cult of his associate to the end: see the fulsome tribute – Cadorna was 'among the greatest and most luminous figures in the history of Italy' – in *Venti anni di vita politica*, Vols II/III, pp. 183–8. He even took pains to belittle Cadorna's replacement Armando Diaz – 'who had nothing to show he was worth more than others of his rank', was 'appreciated more for his political than strictly military gifts', and 'rightly thought malleable' – in order to place his friend on the summits of Italian strategic valour: II/III, pp. 63, 449.

In the event, peace brought the reverse of harmony to the nation, or satisfaction to Albertini. Already in the last year of the war, a split had opened up in the camp that had launched it, once the deal struck in London was published by the Bolsheviks and Wilson issued his Fourteen Points. The Treaty of 1915 accorded Italy territory on the other side of the Adriatic populated by some 700,000 Slavs, in contradiction to what was widely (if inaccurately) believed to be Wilson's proclamation of the right of national self-determination in his Fourteen Points. Interventionists who had backed the war in the name of democracy repudiated the treaty, renouncing Italian claims to Dalmatia; interventionists who had backed the war in the name of Greater Italy demanded fidelity to the treaty. But the treaty itself had neglected to include the port of Fiume, today's Rijeka, in the gains it promised Italy, though the majority of its inhabitants were Italian. D'Annunzio promptly denounced this omission as a 'mutilated victory', and with the help of the army staged a coup giving him control of Fiume. Yet at the Peace Conference in Versailles even the treaty was set aside by Wilson, in favour of the claims of a newly emergent Yugoslavia to the whole of Dalmatia. Nationalist uproar ensued in Italy, which had occupied much of it. Albertini knew of the provisions of the Treaty of London, and approved them at the outset of the war. But for Italy to become what it should be, a Great Power, expansion into the Balkans was not essential: he supported irredentist claims where he felt territory could be held securely, and could dispense with them where not. Decisive for him was Wilson's opposition to these in Dalmatia, for not only had in his eyes the victory of the Entente depended on the United States, but since October 1917 America had become a vital barrier against Communism. When Orlando threatened to pull out of Versailles in protest at Wilson's opposition to the Treaty of London, Albertini upbraided him for paying no attention to the spreading danger of revolutionary socialism, which was what Italians cared about. If his change of heart about Dalmatia found few allies who were acceptable to him, his steadfast warnings of the menace of Bolshevism earned him an increasing number of them.[20]

Far more dismaying than the international situation was the domestic scene. Orlando, unable to make any headway at Versailles, quit in the summer of 1919, replaced by Nitti, an economist from Basilicata to whom Albertini had once been close, but had served under Giolitti. In November he called elections. The result came as an unpleasant shock to Albertini's brand of liberalism. Socialists and Catholics made up half the Chamber, and for Nitti to carry on, the latter had to be integrated into the government. When they pulled out, he was soon gone. What followed was worse: Giolitti in office once more. Impenitently reminding the country of his warnings about the war, he was soon returning to his old tricks – complaisantly presiding over sedition in factories and fields, occupations by workers in Turin and strikes by *braccianti* in Emilia, while courting the Socialists and confecting a promiscuous 'National Bloc' to win a sweeping electoral victory in November 1920. But though Giolitti checked industrial and rural rebellion with nominal concessions damping each, old-style parliamentary *trasformismo* from above was no solution for the radicalization from below that was soon seething in the wake of his apparent initial success.

---

20. 'We are convinced that Wilsonism is the best remedy against Bolshevism': *Corriere*, 1 January 1919; 'Who believes the country is thinking only of the Yugoslavs and Dalmatia? . . . when public opinion is preoccupied by something very different: the stain of Bolshevism spreading at vertiginous speed, revolutionary propaganda in Italy swelling to an unsurpassable diapason': letter to Orlando, 25 April 1919. See Renzo di Felice, *Mussolini il rivoluzionario: 1883–1920*, Turin 1965, p. 525.

Catholics and Socialists (a reformist, interventionist minority aside), the only two mass parties in the country, had rejected the war. Liberals had never formed more than a slender amoebic elite. That left one key post-war constituency adrift: those who had fought in the war, and emerged without reward, enraged or embittered from it, and now supplied the cadres of nascent fascism. The first squads appeared in Trieste and Venezia-Giulia in the northeast, then spreading into Emilia-Romagna, where a violent mob attacked the socialist mayor of Bologna in October 1920. By the spring of 1921, fascist detachments were rampaging across the Veneto, Lombardy, Tuscany and Umbria, bombing and burning socialist offices, killing officials and members of the demoralized Socialist Party under the complaisant watch of Giolitti. In May he called another election, this time incorporating – the fruit of direct talks with Mussolini – fascists into his National Bloc, and his new majority included thirty-five fascist deputies. But Socialist and Catholic votes held up, and the result did not much strengthen his hand. So in a *reculer pour mieux sauter* to which he had often resorted in the past, he resigned with the intention of returning at a more favourable moment. He was succeeded by Ivanoe Bonomi, a long-time admirer of Giolitti and the most right-wing of the deputies expelled from the Socialist Party in 1912, whose tenure saw the formal creation of a national Fascist Party at Naples, uniting its competing factions. In February 1923, Bonomi quit and Giolitti's colourless servitor Luigi Facta became Italy's last liberal prime minister, as fascist violence escalated across the country. In August, a feeble attempt at a general strike by the trade-unions was quickly crushed by *squadristi*, who then fanned out across the north, defenestrating socialist councils in Milan, Genoa, Livorno, Ancona, and rallying shopkeepers, landowners, bureaucrats, students and professionals to the cause of fascism. By October, Mussolini was openly preparing a march on Rome. To block it, Facta sought the consent of the king to declare martial law, and when it was refused, resigned. Mussolini himself had no need to march. He waited a day while Salandra, the king's first choice, tried and failed to form a government, then simply boarded the overnight train from Milan to Rome, was received by the king, and appointed prime minister.

Albertini's liberalism had no time for socialism or Catholicism. His reaction to the eruption of fascism? In the first post-war election of November 1919, Mussolini's list was a complete fiasco, gaining less than 5,000 votes out of 250,000 cast in Milan, the city where his *fasci di combattimento* had been founded in the spring, and failing to win a single seat. Two days later, police found arms in Mussolini's office and he was arrested. But he was not short of sympathy in high places. Albertini came to his help immediately, securing his release within twenty-four hours after a phone call to Nitti.[21] He did so for two reasons, which remained constant for another five years. Fascism too had exalted the Great War, his political touchstone; and it was an implacable foe of socialism. Personally, Albertini disdained Mussolini as a plebeian rabble-rouser with a dubious past; and when his movement got off the ground, never entirely trusted fascism. But politically, it could be of service in stamping out sedition. In the spring of 1919, reporting the birth of a new group in Milan composed of admirable young patriots moved by love of country, the *Corriere* informed its readers that 'Professor Mussolini' held high 'the value of the war and those who fought it'; and when they were a growing force two years later, Albertini would declare: 'fascists are the

---

21. The *Corriere* deplored the 'political vendetta' of which Mussolini had become a victim: 'Perquisizioni al "Popolo d'Italia". L'arresto di Mussolini', *Corriere*, 19 November 1919. For his arrest and release, see Seton-Watson, *Italy from Liberalism to Fascism*, p. 570.

extreme wing of a great national party which wanted the sacrifice of war for the good of Italy and did not want Italy to perish suffocated by a stolid and, for civil persons, now superseded utopia'.[22] His usual way of referring to socialism was blunter: socialists aimed at nothing less than 'civil war' – a 'red terror in which all the rights of existing society will succumb'. When fascism, recovering from its electoral humiliation in 1919, swept northern Italy with a deluge of violence in 1920, Albertini did not flinch. Giolitti was now back in power, and once again dandling the socialists. They should be given no quarter. It was nonsense to speak of fascist violence as a white terror. It was 'a legitimate reaction' to the misdeeds of socialism, whose control of the city council must at all costs be overthrown. 'Everyone to the polls to save the commune of Milan from Bolshevism – Electors! Victory is in your hands: vote!' cried the *Corriere* that November, still in vain.[23]

Nor did its attitude to fascism change when Mussolini's influence grew to a point where in the following year Giolitti thought it astute to enlist him into his National Bloc, awarding him seats in parliament, and then himself withdrawing for a spell to Piedmont. The paper continued to treat Mussolini himself with respect – 'a name dear to us all' was how it termed him that spring.[24] Were the fascists 'to go quiet and re-allow red hooliganism', the 'bourgeoisie would be finished' and

---

22. 'Fasci d'azione fra interventisti', *Corriere*, 24 March 1919; 'Due formule', *Corriere*, 17 April 1919; 'L'appello del paese', *Corriere*, 8 April 1921.

23. Simona Colarizi, *Il 'Corriere' nell'età liberale: Profilo stoico*, Milan 2011, pp. 355–6; the fundamental study for tracking the politics of the paper and its editor in the post-war years, superseding the shrewd but distinctly less critical account of these in Melograni's essay introducing *Corriere della Sera (1919–1943)*, Rocca San Casciano 1965, pp. ix–lix. For Colarizi, 'it is impossible to attenuate the responsibility of the Milanese daily in fostering an ever more favourable opinion of fascism in its *squadrista* form': p. 362.

24. *Corriere*, 18 April 1921.

proletarian dictatorship installed to the applause of pseudo-moderate socialists.[25] In the autumn the first congress of a countrywide Fascist Party was greeted with this sage reflection: 'There was a time when the constitution of a young liberal party was in the air, but the period, it seems, was not propitious for one. Today the fascists find that if they want to be a party, they have to become the party of young liberals', though if they were to live up to liberal ideals, they should be more orderly.[26]

As the crescendo of fascist violence mounted during the autumn of 1922, however, Albertini became alarmed: methods acceptable in dealing with socialists were being extended to those who were not, with little pretence of legality. There was a danger that Mussolini might attempt an unconstitutional seizure of power. In early October, *squadristi* made short work of the authorities in Bolzano and Trento, who had nothing to do with socialism, convincing Albertini that it was now urgent to rein in fascism by what for him was the only practicable way: not by coming down on its black-shirts, but by ushering them into the seats of power in Rome. The right way to respond to fascism was to 'normalize' it by bringing it into the safe haven of government. 'The essential thing is that this [Facta's] unworthy ministry goes as quickly as possible without a parliamentary crisis that would simply cause further confusion and postpone the only solution in sight: a Ministry in which the fascists too take part, averting the danger of a coup d'etat that would be fatal to the country.'[27] When later that month provincial squads mustered for a March on Rome, and the

---

25. 'Legna al fuoco', *Corriere*, 22 April 1921.
26. 'Il congresso fascista', *Corriere*, 12 November 1921. At this time Alberto was running the paper in the absence of Luigi, who was heading the Italian delegation to the conference on naval disarmament in Washington.
27. Albertini, *Epistolario III*, Milan 1968, p. 1589.

Corriere itself was threatened with closure by them, Albertini was initially aghast, but quickly rallied: it was now more urgent than ever to constitutionalize fascism. Mussolini had no difficulty pacifying him. Before catching the train to Rome, he consulted Albertini on the composition of the cabinet he would form once granted office, and Albertini informed the capital that Mussolini should be made prime minister without further ado.[28] The acceptance of his advice was a great relief. 'The essential thing is that the end of the movement can be seen in an apparently legal solution of this grave crisis.'[29] Appearances were everything. Mussolini safely at the helm by royal appointment, Albertini told the Senate at the end of November, speaking as 'an intransigent constitutionalist, an impenitent liberal':

> My conscience tells me – I have often said so here and I repeat it today – that fascism has saved Italy from the peril of socialism, which openly and more or less menacingly weighed on our life and gradually poisoned it for twenty years. Likewise it tells me that in seeking to restore the authority of the state and lend new energies to its leaders, fascist reaction has interpreted the most intense aspiration of all true Italians.[30]

Mussolini should not misuse his authority or act as a dictator, yet he had earned Albertini's support in parliament as prime minister. But

---

28. Seton-Watson, *Italy from Liberalism to Fascism*, p. 628. Lyttleton's comment on the way D'Annunzio was summoned back to Rome in May 1915 – 'Albertini like the sorcerer's apprentice had raised forces which he could not control' (*The Seizure of Power*, p. 25) – is yet more apposite to his benevolent response to Mussolini from 1919 to 1922.

29. Albertini, *I giorni di un liberale: Diari 1907–1925*, ed. Luciano Monzali, Bologna 2000, p. 399.

30. Speech of 26 November 1922: see Paolo Alatri, 'Luigi Albertini', *Belfagor*, 31 January 1953, p. 72.

the illusion of the *Corriere*, and of the entire liberal elite, that fascism would thereby be 'transformed' according to their recipes was soon exposed. Mussolini at first complied, with economic policies hailed by Einaudi as 'classically liberal' and assorted gestures of tactical moderation. But from the start he regarded Albertini as an enemy who enjoyed too much influence in the middle class, however conciliatory he might seem, and at first tried unsuccessfully to get him out of the way by dispatching him to Washington. For his part, Albertini not only continued to lavish praise in the Senate on much the government did – its handling of the economy, its restoration of order, its firm foreign policy – but voted for its blatant rigging of the electoral system, with the Acerbo law designed to give fascism a monopoly of power in the country. But he insisted on independence of the press, which Mussolini was determined to control by intimidation, assault, or purchase. When the *Corriere* resisted the fate of other papers, a volley of imprecations was unleashed against it in fascist broadsheets, with threats of physical attack to follow. In the summer of 1923, Albertini's response was to cease publishing anything of its own about domestic affairs, a self-censorship restricting the paper to international and cultural coverage, but a silence too pointed to appease Il Duce. A year later, in the summer of 1924, thugs in Mussolini's entourage brazenly kidnapped and murdered the Socialist deputy Matteotti, causing a political uproar that threatened to topple the regime. Three years earlier, at a time when Matteotti was the target of a virulent fascist campaign depicting him as a wealthy landowner in a wide-brimmed hat acting the Marat to his peasants, the *Corriere* – rather than printing Matteotti's indignant denials – had dwelt on his vast properties in the neighbourhood. Now it received a flood of letters from readers calling on it to denounce the crime in the strongest possible terms and bring its perpetrators to book.³¹ On 24 November, Albertini broke his silence with a speech in the Senate in which he declared there was a difference between 'abuses committed by minorities or individuals outside the law and the same violence perpetrated by a party responsible for the law and instigated by its leaders themselves'.³²

To dramatize their indignation at the killing, and in the hope of separating the king from Mussolini, much of the opposition seceded from parliament, setting up a nominal counter-assembly on the Aventine. Albertini declined to join it.³³ In a tense atmosphere throughout the country, and considerable turmoil in the ranks of the fascists, a further campaign of threats and harassment hit the *Corriere*, its violence increasing when the paper failed to provide support for the government when elections were held under the rigged Acerbo system in the spring of 1925, though Albertini had voted in favour of the law installing it. In May Albertini then delivered a frontal attack on the regime in the Senate, in the name of freedom and the constitution. It would be his last. In the autumn, the majority shareholders in the *Corriere* found a loophole in the contract they had signed with Albertini precluding his dismissal, and at Mussolini's behest bought him out, paying some 72 million lira, or well over what the Albertini shares were worth to evict him.³⁴ He departed, aged fifty-four, with a famous

---

31. Colarizi, *Il 'Corriere' nella età liberale*, pp. 361–2, 441–2.

32. Alberto Albertini, *Vita di Luigi Albertini*, p. 196. Alatri would observe that Albertini's sad fate could be resumed in the popular saying, valid throughout his career, that 'he closed the stable doors after the cattle had bolted' : 'Luigi Albertini', p. 74.

33. An 'obstinate isolation', expressive in Barié's view of a liberal purism resistant to association with any segment of opinion critical of the constitutional order with which the Historic Right had endowed Italy: *Luigi Albertini*, p. 506.

34. Licata, *Storia di Corriere della Sera*, p. 211.

farewell to the *Corriere*, 'to which I have dedicated my whole existence for twenty-five years', ending: 'I go towards this immense sacrifice with a heart that swells with bitterness, but a head held high. I lose a good that was supremely dear to me, but I preserve intact a spiritual heritage that is still dearer and save my dignity and my conscience.'[35]

In getting rid of Albertini, Mussolini had acquired control over a property by which he set great store, Italy's largest and most famous newspaper, with a circulation approaching 800,000, more than double that of all those previously in his power. Other than issuing his farewell, Albertini went quietly, with a fortune in his bank accounts. Since he was widely respected at home and abroad, nothing was to be gained by further exactions against him. Either shortly before or shortly after his ouster from *Corriere*, he bought a vast estate close to Rome – 3,500 acres: over ten times the size of a holding currently reckoned a latifundium in Italy, to which he later added a further adjacent 2,000 – on which he employed his son and son-in-law to manage Frisian dairy cattle, while he renovated and took up residence in a chateau decorated with eighteenth-century frescoes on the grounds. He was watched by the regime, but could entertain like-minded liberal friends on his estate; still a senator, cast his vote against the Lateran Pact; and after 1930 travel freely abroad – trips to the Middle East and North America, a cruise to Scandinavia, limousine tours around Germany and France, not to speak of Italy itself.[36]

But it was not in his nature to drop his pen. Once he had organized the estate and restored his *palazzo*, he set to work on a history of Italian politics from the time he joined the *Corriere* in 1898 to his eviction from

---

35. Alberto Albertini, *Vita di Luigi Albertini*, p. 218.
36. Ibid., pp. 257–61, 273–5. Albertini initially says he purchased the estate while still at the *Corriere* – that is, in 1925, then on the next page in 1926.

it, based on files of the paper he had kept in his possession. Displayed in heavy leather-bound volumes on a music stand close to his desk, he could consult them regularly and conveniently as he composed his narrative. He had always been a fluent writer, and eventually took the story up to 1918, in a work that would form a pentalogy of 2,500 pages when it was ultimately published, a decade after his death. But once he reached the outbreak of the First World War, he realized that its genesis was not amenable to a purely Italian standpoint: it required a European perspective covering all its major participants, demanding another and broader study. So from 1933 onwards he embarked on a second major work, which would see the light of day a full decade before the first, and become much more famous as *The Origins of the War of 1914*. Neither was finished when he died. The two books were not composed in a clear-cut sequence. So closely was the writing of these enormous enterprises intertwined that Albertini failed to write the final chapter of *Origin*s before he died because he had reverted to a chapter of his account of Italian politics which he felt needed revising, instead of completing his explanation of the genesis of the Great War.

Nevertheless the tenor and spirit of the two works differed profoundly. The first, based on his memories and the files of his newspaper, was an undiluted product of the partisan passions of his years as a political actor and publicist in his own country. The second was a work of immensely diligent and painstaking scholarship, aiming at an objectivity free from any narrowly national or ideological preconceptions. How far it realized that intention in the end is questionable. What is not are the qualities that would make *The Origins of the War of 1914* an unparalleled achievement on the subject: the depth and width of its research, on the evidence then available, and the relative balance and scruple of its judgments, compared with those of other European participants or historians of the time. Albertini worked in no archives, but enjoyed a scale of wealth that allowed him to purchase for his personal library all official and many secondary publications in the different languages of the belligerents, and to pay a collaborator, Luciano Magrini, to travel across Europe to interview key political and military actors in the crisis of 1914, and help him organize the documents, books and articles brought back to him.[37] Impartiality of purpose did not preclude trenchancy of opinion, on memorable display across his three volumes, each of them testimony to the intensity of Albertini's immersion in his labours.

Italy had entered the war on the side of the Entente not at its outset, but ten months later, lowering the pressure for justification of its own role in the drama of 1914 itself, if not of the cause which it subsequently joined. Albertini argued that the Central Powers bore primary responsibility for the conflict, but extended the blame for its outbreak to all four of the other powers that resorted to arms that August. None of the powers of the Triple Entente, Russia, France or England, escape reasoned, often severe judgment, not to speak of Serbia, whose part in detonating the disaster received the most substantial and critical treatment to which it had yet been subject. Culpability was unequal, but it was general. Austria was bent on breaking Serbia, and Germany had backed it to do so, without either state registering the consequences for Europe. Germany, in its haste to strike down France, had blatantly invaded Belgium. Yet it was also

---

37. Magrini was himself the author of a study of the assassinations which set off the First World War, *Il drama di Sarajevo* (1928), which had come out before Albertini embarked on his trilogy. One of the most distinguished reporters of his generation, he played an essential role in the composition of *Origini*, and a decisive one in its publication, for which see Giancarlo Finizio's meticulous study *History in the Making: lettere di Luciano Magrini a Luigi Albertini (1929–1941)*, Trieste 2019. Space precluding adequate treatment of Magrini here, his cursus and achievement will be considered elsewhere.

now plain – as Albertini was the first to trace in detail – that Russia had mobilized for war well before Germany; that France, far from restraining, had encouraged it to do so; and that Britain had signally failed to warn Germany that should war break out, it would fight with France and Russia, throwing away the chance of stopping the descent into a carnage in which it no less blindly joined. No regime had spoken the truth about its part in the debacle: 'all governments abandoned themselves to the most incredible manipulation of the diplomatic actions which preceded it'.[38] None of the politicians at the helm of the leading states understood the dispositions or timetables on which the military planning of their general staffs were based. Statecraft was everywhere in short supply. Most of the rulers of Europe were birds of a feather: weak, indecisive mediocrities overtaken by a logic of events beyond their comprehension.[39]

Writing as an Italian, Albertini enjoyed the advantage over his counterparts in the Entente of not only his country's greater distance from their immediate plunge into the war in August 1914, but also its greater proximity to the theatre of its outbreak. The distance from London or St Petersburg to Sarajevo was about three times, and from Paris twice, that of Rome or Milan. Serbia was just much nearer. For Italy, the Balkans were close by in a way that for England, Russia or France they were not, and they occupy a proportionately – and

---

38. *Le origini della guerra del 1914*, Vol. II, p. 245. The first two volumes were published in Milan in 1942, the third in 1943; references henceforward *OG* (translation of the trilogy into English as *The Origins of the War of 1914*, published by Oxford University Press, came out successively in 1952, 1955 and 1957; henceforward *OW*. The translator, Isabella Massey, had her own views on the war, and did not always respect the Italian original. For example, evidently finding the passage above too strong for her taste as a British patriot, she omitted the term 'incredible' – see Vol. II, p. 244).

39. *OG* II, p. 475; *OG* III, pp. 242–3 [*OW* II, p. 479; *OW* III, pp. 252–3].

appropriately – larger place in Albertini's narrative of the outbreak of the war than in any other account of the period.

At the centre of his story lies the most critical and detailed reconstruction in the literature of the Serb conspiracy that put an end to the lives of the Archduke Ferdinand and his wife – a labyrinth minimized or dismissed in standard Entente apologetics – leaving little doubt of the complicity of the Serbian state apparatus, and foreknowledge of its prime minister, in the scheme. For its part, Austrian reaction to this provocation was in Albertini's eyes rooted in a larger one, its annexation of Bosnia-Herzegovina itself, scene of the crime, staged by Aehrenthal six years earlier in defiance, according to Albertini, of the provisions of the Congress of Berlin of 1878,[40] and compounded by a determination to reverse Vienna's setback in the outcome of the Balkan Wars of 1912–13.

But if Austria's ultimatum of 23 July to Belgrade was calculated to inflict a punitive war on Serbia, behind its resolve to do so lay the connivance of its much more powerful ally Germany, whose emperor not only supplied a blank cheque for aggression at the outset, but whose ministers pressed thereafter for military action when counsels were divided in Vienna, pushing it into what Berlin believed would be swift victory in a local conquest. In this, its course of action repeated its stance in 1909, when Germany backed Austria to the hilt over Bosnia-Herzegovina by threatening to attack Russia if it continued to resist Habsburg annexation of the province, as

---

40. In Albertini's trilogy, the Bosnian crisis of 1908–9 – Aehrenthal and Bülow the originating culprits – is effectively the fulcrum of its attribution to Austria and to Germany the primary responsibility for the Great War. At the time, as he tersely recalls without comment in *Venti Anni*, but does not in *Origini*, he took an opposite view of the crisis, the *Corriere* criticizing domestic enemies of the Triple Alliance who attacked Italy's partners for their conduct of it and complained of the outcome.

Austria itself was not in a position to do. For Albertini, the reality in 1914 was that 'it was war that the Wilhelmstrasse wanted', and it was in Berlin that 'all the acts and all the roles in the tragedy were settled in advance'.[41] Categorical enough? Yet Russia had undeniably played a part too, in mobilizing its army before either of the Central Powers had moved against it. Sazonov had come up with the 'bright idea' of a partial mobilization just against Austria, unaware in his ignorance of military matters that this was not feasible, since in Russia the general staff had plans only for a general mobilization, and Germany was in any case treaty-bound to come to the defence of Austria if it was attacked. On learning and accepting that this was so, Sazonov took a decisive step. 'Let it be clearly established that the responsibility for mobilizing against Austria on the evening of the 29th and against Austria and Germany at 4 p.m. on the 30th rests beyond all doubt with Russia.' Unlike his opposite numbers in Berlin, Sazonov acted in good faith, but his option for mobilization would have 'fatal consequences'.[42]

France was bound to Russia by treaty as Germany was to Austria. The alliance of 1894 between the two states ratified a military convention concluded two years earlier in which the chiefs of both general staffs had declared that 'mobilization is war', and stipulated that each must consult with the other in such an event. No such consultation occurred when Russia mobilized in 1914. Yet France not only made no case of it, but its ambassador in St Petersburg, Maurice Paléologue, plainly incited Russia's decision and helped inspire the mendacious French claim that it was a response to a prior Austrian

---

41. *OG* II, pp. 425, 270 [*OW* II, pp. 430, 268; insufficiently vehement for her, Massey rendered the first sentence as 'the only thing that would satisfy Germany was war'].

42. *OG* II, pp. 570, 294–5 [*OW* II, pp. 574–575, 291–2].

mobilization against Russia.[43] When France itself went to war with Germany, Albertini remarks that its explanation on 4 August of how this had come about was 'as much a distortion of the truth' as that of Germany.[44] Berlin's justifications of its invasion of France, Luxemburg and Belgium were a shameless tissue of lies. Paris's justification of its declaration of war on Austria, however, was also a pure invention – the fabrication that Vienna had sent troops to the frontiers of Germany in aid of its attack on France.[45] Moreover, when war was actually being waged, France forged evidence to sustain its claim that it was entirely innocent of any responsibility for it in a way that no other belligerent did – its Yellow Book far exceeding the German White or Austrian Orange Book in deliberate falsification of the diplomatic record, a scandal exposed by French critics of the government after the war, and one which Albertini made devastatingly clear.[46] Yet the result was a patent contradiction in his own story. For the one figure who escaped his strictures on the European governing class as a whole was the leader who propagated the country's official mythology. 'In strength of will, character, and tenacity, even more

---

43. *OG* II, p. 619; *OG* III, pp. 135–6 [*OW* II, p. 626, *OW* III, pp. 138–9].

44. *OG* III, p. 217 [*OW* III, p. 227]. Massey, having just toned down the Italian phrase 'absolutely untrue' of a claim by Viviani, the French prime minister, then inserted the English formula 'to present its case in the best light', which Albertini did not write, to soften the comparison of Viviani's speech with German pronouncements.

45. *OG* III, p. 513 [*OW* III, p. 542].

46. *OG* III, pp. 138–58 [*OW* III, pp. 141–63 ff]. Predictably, this section of the book so pained the Entente devotion of Isabella Massey that she watered down the bluntness of Albertini's word 'lies' (*bugie*) to the more decorous 'falsehoods'; she herself lamenting, in an early review of *Origini*, the evidence of a 'manifest antipathy for Poincaré – the one instance where Albertini falls somewhat short of his habitual calm judgement.' See 'The Diplomatic Origins of the First World War', *International Affairs*, February 1949, p. 190.

than in intellectual gifts', Poincaré – so Albertini – was no ordinary parliamentarian, but a statesman who occupied 'first place' among those who led the continent to war.[47] Hoodwinked by Paléologue into repeating the untruths the latter had invented, it must have been discomfiting for him to be obliged eventually to disavow them. But even had Poincaré been cognizant of awkward realities he did not disclose at the time, he could not have acted otherwise than he did. France had to stand by Russia if its alliance with her was to be preserved. For a good while, he had believed war was inevitable, and was sure that if the Tsarist empire was left to fight it alone, Germany would turn on France as soon as it dispatched Russia. Better by far to welcome Berlin's declaration of war on both as the chance for a *règlement de comptes*.[48]

In England, Grey was an 'upright and straightforward character', whose professions of his own and his country's commitment to peace were of the 'the utmost sincerity'. But he was also, alas, ingenuous and his conduct of foreign policy so 'inept and dilatory' that it was a

---

47. 'Poincaré impressed himself on all by his formidable powers of work, the clarity of his thought, the exact and logical quality of his oratory'; 'in this cool, hard, methodical, stubborn man of Lorraine love of country, national pride and thirst for revenge against Germany submerged every other emotion', et cetera: *OG* I, pp. 350–1 [*OW* I, p. 333]. Such was Albertini's homage to Poincaré in the first volume of his work; by the third volume, he was forced to concede his lack of honesty. The contradictions of his treatment of Viviani, the prime minister of the time under Poincaré, were more glaring still. Readers of the second volume were told that having met Viviani personally at the Washington conference of 1921, Albertini's impression was of a man of 'passionate temperament and extremely quick, sharp and straightforward intelligence, which moved directly and firmly to where his convictions took him', that war was 'terrible': *OG* II, p. 590 [*OW* II, p. 595]. In the next volume, he appears as a confused booby, emitting a stream of gross untruths: *OG* III, p. 144 [*OW* III, p. 147].

48. *OG* II, p. 620; III, p. 80 [*OW* II, p. 626; III, p. 83].

major cause of the war. For had he warned Germany at the outset of the crisis of 1914 that should a conflict between the Central Powers and the Dual Alliance break out, Britain was bound to enter it on the side of France and Russia, he could have stopped the slide to catastrophe. For such a prospect, in which Germany and Austria would be plainly outmatched, would have deterred Berlin from driving Austria forward, and halted the stumble to general disaster. Indeed, when Grey proposed a four-power mediation between Austria and Serbia, the kaiser was so relieved he thought the danger of war was over. When the proposal came to nothing, and Grey finally issued the threat of English intervention on 29 July, it was too late: between the three Eastern monarchies, the machinery of mobilization and counter-mobilization had started. When the reality of Grey's belated warning sank in, there was panic in Berlin, but by then there was no turning back. For the ensuing debacle, Grey had a 'terrible responsibility', from which – so Albertini – 'he cannot be exonerated' by the excuse that he had no authority to threaten war on Germany without the approval of the Cabinet, since that is what he ultimately did anyway without consulting it. Germany's invasion of Belgium, dictated by its belief in the Schlieffen Plan, allowed Grey to rally the Cabinet and Parliament behind him. Britain was not actually treaty-bound to intervene in defence of Belgian neutrality. Why did it do so? No doubt because Grey felt this was 'the one ground on which he could overcome the repugnance existing in England to entering a Continental war at the side of France', while actually believing defence of Belgium was essential to safeguard 'the position of the British Empire in the world'.[49] For Albertini, that was no cause for criticism of Grey. Reproach must rather 'for ever remain attached to

---

49. *OG* III, p. 489 [*OW* III, p. 517].

his memory' as the politician – personally honourable enough, but 'a man devoid of all political perception' – whose tragedy was 'to be co-responsible for the rivers of blood shed by humanity in the Great War'.[50]

Italy was not a participant in the Great War in the period covered by Albertini's history of its origins, and would not be for another ten months. But it was understandably near the centre of his concerns, featuring in all ten chapters of his first volume, and receiving three full chapters in the next two volumes. His treatment of the country focusses on the Marquis of San Giuliano, a Sicilian aristocrat who was foreign minister from the spring of 1910 to his death in the autumn of 1914. Albertini depicts him as the temperamental and political opposite of Grey. Well-travelled, of quick intelligence, with an excellent command of foreign languages, 'he had great powers of application, plenty of wit and guile and the manners of a lord'. In general outlook he was 'somewhat sceptical, on occasion even seemingly cynical'. His policy was also 'one of utter, unreserved devotion to the Central Powers, inspired by sympathy and admiration for them', especially Germany, and fear of their strength.[51]

Both during the July crisis, and so long as he lived, instead of taking what Albertini regarded as the principled position of an immediate repudiation of the Triple Alliance once Austria's aggressive designs on Serbia became apparent, San Giuliano adopted a stance 'blind to all moral considerations and ruinous to Italian interests and good name', in manoeuvring to connive at Vienna's assault on Serbia in exchange

---

50. *OG* II, pp. 510, 512, 637–8 [*OW* II, pp. 515–16, 518, 644].

51. *OG* II, p. 246 [*OW* II, p. 245]. San Giuliano was not alone in this attitude; the Vatican was unswervingly pro-Austrian, while the Italian upper classes and intelligentsia were rife with Germanophile and Triplicist sentiments: see Magrini's insertion of a section from *Venti anni* into *OW* III, at p. 359.

for territorial compensation to Italy in the Trentino. Thankfully, since Italian neutrality meant departure from the Triple Alliance, Austria rejected any such bargain, for which Albertini had no words of condemnation too strong.[52] His verdict was a logical product of his own stance during the crisis, reflecting an Austrophobia that persisted to the end of his life, to which he gave free expression in his retirement. Vienna had prevented Italy from finishing off its Ottoman foe in 1911 with an assault on the Dardanelles; the Archduke's ambition was to destroy the work of the Risorgimento; Austria sought to strangle Italy in the coils of *Deutschtum*.[53]

Albertini's treatment of the performance of his own country in the run-up to the First World War forms an exception in his account of its origins, falling visibly short of the standards he attained elsewhere; yet it is none the less revealing for that. For if he nowhere furnished any plausible reason for Italy's participation in the war, it was because of a premise that he so took for granted that he had no need to spell it out. To take part was the calling of a Great Power, and the only acceptable choice was for the Entente as the right side; to abstain was to drop out of the ranks to which Italy had to aspire if it was to respect itself. Emblematically, what was at stake in the Russian decisions that set the wheels of European destruction in motion? For Albertini, the answer was obvious: how could anyone expect, after its humiliation over Bosnia in 1909, that 'Russia should have tolerated the humiliation and subjugation of Serbia' in 1914, which could have had 'incalculable

---

52. Pandering to 'Italy's hereditary enemy', San Giuliano's policy 'revealed a total absence of all sense of horror at the tragedy that was about to be enacted and did not raise a finger to avert it. Despite protestations to the contrary it showed not the slightest regard for the feelings of the Italian people': *OG* II, p. 253 [*OW* II, pp. 252–3].

53. *OG* II, pp. 251, 220, 322 [*OW* II, pp. 251, 218, 321].

repercussions in the Balkans'?[54] Such was the logic, common to all its major players, of the international politics of the time. None went to war without the word 'honour' on their lips.

Not, of course, that interstate competition was a contest in which the amour-propre of grandeur was the only value. The requirements of a Great Power were more than simply reputational and moral. They were territorial and material. All five of the major states that fought in 1914 were empires, and described themselves as such. Since Albertini took the rights and obligations accruing to Great Powers for granted, he questioned the reality and necessity of imperialism as little as any other of the other attributes that went with their position. Colonies were the natural froggings of their rank. British identity could not be separated from its possessions on five continents; Russia encompassed the Caucasus, Finland and half of Poland; Germany shared Poland, and booty in Africa; the Ottoman realm covered the larger part of the Middle East; the Austrian half a dozen subject nationalities; France's acquisitions stretched from Indochina to Senegal and Guyana. If Paris took Morocco too, why complain? Rome could compensate itself with Libya.

In bracketing the totality of the imperialism that was the ultimate *Treibstoff* of the struggle for power in Europe, Albertini was unable to fulfil the promise with which he entitled his work. In a key passage, he wrote:

> To attribute responsibility for July 1914 to the Central Powers is not to enter into the merits of the situation which drove Austria into a conflict with Serbia and Germany to support Austria. To assert that Austria and Germany acted as shown and will be shown is not to assert that from their own point of view they lacked good reasons for

---

54. *OG* II, p. 361 [*OW* II, p. 361].

seeking to change a state of affairs that was of extreme gravity directly for Austria and indirectly to Germany. The same holds true of those other powers, like France and Russia, which displayed no great fear of the tempest being unloosed, if not under certain conditions actually welcoming it, perhaps in the hope that it would turn out to their advantage. The fact is that the question of the origins of the war is not the same as the legitimacy of the war, an immense problem which we do not claim to solve.[55]

Well said, but not supplied. The history that Albertini produced was the opposite of what he affirmed. It accused the Central Powers, and absolved the Entente, of responsibility for unleashing the Great War without ever considering the conditions that generated it, focussing exclusively on its conjunctural circumstances, and blotting out its structural propellants. When the trilogy appeared in English, it was Alan Bullock who saw this misconstruction most clearly.[56] Nor, of course, was it without consequence on the conjunctural plane itself. Albertini could not depart from baseline Entente beliefs in Teutonic

---

55. *OG* II, pp. 140–1 [*OW* II, pp. 136–7].

56. 'What is missing is precisely what the title promises, but the book fails to provide – a study of the origins of the war. That is a different question from that of responsibility and war guilt. For the war of 1914 was not made in the chancelleries of Europe and its origins are not to be found in the records of their diplomatic transactions. To understand these, we must probe deeper into the social and economic tensions, the passions, fears, greed, and hatred from which sprang the terrible storm released by the blunders of Europe's rulers.' That said, Bullock paid full tribute to the quality of the monumental work Albertini did produce, narrowly diplomatic as it was – 'it is unlikely any man will ever again combine such mastery of the documentary material with first-hand interrogation of many of the principal actors and personal recollection of the events he described' – and had no quarrel with his allocation of war guilt to the Central Powers: 'If his conclusions come as no surprise to an English historian, they are delivered with an authority and supported by a weight of evidence which no other enquiry into the question has equalled': *International Affairs* 34, I, January 1958, pp. 71–2.

ill-doing without reneging on his own part in propagating them to spur Italy into the war. Calibration of the language he employed to characterize the respective actions of each camp, admittedly neither of them guiltless, makes this clear: more in sorrow than anger on one side, far more in anger than sorrow on the other. In his narrative the combatant and the historian were never entirely at peace with each other. That the tension between them drew Albertini despite himself so unfailingly to the question of what Massey would call 'the rights and wrongs' of the conflict, was not unproductive. For it meant that, unusually for a historian, he could make telling use of counterfactuals within the range of possibility for the actors of the time. If Sazonov had possessed some familiarity with military matters, he would have known that for Russia partial mobilization was not practicable; if Moltke had not taken Schlieffen's purported plan for gospel, Germany might have avoided adding Britain to its enemies; if eleventh-hour signs of sobriety in Berlin had reached Vienna in time, Berchtold might have resiled; if Grey had issued any prompt warning to Berlin, war could have been averted. Or even, after the fighting had broken out, had the Entente made Austria early on the target for a major offensive, it could have shortened the conflict which did ensue. Hypotheses like these are often powerfully argued. Yet they are illustrations of the occasionalist rhetoric to which Albertini's short-term optic was consigned. Even if the answer to some or all of them was yes, had they occurred and Europe been spared the four years of *kataplēxis* that descended in 1914, none of them offered any hope that inter-imperial war of the same kind would not erupt, with the same structural logic, in time to come.

In a sensitive and intelligent introduction to *Venti anni*, written a decade after his father's death, Albertini's son Leonardo observed that his father was essentially a man of action. On being prevented from acting politically in the way that he had always done, editing the country's leading newspaper, at the age of fifty-four he transformed himself into a historian by the exercise of sheer willpower and self-discipline. The confiscation of the *Corriere* remained an 'irremediable fracture' in his life, from which he never ceased to suffer, now utterly separated from the readers he had addressed for a quarter of a century. To reach them again in a future when fascism had fallen, he sat down to write the history of the paper when he had edited it, and found that to do so was to write the history of an epoch in Italy. Planning to cover the whole period when he was editor of the *Corriere*, from 1900 to 1925, he was unable to complete it, the manuscript ending with the armistice of 1918. In part, that was certainly due to the requirement he felt to broaden his account of the onset of the First World War into a full-scale parallel history of the European origins of the war; and in part, of course, the work was cut short by his death sixteen years later, at the age of seventy-one. But if these were the main reasons for its incompletion, they were not the only ones. In the last years of his life, fascism was still in power, his work impossible to publish, and his strength waning, worn down less by age than by the sadness of the time. So too, though he was technically free, saved from a worse fate by his status as a senator, and was not subject to close surveillance, the limitations of his existence meant that he never enjoyed either the material peace or the spiritual calm which he needed to bring his work to its full fruition. Missing from the project as he designed it were the exceptional years from the end of the war to his expulsion from the *Corriere*, which had called upon the 'full measure of his political thought and moral force'.[57]

---

57. Leonardo Albertini, 'Introduzione', *Venti anni di vita politica*, I/I, pp. xiii–xiv, xviii–xxi.

It is an impressive filial retrospect. Yet there is one further reason, obvious enough, why Albertini was unable to bring his Italian story up to 1925, diverting his energies instead to *Origini*. To have written the history of the *Corriere*'s part in the triumph of fascism would have put Albertini's new-found, hard-won intellectual honesty under intolerable strain. Either he would have had to regret and criticize the role he had played in helping Mussolini to power, or he would have to engage in wholesale suppression of the truth: psychologically, alternatives equally impossible for him. We owe the creative feat to which he was diverted instead to that barrier. While local judgments in Albertini's huge work on the Great War sometimes lost their balance, and not all have been uncontested, its overall scale, sobriety and equanimity have to this day earned it the widest spectrum of consensus that any account of the origins of the conflict has ever gained. The commanding posthumous reputation of the book, however, has concealed the extraordinary paradox on which it was based. For this history of the coming of a cataclysm, which it never understates, was the work of an ardent proponent of his country's plunge into the bloody maelstrom and champion of its most notorious military butcher, a writer for whom the war was, in the words of his biographer, 'the culminating moment of the entire existence of Luigi Albertini'.[58]

The fruit of the post-war mortification he then endured was the pair of books at which he laboured on his estate until his death. His work on the First World War ending in 1914, and his retrospect of Italian politics in 1918, fascism could not figure in the narrative of either.[59] The latter,

---

58. Barié, *Luigi Albertini*, p. 310.

59. Though Mussolini's pronouncements during the war are cited and criticized in the last three volumes of *Venti anni*, and his dictatorship after it earns fleeting proleptic reference: viz. II/II, p. 136; II/III, pp 172–4.

however, makes clear why Albertini was capable of the achievement of the former. After commending the speech of November 1918 with which Orlando, the Liberal premier after Caporetto, had hailed the war as bearer of 'the greatest political and social revolution in recorded history, superior to the French revolution', Albertini added : 'so it seemed we were proceeding with full sails towards the most luminous goals set before us, or at least there was an Italian consensus around Wilson's directives for peace'. He then went on:

> Alas! The edifice of ideals raised during the war was about to collapse in ruins. I write these pages thirteen years after the armistice, in the darkest days of world civilization. Instead of living in freedom, a series of European countries are oppressed by the most reactionary dictatorships. Instead of peace and harmony reigning among nations, bitter conflicts dominate the peoples of Europe, impelling the stronger to armaments and the weaker to talk of disarmament the better to wage war on the stronger. No solidarity between the vanquished and the victors, nor among the victors themselves, some of whom make common cause with the vanquished thirsting for revenge. A terrible economic crisis rages in the world. Its signs are the millions of unemployed that every great nation laments, the rising prices of everything, the enterprises that are shutting down, the banks that are failing, the budgets that no longer balance . . . Where are we going? Towards the end of the world, to the collapse of civilization, towards bolshevism? Despite the disastrous results of communism in Russia, its zealots are multiplying in Europe, and the defenders of private property and individual initiative appear dismayed by the spectacle that capitalism and the capitalist states offer of impotence and egoism. Were these the fruits glimpsed after victory? Is that how the solemn promises made on the tombs of millions of the dead, to the mutilated and wounded veterans of so much carnage, were kept?[60]

---

60. *Venti anni di vita politica*, Part 2, Vol. III, Bologna 1953, pp. 479, 482.

Without renouncing in any way the principles for which Italian patriots had fought, Albertini observed a sad truth: 'We won the war and lost the peace, making the immense sacrifices that victory cost us largely in vain.'[61]

Continuous work on *Venti anni di vita politica* came to a stop, for most purposes, in 1931. It was Magrini who devised its posthumous title, accepted by his family.[62] Part of one of its volumes covered the outbreak of the Great War before Italy joined it, if in much less detail than *Origins*, so there was a limited overlap between the two.[63] The connexion between them, however, was in a more important sense very close. Read together, they explain the puzzle of Albertini's trajectory. It was disappointment at the outcome of the crusade on which he had embarked in 1914 – the failure to achieve the gains from the war he and others promised the country for entering it; the destruction of the liberal order in Italy after the war; the depression that engulfed the civilization of capital in its wake – that prompted detachment from its passions, without renunciation of what he contended were its reasons. The judicious balance that gave authority to so much of his great compilation was hard come by, and never complete. But it ensured that it would stand the test of time, as Albertini's personal politics did not.

---

61. Ibid., p. 484.
62. See Barié, *Luigi Albertini*, p. 527. As his son noted, Albertini's original intention had been to take the story up to 1925.
63. For the way in which the process of working on the first book led to concomitant research on the second, see his brother's account: *Vita di Luigi Albertini*, pp. 263–4.

3

FRITZ FISCHER

The Second World War naturally diminished interest in the First, its aftermath giving rise to no comparable debate about what power had unleashed it: the role of Nazism in setting Europe on fire was all too plain. In Britain alone, which emerged once more undefeated and unoccupied, there was a significant retrospect linking the two conflicts. There in 1944 a young, so far relatively little-known, lecturer at Oxford, A. J. P. Taylor, had been engaged by the political warfare executive, the propaganda arm of the state, to produce a chapter on the Weimar Republic for a handbook to serve British troops in occupying post-war Germany. When, ironically, it was rejected as too dismissive of democratic traditions in the country, Taylor expanded it into a short book, *The Course of German History*, which appeared in the summer of 1945, shortly before VJ Day. In it, he argued that Bismarck's unification of Germany had created so rigidly authoritarian a structure of politics at home, a system in which he monopolized decision-making, that middle-class energies were forced outward into a 'world policy' threatening every neighbour, not least Britain, with a naval build-up of no defensive use, but hugely popular as a German cause distinct from an army that remained overwhelmingly Prussian. In this system, all parties – Conservatives,

National Liberals, Catholics, Progressives, Social Democrats – were rendered largely impotent by the Iron Chancellor, and the state was left adrift when he was gone, 'political incompetence and incapacity' spreading in what passed for an opposition 'as by an infection, from the German middle classes to the German workers', both equally 'awed by power dutiful in the face of authority'.[1] In 1914 responsibility for the country's drive over the precipice of war was general, the Reichstag united as it had never been behind Bismarck himself. But no premeditation was involved. 'To accuse Germany of having consciously planned and provoked the outbreak of war in August 1914 is to credit Germany with more direction than she possessed.' In Berlin, no-one ruled – not Bethmann Hollweg, not William II, not Moltke. 'This was an abdication of the whole German people.'[2] Two years later, in August 1916 the High Command took power, and in pursuit of German domination of Europe not only knocked Russia out of the war but left a million troops to secure control of territories it had conquered in the East, who might have saved it from defeat in the West. When collapse came, the generals sacrificed without compunction the dynasties of the Second Reich, the SPD hopes of the Republic that replaced it.[3] Hitler was the natural outcome.

Taylor's caustic philippic, judged inadvisable by the authorities in the UK, was a commercial success in Britain, reflecting as it did common unofficial sentiment, even if its impact was brief. Across the Channel, the pattern differed. There as early as 1950, France – formally, if not in the same way psychologically – also a victorious power, issued the Schuman Plan, designed to lay the foundations for

---

1. *The Course of German History; A Survey of the Development of Germany since 1815*, London 1945, p. 153.
2. Ibid., pp. 163–4, 166.
3. Ibid., pp. 170, 174, 181.

a durable reconciliation with Germany, and in its wake pre-war ideas for bringing historians of the two countries together revived. These had aimed to produce textbooks for schools superseding animosities of the Great War, a vision promoted by Jules Isaac and aborted by the Nazi regime in 1937. Now, in occupied West Germany where the crimes of the Third Reich were denounced by distinguished historians – Meinecke and Dehio among them – who had not been critics of the Second, there was little basis for another instalment of the disputes of the inter-war period, or reason for an acrimonious return to them. In May 1951 a bilateral meeting was held in Paris, at which Renouvin – whom Isaac had recruited for his scheme in the thirties – played a leading role. In October a second meeting convened in Mainz, where the dominant figure in the German delegation was Gerhard Ritter, also a veteran of the First World War, who had become a prolific historian of conservative temper, imprisoned for anti-Nazi sympathies towards the end of the Second World War. Without agreeing on the Great War, Renouvin and Ritter came to respect one another, and after sometimes heated arguments in Mainz and months of correspondence thereafter, they produced in the spring of 1952 a Franco-German Historians' Agreement, denying any premeditated plan to provoke war by either country, as a basis for textbook reform in each.[4]

Within a decade, however, eirenic diplomacy of this sort was unexpectedly put out of court by the publication in Germany of a massive volume offering, in the candid words of an admirer, 'powerful confirmation of the much-hated decision of the victorious allies in

---

4. For particulars, see the detailed account by Mona Siegel and Kirsten Harjes, 'Disarming Hatred: History Education, National Memories and Franco-German Reconciliation from World War I to the Cold War', *History of Education Quarterly*, August 2012, pp. 370–412.

1919 to make Germany responsible for the war'.[5] Fritz Fischer's *Griff nach der Weltmacht*, based on access to diplomatic and military documents held in the DDR and hitherto inaccessible to historians, set out to show that within a month of the outbreak of hostilities, in September 1914, a memorandum by Bethmann Hollweg revealed German plans to dominate the continent by sweeping conquest and annexation, escalating by early 1918 to the project of a vast 'Mitteleuropa surrounded by a ring of vassal states' from Belgium to Lithuania, flanked by a 'central African colonial empire safeguarded by naval bases and linked to the Near East through the Sudan and Suez', amounting to an 'imperium of grandiose dimensions' giving Germany 'an impregnable position of world economic power'. In so doing, 'it shook Europe and the world to their foundations'.[6] Four years later, a sequel radicalized these findings. Well before 1914, the country's military and political leadership planned to unleash a continental war, for which 'the German people had been prepared'. Resolved on 'a violent confrontation with the ever more threatening Russian colossus and its financial backer France', Fischer would later declare, 'it was essential that Austria-Hungary draw Russia into a blitzkrieg in the Balkans', where German leaders were confident 'a general conflagration could be made to order at any time'.[7]

In a second large volume expounding the socio-economic and political forces driving Germany's quest for hegemony in Europe,

---

5. Annika Mombauer, 'The Fischer Controversy 50 Years On', *Journal of Contemporary History*, April 2013, p. 232.

6. *Griff nach der Weltmacht. Die Kriegzielpolitik der kaiserlichen Deutschland 1914/18*, Düsseldorf 1961, pp. 817–19, 12 [*Germany's Aims in the First World War*, London–New York 1967, pp. 607–8, xxii].

7. *Weltmacht oder Niedergang. Deutschland im ersten Weltkrieg*, Hamburg 1965, pp. 51, 53, 57 [*World Power or Decline. The Controversy over Germany's Aims in the First World War*, New York 1975, pp. 20, 23, 28–9].

Fischer produced a document to demonstrate that the Kaiser and von Moltke, his chief of staff, were plotting a preventive war as early as December 1912, a conflict to be staged 'the sooner the better'.[8] Germany's part in igniting the First World War was thus not just, as suggested earlier, 'substantial'.[9] It had become total. In 1914 Germany's politicians neither stumbled blindly into war, nor perforce just accepted war. They deliberately 'unleashed' a war they had wanted and prepared in advance. The verbs Fischer chose for their performance – *wollen, vorbereiten, auslösen* – allowed for no ambiguity. Should the message not be clear enough, he dotted the i's and crossed the t's for the West German public at large: 'There does not exist a single document in the world that could weaken the central truth that in July 1914 a will for war existed solely and exclusively [*einzig und allein*] on the German side and that all arrangements on the Entente side served only the defence of their alliance.'[10]

The Second Reich, moreover, had not just deliberately launched the Great War in pursuit of an imperial domination of Europe, but – Fischer went on to argue – laid the ground-plans for the expansion of Germany by the Third Reich from the Channel to the Caucasus. For the Nazi state inherited both its territorial ambitions and its racial obsessions from the Second Reich. The continuity between the two did not, of course, mean that they were identical. In its own distorted fashion, the Wilhelmine political system had remained a species of *Rechtsstaat*, where Hitler's rule was a violent dictatorship whose purposes and methods exceeded

---

8. *Krieg der Illusionen. Die deutsche Politik von 1911 bis 1914*, Dusseldorf 1969, pp. 232–5 [*War of Illusions: German Policies from 1911 to 1914*, New York–London 1975, pp. 161–4].

9. *Griff nach der Weltmacht*, p. 97 [*Germany's Aims in the First World War*, p. 88].

10. 'Von Zaun gebrochen – nicht hineinschlittert', *Die Zeit*, 3 September 1965.

its predecessor's. Yet it was essential to 'analyse the enduring structures and aims of the Prusso-German Empire born in 1866–71 and destroyed in 1945', and so grasp 'the continuum within its changes and its impact on the international system'. Oblivious of the fact neither its European neighbours nor the United States would ever accept a reversal of the verdict of 1918–19, the Second World War was 'a refusal on the part of the leading strata of the German Empire to accept the outcome of the First World War'.[11]

In his final book, published three decades after his first, Fischer rammed the message home. The Führer was no 'occupational accident' of German history. There was a 'straight line' from the Treaty of Brest-Litovsk to Hitler's milieu in Munich. Power consolidated in the summer of 1933, Hitler forged an alliance with the 'social and economic pillars of Wilhelmine Germany' – the army and its largely aristocratic officer corps; heavy industry which alone made possible the armament of a modern offensive army; large East Elbian landowners capable of producing the necessary food supplies in case of war; the bureaucracy and reactionary judiciary; and the Catholic church. 'Hitler sprang neither from heaven nor from hell.' Rather, 'measured by the preconditions making possible his actions and performances, and by his thought-world, he belongs deep in German history of the nineteenth and twentieth centuries'.[12] For a long time, traditional historians had suppressed all acknowledgment of this. But then a 'breakthrough' had occurred, which had prevailed over all attacks and criticisms, effecting a lasting

---

11. *Bündnis der Eliten: Zur Kontinuität der Machtstrukturen in Deutschland 1871–1945*, Düsseldorf 1979, pp. 93–5 [*From Kaiserreich to Third Reich*, London 1986, pp. 97–8].

12. *Hitler war kein Betriebsunfall*, Hamburg 1992, pp. 178–81; text published in 1989.

change in German conceptions of history. What was this? 'My own writing since 1959.'[13]

Criticism Fischer's work certainly attracted. There was vehement, at times enraged, rejection of it by an older generation of German historians, Gerhard Ritter foremost among them – traditional conservatives committed to the notion, standard in every other belligerent state, that the country was innocent of any malign or aggressive design in 1914. Cooler dissent also came from incisive younger scholars like Wolfgang Mommsen. The charges Fischer's work incurred were essentially two: that his use of evidence was simple-minded and selective, putting more weight on his pick of documents than they would bear, neither of his prize exhibits supporting what he claimed of them; while ambitious war aims were common to every power once fighting started, just as senior officers in every country looked forward to its onset. As for a straight line from Brest-Litovsk to Barbarossa, between them lay Versailles – the peace conspicuously absent from Fischer's roster of the preconditions for Hitler. Beyond his handling of key pieces of evidence was the obvious absence of any serious comparative dimension in his work, noted from the start by Ludwig Dehio and Klaus Epstein, and later underlined by Jonathan Steinberg.[14]

---

13. Ibid., p. 18. For a similar, unmitigated presentation of his work for a foreign audience see 'Twenty-Five Years Later: Looking Back at the "Fischer" Controversy and its Consequences', *Central European History*, September 1988, pp. 207–23.

14. See Dehio, 'Deutschlands Griff nach der Weltmacht?', *Der Monat*, February 1962, p. 65; Epstein, 'German War Aims in the First World War', *World Politics*, October 1962, pp. 174–5; Steinberg: 'German Fischerite scholarship was for the most part entirely ignorant of (and uninterested in) the politics and policies of the other great powers and thus had no way of verifying the extent of German responsibility for the outbreak of war': 'On Knowledge and New Research: A Summary of the Conference on the Fischer Controversy Fifty Years On', *Journal of Contemporary History*, April 2013, p. 246.

Focussed just on the Second Reich, its adversaries received little more than mentions in so far as they featured in German calculations, even its Austrian ally treated as a mere object of diktat or pressure from Berlin. Loose claims of the uniqueness of German defects, 'the only people who did not themselves create the state from below by invoking the forces of democracy [*im Bunde mit der Demokratie*] against the old ruling groups', as announced in the very first paragraph of *Griff*,[15] lacked any rudiments of an international compass – as if Romanov rule in Russia or Habsburg in Austro-Hungary, or for that matter Bourbon or Tudor dynasties in France and England, all unmistakeably state-creating, had 'invoked the forces of democracy'.

Not that depictions of Germany in this vein were outlandish. Their tenor was common currency in the Entente apologetics of the Great War and inter-war periods, and could be found even in writing by historians after 1945. Taylor had matched or outdone Fischer's most extreme pronouncements. But what was familiar enough abroad was far from banal in post-war West Germany. There the impact was huge. Virtually from the start a *cause célèbre* in the Federal Republic, Fischer's construction quite soon became a standard consensus across much of the West. There were a number of reasons for its success. The first was straightforward. Although Fischer's judgment of German guilt for the First World War conformed to prior Allied belief, his archival work in hitherto secret official files was quite new – terrain neither Renouvin nor Fay, Schmitt nor Albertini, let alone Taylor, had been in a position to explore – and commanded widespread respect among historians abroad, above all in the English-speaking world,[16]

---

15. *Griff*, p. 15 [*War Aims*, p. 3].

16. Reaction was much cooler in France. Renouvin, who cannot have been pleased by Fischer's denial of the Franco-German historian's agreement he had reached with Ritter that no power deliberately planned the First World War,

which after victory in the Second World War enjoyed a degree of international cultural dominance without equivalent in the pre-war era, and mattered greatly for the fate of Fischer's work in Germany itself. There, establishment reaction to his first book was so hostile that in 1964 the ruling Christian-Democratic Party blocked funds from the Goethe Institute for a speaking tour by Fischer in America, upon which a dozen distinguished historians of Germany in the US not only protested but financed the trip themselves. But these were the last years of the CDU's post-war reign of power. Fischer's second major work appeared in 1969, the year of the *Wende*, when Brandt took office as chancellor for the SPD. It has occasionally been suggested that Fischer's triumph, in public reputation and in the profession, owed something to the generational revolt of the sixties that exploded in the second half of the decade. But no friend of the radical left, he was hostile to the student rebellion of the period. What he benefited from was the liberal turn of the time – Habermas's 'unconditional orientation to the West' – and its administration by Brandt and Schmidt, who made short work of subversives. A major change of public mood and political sensibility could now canonize Fischer as a symbol of the better Germany emerging after its entry into the Atlantic fold. It was an apotheosis that lasted. As late as 2015, an Anglo-German historian of note devoted to his memory could write: 'The Fischer controversy of the 1960s was always more than just an

---

pointed out that while Fischer's work in the German archives was meritorious, his overall view of the conflict added little to truths established in Paris forty-five years earlier, and his writing was unnecessarily shrill – 'the reader would sometimes wish for greater serenity': 'Nationalisme et impérialisme en Allemagne de 1911 à 1914', *Revue Historique*, January–March 1971, p. 72. In an obituary of Fischer, his pupil Jean-Claude Allain was less diplomatic. Fischer's documentation was selective and interpretation of the chosen documents 'peremptory' in ways that were counterproductive, whatever his other deserts: *Francia*, 2000, 27:3, p. 234.

academic dispute about scraps of paper in the archives. It marked the point at which civil society in the Federal Republic admirably turned its back on a difficult past to embrace Western values and share its destiny with that of its neighbours. The transformation was profound and lasting, making Germany a model democracy and its people the most peace-loving in Europe.'[17]

When Fischer died in 1999, tributes were virtually universal. Four years later, in a recondite journal on the history of theology, a young historian published his findings on Fischer's past in the Third Reich. It was always known that he had joined the Nazi Party in the late thirties, for which he was reproached by Ritter.[18] But taking the party card to advance a career was so common among ambitious Germans at the time, when membership might be a condition for a sought-after job, that it was not held against him. The top ranks of post-war Christian Democracy itself were, after all, filled with former members of the NSDAP, not least the last CDU chancellor of the Federal Republic in the sixties, Kurt Kiesinger, during the war a henchman of Ribbentrop. Why fuss over a pro-forma gesture at a far lower level? Understandably, nothing was made of it. So the posthumous revelations of Klaus Grosse Kracht were a bombshell, which attracted considerable public attention. Working on religious

---

17. John Röhl, 'Goodbye to All That (Again)? The Fischer Thesis, the New Revisionism and the Meaning of the First World War', *International Affairs*, January 2015, p. 166. The same article expresses its uncertainty as to foreknowledge by the high command in Berlin of the fate of the heir to the Habsburg monarchy in Bosnia: 'The German general staff may or may not have had had prior knowledge of the plan to assassinate Franz Ferdinand in Sarajevo' (*sic*).

18. Ritter, for his part, was arrested in 1944 for his anti-Nazi ties to the Goerdeler group planning the overthrow of Hitler, escaping execution only because the court charged with the case was destroyed and the judge presiding over it killed in an Allied bombing raid.

history, he had been in search of what the state archives in Koblenz might contain about Fischer's work on church affairs in nineteenth-century Germany, written prior to the Second World War. But on coming across a CV of Fischer's dating from 1942, he realized he could not look away from what it showed, and had led up to it. The article he published on what he had found was a model of cool precision and restraint. Research in the archives told a story at startling variance with the post-war image of the historian. From a very early age – not even yet a teenager – Fischer had been active in right-wing youth movements in the *mouvance* of Ludendorff and the Stahlhelm. In his teens, he had been a member of the militantly anti-Semitic organization Bund Oberland, in which he received 'pre-military training' in his native Franconia. He had participated in the 'Deutsche Tag' of September 1923 organized by the NSDAP, the Stahlhelm and Bund Oberland in Nuremberg, two months before Hitler's attempted putsch in Munich. He had worked for the 'national cause' among *Volksdeutsche* outposts in Bohemia and Transylvania. He had joined the SA in November 1933 and the Nazi Party on 1 May 1937, as soon as the ban on admission of new members was lifted, and had volunteered for the occupation of the Sudetenland by the Wehrmacht in 1938.[19]

Majoring in church history and theology at the University of Berlin, Fischer was mentored by Erich Seeberg, a former military chaplain and authoritarian Protestant divine who hailed the Nazi rise to power as 'a world-historical turning-point' and joined the NSDAP in 1933. Under him Fischer authored a dissertation on Bethmann Hollweg's Lutheran grandfather – a figure positive enough for his

---

19. Klaus Grosse Kracht, 'Fritz Fischer und der deutsche Protestantismus', *Zeitschrift für neuere Theologiegeschicht*e, 2003, 10, pp. 229–30, 239.

time, since he had stood for the unification of all Prussian Protestants in a single church, yet one who was too much a moderate, lacking 'the excess and injustice and toughness that belong to true life, and the will to perform and to suffer them'.[20] In 1939 he was awarded a grant for research on religion and politics by the historical institute that was a fief of the high-flying Nazi ideologue Walter Frank. His project, he explained, would show how two distinct historical trends in German Protestantism, each equally 'natural law–moralistic' and 'pietistic-humanitarian', but one committed to a 'concept of right', the other to an 'ethic of love', had both of them always been hostile to the Reich, from the time of the elder Bethmann Hollweg under Bismarck to that of the last Wilhelmine chancellor, down to the era of 'Adolf Hitler today'.[21] While serving in an anti-aircraft battery in Berlin during the Second War, in 1941, he told Frank's deputy Erich Botzenhart that he regretted not being able to take part in the Great Eastern campaign of the Third Reich, but was proud to be lecturing to his unit on themes as central to the work of the Institute as 'Jewish penetration into German culture and politics in the last 200 years, Jewish blood in the English upper class, and the role of Jewry in the economy and society of the USA.' Appointed professor of history at the University of Hamburg at the end of 1942, he thanked Frank for his help in securing the post, saying he hoped to stay in touch with the Institute after the end of the war 'in the confrontation with old-British and new-American imperialism and their Christian-moralistic and human-rights ideologies', ending his letter with a loyal 'Heil Hitler!'[22] Military duties preventing assumption of his chair in Hamburg, he

---

20. Ibid., pp. 231, 233, 235.
21. Ibid., p. 238.
22. Ibid., pp. 239, 240.

was captured by the US Army in April 1945. Frank committed suicide a month later, explaining that with the death of Hitler life had lost its meaning for him.

Held for two years by the US in a case of mistaken identity, Fischer was cleared and released in 1947, and in 1948 delivered his inaugural lecture at Hamburg, attacking Lutheran traditions in Germany for their want of a 'natural law and moral conception of rights'. Where once he had upheld the opposition between Luther and Calvin as characterized by Seeberg, dubbing Germany's defeat by England and America in 1918 the bitter 'victory of Calvin over Luther', now he reversed it, criticizing Lutheran traditions for blind obedience to the state and lauding Calvinist principles of human rights and resistance to unjust rulers as foundations of the Western democracy that Germany had so tragically lacked.[23] Moving from religious to political history after trips to England and America in the early fifties, he embarked on the research in captured German archives held in the DDR which yielded the book of 1961 that made him famous for the rest of his life as an iconoclastic champion of democracy. How then was Fischer's post-war trajectory to be judged? Without question, Grosse Kracht concluded, in these years he rallied to Western political values. But his critical impulse, applied to such celebrated effect in his work on German elites in the Second Reich and beyond, hit limits where it was a question of his own past. The result was a 'performative self-contradiction', as he sought to change the political-historical culture

---

23. 'Die Auswirkungen der Reformation auf das deutsche und westeuropäische-amerikanische politische Leben', collected in *Der Erste Weltkrieg und das deutsche Geschichtsbildung: Beiträge zur Bewältigung eines historischen Tabu*s, Düsseldorf 1977, pp. 37–46; arguments further developed in his contribution to the Conference of German Historians in Munich the following year: 'Der deutsche Protestantismus und die Poltik im 19. Jahrhundert', ibid., pp. 47–88.

of Germany while keeping silent about his own part in it, including its anti-Semitism. Such schizophrenia was only possible in the early years of the Federal Republic, when the common survivors of a criminal past created a personal 'zero hour' for themselves. What distinguished Fischer's case was 'a body of work that broke through the very silence to which it was indebted'. It was not any self-criticism, but his radical critique of his own original Protestant background that did more for the liberalization of the political culture of West Germany than many a pious 'confession of guilt' of that or other times.[24]

How was the news of Fischer's long-standing pre-war record – evidence of twenty years of entanglement with the politics of the far right – received in Germany when it broke? It was given prominent coverage in major organs of the press – the *Frankfurter Allgemeine Zeitung*, *Süddeutsche Zeitung*, *Frankfurter Rundschau*, *Die Welt*, *Die Zeit*[25] – to unanimous regret that Fischer had not been more candid about his past, accompanied by varying degrees of assent or reservation about Grosse Kracht's assessment of this. Replies came in letters from his pupils questioning or minimizing the case against him – Fischer had never concealed his membership of the SA or NSDAP, a formality he had been obliged to accept for financial reasons, which had not stopped him being openly critical of the Third Reich, nor was there any proof he had ever given the talks allegedly incriminating him. The most substantial response was an article in a scholarly journal by a friend and former assistant of Fischer in

---

24. Kracht, 'Fritz Fischer, pp. 251–2.
25. Johann Hinrich Claussen, 'Umgepoltes Denken', *Frankfurter Allgemeine Zeitung*, 7 January 2004; Volker Ullrich, 'Griff nach der Wahrheit', *Die Zeit*, 15 January 2004; Rudolf Walther, 'Im kollektiven Beschweigen eingerichtet', *Frankfurter Rundschau*, 16 January 2004; Sven Felix Kellerhoff, 'Gewissermassen schizophren', *Die Welt*, 7 January 2004.

Hamburg, contesting Grosse Kracht's view that he had reversed his judgment of Lutheranism and Calvinism after the war. Fischer's pre-war books showed he had not. He had, of course, made some 'concessions to the Zeitgeist'. But it was wrong to claim he had made no self-criticism after the war; on the contrary, in private and in public he had striven to be subjectively honest about it.[26]

Six years later, the first book-length treatment of Fischer's past in the Third Reich appeared, based on a doctorate completed at the University of Bayreuth, *Fritz Fischer im Nazionalsozialismus* by Bernhard Olpen. Though the most thoroughly documented account of Fischer's early years to appear so far, it was ignored by the media and the profession in Germany. This was perhaps in some part due to the fact that it offered no sudden sensation for the press, as Grosse Kracht's revelations had done. In all probability, however, its lack of reception was more a function of the status of its author, and the nature of his conclusions. Olpen was a scrupulous scholar, his book based on a doctorate, but in a land where titles bestowed by the university have the status of those that are hereditary in Britain, he was not an academic but a Lutheran pastor; while his verdict on Fischer, avoiding recourse to extenuation or euphemism, was inevitably more uncomfortable to conventional opinion, which perhaps found – as so often in such cases – silence the better part of valour.

The strengths of Olpen's work lay in the empirical range of his investigation, the common sense he brought to his analysis of it, and – especially – the balance and acumen of his final judgment of Fischer.

---

26. Among letters, see Hartmut Pogge von Strandmann, 'Aus akutem Geldmangel in die Partei eingenommen', *FAZ*, 4 February 2004 and Imanuel Geiss, 'Über das Ziel hinausgeschossen', *FAZ*, 3 February 2004. The extended rejoinder came from Manfred Asendorf, 'Griff nach Fritz Fischer', *Blatter für deutsche und international Politik*, 2004: 8, pp. 933–46.

The result is a more considerable account – in a Geertzian idiom, if you will, a thicker description – of the probable character and extent of Fischer's imbrication with organizations and ideologemes of the far right in Germany between the wars than possible in article form. Building on the material Grosse Kracht found and extending it, Olpen looked in greater detail at the political and cultural setting in which Fischer grew up, the Bavaria of the twenties, showing that in these years it was through his religion that Fischer acquired his ideological bearings: a violently nationalist brand of Protestantism that in Germany not infrequently served as a conduit towards proto-fascism. But he was also an academically accomplished and ambitious schoolboy, who – according to his own account a dozen years later – ceased to be politically active in 1923, the year Hitler's attempt at a putsch proved a fiasco in Munich. Yet, Olpen points out, once the eighteen-year-old got to the University of Erlangen in 1926, he joined the Uttenruthia Verband, membership of which in subsequent years he would often record in his favour: a militant student association of the anti-Semitic right offering weapons training, homage to Hitler, and propaganda work in the Volksdeutsche populations of Transylvania and elsewhere, in which he took part.[27]

At Erlangen Fischer studied church history and theology, though his reading was clearly wider, and in 1929 transferred to Berlin, where he graduated in theology in 1931. By then he already had a dissertation in hand on a Prussian official of the early nineteenth century concerned with religious affairs, Georg Nicolovius, for which he was given a further degree in 1932 under Seeberg, whose doctrinal views were akin to those of his own adolescent background in Bavaria. The

---

27. Bernhard Olpen, *Fritz Fischer im Nationalsozialismus*, Saarbrücken 2010, pp. 26–8.

following year, when the Nazis came power, Fischer embarked on a doctorate for his *Habilitation* as a university teacher, selecting as his topic the early career of Bethmann Hollweg's devoutly Lutheran grandfather August, minister for education and culture in Prussia in the mid-nineteenth century, and in 1935 was awarded the necessary degree. By 1936, at the age of twenty-eight he was lecturing in the theology faculty at Berlin. But it had become his 'passionate wish', he confessed, to change his field to political history, which he could teach only if the Ministry of Education would grant him the formality of an *Umhabilitierung* to the philosophy faculty. That, however, was going too fast. His application, judged 'premature' by a senior historian at the university, was rejected, not for the last time. In 1937, when the ban on new admissions to the party was lifted, he enrolled as a Nazi, and then in short order brought out enlarged versions of both prongs of his post-graduate research as books, on Bethmann Hollweg in 1938 and on Nicolovius in 1939, the latter dedicated to Seeberg.[28]

Frustrated in his desire to switch from dealing with articles of faith to questions of power, and dissatisfied with official responses to his request for side-payments to top up a salary which left him, he complained, continually straitened, Fischer turned for betterment to the Institute for the History of the New Germany. Created by the Nazi regime in 1935, this centre was run by the high-decibel anti-Semite Walter Frank, a slightly older contemporary of Fischer's who also came from Upper Bavaria. In 1939 Fischer sent him a

---

28. *Moritz August von Bethmann Hollweg: Religion, Rechts- und Staats-Gedanke*, Berlin 1938; *Ludwig Nicolovius: Rokoko – Reform – Restauration*, Berlin 1939. The two books, though their concerns are obviously related, differ in other ways. The study of Nicolovius is substantially longer than that of Bethmann Hollweg, and as its subtitle suggests, wider in scope, covering the family, friends, and intellectual and political milieus of its subject in more typically biographical detail.

research proposal: he wanted to extend the important work of a recently deceased scholar, Christoph Steding – whom Frank had edited – on the 'external enemies of the Reich' in the belt of neutral countries around Germany.[29] Fischer would complement that with a study of the Reich's 'inner enemies' in the field of religion: the 'Lutheran-confessional' tendency and the 'charitable-humanistic supra-confessional' tendency. The former 'narrowed' the creed proper for the Reich, the latter 'softened' it. Both were in conflict with Bismarck in the nineteenth century, and now with Hitler, the 'fulfiller of popular longing' for a true faith in the twentieth.[30] This was a prospect calculated to appeal to Frank, and Fischer was duly rewarded with a monthly stipend that he received till he was called up later that year, when the Second World War broke out, for service in the artillery arm of the Luftwaffe. Stationed in an anti-aircraft system of the capital and subsequently in Bremen, he remained, however, in close touch with fellow spirits of influence in Berlin and elsewhere, securing *Umhabilitierung* at his fourth attempt in 1940, and eventually the rank of professor at Hamburg in December 1942. His appointment was highly political, the result of a concerted intervention by leading lights of Frank's Institute – three out of the four recommendations he secured for it; while in Hamburg itself he had been cultivating its first Nazi rector, Adolf Rein, historian and theorist of colonial expansion, and in the wings Kleo Pleyer, holder of chairs in Königsberg and Innsbruck, and exponent of an implacable racism. Fischer was in correspondence with all five.

What changed his political outlook, when a little over two years later the war in Europe ended with the defeat of Germany, and Fischer

---

29. Olpen, *Fritz Fischer*, pp. 60–2.
30. Koblenz, N 1422/44, 'Exposé', pp. 2, 5.

was captured by American troops? The standard account, offered by Fischer and generally accepted, is that it was his shock at learning of Nazi atrocities, and witnessing the lack of remorse among veterans of the SS held prisoner together with him at Dachau, which transformed him: a trauma that produced a radical conversion – intellectual, moral and political – that made him the fearless democratic historian he became after the war. Olpen does not question the change itself, but does cast doubt on this version of how it came about. For after capture by American troops in Jena during the US occupation of Thuringia in 1945, Fischer was not held at Dachau, but transferred to a camp for officers and officials of the Third Reich run by the US army in Zuffenhausen outside Stuttgart, where – not unlike Braudel's experience in a German camp – he lectured on history to fellow prisoners three times a week, talks mainly concerned with the First World War. It was not until the end of the year that, mistaken for a Nazi doctor of the same name – a very common one in Germany – he was held at Dachau for another eight months on suspicion of war crimes, before he was released in the autumn of 1946. Formal clearance to resume the chair at Hamburg he had not been able to take up during the war lasted through most of 1947 because his denazification was delayed, not by the university but by the occupation authorities. It was not till 1948 that he could give his inaugural lecture – topic: 'The Effects of the Reformation on the Political Life of Germany and of Western Europe–America'. With that opening of a new career, the subject of Olpen's book ends.

What does he make of it? Without being judgmental, his account of Fischer's pre-war career makes clear how little his post-war depiction of it corresponded to the reality of those years. His fabrications leave 'an unpleasant aftertaste'. Though not uncommon in his generation or its elders, they are immaterial to his record at the time. How should that be defined? Olpen rejects a couple of ready labels. Fischer, he argues, was neither a 'convinced Nazi' nor a mere 'opportunist' – a *Konjunkturritter* in the vocabulary of the time. Rather, his path through the Third Reich was the result of two distinct motifs. One was his right-wing religious formation in Bavaria, which propelled him into a thought-world close to what became Nazism, while remaining culturally distinct from it, with many overlapping – not least anti-Semitic – themes, but no comprehensive identification. The other was an unbridled intellectual ambition, the drive to 'make a splash' – *ein grosse Wurf* – in the world of scholarship. As a historian, that meant coming up with a new and striking scientific vision of the past, which in 'politically warped times' could have grave consequences. Frank recommended Fischer to Hamburg University as 'one of the great hopes' of historiography in the Third Reich, and Fischer was impatient to fulfil that hope. This was the fatal combination, of formation and ambition, which led him to the brink of disaster, as he spelt out the future collaboration with the Institute for the History of the New Germany to which he looked forward, from which he was saved at the last minute by the Second World War, that suspended this prospect. 'No, Fischer was not significantly more absorbed into National Socialism than other scholars of his time. But nor was he less so. His adaptation was far-reaching, his overlap with Nazi positions not trivial.'[31]

Olpen conducted his research in the state archives in 2007–8. The following year, a young German historian working in England, Stephan Petzold, became the third scholar to study them, and in 2013 published an article on Fischer's pre-war life based on a doctorate at the University of Aberystwyth about the controversy his post-war writing had set off. In his article, he stressed the intellectual

---

31. Olpen, *Fritz Fischer*, pp. 101–7.

consequences of what he argued was a youthful revolt against the national-conservative brand of Lutheranism in which Fischer had been brought up. It was this rebellion that made him sympathetic to the radical strands in National Socialism, and those Protestant thinkers who sought to adapt their Evangelical faith to Nazi doctrine and practice. True, he did express loyalty to the regime during the war, contrasting the lack of any 'great slogans' capable of rallying rank-and-file soldiers to their leaders in 1917–18 with the 'coherent ideology' galvanizing them in 1943, in a struggle that might yet end with Europe in 'subjugation to Asia, the rule of blood over the leading classes, their decimation and enslavement to American bankers and Jews'. But after the fall of the Third Reich, his two years as a POW changed his life, making him realize the 'fateful effects that the traditions of unconditional obedience' had left on German history. What was already a 'deeply internalized sceptical disposition towards national-conservative histories' now allowed him to reject the restored consensus around these in the post-war era. In this intellectual turn there was thus a 'significant continuity in his positioning within the historical profession', as Fischer put his pre-war sensibility to positive purposes in peacetime Germany.[32]

Petzold's findings, published not in the Federal Republic, but in Britain's *Journal of Contemporary History*, a leader in its field, appeared side by side with essays by many a scholar of renown, in a special issue

---

32. Stephan Petzold, 'The Social Making of a Historian: Fritz Fischer's Distancing from Bourgeois-Conservative Historiography 1930–1960', *Journal of Contemporary History*, April 2013, pp. 271–89. The doctorate behind this essay, completed in 2011, is under embargo, a not unusual precaution when a dissertation is being prepared for publication, and the reason registered by Aberystwyth for its unavailability. The date at which it is to be released, however, is the end of this century, by which time its author is unlikely to be alive, so some other consideration, perhaps related to the family, must be at work.

devoted to the international impact of Fischer's work. In Germany, although some of its findings and all of its analytic cases were new, it attracted no visible notice. What Petzold made clear, however, was that the documents from the time of the Third Reich held in Koblenz had not been fully used by either Grosse Kracht or Olpen. For neither had broached the notes or 'war diary' Fischer composed in 1942–43. Yet these form essential evidence for Fischer's political outlook at the turning-point in the Second World War. Two features of them, closely connected with what we know of his interests and activities on the eve of hostilities, stand out. These are the ideological sources of his admiration for Kleo Pleyer, and the autonomy from purely NSDAP blinkers that he shared with Adolf Rein. What was the trajectory of this duo, who figured so largely in his mental environment at the time?

Pleyer, born in 1898, son of a blacksmith in Bohemia and largely self-educated, fought for the Austro-Hungarian armies in the First World War from the age of seventeen on the Galician and Italian fronts, and was decorated twice. In post-war Czechoslovakia he joined the Sudeten version of far-right German nationalism, the DNSAP, writing its marching song 'We Are the Army of the Swastika' for it; was an anti-Semitic activist at Prague University; transferred to Germany where he joined Bund Oberland and participated in the Munich putsch of 1923; expelled from Bavaria, he pursued his studies in Baden and then Berlin, producing a dissertation so dismissive of the idea that there was ethnically such a thing as a French nation that when published as a book it was impounded by the foreign office of the Third Reich itself, as a provocation capable of compromising relations with Paris.[33] Nevertheless, equipped with his *Habilitation*,

---

33. More than half of the territory of France was occupied by people not ethnically French in origin, Pleyer claimed: Peter Schöttler, *Du Rhin à la Manche: Frontières et relations franco-allemandes au xxe siècle*, Tours 2017, pp. 83–4. For

he became in 1934 an instructor in the historical seminar at Berlin attended by Fischer, and at a conclave of historians in Erfurt organized by Frank the following year, delivered a speech on Greater Germany so electrifying that he was regarded by some as the only orator whose power could be compared with Hitler's. Brigading him into his Institute, Frank avoided such a risky tribute, preferring to speak of a new Pericles. In 1937 he was awarded a chair at the university of Konigsberg, in 1939 a sequel in Innsbrück.

When the Second World War broke out, Pleyer volunteered for service in France, and after victory there was transferred to the Russian front, where he was killed south of Novgorod in March 1942. On his last Christmas leave in Königsberg in 1941, he finished a book, *Volk im Feld*, whose manuscript he entrusted to Frank and which was published posthumously in Hamburg in the spring of 1943. Three chapters recorded his time during the conquest of France; in the occupation of Normandy; and in Army Group Centre of Operation Barbarossa in Russia; two others dealt with the discipline of the warrior and the meaning of the war. The book extolled the 'unconditional obedience that is the axis of German existence', and the lethal duties of the army in the East – 'the German soldier kills, so that his people can live'. It described the people of Paris as 'sub-racial humanity', 'living lees, population-political trash'. It exalted the annihilation of the Jews: 'The prophecy of the Führer is fulfilled: the war which the Jews wanted ends with the extermination of Jewry.

---

particulars of the fortunes of the book when it came to the attention of the Foreign Office, see Helmut Heiber's scathing account of Pleyer in his cyclopean study of Frank and his associates, *Walter Frank und sein Reichsinstitut für Geschichte des neuen Deutschlands*, Stuttgart 1966, pp. 389–400, the subject of a typically effective review by Klaus Epstein (*History and Theory*, 7:1, 1968, pp. 114–39), though his own comments on Pleyer err in the opposite direction.

Europe will emerge cleansed in body and soul from this war. Parting from the Jews will not be difficult for the peoples in the space of the East, since they are innate opponents of the Jews.' Since Bolshevism was Jewish, the war in Russia was pitting 'Aryan against Jewish-Bolshevik world revolution' in a fight whose stakes were 'physical annihilation', where 'each side knows that it must either eradicate the other or be eradicated itself'. Pleyer had little doubt which would prevail: 'The central front of Bolshevism is smashed, the road to Moscow lies open. Stalin has abandoned the Kremlin and moved the government far inland. While the legs of the Bolshevik monster in the south have been broken and its throat at Petersburg is pressed hard, we have led the main thrust against its heart. The largest army ever seen is shattered. The modern Mongol storm is choked in blood.'[34] Posthumously awarded the Kant Prize, the book became a war-time best-seller: towards the end of 1944, the High Command distributed 700,000 copies of its first chapter to German soldiers on all fronts of their retreat.

Thirteen years older than Pleyer, son of a university professor, Adolf Rein was in background and career a different example of adherence to Nazism. After schooling in Jena and graduation in Leipzig, he spent a year in England in 1910–11, where he was greatly impressed by Seeley's work on the British Empire, on which he published a book on his return, and a semester in 1912 as a junior teacher at Syracuse in America. In 1914 he earned a doctorate at Strasburg for work on the US constitution and a position at the university there, then served

---

34. But though 'the outcome of the war has been decided', he told his company, 'the struggle in the East is not yet at an end': *Volk im Feld*, Hamburg 1943, pp. 15, 33, 83–4, 159, 193–4, 219, passages illustrating Schöttler's description of a 'genocidal ultra-Nazi'.

in an artillery regiment during the war. In 1918 Strasburg reverted to France, and Rein found a post in Hamburg, initially as a lecturer on the constitutional arrangements of the United States, and subsequently on the foreign policies of the Great Powers more generally. What had attracted him in Seeley were his ideas on imperialism, which he developed into proposals for a German version, acquiring in 1927 a chair in colonial and overseas history and in 1931 publishing a book on *The Spreading of Europe across the Earth*. A year later he wrote a manifesto for higher education in Germany. From the Middle Ages to the Reformation, the master discipline of the university was theology, its enemy heresy; in the age of the Enlightenment it had been philosophy, its enemy unreason; now, when the German universities had become a warehouse of specialisms, it must be politics, whose enemy was nihilism – politics, which alone could unify in a single comprehensive faculty all the sub-fields into which humanism had declined. That meant scholarship needed the state as the highest expression of politics, and so after Germany's recent defeat at the hands of its adversaries, the nation needed a political culture if Germans were to have something decisive to say to the world.[35]

Though his own politics had more in common with thinkers of the 'conservative revolution' than with the radicalism of the NSDAP, when Hitler took power in 1933 Rein enrolled in the Nazi Party. Within a year he had become the rector of Hamburg University, where he launched a wholesale purge of Jewish professors before it was even commanded by the state, and could boast of having created the first National-Socialist university in Germany, a model for the rest of the country. In early 1938, when the Ministry of Education

---

35. Adolf Rein, *Die Idee der politischen Universität*, Hamburg 1933, pp. 5–7, 11–12, 20, 37–9.

restricted the term of a rectorate henceforward to three years, he requested his release from the position, but continued to be active from his chair in Hamburg and as a member of the board of Frank's Institute in Berlin. In 1940 he was quick off the mark with a volley against England, whose aim in the new war was to inflict a second Versailles on Germany.[36] But under Adolf Hitler, he would write in the autumn of 1941, a Europe united from Sicily to the Crimea, Crete to the Channel was taking shape, fulfilling the destiny accorded it by the Almighty, which had begun with Charlemagne, seen the adventure of Napoleon, the vision of Metternich, the system of Bismarck, and now the advance by Germany, the most powerful and central state of the continent, towards a goal beyond the reach of Hohenstaufen or Hohenzollern – an empire of security, of welfare and of peace encompassing all the peoples of Europe.[37]

Though by the time of the war both Pleyer and Rein were committed, vocal members of the NSDAP, neither's outlook coincided fully with the ideology or sensibility of its leadership. There were a number of ways of being a Nazi, of which they represented different variants. Pleyer had always been an ardent fascist, and by 1940 was a fanatic. But he was not particularly orthodox: he had broken with Hitler in the mid-twenties, his ideas of a supra-*völkisch* empire along Habsburg lines were anathema to mainstream Nazism, and he was capable of a rousing call for historians to realize that the state might be man's work, but men were only half of humanity, and must reckon with women as the other half: *Erst Volksgeschichte ist hierin Vollgeschichte*. Rein was the opposite, a historian for whom history was not a plaything of

---

36. *Warum führt England Krieg?*, Berlin 1940, p. 37.
37. *Europa und das Reich*, Essen 1943, pp. 7–9, 65 ff., 74–5, 84–7.

peoples. It had always been made by states and the conflicts between them, and remained so.

How does this pair figure in Fischer's 'war diary'? The folder in Koblenz containing it opens in December 1942 with an entry headed 'On reading Walter Frank's obituary of Kleo Pleyer'.[38] Fischer's reflections? 'Pleyer demands a blood-history, a population-history. What does the *blood-loss* of 1914–18 and 1939–44 mean for the reduction of the substance of the German people?' It meant an 'undermining' of its substance by racial mixture with surrounding elements: Baltic; Finno-Ugric; 'Stray-German'; Slav (Croats, Slovenes, Poles, 'servant girls and labourers from Ukraine'); Scandinavian (Norwegians and 'dirty neutral' Danes); Celtic Swiss; Netherlandish; French; Luxemburger and Lorrainer-Alsatian ('catholic-crippled, narrow-minded', unwilling to learn proper German); large numbers of Italians, Sicilians and Spaniards ('dirty, flabby, superficial', ultra-mixed). 'Legal marriages are few, illegitimate children numerous, and many of these worker-immigrants will remain forever in Germany.' When Pleyer taught at the university of Berlin, Fischer went on, 'I heard him in the winter semester of '34–'35 and it was *the* lecture (on modern German constitutional history) that in the decisive summer of 1935 mentally shaped and guided me. Then his speech at the Historians Conference in Erfurt in the summer of 1937, when the breakthrough of 1935 found the completion of its outer aim *and* inner deepening: the revolt of the English and Germano-neutral-belt of states and their religion against the Reich.' National-Socialism, Pleyer had argued, was capable of

---

38. 'Ein Kampf um das Reich', *Historische Zeitschrift*, 1942, 3, pp. 507–55. This threnody for a national hero was Frank's last quasi-academic publication. That December he was dismissed from the Institute on the instructions of Bormann, by then head of the Nazi Party, a friend of Frank's enemy Rosenberg.

creating a supra-*völkisch* new order. His was 'the popular vision of a border German and the state vision of a former Austrian', who saw in the Habsburg Empire 'the good of a supra-völkisch new order and role model of a law of nationalities (whatever its reality and how it was experienced by those subject to it, especially in Hungary with its policy of oppression). What of Russia now?'[39]

In late January 1943, Fischer set down a much longer set of notes. On January 25, he had been in Hamburg for the formal confirmation of his appointment there. 'Bright winter's day, east wind, the life of the harbour.' But on the same day 'the Wehrmacht announces that the Sixth Army is locked at Stalingrad in a communiqué speaking of a "fight to the finish", that is to the bitter end. I am happy at the consolidation of my personal life and its future, and depressed by the dire position of the war in the East and gloomy future in general.' There follows 'Conversation with Prof. Rein' — a long exchange, at first personal, then about the causes of the looming disaster in Russia, in which Rein made no secret of his pessimism. In his view, Hitler — a man of will — needed men of restraint around him to avoid the needless consumption of manpower. The sacrifices incurred in the summer campaign of 1942 had been in vain, reaping the mistake of autumn 1941. Each time the offensive had gone on too long, as at the Marne in 1914. In Russia, there was a strategic choice to be made: either drive towards Stalingrad or towards the Caucasus. To attempt both was beyond our forces, and Halder as chief of staff had opposed such a course, but the Führer overrode his forebodings. Halder was proved right. Rein expressed further scepticism about the position in North Africa, where Rommel had been forced after El Alamein to

---

39. Bundesarchiv (Koblenz), N 1422/105, December [undated] 1942; henceforward Koblenz.

retreat to Tunisia. Fischer seconded these views, comparing the likely outcome at Stalingrad, worse than that for the French at Sedan or Metz in the Franco-Prussian War, to Thermopylae or the fate of the last king of the Ostrogoths on the slopes of Vesuvius. They agreed that official coverage of the war on the radio and in the press, aimed at concealing successive setbacks with inflated rhetoric and 'heroization' of defeats, was of no avail. People knew the war was going badly. In subsequent entries, Fischer reported criticisms of Hitler by peasants, and by men in his own battery; compared illusions among the German leadership about Russian strength to earlier English illusions about German strength. Britain and France certainly had the advantage of their colonies over Germany, which had none, and had suffered far fewer losses on the battlefield. Victory might not be possible in this war, the best feasible outcome a compromise with Russia. Could an economic quest for raw materials and other riches in Soviet territory have outweighed ideology in the war against it? Yet however that might be, 'we must win' or 'go under'. For the demonic Bolshevik dictatorship was the worst enemy of Germany, and an Asiatic menace to all Europe. In alliance with World Jewry and America it threatened 'a reign of blood' that would consign the elites of the continent to slavery or the grave. 'So we must prevail, or at any rate survive the war as a people and a Reich, as Prussia did in Frederick's time.'[40]

On 1 February, the notes suddenly cease, the day before the surrender of the German army at Stalingrad. In May, they resume after the Allied landings in Italy, and end in August after the fall of Mussolini.[41] In this section, claiming it was universally believed the

---

40. Koblenz, N1422/10: 26, 27, 30 January 1943.

41. Fischer headed this section 'Long break in my notes. In the interim, first lieutenant, head of the battery, service medal' – 'in February on leave with Margrit in Münchberg'; Koblenz, N 1422/105, 5 May 1943.

country couldn't win, Fischer's criticism of German conduct of the war predictably became much sharper, attacking official excuses for the strategic retreat in North Africa, failure to organize an evacuation of German troops like Dunkirk, disastrous trust in the Italian army and monarchy, and the inadequacy of anti-aircraft defences against the Allied carpet bombing of German cities.[42] But along with tirades against Italian treachery came praise for Berlin's belated decision to privatize land in Russia, delivering the liberation the Russian peasantry had always longed for, and advocacy of a ban on German marriage with Finns, Baltics and German 'driftwood' in the East, which would weaken the nation's racial stock. To 'preserve German blood', the families and regiments of the nation had to be protected from alien admixture. '*Pleyer's lesson*' – underlined – must become the 'highest guideline of all legislation and public care.'[43]

The 'war diary' is the longest and most substantial document predating 1945 in the archive that Fischer bestowed on Koblenz. What does it suggest? To unravel this, a sense of the character of the *Nachlass* itself is needed. Paradoxically, none of the historians who have so far worked on its holdings have commented on these. The *Nachlass* originated in 1991, when Fischer – then in his mid-eighties – let the Bundesarchiv know he intended to give his papers to it. In the spring of 1992 a functionary from Koblenz consulted a professor and former pupil of Fischer's on the matter, who told him that Fischer was currently examining his papers in detail, but 'feared that in doing so he would destroy assorted documents' – some of his correspondence with colleagues with whom his relations had their ups and downs, 'or other material whose perusal by third parties might create an unfavourable

---

42. Koblenz, N 1422/105, 13 May, 7 July, 5 August 1943.
43. Koblenz, N 1422/105, 21 May 1943.

impression'.⁴⁴ Fischer was, after all, known as 'both contentious and not quite free of a certain vanity'. In July an envoy from Koblenz was received by Fischer, who had readied thirty-three binders of materials for the Bundesarchiv – thirty-two of which dealt with his career since the war, a single further binder covering the entire pre-war period: 'evidently what remains from a drastic prior selection', noted the emissary.⁴⁵ In August a contract was signed, stipulating that the papers could not be consulted without the permission of Fischer or his heirs until 2010, and the binders were transferred to Koblenz. There they were examined, their contents reorganized and decanted into 146 boxes. Fischer subsequently altered the date at which these would become accessible, from 2010 to 2000. He died in 1999, and in the new century Grosse Kracht became the first scholar to study what was held at Koblenz.

What the *Nachlass* makes clear is that, by temperament or habit, Fischer was someone who quite carefully preserved correspondence, notes, drafts, proposals, statements for officialdom, reactions to his work, and materials bearing on it. The volume of all that he kept is impressive, nearing a thousand pages. But if it is striking how little from the pre-war and war years survives, all the more so is what does. It is clear that Fischer purged his papers, as his former pupil and the envoy from Koblenz suspected, before giving them to the Bundesarchiv. It is highly probable, for example, that he destroyed the drafts or texts of the talks denouncing the Jews he gave as a cadre of the SA to his battery during the war, and virtually certain that he expunged a good deal of his 'diary' itself, which begins well after Germany's victory in France and rapid advance into Russia, stops

---

44. Koblenz, 'Dienstakte – Prof. Dr. Fischer, Fritz', p. 4.
45. Ibid., p. 17.

so precisely before the surrender at Stalingrad, and resuming after three months, ends so abruptly with the Allied advance towards Rome. It is not difficult to imagine what he might have written about any of the periods in these gaps – triumphalist in 1940 and 1941, dubitative in 1942, increasingly disillusioned in 1943, as would have been the feelings of a good many of his compatriots. He may also have rewritten parts of the diary during the war, as suggested by a reference to losses in '1941/44' in an entry dated December 1942, and an accompanying proleptic parenthesis.

More perplexing, it might be felt, is the fact that Fischer nevertheless allowed so much evidence to remain that certainly compromised him. Why did he not do away with all of this too? Only conjectures are possible. He may have realized that there were documents revealing his political past in other archives, held by the Humboldt or Hamburg universities, that were beyond his reach, and thought that if these came to light, his own would not add much to them. Or advancing years and a lessening attention span could have made a cleansing of his record more erratic than it would otherwise have been. Perhaps too, he may have felt confident enough of his public standing for survivals from that earlier time to be immune to much objection, since after all his membership of the party had always been known and had not damaged him, Ritter being unable to make much trouble about it given that his principal allies in the contest with Fischer, the historians Egmont Zechlin and Karl-Dietrich Erdmann, were compromised by Nazism as well. In the case of the war diary, he might have regarded his sharp criticism of the military and other blunders of the Nazi leadership as sufficient evidence that his sympathies lay with the Anglo-American Allies rather than the Axis, to be kept as potential protection after the war. These can be no more than guesses. What the documents show that is not speculative but deductive is the instability of Fischer's outlook under the 'warping' pressures of the Third Reich. That he remained in large measure an outcrop of Bund Oberland and the luxuriant vegetation of the far right in which he had grown up is plain. But this was not a tight-knit Weltanschauung, and permitted other impulses and reflections of a contrary character. Asendorf could legitimately point to passages in his book on the elder Bethmann Hollweg that anticipated just the contrast he would make after the war between a Calvinism that upheld the rights of resistance and civic freedoms and a Lutheranism that preached a piety of obedience, ascribing Bethmann Hollweg to the first rather than the second.[46] In the same years Fischer could write to Seeberg that he feared universities were going to be squeezed between 'the two pillars of the Third Reich', the Army and the Party (of which Frank's Institute was an arm) – 'no pleasant prospects'.[47] In the war diaries, he criticized the treatment of Soviet POWs in Germany, contrasted the logic of Great Power strategy with the suffering of mothers losing their sons in the war, and condemned the unnecessary sacrifice of lives at Stalingrad and in North Africa: notes discordant not only from official propaganda, but from the virulent chauvinism and racism of entries in the diary alongside them. A mixture like this lent itself, with a change in circumstances, to volte-faces.

These did not come complete overnight with the end of the war. To be cleared for resumption of his chair in Hamburg, Fischer had to falsify

---

46. Asendorf, 'Griff nach Fritz Fischer', p. 7.

47. Koblenz, N 1248/9, 21 March 1937; cited by Grosse Kracht. For his part, Seeberg, too, though not a fellow-traveller but a 'decisive propagandist for national socialism', could tell Fischer that the Nazis were interested in the Christian religion only as a cultural phenomenon of concern to the state, not as an affair of the church, and mistrust was always 'their first characteristic': letters of 23 and 15 February 1940, in Thomas Kaufmann and Harry Oelke, *Evangelische Kirchenhistoriker im 'Dritten Reich'*, Gütersloh 2002, pp. 262, 265.

his past. But whether he had shed it altogether by the time he reversed his verdict on mainstream Lutheranism and Calvinism with such éclat in 1948 is ambiguous. Traces of it still clung to him. Pleyer and Frank were safely dead; Botzenhart ostracized, with suicide to come. Rein, however, was still alive and in Hamburg, actively pursuing his own rehabilitation, and gathering pre-war associates around him. Barred from recovering any academic position, in 1950 he set up a parallel forum for the discussion of serious historical and contemporary issues, the Ranke Society, which soon had its own journal and national presence, of a national-conservative bent.[48] Among those he invited to join it was Fischer, who did so. The Rein and Fischer couples remained on good terms after the war, supping together in each other's homes.[49]

Five years later, Rein sought to secure the title of emeritus, with the financial and reputational advantages it yielded, at Hamburg University. A leading ally in his campaign was the jurist Hans-Peter Ipsen, a former member of the SA and NSDAP who during the war had served as Nazi commissar for the control of universities in occupied Belgium, but who unlike Rein had survived denazification and would go on to become Germany's leading authority on the constitution of the European Union. To achieve *Emeritierung*, Rein needed affidavits from respected scholars approving his application, and explaining why they did so. Fischer was among those he asked. He complied with brio. Rein's pre-war writings on European expansion, he wrote, were completely independent of National-Socialism, and the work Rein had published in 1941, *Europa und das Reich*, could be said to look forward to the day when a united Europe took its place as a force of its own

---

48. For an account of the creation and activity of the Society, see Arnt Goede, *Adolf Rein und die Idee der politischen Universität*, Berlin/Hamburg 2008, pp. 230–73.

49. Goede, *Adolf Rein*, pp. 209, 237.

on the great political chequerboard of a divided world. If the book ended by declaring that 'Hitler has become the shaper of the Reich and therewith the saviour and benefactor of Europe', that should not be held against it. 'The hope that Prof. Rein shared with many Germans that Hitler would justify victory over Soviet Russia with the emancipation of peoples of the East from the Baltic to Ukraine, as today is often demanded under the slogan of Liberation, was not completely absurd. That sentence, like the mistaken political judgment of the greatest minds of our history, Goethe and Hegel, about Napoleon, should be seen as an expression of the expectations and hopes of the time.' Nor should Rein's *Idee der politischen Universität* be condemned indiscriminately, since after all it raised scientific and pedagogical problems that had still to be resolved.[50] Such emollient counsel was not enough to secure agreement from Hamburg University. Two of the most eminent victims of Rein's extrusion of Jews from it were Ernst Cassirer and Erwin Panofsky. Cassirer's widow lodged a vehement protest against granting Rein his wish, and Panofsky said his name must be removed from the directory of emeriti if Rein was made one. But Fischer's voucher for his friend was not in vain. The following year the city of Hamburg overruled the university and retrospectively awarded Rein the rank and emoluments he sought.[51] In the early sixties, the explosion of controversy over Fischer's work on the First World War brought relations between them to an end. Never a likely ally in that conflict, Rein cut all ties with him.

Lingering attachment to Rein did not mean that Fischer was

---

50. 'Gutachten über die wissenschaftliche Persönlichkeit von Prof. Dr. Ad. Rein', 15 January 1955. For this episode, see Goede, *Adolf Rein* pp. 208–11. After the war, Rein let it be known that his first name was actually Gustav, by which he preferred to be called.

51. Goetz, *Adolf Rein*, pp. 212–16.

unchanged since they conferred together in the war, when after all both had been critical of its management by the Third Reich. There is in any case no reason to doubt that the post-war revelation of Nazi crimes shook Fischer, as it did many former loyalists of the regime. But the transformation that produced *Griff nach der Weltmacht*, a new direction for work hitherto focussed on revision of his pre-war positions on church history, had more specific origins. There, direct encounter for the first time with the Anglo-Saxon world, which in the past he had stigmatized as the deadly antithesis of Germany, was decisive. In 1950, invited to a small Anglo-German gathering of historians in Oxford organized by Ernest Barker, he spent three weeks in England, on his return setting down his impressions. He found the country a fundamentally conservative society, where Labour had introduced a number of reforms that left much of the intelligentsia, in thrall to *Salonbolschevismus*, discontented, but workers themselves better off, though their gains would only last if higher taxes and statist interference in the economy did not damage overall growth.[52] The trip was too short to yield many contacts. The opposite was true of his next trip abroad, to the United States, an altogether different experience.

In 1952 Fischer received an invitation from a 'Government Affairs Institute' in Washington DC that would give him nearly eight and a half months in America. The terms of the invitation seem unknown, and the reasons for his selection by the host institution remain obscure, but a reasonable conjecture is possible.[53] The Institute was created in 1950 at the initiative of Edward Litchfield, then executive director

---

52. Koblenz, N 1422/90, 'Betrachtungen über England', April 1950, based on a handwritten diary recording his experience in the country, written in March.

53. The absence of any correspondence from the institute, though there are letters of Fischer to it, is a puzzling omission in his *Nachlass*.

of the DC office of the American Political Science Association, who became its chairman. After teaching political science at Michigan and Brown during the war, Litchfield had been picked by General Lucius Clay in 1946 to head the Civil Affairs Department of the American occupation of the US zone in Germany, where together with Carl Friedrich, seconded from Harvard, he advised the convention writing the constitution of the future *Bundesrepublik*. After his return to the States, he edited a 700-page compendium, *Governing Postwar Germany*, dedicated to Clay,[54] and set in motion a study of US military government in the country by the GAI. A plausible surmise might be that in the course of his duties in Germany, Litchfield met and talked with Fischer, forming such a good impression of him that once the GAI was set up in Washington, he arranged for him to be invited to it. For his part, Fischer had the good luck to be stationed in Bremen during the latter part of the war, for the city – though situated in the British zone of occupation, was an American exclave within it, required by Washington to have access to the sea. So he would have been in touch with US rather than UK authorities after his release, and in a position to further the image of ardent admiration for America he had been fashioning as a POW.[55]

---

54. Cornell University Press 1953.

55. In the papers held by the Bundesarchiv dating from his time of captivity, there is a veritable hymn to America Fischer composed in English, probably intended as evidence of his political reliability, adjoining a list of those who could vouch for his conduct under the Third Reich, and a request that he be released from the undue hardship of continued imprisonment. It reads: 'There is a country of hope, there is a country of freedom. There is a country where *all sorts of different people, drawn from* every nation of the world, *get along together* under the same big sky. They go to the church they choose and no men *may be persecuted* for his religion [sic]. The men and women of this country *elect* their representatives they wish to govern them, remove them by vote – not by revolution – *if they feel* their representatives have done badly, *speak their minds* about their government and

On arrival in Washington in September, Fischer was given a briefing course at an 'International Center', perhaps of the Governmental Affairs Institute, and letters of introduction to scholars and universities around the country. He then set off on an imposing tour of campuses across the land, all expenses presumably paid. After ten weeks at the University of Virginia, he spent seven at Princeton, Yale and Harvard, then fourteen weeks visiting universities in the Midwest, West, Southwest and 'Old South' – two in Chicago, one in Madison, five in Berkeley, taking in liberal arts colleges – Swarthmore, Smith, Reed ('the best') – along with Syracuse, Cornell, Ann Arbor, Denver, Seattle, Stanford, UCLA, Albuquerque, Tulane, Austin, Duke, Chapel Hill, Johns Hopkins and Columbia. In the course of his trip, he met and conversed with luminaries at every stop, among them Gordon Craig, Hajo Holborn, Carl Schorske, Samuel Beer, William Langer, Franz Neumann, Hans Morgenthau, Quincy Wright and Carl Friedrich, of whom 'the most impressive' for Fischer was the last.[56] Contacts were arranged for him essentially in political science and international relations departments. After getting back to Hamburg in May 1953, he submitted a report to the Governmental Affairs Institute on lessons he had learnt in the States that could be applied in German universities, starting with the introduction of American-style political science.[57] He would return to the US in 1955 for a semester, teaching a course at Notre

---

about *the running of their country* at all times, *stay themselves* and yet *stay loyal to* one cause, one country, and one flag' (emphases in original): Koblenz 1422/133, p. 19.

56. Koblenz, N 1422/50, 'Report on my experience at individual universities in the USA from September 1952 to May 1953', sent to the Governmental Affairs Institute on 19 August 1953.

57. Koblenz, N 1422/50, 1 August 1953.

Dame in the political science department, and this time keeping a full diary of his stay.[58]

Fischer's extended sojourn in America came at the height of the Cold War. In 1950, the Korean War had spurred Acheson to press for the rearmament of West Germany. French reticence at this prospect led to the signing of a treaty for a European Defence Community in March 1952, binding the BRD into a military pact between the six future members of the Common Market, which would later be blocked by the French Assembly. In September, when Fischer arrived in Washington, the election campaign for the presidency was in full swing, won by Eisenhower in November, who appointed John Foster Dulles his secretary of state. In March Stalin died. It is likely, therefore, that the Governmental Affairs Institute was set up by Litchfield under the Truman Administration at least in part to serve its foreign policy goals of the time.[59] Why Fischer was chosen for such a lavish welcome by it is not explained by his standing as a historian, since he had not yet published any work of significance in the BRD. But in detention, or on release from it, he no doubt impressed the occupation authorities sufficiently for him to be viewed in Washington as a promising recruit for the new Atlantic order. He left no personal diary of his experience in the

---

58. Koblenz, N 1422/146. It was during this stint that he wrote his recommendation of Rein and sent it to Hamburg.

59. For Litchfield's own firm opposition not just to communism but to 'the very bad' positions taken by the SPD at the post-war constitutional convention, see Jean Edward Smith (ed.), *The Papers of General Lucius D. Clay: Germany 1945–1949*, Vol. II, Bloomington–London, 1974, pp. 1116–17, about which Clay commented: 'It may not prove as bad as Litchfield thinks. He reacts quickly and always strongly in one direction or other.' He would later serve on the US delegation at post-war meetings of the Council of Foreign Ministers in Moscow and London, and as an adviser to the Pentagon.

US in 1952–53, unlike his subsequent visit in 1955. What is sure, however, is that he would have been deeply impressed by the power and wealth of America, the quality of its premier universities and the scholars they contained, not to speak of the scale of the hospitality he received. It was a watershed in his life, its effect clinched by his time at Notre Dame soon afterwards. It was in the United States, his pupil Imanuel Geiss would report, that Fischer discovered the work of Albertini. When he got back to Germany, he worked flat-out from 1953 to 1959 on the research and writing that became *Griff*.

His pre-war record shows that Fischer was not someone who took risks, if he could avoid them. Publication of his big tome on the First World War, plainly echoing – as his conservative critics were right to point out – the charge of war guilt levelled against Germany in the Treaty of Versailles, caused an uproar in the profession to which he belonged, the furore around his claims lasting for a decade or more. But though Chancellor Erhard and Speaker Gerstenmeier condemned it, the book was not such a huge risk at the time. The Christian-Democrats were at the fag end of their long period of rule, and the intelligentsia becoming restive. Most of the media were well disposed to *Griff*, which received favourable reviews in major dailies, while excerpts from it were read aloud on the radio. The most influential single platform of the press, the weekly magazine *Der Spiegel*, which unlike most newspapers had a national circulation, not only praised it from the outset, but – once it emerged that the *Aussenamt*, instigated by the book's opponents in the academy, had blocked funds for a lecture tour by Fischer in the US – became something like a continuous publicity machine for him, to the point of publishing an advance version of his revision of the book's chapter on the crisis of July 1914 before its second edition had even appeared.[60] Fischer could not have foreseen the speed of this local consecration. But that America, where he was welcomed with open arms, was master of the Atlantic world, and a cultural lodestar of far greater attraction than anything the domestic scene could muster in a political and military dependency of the US, was obvious. Betting on its opinion about a war against Germany in which it had been a victor in 1918, and a victor squared in 1945, was an eminently safe option; and so it proved. Fischer's second book on the Great War, *Krieg der Illusionen*, was published in the same year that the reign of the CDU and the national-conservative consensus over which it had presided came to an end. By then, Fischer's ideas were by and large received wisdom, as they have remained.

In 2004, Grosse Kracht's discoveries caused something of a stir, and a modicum of argument. What no-one, whatever their view of his essay, queried was his conclusion that Fischer had helped to transform the country into a mature democracy. He might have dissembled about his own past, but in demonstrating German responsibility for the First World War and its concatenation with the Second, he had spoken truth to and about the nation. Recipient of three successive *Festschriften*, he was awarded the *Bundesverdienstkreuz* in 1974, and promoted to Class One in 1987: official recognition of his towering achievement as a historian, which was that of a citizen too. In this century, all could agree about this eminence. If there was less unanimity about his life story, Grosse Kracht had supplied an ingenious formula for redeeming

---

60. For the contrast in the book's reception by the profession and by the press, see Hartmut Pogge von Strandemann, 'The Political and Historical Significance of the Fischer Controversy', *Journal of Contemporary History*, April 2013, p. 257; he notes that it was the publisher rather than the author who devised the title of the book (toned down when it appeared in the Anglosphere), with an eye to the sensation it was intended to cause.

it. True, Fischer had hidden his past, but in doing so he had protected the higher good of liberalizing German democracy by his research into the culpability of the Second Reich for the Great War, without compromising the credentials of his exposure of that by admission of what he had himself been during the Third Reich. Petzold, whose essay abroad was little noticed, would go further: Fischer's youthful impatience with bourgeois conservatism formed a productive bridge between his pre-war and war-time Nazism and his post-war liberalism, hostility to the intellectual and political establishments of Weimar Germany morphing creatively into rebellion against those of the era of the *Wirtschaftswunder*.

Revelations that some might consider, verbally at least, more damaging about himself than the charges he levelled at the younger Bethmann Hollweg were thus absorbed and repressed with scarcely a ripple in the Federal Republic. His pupils were unperturbed. In Imanuel Geiss's words, 'Fischer never spoke of his emotional life, the tension between his Nazi past, of which we knew nothing, and his work on *Griff nach der Weltmacht*. Nor did we ask him about it. Why should we?'[61] The ideological and political capital invested by the *Bundesrepublik* and its admirers abroad in the icon of Fischer remained so large that any frank accounting with the reality of his career continues, in an ironic replication of the Wilhelmine icons that were once the target of his work, to be for the most part taboo.[62] To

---

61. 'Zur Fischer-Kontroverse – 40 Jahre danach', *Zeitgeschichte als Streitgeschichte: Grosse Kontroversen seit 1945*, Martin Sabrow, Ralph Jessen, Klaus Grosse Kracht (eds), Munich 2003, p. 54.

62. Without any specific reference to Fischer, the author of the major study of his principal adversary, Ritter, has commented that while the controversy of the sixties may have contributed to a lifting of taboos in German historiography, since 'none of those who took part in it disclosed their involvement in the Nazi regime at the time, or afterwards', the claim that taboos were a thing of the past was, as he

break it involves no aspersion on the sincerity of Fischer's political conversion after the war. It was quite possible to be a regular Nazi, of which there was a range of different types, up to 1943 or 1945, and to be so shaken by the evidence of Nazi atrocities in 1946 that henceforward complete revulsion from all that the Third Reich stood for and a deep commitment to liberal democracy were genuine. There is no reason to doubt the existence of such cases.

Whether in the instance of Fischer, the reasons for his change were, from the start, so unmixed is another question, which Olpen's work would raise. The nemesis of a long-standing patriotic conformism in German historiography concealed his part in its worst paroxysm. Nor did Fischer just keep quiet about his past. He gratuitously lied about it. In the summer of 1988, in a long interview with the *Norddeutscher Rundfunk*, he recounted a blameless youth cleansed of any hint of Bund Oberland, any mention of the *Sturmabteilung*, any reference to the seizure of the Sudetenland. Claiming, on the contrary, to have belonged to a circle of 'religious socialists' and voted for the SPD, he explained that only financial need had taken him into the Nazi Party after the Anschluss – he was so poor that as a child he had been forced to beg, and as an adult could scarcely get by on a pittance from the university. Those who inspired him were not Seeberg or Steding, but his mentors Oncken and Spranger.[63] Without

---

puts it politely, 'not entirely convincing': Christoph Cornelissen, *Gerhard Ritter: Geschichtswissenschaft und Politik*, Düsseldorf 2001, p. 622.

63. Manfred Asendorf and Wolfgang Bombosch, '"In Weimar hätten sie mich erschossen . . ." Ein Gespräch mit Fritz Fischer', *Zeitgeschehen*, Heft 1, 2000, pp. 143–59. A prefatory note explains that Asendorf submitted a typescript of the interview to Fischer almost two years after it was conducted, and after some alterations to the text, Fischer approved it for publication in May 1990. After that, however, the publication project fell apart, recounts Asendorf – reasons unexplained. But in early 1996, after an evening lecture in Hamburg on National

a syllable about his pronouncements on world Jewry or the greatness of the Eastern campaign to save Europe from the Asiatic menace of Russia, he ended on a note of the sheerest self-dramatizing fantasy. In Weimar times he 'would have been shot' for the heresies of *Griff nach der Weltmacht*; as if any historian had actually died for their views under the Republic. The following year, he published a memoir whose immaculately cloying title says enough about it, 'Sunny Days of Childhood': sleigh-rides at Easter and cranberries in summer, a mother's light voice trilling 'when in the dale wild roses bloom', no word of the *Deutsche Tag* in Nuremberg.[64]

What weight, or lack of it, should be given to such denegations? It is possible that the startling mixture of *suppressio veri* and *suggestio falsi* in his interview of 1987 may have given pause to Fischer himself when he saw it in typescript, and explains why it never saw the light of day while he was alive. Yet what it suggests is the unreliability of his relation to the past. Would any trustworthy historian be capable of the fictions contained in it? So many German historians were in one way or another implicated in Nazism, and so vanishingly few came clean about what they had said and done at the time, that the answer is not straightforward. At least two of the most distinguished and productive scholars of the post-war period, Theodor Schieder and Werner Conze, both stalwarts of the SA and NSDAP, concealed their part in preparations for 'dejudification' and 'depolonization' –

Socialism during which Fischer's scientific work on the First World War was not mentioned, an omission at which Asendorf protested, a conversation between the two men took place in which 'Fischer confirmed to Asendorf that he stood by everything he said in 1988 and regarded it as an authentic expression of the scientific achievement of his lifetime'.

64. 'Sonnige Kindertage im nördlichsten Zipfel Frankens', in Rudolf Pörtner (ed.), *Kindheit im Kaiserreich: Erinnerungen an vergangene Zeit*, Düsseldorf 1987.

their terms – in the East, actions more incriminating than anything recorded of Fischer,[65] without the value of their post-war work being in question. Each became rector of his respective university, Cologne and Heidelberg, as indeed at Hamburg did their Austrian colleague Otto Brunner, perhaps the finest mediaevalist of his generation, less practically culpable if just as ideologically compromised. Two factors, however, set Fischer's case apart from these. They were interconnected. Unlike them, he was a public figure, celebrated as an inspiration of civil and political courage, who went to considerable lengths to falsify the truth about his past. The lies he told were a function of the fame he enjoyed, a reputation that had to be cooked if it was to be kept. Do they cast any shadow on the work he published? Fischer's books, where his personal past was not at stake, were free of the inventions he told about himself. But though diligent and painstaking, the handling of argument and evidence in them reveals something of the same propensity to omission and exaggeration, a loose joint of mind or character to which his admirers, for reasons not of convenience but of principle, as a political *point d'honneur*, would shut their eyes. There is no mistaking the *parti pris* which powered Fischer's writing on German responsibility for the Great War. He picked the evidence he wanted to demonstrate it, and ignored what did not. He adjusted his claims of the war guilt of the Second Reich on a sliding scale of judgment – considerable – decisive – exclusive – according to the needs of the moment.[66] That he made no attempt to assay the role of the other Great Powers was not, as occasionally suggested, out of a certain provincialism, understandable enough

---

65. Conze destroyed all his papers before dying; Fischer just some of his.
66. For these, see Klaus Grosse Kracht, *Die ʒankende Zunft: Historische Kontroversen in Deutschland nach 1945*, Göttingen 2005, p. 63.

in the early *Bundesrepublik*; his unpublished papers show plenty of interest in international affairs. Rather, to do so would too obviously have undermined his construction, so large was the gap between what he could actually show and what he made of it. But if the renown he earned outran his achievement, which as a historian was middling, it was a product of the time as much as of his own desire for it. Germany needed in the Cold War the absolution of its present that Fischer's execration of its past in the belle époque seemed to offer, and which Anglo-America could welcome as the token of a new loyalty to the West. He cannot be blamed for that.

That Fischer's image remained largely intact in the *Bundesrepublik* is hardly surprising. In its own way, much the same can be said for the Anglosphere which secured his international reputation. There, his work did more than reinforce traditional contrasts between German addiction to aggression and Entente devotion to peace. It vindicated the moral education of Germany in Western values by the Allies after the Second World War: proof that the verdict of Versailles had been just, and its lessons were now well learnt by Germans themselves. Tactful guidance of the *Bundesrepublik* and its political culture from afar could seem like deliverance from their own history, lived as the self-understanding of freedom. From a strictly historiographic point of view, Fischer added little that was new. With one exception, all his principal griefs against the Second Reich – *primum movens* of the Great War, greed for vast territorial annexations, unhinged drive towards domination of Europe – were rehearsed far more pithily by Taylor while Fischer was still an Allied prisoner, with an economy and panache Fischer's sprawling, cumbersome tomes could not match. The exception was the idea that had to be dropped by Fischer's followers most quickly, that the war had been deliberately planned by Germany two years before its armies unleashed it. Taylor would himself in due course take some distance from Fischer, whose success he decided was less than fully deserved, and though Fischer found his first and most balanced champion in another historian at Oxford, James Joll, whose own view of the First World War was considerably more complex, Fischer's overall impact in Britain was limited. Where it loomed far larger was in the United States, with its numerous leading scholars, many of Jewish origin, who had arrived from Germany as refugees from Nazism in the thirties. Since America was now the premier global power, it was the US reception that sealed Fischer's international standing.

The paradox of the aura his work so acquired was the intellectual regression it brought to the field in which it did so. For twenty-five years after it ended, all the major studies of the origins of the Great War – Renouvin, Fay, Schmitt, Isaac, Albertini – had been continental in scope, adjudicating the role of each of the principal six belligerents in its outbreak. Fischer reversed this pattern with a body of work focussed on just one participant, to the exclusion of all others save where they impinged on Germany. But such was the prestige that this example came to enjoy that it altered the direction of the field. By the time Fischer produced what he termed his most important work, *Bündnis der Eliten*, in the early eighties, studies devoted to the part played by single countries in the inception of the conflict – France, Russia, Austria, and Britain, as well of course as Germany itself – were beginning to roll off the presses in a stream that would last a full two decades. Most of these, whatever their political standpoint, were valuable contributions to historical knowledge of the times, while also representing a contraction of focus within them. The example set by Fischer's major works had a further narrowing effect. For subsequent contributions were not just, as his had been, confined geopolitically to Germany, but were concentrated chronologically on the years immediately preceding the war – in effect 1911–14. As such they gave renewed impetus to what had already marked the work of Renouvin, Schmitt and Albertini, attention to the short-range precipitants of the conflict at the expense of the longer-term pressures building up towards it. Once the centenary of the onset of the First World War approached, the publishing industry in all the belligerents inspired a plethora of works recounting in detail, sometimes day by day, just the last six weeks, from the attentat in Sarajevo to the exchange of ultimatums between the Great Powers, before Europe descended into mutual destruction. It was a convenient myopia: one that honours the few who have escaped it.

KEITH WILSON

In Britain, victory in the Second World War came as a confirmation of the national verdict on the First. In both conflicts, Germany was the aggressor, in both England, alone unsullied – as France was not – by invasion or occupation, had defended the liberties of Europe together with its own. After 1945 the leading historical voice in such patriotic reflection was A. J. P. Taylor, all the more effective for positioning himself as an inveterate dissenter from orthodoxy, author of *The Trouble Makers*, an admiring study of critics who from the time of the French Revolution onwards had opposed successive ruling conventions of British foreign policy. Thankfully, however, even they had rallied to the cause of freedom in 1914.[1] Two years earlier, in *The Struggle for the Mastery of Europe*, Taylor had explained that if Britain had not entered the First World War, 'the inestimable value of moral superiority' would have been lost, while in his subsequent history of England the hero of what ensued becomes the politician who led the

---

1. 'Fundamentally, contemporaries saw the overriding fact which was afterwards obscured by many ingenious arguments: whatever the rights and wrongs of the Sarajevo assassination or of Russia's mobilization, or more broadly of the Franco-Russian alliance, the war came about when Germany declared war on France and Russia.': *The Trouble Makers*, London 1956, p. 129.

country to final triumph in that struggle, Lloyd George.² Four years later, wrapping the story up in a sentence, Taylor announced: 'When cut down to essentials, the sole cause of the outbreak of war in 1914 was the Schlieffen Plan'³ – the premeditated assault on Belgium by Germany that sent Britain to the rescue.

Such was the generally accepted version of the Great War when the scholar who would become the most original mind in the historiography of England's entry into it arrived to study in Oxford in 1963. Born to a lower-middle-class family – his father headmaster of a grammar school at Dewsbury in Yorkshire – Keith Wilson took history at one of the least fashionable of colleges at the university, Keble. There he earned a first in 1966, followed by three years' research for a Ph.D. at Nuffield. At the end of these, he was appointed a junior lecturer at Leeds University, though his dissertation was still some way from completion – not unusual at a time when doctorates were still a relative rarity in England, and a successful Oxbridge graduate could get a job with just the informal recommendation of a tutor. On the evidence of Wilson's thesis, his supervisor probably knew the founder of International History as a student at Leeds, assuring his appointment.⁴ It would be another

---

2. 'The most inspired and creative British statesman of the twentieth century', *English History 1914–1945*, Oxford 1965, p. 192.

3. *The Struggle for the Mastery of Europe 1870–1914*, Oxford 1954, p. 520; *English History 1914–1945*, Oxford 1965, pp. 73, 192; *War by Time Table*, London 1969, p. 93.

4. His tutor at Oxford was Alec Campbell, who had started his career in the Foreign Office, before becoming a historian principally of North America, where he later moved, before returning to England after marriage to the British ambassador to Luxembourg. At Leeds the scholar responsible for hiring him was a refugee from Nazi Germany, who arrived at the age of eleven in Britain as Hans Guhrauer in 1939, and became a leading authority on European politics of the late nineteenth century as John Grenville. In the autumn of 1969, he transferred to a chair in Birmingham just as Wilson took up his position at Leeds.

three years before he submitted his dissertation, getting his doctorate at the beginning of 1973.

The Role and Influence of the Professional Advisers to the Foreign Office on the Making of British Foreign Policy from December 1905 to August 1914 is the longest continuous text – 382 typescript pages, 130,000 words – Wilson ever wrote, and displays already some of the hallmarks of what would become his kind of scholarship. A study of the senior officials in the Foreign Office and its principal embassies abroad and their relations with the Liberal governments and political system of Edwardian England, it is based on meticulous analysis of primary sources of the time. Official papers formerly or newly released, published memoirs and private documents distilled from diaries or correspondence of diplomats and politicians, are examined with a *pointilliste* density of quotation and illustration beyond post-graduate expectation. Wilson explained at the outset that his intention was to offer neither an administrative history nor a sociological analysis of Britain's diplomatic elite, but rather to trace the leading 'ideas and opinions' current in the Foreign Office, and assess their influence on British policies abroad.

The Agadir crisis of 1911, when Germany challenged France's tightening grip on Morocco by sending a gunboat to take a port on its southern coast, supplies his opening example. Though the Liberal government, anxious to preserve the Entente Cordiale with Paris it had inherited from its Conservative predecessor, backed France in the dispute, the Foreign Office was highly critical, from a more pro-French and anti-German position, of what it regarded as the Cabinet's weakness in doing so. In the event, after threats from London, Germany backed down. Not so much, however, due to exertions of the FO, whose contribution to the outcome of the crisis was slight, but rather to the ability of its Liberal Imperialist ministers to bounce the Cabinet into a firm stance against Berlin. Yet if its diplomats failed on this occasion to secure adoption of a still more hawkish line, they were far from a *quantité négligeable* in the formation of British foreign policy. For they possessed an influence which did not derive from their particular views of the course to be taken at any given time, but from the authority of a fund of long-standing 'principles and traditions' that had guided London's relations with the outside world for the better part of a century, to which Wilson devotes most of his study.

These rested on the axiom of 'continuity' in British foreign policy, whatever government was in power, dating back at least to 1870, comprising three basic principles. The first and most important of these was that Britain must keep a 'free hand' in European politics – that is, avoid any formal alliance with other powers: what written agreements the country had reached with foreign governments in the past should be respected, but minimized. The second was maintenance of a 'balance of power' in Europe by a diplomacy designed to check the danger of any one continental power becoming so strong that it was in a position to dominate all others. The third was preservation of the naval supremacy of Britain, a global command of the seas ensuring the immunity of the home country and its empire from armed invasion. The free hand had precedence over the balance of power as the flexible means of securing it. But if a threat to the balance were to extend from Europe to the world where Britain held sway, a free hand would be no longer possible, requiring intervention on the continent.

There had been a time, after the Congress of Vienna had sealed the defeat of Napoleon, when a concert of powers that included all the major states of Europe had kept the peace between them. But by the 1890s, while the Concert of Europe was still occasionally invoked, it had lost any reality with the crystallization of two rival military blocs on the continent – the Triple Alliance of Germany, Austro-Hungary and Italy on one side, pitted against it on the other the Dual Alliance of France and Russia – and was dismissed as an anachronism by the Foreign Office. When he became foreign secretary in December 1905, Grey was not quite so categorical, imagining at moments that Britain could act as a bridge between the two blocs and opposing deductions from either that could alter the rough balance between them. But he had inherited from Lansdowne, his Conservative predecessor, the Entente Cordiale between Britain and France, an informal understanding to which he remained firmly committed; and he shared with his subordinates in the Foreign Office their fears of German ambition for hegemony in Europe.

These were sufficiently pronounced to give rise to the 'legend' among Radicals of an incorrigible anti-Germanism in the FO. In fact, there was no such thing. The Foreign Office was just pro-British, and its hostility to Germany based not on myths but realities – 'nefarious projects' of Berlin, that were leading to its 'self-encirclement'.[5] Grey saw through these too, but with an independent mind did not draw the same conclusions. More insular than his advisers, he did not envisage British naval supremacy as a potential weapon of intervention to protect the freedom of every state in Europe from German domination, but rather as the shield of Britain itself and its overseas possessions. He was also aware, however, that it could no longer be upheld against all comers without excessive cost, and that it was essential to prevent a growing German fleet from combining with the fleets of Russia and France to outgun the Royal Navy on the high seas. That required the extension of Britain's entente with Paris

---

5. *Role and Influence*, pp. 222, 234, 237, 239.

to a parallel understanding with St Petersburg, which he achieved in 1907, giving birth to what he and the Foreign Office would call the Triple Entente.

For its critics, this was just the kind of foreign entanglement that Britain's free hand was supposed to preclude, and resistance to it was anticipated by the Foreign Office. Potential impediments were two. One was public opinion, against which its diplomatic personnel – 'reluctant democrats', but aware that this was a force that mattered – were always on their guard, as capable of causing trouble in Parliament or the press. The other was Radical opposition within the Cabinet, which contained many a minister mistrustful of the direction the Liberal government was taking abroad. In the event, neither proved much of an obstacle. In the case of the first, it was an unspoken assumption at the Foreign Office – less spoken even than those for which James Joll had coined the term – that public opinion was confined to 'the political nation', which thought much as the FO itself did. It was the answer the country would give about anything if it was asked. 'This being so, there was never any real need to actually ask the question.'[6] As for the second, the Foreign Office had two safeguards against being *roulé* by Radicals in the Cabinet. One was simply the 'untravelled' quality of Radical ideas about foreign policy itself, vague notions that had never been put into practice, incapable of 'envisaging the ultimate aims of Germany which were only too real for the Foreign Office'.[7] The other was the knowledge that even if Radicals, Irish Nationalists or Pacifists opposed the government's conduct of foreign policy, Conservative support could be relied on to proof it against any challenge. The upshot was that, in the end,

---

6. Ibid., p. 277.
7. Ibid., pp. 308, 349.

FO fears that the country's foreign policy might change never materialized. The Radicals were carried along with everyone else on what Churchill aptly called the 'howdah' of its doctrinal continuity.

Wilson's cool-minded conclusion was that from 1906 to 1914 the Foreign Office had neither the kind of influence it wanted nor was ascribed to it by attacks on its record. What influence it did enjoy was based simply on the accumulated fund of traditions it conveyed, as these adapted to the new situation in which it found itself. For the underlying reality was that in this period Britain's relative position in the world declined, and the result was a foreign policy that became more conservative just as domestic politics were becoming more radical. The Foreign Office viewed association with Russia as an insurance against failure to deal with Germany short of war, while the Radicals saw tsardom as a bogey. In England, the result took on the semblance of a 'contest between experience and experiment, logic and sentimentalism, power and ideology, Might and Right, a contest which involved the avoidance of Armageddon and the achievement of the Millennium'. If Grey's advisers did not make the lines on which foreign policy ran, which were set by principles rather than personnel, they maintained them by 'constantly drawing attention to the awful consequences of crossing them'.[8] No consensus on the way to preserve peace was achieved.

Wilson's doctorate, written when he was in his twenties, delivered its unconventional arguments with considerable authority. Setting the text apart within the form of the time to which it belonged was not just the granular extent of the evidence on which it drew, but the conceptual stamp it set on the research it displayed. It could have been published as a quite striking book as it stood. The reason why it was

---

8. Ibid., pp. 343, 350–1, 354.

not lay, no doubt, in the last paragraph of Wilson's introduction to it. There he noted that 'in the course of my work a book was published which attempted, according to its Preface, to trace and detail the influence which the civil servants who staffed the Foreign Office had on diplomacy in the pre-war period'. This was Zara Steiner's *The Foreign Office and Foreign Policy, 1898–1914*, released by Cambridge University Press in 1969. 'Neither Mrs Steiner's approach nor her conclusions', he went on, 'were such as to persuade me to abandon what I was doing.'[9] The standing of Steiner's book, however, was probably enough to deter any publisher from considering another whose subject might have seemed virtually identical.

In fact, the two were quite distinct. By origin an American, and a generation older, Steiner had pioneered modern research on the British Foreign Office with a work covering twice the timespan of Wilson's study, from the late Salisbury to the outbreak of the First World War, and encompassing not only its administrative history but the sociology of its staff and its dominant personalities, questions Wilson had set aside. Critical of the unduly narrow class background of its officials and the restrictions of their outlook, she was nevertheless in little doubt of their talents and influence. Reforms attributable to Grey's first permanent under-secretary, Charles Hardinge, gave them a degree of autonomy and self-confidence they had never known before. In consequence, she thought, in the pre-war years 'the Foreign Office reached the peak of its power',[10] its senior men advising and arguing with Grey as they had no chance of doing under Salisbury. Nor were the policies they pressed misconceived: as Grey, too, understood, Germany was a threat to England that had

---

9. Ibid., p. xiv.
10. *The Foreign Office and Foreign Policy, 1898–1914*, p. 209.

to be met by forging close ties with France and Russia. Foremost in dissecting that threat and urging resolute measures to deal with it was the 'vivid figure' of Eyre Crowe, whose 'brilliance and energy' fascinated Steiner. Half a century later, she would report her longing to write a biography of him, in an essay making clear the extent to which she felt at home in the company of the Foreign Office.[11]

Wilson's treatment of the institution was in marked contrast. Showing no particular identification with it, his central theme lay in the ideas, patent or latent, that shaped its practice, rather than the persons who carried it out, and his assessment of them was more critical, lacking any obvious note of complaisance. How distinctive this way of looking at the Foreign Office was remains clear if its results are compared with a work that appeared forty years after Steiner's, from a historian a generation younger than Wilson, *The Foreign Office Mind* by Thomas Otte, covering a still longer timespan, from 1865 to 1914. Hailed by Steiner as an outstanding achievement, it is a formidable successor to her work – comprehensively researched, stylistically polished and substantively self-assured: by any standard a major contribution to the diplomatic history of Britain. Its title, however, is somewhat misleading. Disavowing at the outset any suggestion that it implies a hypostasized, invariant outlook inhabiting the institution across seventy years – 'this is not the place for a "high-flown think piece"' on abstract elite *mentalités* or bloodless

---

11. *The Foreign Office and Foreign Policy*, pp. 109–17. For a lifelong *engouement* with Crowe, see Steiner's memoir 'Beyond the Foreign Office Papers: the Making of an International Historian', *International History Review*, May–June 2017, pp. 550–3 et seq., where she describes the mortifying audience with Crowe's daughter Sybil at which she was told that she would not be allowed access to his papers since a filial biography of him was under way, and recounts her pursuit of assorted eminences who had known Crowe, concluding that 'we still need a proper life of Crowe to replace his daughter's biography': p. 560.

world-political *Weltanschauungen*' – the book fills out the sociology of recruitment to the Foreign Office sketched by Steiner, and gives analytic pride of place not to conceptions but to generations – High Victorian, Late Victorian, Edwardian, incipiently post-Edwardian – as the most significant markers of the mind it conjures up. Ideas? – 'hatred of Germany' was an 'article of faith' among the younger levy of Edwardians.[12] Performance? Yet more approving than Steiner. This was a body of 'able, conscientious, intelligent public servants', who believed in 'fair, straight dealing', attached to notions of 'honour' and 'prestige' as 'a form of "soft power"', 'a currency readily convertible into real influence', reflecting 'Britain's political and financial power'. It was this collective mind-set 'that provided the energetic impulse that, in turn, powered the machinery of British foreign policy'.[13]

So Wilson was not wrong in thinking that after Steiner, 'still there were a few things to be said', which her successors were unlikely to say. That he himself had not said his last word on the foreign policy of pre-war Britain can be judged by what followed his thesis. In that, along with its strengths, there were evident limitations. His dismissal of the charges against the Foreign Office of an engrained hostility to Germany, contradicted by much of his own evidence, was one. Two others were more fundamental. Though the timespan he chose was that of rule by the Liberal Party, in his doctorate there is no discussion at all of Edwardian Liberalism as such; and while divisions in the Cabinet are treated, the roots, ramifications and consequences of an ideological stock that all factions in the party shared are absent.

---

12. *The Foreign Office Mind: The Making of British Foreign Policy, 1865–1914*, Cambridge 2011, pp. 5, 276.

13. Ibid., pp. 394, 396, 407.

Gropings among Radicals for another foreign policy are, furthermore, dismissed or deflated. A more glaring omission is any consideration of imperialism itself as a leitmotif of British foreign policy in the period. Morocco reduced to a dispute between Paris and Berlin, the horizon of the thesis is Europe. The colonies are enveloped in amnesia; empire scarcely figures. Finally, of course, the genesis of the war whose outbreak closes the period is never brought into the scope of the thesis, leaving it open to a reading that Wilson, accepting without apparent demur Crowe's conviction that Wilhelmine Germany was a deadly threat to England,[14] had no quarrel with the general belief in England that Berlin was responsible for the First World War.

Once he was teaching at Leeds, it had taken Wilson four years to complete his thesis. His exact contemporary Paul Kennedy, who started his doctorate at Oxford at the same time, at first a bit slower to find a job, finished his much faster, in 1969. It would be another twelve years before Wilson's first book appeared. Extreme scruple and thoroughness in the archives, and the gradual alteration of his ideas as he worked in them, would certainly have been the main reason for the intermission. But from the evidence of those who knew him, it would be a mistake to imagine a life of unrelieved toil in dusty remnants of the past. A good athlete, he played football in his youth for Huddersfield, enjoyed tennis, and developed a liking for all manner of Americana – Raymond Chandler, Edward Hopper, Art Tatum, Ella Fitzgerald. Often held unsociable, he could charm women throughout his life: three of his books were dedicated to

---

14. Agadir: 'Neither individually nor collectively did the Cabinet match the insight and forthrightness of, for instance, Eyre Crowe who discerned the issue as one of peace or war at the outset': *Role and Influence*, p. 40. Formulations like this might be regarded as cases of a deadpan ambiguity to which Wilson on occasion resorted; without, however, relevantly implied opposites in play here.

successive flames. Though soft-spoken, needing a microphone to lecture, he could be cutting; he had a short fuse, yet a wry sense of humour. His life as a scholar would be no less contradictory.

The decade following his thesis were not fallow years. Drawing on its material, his first article in a scholarly venue appeared before it was accepted, a piece on the Agadir crisis, from which he would take his distance in due course as 'youthfully pretentious' when it was collected in book of essays.[15] Two further texts, on military plans and cabinet divisions prior to 1914, appeared in the seventies in the *British Journal of International Studies*. The order in which another eight such pieces came out in the early eighties were composed is obscure, Wilson observing that 'date of publication is not a sound guide to time of writing' and when brought together, 'the diversity and multiplicity of interests, the simultaneity of concerns, the different speeds of progress in different directions and at several levels' in them, their effect had 'none of symmetry of the kaleidoscope, none of the geometry of progression. Rather it resembled strobe lighting, programmed to a random sequence'.[16] Such was the preamble to a collection of texts most of which were in print before his first, decisive book was published.

The Policy of the Entente, which came out in 1985, was Wilson's début as an author. In a work joining originality of argument with depth of research, he made his entry at a stroke into the ranks of major historians of the run-up to the First World War. The combination, rare enough in itself, was not the only unusual feature of the book. It was a slim volume, a mere 147 pages of text; backed by some forty

---

15. 'The Agadir Crisis, Mansion House Speech, and the Double-Edgedness of Agreements', *Historical Journal*, September 1972, pp. 513–32.

16. Prefatory note to *Empire and Continent: Studies in British Foreign Policy from the 1880s to the First World War*, London and New York 1987.

pages of endnotes sourcing its case. It opens with a matter-of-fact description of the received view of British foreign policy in the Edwardian era – one that still prevails today – and an enumeration of the leading historians whose writing encouraged versions of it at the time: Monger, Steiner, Robbins, Hinsley, Kennedy. It then calmly proposes to explore 'the actual content and real determinations of British foreign policy', notifying readers in advance that in his view, so unbridgeable was the gap between commitments and assets of the period that its major principles were incompatible with each other.[17]

What was the orthodox version of Britain's foreign policy? In keeping with its self-image, that it was essentially 'straightforward, honest and open' in its dealings with other powers, as were those who conducted it, and 'to a large extent self-contained', unaffected by domestic concerns or changes, if adjusting to alterations in its external environment. After 1900 a shift in its orientation had occurred with the ententes reached by Lansdowne with France in 1904 and by Grey with Russia in 1907, each a response to the threat to England of a German domination of Europe, which in due course plunged the continent into war in 1914, obliging Britain to come to the aid of France and Belgium when both were attacked by the German army. Entry into the war was a logical outcome of the transformation of 'values and emphasis' in British foreign policy in the new century from the Empire to the European continent.

Point by point, Wilson overturned this self-satisfied vision. Though it possessed the largest empire and biggest navy in the world, Britain had struggled to defeat the small Boer republics in South Africa, and faced the rapid growth of other industrial powers in Europe, Asia and America,

---

17. *The Policy of the Entente*, Cambridge 1985, pp. 1–3. Taylor is absent from the roll call of the received view.

all with imperial ambitions of their own. It could therefore no longer afford, either strategically or financially, to hold what it had without allies, for fear that it might now face a combination of rivals capable of besting it. Dropping insistence on the principle of a free hand, in the Far East Britain signed a pact with Japan in 1902. Two years later a deal was reached with France, swapping cession by Paris of continued control over Egypt to London, in exchange for cession by London of novel control over Morocco to Paris. Putting an end to the colonial rivalry that had previously brought them to the brink of war over Sudan, such was the baptism of the Entente-Cordiale between the two countries.

These were initiatives taken by the Conservative government of Salisbury's nephew Balfour. The Liberal government that succeeded it consolidated them by an agreement with Russia, long regarded as potentially an even greater danger to the British Empire than France. Grey, the architect of this understanding, had been so committed to an alliance with France that he had threatened to resign if Britain failed to show resolute support for Paris against Berlin – to the point, if it came to that, of war – in French appropriation of Morocco. For in his eyes France was not just a valuable partner as a naval and imperial power in its own right. For over a decade it had enjoyed a formal military alliance with Russia. Entente with France was thus a vital stepping-stone to what under Grey became the primary long-term objective of British foreign policy, an understanding with Russia that would safeguard the empire in Asia, above all in India. France and Russia had been the two major geopolitical dangers to British interests since the eighteenth century, and the two Great Powers with which Britain had been close to war in the 1890s, when Grey had served as under-secretary at the Foreign Office. In the increasingly difficult situation in which the country found itself in the early twentieth century, the paramount need for London was to neutralize them.

The German empire Bismarck had created was now the most formidable military force in Europe, and some British politicians – Chamberlain was one – had toyed with the idea of an alliance with it, rather than the nation's traditional adversaries. But as Salisbury, no Teutophobe, had seen, Germany could offer Britain very little: it was not a significant colonial power, and if its own alliance with Austria led to war with Russia, as several times had seemed possible, Britain was in no position to help it in the Pripet Marshes. On the other hand, by Edwardian times its economy was growing much more rapidly than Britain's, and it was building a major navy. It was a parvenu state, its diplomacy after Bismarck often blustering and clumsy, a natural object of aversion and suspicion to France, whose alliance with Russia was designed as a shield against it, though actual conduct by Germany was in general quite restrained: no actions comparable to those of Britain in South Africa, France in Morocco, Italy in Libya, or any attempt to take advantage of Russia's near collapse after defeat by Japan and revolution at home in 1906–07. If the Foreign Office nevertheless constructed a lurid image of Germany as bent on the hegemony of Europe, graphically depicted by Crowe in 1907, shared by all its senior officials and entertained by Grey, this served a purpose: to present a foreign policy whose ultimate aims were preservation, and where required extension, of the British Empire as a vigilant guardian of the peace and liberty of Europe. A largely imaginary Germany was invented to cover an abiding concern to parry Russia.

There was a difficulty, however. An alliance in the remote Far East was one thing: it touched no domestic nerve. Alliances in Europe were quite another. In peacetime, military agreements with other states were incompatible with the principle of the free hand. How were the arrangements with France and Russia to be reconciled with it? By putting – Grey's expression in 1914 – 'nothing in writing'. An entente was nominally just that, a friendly rapport without institutional commitment. For practical purposes, of course, it meant a great deal more. Grey authorized clandestine military talks with France virtually as soon as he came to office, and was soon privately saying that if Britain failed to back France over Morocco with force, it would lose all credit in the world and he would quit. The talks were a state secret, knowledge of them withheld even from the Cabinet. Repeatedly, Grey told intimates that Britain was – morally – 'bound', by honour if not by letter, to stand by France if war came.

In other words, Wilson observed, the 'free hand' had become a fiction, while the balance of power that it ostensibly ensured was a dissimulation, since if a continental war broke out Britain's army was too small to affect the issue, as uniquely among the Great Powers of Europe it lacked conscription. There, indeed, lay the reason why the country's foreign policy was not self-contained, but subject to at least one immovable domestic constraint. Conscription was so unpopular in Britain that no party dared openly advocate it, though there were Tory voices that did so. *Innenpolitik* could not be discounted by any government, least of all a Liberal one with a significant Cobdenite contingent. The course of the coterie in charge of foreign policy had therefore to be largely hidden from Parliament, and the Cabinet only partially privy to it. Deception was a condition of its pursuit, and self-deception of the calculations on which it was based. Joining the conflagration in 1914, Grey told the Commons, would cost the country no more than staying out of it. Wilson's verdict? 'Participation in a great European war was the price Britain paid for "the policy of the Entente". This price could have been paid at any time. It was paid not over Casablanca or Scutari, but over Sarajevo. It was paid in the form of casualty returns.'[18]

The contrast between Wilson's first book and his thesis was thus in many ways marked. *The Policy of the Entente* differs from *Role and Influence* in three major respects. First and foremost, the empire that was largely absent a dozen years earlier was now central to his case, explicitly set over against, and above, Europe in the calculus of British foreign policy. Concomitantly, the position occupied by Germany in the outlook of Whitehall is reversed. In 1973, there was no Germanophobia in the Foreign Office, but an accurate calibration of the growing danger that Berlin represented, not only to the country whose interests the FO was determined to defend, but to the freedom of every other country in Europe. In 1985 Germany was not out to subjugate Europe or the world, where its conduct on the whole was quite moderate, but was demonized in the Foreign Office as a mask for anxieties about Russia and justification for discarding the free hand which Britain had in the past upheld. So where once the politician at the helm of Britain's foreign policy before the Great War could be praised for his clarity of vision, balance, and independence of mind, he now emerged in a far less favourable light, as a figure who misled Parliament and circumvented the Cabinet in pursuit of aims he could never publicly avow and entanglements that eventually pitched the country without preparation into a European war.

Wilson returned to Grey's performance at the Foreign Office repeatedly on subsequent occasions, at greatest length in the essays he wrote shortly afterwards for the volume he edited on *British Foreign Secretaries* (1987) and again towards the end of his life in a symposium on Grey held at the Foreign Office itself and published

---

18. Ibid., p. 98.

in the *International History Review* in 2016. In these he developed and reinforced the evidence for the image left of him in *The Policy of the Entente*. Before he even took office, Grey was writing in private that better relations with Russia were '*the* thing to be striven for', and within forty-eight hours of taking office was instructing the British embassy in St Petersburg to make an overture to the Tsarist regime. By March 1906 he had made it clear that what London expected from a mutual arrangement was that 'repose should be guaranteed on our Indian frontier'.[19] In the past, as he would recall a few years later, while Germany had certainly caused trouble for Britain, 'the situation was very much worse' with France and Russia, where the country was 'constantly on the brink of war' with one or the other. Since then it had thankfully reached understandings with each, Russia above all 'scrupulously abstaining from doing anything prejudicial to the security of our Indian frontier'. But if the Triple Entente were to lapse, the outcome would be deadly; for then, 'sooner or later there must be war between Russia and ourselves over these Asiatic questions'.[20] Insistently, again and again Grey framed an embrace between the two powers as the indispensable condition for tranquil possession of the British Empire in the subcontinent. 'The pride of England would be broken if India were lost,' he told the Canadian prime minister in 1908.[21] Its security was thus 'the *fons et origo*', the 'real raison d'être', 'the primary and cardinal object' of the

---

19. *The Limits of Eurocentricity: Imperial British Foreign and Defence Policy in the Early Twentieth Century*, Istanbul 2006, pp. 26–7; 'Grey and the Russian Threat to India 1892–1915', *International History Review*, March–April 2016, p. 277.

20. *The Policy of the Entente*, p. 108; 'Grey and the Russian Threat to India', p. 276; *British Foreign Secretaries*, London 1987, pp. 179–80.

21. *Problems and Possibilities: Exercises in Statesmanship 1814–1918*, Port Stroud 2002, p. 179.

Anglo-Russian conventions of 1907. From them had sprung a friendship that by 1914 was 'the cornerstone' of British foreign policy as a whole. Should it be brought to an end, as frictions over the division of Persia threatened to do that summer, the result would be calamitous. To avert that misfortune, Grey was willing to sacrifice Constantinople itself – 'the greatest prize of the whole war', he termed it – to Russia in March 1915.[22]

In the discourse of the Foreign Office, the function of the Triple Entente was to assure a balance of power in Europe by acting as a counterweight to the alliance of Germany and Austria, thereby helping to preserve a general peace of which at home Grey was widely seen and admired as the architect, and saw himself as a committed guardian. Image and reality did not correspond. Behind the screen of confidentiality which went with his office, he was a consistent advocate of resort to arms where he judged them necessary, who believed that nations had recourse to them at regular intervals, more or less inevitably. As early as the first Moroccan crisis of February 1906 he was threatening resignation if Britain shrank from joining France in battle with Germany: 'We ought in our own minds to face the question now, whether we can keep out of the war, if war breaks out between France and Germany. The more I review the situation the more it appears to me that we cannot, without losing our good name and friends and wrecking our policy and position in the world.' To leave 'France in the lurch' would incur the contempt of the United States, alienate Russia and Japan, and make his own position intolerable.[23] Three months later, he had the Ottoman Empire in his sights, proposing an attack on

---

22. 'Grey and the Russian Threat to India', pp. 278, 279, 280.
23. *The Policy of the Entente*, pp. 94–5.

the Dardanelles to punish it for daring an incursion into Egyptian territory, Britain's pendant to Morocco.[24]

In 1908 he could write: 'After a big war a nation doesn't want another for a generation or more, but after 40 years of peace, if a nation is strong enough it begins spoiling for a fight. It was so with us between 40 and 50 years after the Crimean War, and it was so with Russia; and it was so with the United States nearly forty years after her Civil War.' After these candid if tactful allusions to the Boer, Russo-Japanese and Spanish-American wars of late, he noted that it was now '38 years since Germany had her last war'. It had become 'strong and restless', too big for its boots, so 'it will be difficult to keep the peace in Europe for another five years'.[25] Three years later, he told the Russian ambassador during the Agadir crisis: 'In the event of war between Germany and France, Britain would have to participate. If this war should involve Russia, Austria would be dragged in too', hence 'it would no longer be a duel between Germany and France – it would be a general war'.[26]

When the first Balkan War broke out the following year, he summoned Lichnowsky, the German ambassador in London, and warned him that if 'a European war were to arise through Austria's attacking Serbia, and Russia, compelled by public opinion, were to march into Galicia rather than again put up with a humiliation like that of 1909, thus forcing Germany to come to the aid of Austria, France would inevitably be drawn in and no one could foretell what further developments would follow'. The menace in the last clause, Lichnowsky reported to Berlin, was 'unmistakeable'.[27] Grey had

---

24. *The Limits of Eurocentricity*, p. 123.
25. *The Policy of the Entente*, p. 173.
26. *The Limits of Eurocentricity*, p. 164.
27. *Empire and Continent*, p. 143.

predicted exactly the scenario of August 1914, and indicated the role Britain would play in it. When the crisis came, his threat to resign if it did not – 'we have led France to rely upon us and unless we support her in her agony, I cannot continue at the Foreign Office'[28] – cowed doubters with the spectre of a split in Liberal ranks, the fall of the government, and its replacement by a coalition with the Tories, clinching the decision he sought. 'There were over eight years of peace in Grey's time', Wilson observed, but was that a personal achievement? His answer was unambiguous. The character of Grey's stamp on British foreign policy was such that 'he can be given no credit for the duration of peace among the Great Powers'. His rigidity and brinkmanship did nothing to prolong it.[29]

In the eighties, Wilson's writing on British foreign policy prior to the First World War was a frontal challenge to the conventional wisdom about it then, as it remains today. How was it received? Such notices as appeared at the time complained that it paid virtually no attention to the reality of the German threat to Europe, and while containing some unorthodox ideas and insights, had failed to integrate these into any cogent alternative to the line taken by Grey.[30] The two historians of the First World War who dominated the subsequent literature on it in England, Zara Steiner and Thomas Otte, would consign Wilson to minuscule dismissal.[31] The one exception was

---

28. *The Policy of the Entente*, p. 138.
29. *British Foreign Secretaries*, p. 193.
30. For example, Michael Dockrill, *Albion*, April–June, pp. 339–41; Samuel Williamson, *The American Historical Review*, June 1986, pp. 669–70.
31. Zara Steiner and Keith Neilson, *Britain and the Origins of the First World War*, endnotes pp. 312 and 328 – explaining right away in the endnote following the last that 'the most important defence of Grey is Zara Steiner, *The Foreign Office and Foreign Policy 1898–1914*'; T. G. Otte, *Statesman of Europe: A Life of Sir Edward Grey*, London 2020, p. 690: 'The scholarly works of Keith Wilson remain the *fons*

Paul Kennedy, in whose judgment *The Policy of the Entente* was a tour de force. Wilson had produced a 'skilful, elegant and sophisticated work', based on years of intellectual reflection, archival research and fresh evidence he had brought to light. His stress on the fixation of the Foreign Office with the danger of Russia, though credible enough in the case of some of its leading lights, swung the pendulum too far from the alarm at Germany which was uppermost among much wider layers of the political and officer class in Great Britain. Yet, as among those identified by Wilson with the argument for the primacy of the German threat, he nevertheless had no hesitation in saying that Wilson's book should be read by anyone interested in the question of the British role in the origins of the Great War.[32] It was an isolated judgment.

The most effective response to any body of ideas unwelcome to established opinion is typically silence, and hostility was certainly the principal reason for the muted reception of Wilson's work. But it was not the only one. *The Policy of the Entente* was composed, as critics pointed out, of overlapping essays, each closely argued and documented, but lacking the form of continuous narrative or a consecutive case, or a classical conclusion. The analytic intensity of Wilson's research came at the expense, not just of a range of subject matter, but of a bent for synthesis. A comparison with Kennedy's own work, which had come out five years earlier, underlines the difference. Over triple Wilson's book in length, *The Rise of Anglo-German Antagonism, 1860–1914* developed a sustained, comprehensive comparison of the economy, society, politics and culture of two countries, without equal

---

et origo of most critiques of Grey's policy, though Wilson has shifted his position frequently, advancing and retracting positions over time.'

32. *English Historical Review*, April 1986, pp. 454–7.

to this day. *The Policy of the Entente* is a slim study of the diplomacy of just one. Kennedy's book ends with a conclusion anchoring the conflict between Edwardian England and the Second Reich in the uneven economic development that saw the latecomer, once united, growing faster than the pioneer of the first industrial revolution and challenging its global primacy with a major fleet of its own, a short distance – unlike the United States – away from it, making a clash between them inescapable. But if that was the long-term logic of their rivalry, the immediate responsibility for the war that pitched them into battle in 1914 lay in the truculence and stupidity of Germany's military caste, which unleashed fighting in East and West alike, and the ideology of force – 'blood and iron' – that had presided over the country's unification from the start. Whatever their own failings, or the expansionist violence that had once created the British Empire, the liberal rulers of Edwardian Britain were less imprudent, managing their affairs better. It was no good blaming them as well.[33] Abstaining from comparison, or any opinion about relative guilt for the war, Wilson offered no such measure of patriotic consolation.

If a disinclination for synthesis – hard labour at the coal face of archives more compelling than easy recoil to a bird's-eye view of the landscape? – was one element in the reputation Wilson earned, another was a perhaps surprising absence of polemical appetite. What he published was generally combative in substance, and in an understated way could be quite sharp, but it rarely if ever took direct issue with any other historian. Given how historiographically controversial were his positions, that abstention reduced his impact. Cambridge unwisely announced *The Policy of the Entente* as an English counterpart to

---

33. *The Rise of Anglo-German Antagonism 1860–1914*, London 1980, pp. 456–7, 464–9.

Fischer's work in Germany, whereas in method and character they differed completely, and their authors were at opposite poles in *animus pugnandi*. Last but not least, though his diplomatic history was intensely focussed, his interests were quite dispersed, yielding an output whose directions were more heterogeneous than many a colleague's. That too confounded any obvious identikit of him.

Over the years that followed his brace of books in the mideighties, Wilson's writing can be divided, broadly speaking, into three categories. The first was composed of collections bringing together essays by fellow scholars, as well as one of his own, which he edited and in a couple of cases introduced: beginning with *British Foreign Secretaries* (1987), and continuing with *Decisions for War* (1995), *Forging the Collective Memory* (1996), and *The International Impact of the Boer War* (2001); the first two, outcomes of conferences he organized in Leeds. A striking feature of the set is their ecumenical composition. The two bearing most directly on Wilson's concerns in *The Policy of the Entente* both contained much that was at variance with his own positions. The longest essay in *British Foreign Secretaries* supplied an admiring portrait of Palmerston, to whom Wilson was understandably averse. Six out of eight of the contributions to *Decisions for War* took Entente-inflected views of 1914 (the other two, on Japan and the Ottoman Empire dealt with extra-European powers), while the tenor of the volume as a whole was set by an introduction from Harry Hinsley, intelligence operative turned don, bluntly declaring that the cause of the First World War lay in the paranoia of Germany's rulers, whose bid to lord it over Europe by violence opened the road to Hitler. The only clearly dissentient contribution was Wilson's account of the neutralization of the Liberal Cabinet in the crisis of 1914 when, as he wrote, 'Grey's personal decision for war was made as soon as the Russian government made it clear that they would not tolerate a forcible Austro-Hungarian solution of the Serbian problem. The Cabinet, as such, never did make a decision for war.'[34]

In a second category came two books Wilson authored in the nineties. The first (1990) was *A Study in the History and Politics of the* Morning Post *1905–1926*. Until Northcliffe slashed the price of *The Times* to attract circulation, the *Post* was the largest newspaper in Britain read by the propertied classes, and once inherited by Countess Bathurst – 'the most powerful woman in the country after royalty', according to Northcliffe – an organ of die-hard right-wing opinion. Wilson's choice of the paper for a work on the press was characteristically heterodox and acute. Neither Steiner nor Kennedy, in their respective coverage of the national press, had paid any attention to it, each largely confining themselves to consideration of *The Times*. Wilson's book on it was not a narrative history of this ultra-Tory daily, taking instead the form of a sequence of chapters on different aspects – economic, journalistic, editorial, political – of its record before, during and after the First World War. The majority revolve around its editor from 1911 onwards, the journalist H. A. Gwynne, an intimate of Kipling's and veteran of reportage on the Boer War with numerous contacts at the highest levels of the political and military establishment in Britain. Gwynne's flow of letters to his proprietor during the war, documenting the ease and extent of his intimacy with the rulers of the country, and his efforts to oust first Asquith, then Lloyd George (later even Curzon) from office, had been published by Wilson two years earlier as *The Rasp of War*. He emerges in a still more vivid light in the twenties. The *Morning Post* was ultimately absorbed by the *Daily Telegraph* in 1937.

---

34. *Decisions for War*, p. 201.

Wilson's other book in these years was a study of the fate of projects to build a tunnel to France under the Channel,[35] reckoned to be feasible as early as the final decades of the nineteenth century, when leading politicians of both parties – Gladstone for the Liberals, Lansdowne for the Conservatives – favoured them. In the decade preceding the Great War, the scheme was actively debated in Parliament and Whitehall, when Campbell-Bannerman, after earlier voting for the idea in the Commons, backtracked as prime minister in the face of military, bureaucratic, intellectual and not least royal opposition to it as a threat to national security, facilitating an invasion of Britain by a continental foe – once conceived as France, now Germany. Victory over the latter in the Great War revived the plan, Lloyd George and Woodrow Wilson including it in a twelve-point programme for Versailles devised in the spring of 1919. But once again, despite support even within the General Staff, xenophobic fears fanned by the arachnid fixer Maurice Hankey, secretary to the Committee of Imperial Defence, stymied the scheme in London, the Commons in the end voting it down by seven votes in 1930. *Channel Tunnel Visions* was released in 1995, a few months after an underwater connexion to the continent was finally built.

A third category of texts were what could be described as further needlework on the tapestry of Wilson's work on British diplomacy in the belle époque. Two collections of papers subsequent to *Empire and Continent* appeared before he died. Each contained around a dozen

---

35. Encouraged by Wilson's wife, née Sally Scott, daughter of a Scottish doctor in Northern Rhodesia, an enlightened foe of racism, who was elected as an independent member of its parliament. Her elder brother would become the first white head of state in a decolonized African society, as president of Zambia. His sister, a popular figure at the University of Leeds, rose to the position of director of human resources there.

articles, about half of them unpublished; the second adding seventeen book reviews from assorted various journals. Of these extensions to *The Policy of the Entente*, four develop important arguments that are substantially or completely novel: respectively, a development of Wilson's original account of the Anglo-French Entente, focussing on the Liberal-Imperialist 'cabal' in the British Cabinet, and its effects; a consideration of the abortive inter-departmental committee on Persia set up in 1915, nominally under Curzon, and tractations with Russia and the Indian office about the country; a critical account of Austrian and German actions in the Balkans after the assassinations in Sarajevo, viewed as a classic terrörist action in a nationalist cause, comparable to the Indian attentat against Hardinge as viceroy two years earlier, or in this century Iraqi resistance to American invasion; and a powerful reflection on the duties and difficulties of the study of international history inaugurated after the First World War.[36]

One great exception stands out in Wilson's repertoire as a diplomatic historian, a work published in 2003 unlike anything else he wrote in his career. Its deceptively flat, uninformative title was *Problems and Possibilities*, not greatly illuminated by the bland subtitle *Exercises in Statesmanship 1814–1918*. What it amounted to was Wilson's contribution to a genre of which cases are quite rare: single-volume histories of a century of interstate relations in Europe, not composed or designed as a textbook, but as an original interpretation

---

36. 'The Anglo-French Entente Revisited, 1906–1914' and 'Curzon outwith India: A Note on the Lost Committee on Persia 1915–1916', in *The Limits of Eurocentricity*, pp. 139–72, 199–212; 'Austria-Hungary and Germany: Hamlet without the Prince: Terrorism at the Outbreak of the Great War' and 'The Study of International History in Britain in the Aftermath of the Great War', in *Directions of Travel: Great Britain and the Great Powers before and after the Great War*, Istanbul 2014, pp. 81–92, 127–33.

of its subject. The nearest recent equivalent was perhaps a work co-authored by one of his colleagues at Leeds, Roy Bridge, with Roger Bullen of the LSE, some twenty years earlier.[37] Wilson's book was an anomaly both within his own oeuvre, and within the genre. It is the only work of diplomatic history he wrote that takes the form of a chronological narrative and, uniquely in his oeuvre, has no footnotes. The narrative is selective, as any attempt at one will be, but the principles organizing it were unusual. A foreword explains that the book's focus will be the leading problems confronting the rulers of Europe between the Vienna Congress and the Conference at Versailles, and how they sought to handle them. The actors concerned, Wilson remarks at the outset, were less than twenty. The lens through which European history in this period is seen is theirs: the perspective is top-down. As its title indicates, the book covers the range of options before them, not just those paths that were taken, but others that were canvassed and might have been. The result is often an unexpected story, in more ways than one.

Wilson divides his century into three periods. In the first, extending from the defeat of Napoleon I to the arrival of Napoleon III, the problems that preoccupied European statesmen were how to maintain the Vienna settlement, and to cope with the major power excluded from it, the Ottoman Empire. In the second, they became consequences of Napoleon III's rejection of the Vienna settlement, issuing into the Crimean War and Italian unification, followed by the victories of Prussia over Austria and France. In the third, they were how to adjust to the disappearance of the buffer states set up at Vienna to preserve

---

37. *The Great Powers and the European States System, 1814–1914*, London 1980; Wilson was among those thanked in the preface for help and guidance. A quarter of a century later, Bullen since deceased, Bridge published a revised version of the book, nearly twice the length of the original, in 2005.

peace between the Great Powers, to react to the accelerating decay of Ottoman rule in the Balkans, to deal with European expansion in Asia and Africa, and to reckon with the rise of the United States and Japan as new forces in the world. In each of these phases, Wilson has some surprises for the reader.

In the first period, Wilson depicts Castlereagh with visible appreciation as the most reasonable and level-headed of the architects of the Vienna system, who resisted unnecessary calls for armed interventions to defend it; has warm praise for Metternich's defence of the Ottoman Empire in 1835 in the name of the public law of Europe, as his 'finest hour'; and hails Nesselrode's 'staggering achievement' in checking nationalist impulses in Russia and therewith reviving the Concert of Europe into the 1840s.[38] Not that the arrangements of Vienna were sacrosanct. At least two schemes for a radical alteration of them were proposed within the Pentarchy itself, each little known and one treated with sympathy by Wilson, the sweeping but relatively fair and balanced redistribution of territories, east and west, by Polignac in 1829, and the offer by Nicholas I to let Austria take possession of the Balkans in 1843 and 1845, declined by Metternich.

In the second period, Napoleon III's foreign policy in the 1850s was actuated not simply by the long-standing French ambition to revise the Vienna settlement, a constant since the Restoration, but by his genuine wish for a new Concert of Europe, the Pentarchy to confer together once again in a regular series of amicable congresses as after 1815, but now acknowledging the importance of national principles: a vision scotched by all four of the other Great Powers, as in a reversion to the Quadruple Alliance that had put paid to his uncle. This was not to be Louis Napoleon's last overestimation of

---

38. *Problems and Possibilities*, pp. 25–8, 36, 42.

the position of France in Europe. When Prussia defeated Austria and became master of North Germany, he felt it incumbent on French standing to challenge it, launching the Franco-Prussian War of his own volition, rather than being tricked by Bismarck into doing so, partly also in fear of an excitable domestic opposition if he did not. The result was to bring down the Second Empire and usher in the final set of problems with which European rulers had to grapple.

Germany now dominated the continent, and Bismarck the diplomatic scene. Aware that its geographical position at the centre of Europe left it open to attack on all sides, he sought to safeguard its eastern flank by cementing alliances with Austria and Russia, and its western flank by diverting France from thoughts of revenge by encouraging expansion of its empire overseas. But the weakening of Ottoman control in the Balkans fuelled rivalry between Russia and Austria for dominion over them, and when Russia rolled up Turkish arms decisively in 1878, Britain threatened to intervene. At a Congress convened in Berlin to settle matters in the Balkans, Bismarck had to choose which side to offend less, opting to placate Austria at the price of alienating Russia. His subsequent efforts to patch up relations with St Petersburg did not outlast him. Once he was gone, Russia formed an alliance with France, and Europe divided into two antagonistic blocs, neither of them capable of controlling insurgent nationalisms in the Balkans or the competition between them.

Britain remained apart, tied to its empire rather than to either continental camp. Willing to reverse its tradition of protecting Turkey against Russia, Salisbury came to the conclusion that the best way of defending British interests in Asia would be to divide Ottoman domains with Russia, granting it control of the Black Sea and the Straits in exchange for British penetration of the Levant and security for India, another bold solution for the Eastern Question which came to nothing. In Africa, where even minor European states joined in the partition of the continent, Britain secured the lion's share of territory that was valuable. Yet though the late nineteenth century saw a major expansion of its empire, the New Imperialism of the period did not ultimately favour it, as industrialization modernized rival predators and bred doctrines of *Weltpolitik* holding a redistribution of the Earth inevitable in the twentieth century, in which it was going to be the definition of a Great Power to acquire a large stake. The New Imperialism, while it set off intercolonial wars in Asia, Africa and the Americas, did not generate armed conflicts in Europe itself, where the fear of the Vienna system that war led to revolution had not entirely faded – the Paris Commune was still a fresh memory. But after Salisbury these changes were enough to eject England out of its diplomatic isolation into an alliance with Japan in the Far East and an entente with France in North Africa. Yet if Europe itself still remained at peace, that was not because there was a balance of power between its two blocs – the combined force of Germany and Austro-Hungary was preponderant; it was due rather to the displacement of European tensions overseas with the spread of *Weltpolitik*. But by 1912, as Russia's recovery from the war with Japan accelerated, the military imbalance in Europe was visibly subject to erosion. Two years later fighting broke out.

To call the conflagration that followed the Great War or the First World War was for Wilson a misnomer, as if it was a single conflict. There were in fact several wars, which overlapped and intermingled, but were causally and analytically distinct. The first was an Austro-Serbian War, consequence of the Balkan Wars of 1912–13 that had finished off the Ottoman Empire in Europe, doubled the size of Serbia and detached Romania from its alliance with the Habsburg Empire. Austria-Hungary attacked Serbia to crush the South Slav threat to itself, and to recuperate Romania. The second was a German–Russian War, unleashed by Berlin on the pretext that St Petersburg responded to the prospect of an Austrian invasion of Serbia with an order for general mobilization of its armies, deliberately misinterpreted by the German high command, which knew it would take six weeks to implement, as an act of war rather than a diplomatic move to buy time for negotiations. Germany had for two years pre-planned a war against Russia, to overwhelm the country before its rearmament was completed.[39] The third was a German–English War contemplated much earlier, from the turn of the century, but envisaged as breaking out in a much more distant future, when the German navy was in a position to challenge British global command of the seas. Since England lacked a land army of any appreciable size, should it decide to resist Germany's attack on Russia, and so necessarily its ally France too, it could be discounted as a military factor. The fourth war was the obverse – an English–German War, also long expected and like its counterpart in Germany impatiently awaited by a significant number of officers, diplomats and publicists as the sooner the better. They were not, however, responsible for the decision to wage war in 1914. That was taken by Grey as foreign secretary, in conjunction with Asquith as prime minister, on other grounds: to avoid the isolation of Britain and keep the friendship of Russia, whose restraint in Central Asia was held critical for India.

Kindred concerns actuated every major state of the time:

Imperial considerations constituted the factor common to all the Great Powers. In 1914 the wars of the distant and the more immediate

---

[39]. An uncritical reception of Fischer's work, at its most contestable, is evident here; for which see too his account in *Directions of Travel* of Austria-Hungary and Germany in 1914, atypical in its extravagance, referred to above.

future merged into what became known as the Great War, because no Great Power, no regime, no body of ministers was prepared to curb its imperial inclinations, tendencies or pretensions – whether these related primarily to eastern Europe, as in the cases of Austria-Hungary and Russia, or whether they related primarily to regions outside of Europe altogether, as in the cases of Germany, France and Great Britain.[40]

Once their several wars were unleashed, moreover, the territorial aims of each expanded in the general melée, pitting not only enemies but often allies against each other, in a contest resembling a Hobbesian state of nature, 'the war of all against all' – in which a revolution erupted in the largest belligerent, Russia, overthrowing its monarchy as conservatives had always feared in due course it might. When peace eventually came, the victors were nearly as lenient at Versailles as their predecessors had been at Vienna, and for a not unrelated reason: fear of Russia, military in 1815, ideological in 1919.

Problems and Possibilities was Wilson's most important work after *The Policy of the Entente*, and as history least like it. Nothing he had previously written gave any indication that his learning extended in much depth beyond his native country. However historically critical of its foreign policy in his chosen period, intellectually the focus of his work was thoroughly Anglocentric. *Problems and Possibilities* revealed another side of him: in scope and grasp a mind fully European, as interested and knowledgeable about the east as the west of the continent, and as naturally given to non-banality here too. Avoidance of the familiar or the obvious, of course, was not thereby immune to contradiction or error. What was unorthodox could also induce it. So many striking observations were unlikely to

---

40. *Problem and Possibilities*, p. 203.

be all consistent. Wilson's opening section on the Vienna system – he doesn't use the term 'Restoration' – is an example. Castlereagh is given high marks for his good sense in distancing Britain from the Holy Alliance and its repressions, but what then of praise for Metternich's patronage of Ottoman rule or Nesselrode's record? How compatible with any of these is approval of Gentz's scathing depiction of the Congress of Vienna, upheld against modern admirers of it? The overall tenor of Wilson's approach to the nineteenth century, and the way his narrative is framed, are unmistakably realist. Yet three pivotal chapters of the book are entitled 'Responsibilities', a term of moral judgment generally held foreign to realism, and in each he delivers a somewhat unconventional verdict, criticizing Britain for bringing on the Crimean War, acquitting Bismarck of any blame for the Franco-Prussian War, and excluding France and Russia from the detonators of the First World War, an omission to invite the term 'bewildering'. Yet the same chapter ends by impartially, and correctly, ascribing imperialist drives to all the Great Powers in precipitating the carnage, and the next concludes with French insistence on dispatching, at a time when Germany occupied a substantial belt of France itself, a third of a million soldiers to the Balkans in preparation for post-war expansion by France in the Near East.

Problems and Possibilities, which no doubt drew on lectures Wilson had been giving for a good while at Leeds and reading he had done for them, was ignored on publication. Perhaps in academic journals because it lacked footnotes, which might have been a requirement by the press that brought it out in an obscure corner of the West Country; or conceivably a result of haste to get it into print for a belated promotion in his department, repeatedly denied him by the university. Leeds may not have treated him particularly well, perhaps holding a lack of recognition to which it contributed against him. After he died, it declined to keep his papers, which were destroyed. An increasing marginalization can be traced in the places where he published. *Channel Tunnel Visions* – Lampeter; *The International Impact of the Boer War* – Chesham; *Problems and Possibilities* – Stroud; *The Limits of Eurocentricity* and *Directions of Travel* – Istanbul: effectively, the casting of an outsider to successively further rings of the periphery.[41]

Might his fate have been in part political? Unlikely. That in some sense he was a man of the left is clear. But in what sense? The historical scholarship for which he is best known made short work of self-serving official mythology about British foreign policy in the Edwardian era, putting empire at the centre of it without any explicit political comment. The two books that strayed from the terrain of the Foreign Office are in that regard more suggestive. His study of the *Morning Post* exposed the anti-Semitism of both its proprietor and its editor – principal purveyors of *The Protocols of the Elders of Zion* in the British press – and the key role of the latter in manning the *British Gazette* as the government's propaganda weapon for breaking the General Strike of 1926, leaving no doubt of Wilson's opinion of this record. His sequel on plans for a Channel tunnel was openly hostile to the jingoism of those who blocked it on xenophobic security and cultural grounds, lacking 'the vision, generosity of spirit, optimism or determination to create a new and better world' of its champions – chief among them Churchill, the fire-breathing strike-breaker of

---

41. Likewise his editions of two unfinished manuscripts, the autobiography of the diplomat Sir Charles Marley and the final volume of the life of Salisbury by his daughter: Istanbul 2010 and 2017 – a 'periphery', of course, only in European terms of reference: editing standards at the Isis Press put not a few academic houses in the Anglosphere to shame.

British Gazette fame: an example of the discrimination he could bring to his judgment of individuals.[42]

These were still particular descriptions. *Forging the Collective Memory* contains the one occasion when Wilson became unambiguously declaratory and prescriptive. There he concluded a general attack on all governments involved in the First World War for concealing, doctoring, or fabricating official documents that cast a less than favourable light on themselves, with a credo: 'My own view is that the true role of the historian, and the true internationalism of the international historian, is to be found in being objective enough not to write "national" history. This is a challenge which has not diminished.'[43] It was an issue about which he felt very strongly, and may have been one of the reasons for a solitary expression of approval for a contemporary politician. Reprinting the passage in the last chapter of *Directions of Travel*, Wilson added the most forthright indication of his political convictions to be found anywhere in his writing. After listing all the major wars waged around the world in his lifetime, Africa excepted, he noted that several had been longer than the Great War itself, and the longest of all the American wars in Indochina, 'out of which, thanks to Prime Minister Harold Wilson,

---

42. Though by 1914 the most aggressive warmonger in the Liberal Cabinet, Churchill is treated more mildly than Grey, Haldane or Asquith in *The Policy of the Entente*, Wilson evidently unable to contain some admiration for him. In similar fashion, after an unsparing balance-sheet of Gwynne's political and ideological performance at the helm of the *Morning Post*, he ends by acknowledging that nevertheless Gwynne 'could not be shut up, bought off, diverted or subverted'. A figure neither intimidated by threats nor corrupted by blandishments, in conditions of official pressure during the war his voice was 'a real, and necessary, contribution to the preservation of civil liberties': *The Rasp of War*, p. 328.

43. *Forging the Collective Memory*, p. 23. The same introduction to the volume contains a blistering attack on the 'impudence' of Crowe's glossing of gags and mendacities by officialdom: pp. 6–8.

Britain managed to stay. Credit where credit is due' – whereas Britain had joined the United States in 'a completely gratuitous attack on Iraq' under Blair, claiming ignorance of the Project for the New American Century that lay behind it.[44] Keith Wilson was a student in Oxford in the sixties, at the height of the campus revolt against the established order, which did not spare Labour's inability to break with the war in Vietnam. There is no sign he was affected by the unrest, and he seems to have voted steadily for the party thereafter. New Labour, however, was evidently less to his liking than what it replaced.

How then should his writing on the First World War be judged? Those who took exception to it made no attempt to engage or argue with it; easier to bury it in the small print of an endnote. Others, less hostile, would make use of its findings, without much consideration for the character of his work as a whole. The fragmentary, disparate form it took contributed to casual or muted reaction to it; modest in volume, it lacked the mass that is generally a feature, though not a requirement, of a major reputation. Yet certain things are clear about Keith Wilson's oeuvre. Sticking to his last in primary sources, his focus on British foreign policy was tightly circumscribed. But its implications always extended beyond them.

Of the three pillars of continuity at the Foreign Office he identified at the start of his career, the free hand and balance of power had lapsed by the time Grey took charge of it, but the third – naval supremacy – had not. It was to retain command of the seas and so of its empire that Britain, as he showed, had to reach its understandings with France and Russia. It was open to others to

---

44. *Directions of Travel*, pp. 132–3. In 1965, Wilson's government had also abolished the fifty-year rule forbidding access to official documents less than half a century old, reducing it to thirty years. *Forging the Collective Memory* reprinted his memorandum recommending the change in an appendix.

point out that those seas also surrounded Britain itself, command of home waters explaining phobias of Germany, and so connecting rather than counterposing Empire and Continent in its strategic outlook. No-one has ever explored with such precision and detail the inner workings of the Liberal Cabinet which took Britain into the First World War, and their origins in the domestic political checkerboard. Successors could, if they wished, follow that trail to its logical conclusion: the ways in which liberalism in England, as elsewhere but with particular local clarity, had become inseparable from imperialism as a political force, uniting overt warmongers and ostensible pacifists in what proved a common suicide, as they plunged into the slaughter that would destroy the party whose hold on power they thought they were saving in 1914. Wilson drew an indelible portrait of the politician who pulled them over the precipice. But it was a deliberately partial one, confined to his public office from 1905 to 1914. Left to contemporary and later levies to consider was evidence of the early depth and ruthlessness of Grey's commitment to empire, the central passion of his political career, generating his intense determination to keep faith with France and Russia, and the private roots of an abiding antipathy to Germany.[45]

---

45. In 1894, when Grey was undersecretary at the Foreign Office under Rosebery, he had in all probability an illegitimate child – his younger brother 'married' its mother for him – whom to protect his career he exported to Germany, where she was brought up in Bremen under an assumed name, living the rest of her adult life as a German. For documentation, see the article by her son Hans-Joachim Heller, 'Sir Edward Grey's German Love-Child', *Journal of Liberal History*, Spring 2005, pp. 12–15, and for reflections on it, Michael Waterhouse, *Edwardian Requiem*, London 2013, pp. 43–8. The common enough logic of guilt smothered into aggression is easy to imagine. Subsequent claims from a grand-nephew that genetic evidence disproves any such connexion, piously retailed in sources sympathetic to Viscount Fallodon, have wanted any comparable evidence.

Two emotions that mingled as Britain set about crushing Boer resistance in South Africa, where he tingled with excitement – 'a stirring all down the back-bone' – at the prospect of a 'war for freedom' on behalf of 'the greatest empire the world has ever seen', commended Kitchener's concentration camps and comminated the Kaiser's 'vile lie' about them.[46] Another theme in Wilson's writing about the direction of British foreign policy in these years was that there was nothing inevitable about it. 'There were always alternatives. There always are.'[47] Critics had reason to point out that *The Policy of the Entente* did not explain what the alternatives of which he had written actually were. When Wilson came to write *Problems and Possibilities*, by contrast, he spelt out clear-cut alternatives to conventional solutions of the Eastern Question proposed by statesmen from the 1830s to the 1890s, from Polignac to Salisbury, if not to the course pursued by any of the Great Powers in 1914, including Britain. But his case was in due course made good by a historian of a very different outlook, with the appearance of Niall Ferguson's *Pity of War* in 1998, which argued that the Great War was not inevitable, and if Britain had stayed out of it, as it could and should have done, the conflict would have remained a continental conflict, won in half the time by Germany and with far less damage to all parties and to posterity. The title of his conclusion is 'Alternatives to Armageddon'. A historian of the Right, in his book Ferguson makes some fifty references to Wilson's work. On the Left, Douglas Newton would later expand Wilson's analysis of the Liberal Cabinet in the last week before the war into the finest,

---

46. See H. C. G. Matthew, *The Liberal Imperialists*, London 1973, pp. 182–3, 207; T. G. Otte, *Statesman of Europe*, p. 155.
47. *British Foreign Secretaries*, p. 19.

fullest work yet written on the way the country entered it.[48] Wilson himself, looking back at his starting-points, might at times have wondered whether Salisbury could ever have allowed it to come to the pass where Grey took it, so enormous was the difference between the two in mental stature, audacity and mediocrity personified.[49] Admiration for one and disdain for the other could have tempted such thoughts; his parenthesis of personalities would have resisted them.

What of his combustible central thesis, that from the time of Salisbury onwards the overriding long-term concern of British governments was with Russia rather than any other European power, France or Germany? In the literature on the origins of the First World War, it was a Copernican move. But in due course vindication would come from the ranks of orthodoxy itself. A decade after *The Policy of the Entente*, the Canadian historian Keith Neilson published *Britain and the Last Tsar*, a work greeted with such admiration by Zara Steiner she invited him to co-author a revision of her 1977 book on the origins of the Great War, the new version becoming the standard mainstream study of its subject, and he was soon co-authoring works with Thomas Otte too. *Britain and the*

---

48. *The Darkest Days*, London 2014, which salutes Wilson as an inspiration, while itself eschewing any counterfactuals. For an acute assessment, see Alexander Zevin, 'The Snuffer of Lamps', *New Left Review*, July–August 2015, pp. 127–40.

49. In the prefatory note Wilson wrote to the last book he edited, Gwendolen Cecil's life of her father, he remarked that Salisbury's papers held at Christchurch, directed to them by his tutor, were his first encounter with primary sources, but on realizing he was in no position to challenge the authority of Grenville's work on Salisbury's foreign policy, he turned to Grey instead. His own contribution to the first book he edited, *Imperialism and Nationalism in the Middle East: The Anglo-Egyptian Experience 1882–1982* (London 1983) would be 'Constantinople or Cairo: Lord Salisbury and the Partition of the Ottoman Empire 1886–1897'.

Last Tsar did not question the Entente tenet that Germany aimed at hegemony over Europe, or the high regard in which Grey was held for his 'honesty and simplicity of character' and the 'even-handed' way in which he handled diplomatic relations with other powers in Europe.[50] But on examining the record, Neilson had to admit that 'Russia was the most significant long-term threat to British interests in the twenty years before the First World War and that a driving force – perhaps *the* driving force – in British diplomacy was the effort to reach an accommodation with Russia', relegating Anglo-German antagonism to 'the status of a short-term threat to Britain, of major – but not exclusive – importance in the period after 1906'.[51] Keith Wilson might have advanced some 'fundamental truths', but of course these were 'flawed in emphasis and interpretation'. For 'the British were not *afraid* of Russia', they were just frustrated by the fact that 'solely out of British resources', they were 'relatively powerless to strike a direct and decisive blow at Russia'.[52] Why they should have wanted to attack a state of which they had no fear is not expounded. Nevertheless, the underlying reality was, in Neilson's words, that 'the Anglo-Russian relationship was the dominant long-term determinant' of British foreign policy 'largely by its own dynamics, independent of Anglo-German relations'.[53] Just as Wilson had long contended.

Of all the major landmarks in the historiography of the origins of the First World War, Wilson's is the least conspicuous: smallest in

---

50. *Britain and the Last Tsar*, Oxford 1995, pp. 14, 317. For Neilson's own account of Grey's tenure at the FO, see his contribution to T. G. Otte (ed.), *Makers of British Foreign Policy: From Pitt to Thatcher*, London 2002, pp. 128–50.
51. *Britain and the Last Tsar*, p. xiii.
52. Ibid., p. 371.
53. Ibid., pp. 14, 317, xiii, 370–1.

output and narrowest in gauge. For the most part it dealt only with selected aspects of the diplomacy of just one of the belligerents, without attempting so much as a narrative or resumption even of these. As an aperture onto the conflict, it could be regarded as an arrow-slit. But the mind that opened it was the opposite of narrow: internationalist and anti-imperialist as few profound scholars of the conflict have been; and the landscape to which his work gave entry was as wide – Western in stamp and global in reach – as the interstate system of power, pride and greed that unleashed the carnage. Of the largest of all its predators, the secretary of state for India could write at the turn of the century: 'We are like an octopus with gigantic feelers stretching out all over the habitable world, and constantly interrupting and preventing foreign nations from doing that which we in the past have done ourselves'.[54] Wilson's work could be billed an exercise in marine zoology, with a microscope.

---

54. Lord George Hamilton to Curzon, 2 November 1899, cited by Neilson, *Britain and the Last Tsar*, p. 366, apparently without being aware of the implication for his own case.

CHRISTOPHER CLARK

1. 1892–1914

A couple of years prior to the centenary of the First World War appeared a work which has transformed public understanding of its outbreak as no other has done since it came to an end, Christopher Clark's *Sleepwalkers*. The tributes it earned, though not quite universal, were overwhelming in register and extent, translations and sales of another order from any previous history of the conflict. All but immediately its title became a catchword for politicians warning of the dangers of any repetition of what had brought it about, and the need to ensure against it. The book that met with this response was the work of a historian born, unlike any of those considered earlier here, well after the Second World War, in 1960; and in a country that had entered the First World War not as a Great Power, or even as an independent participant, but as an auxiliary of the most global of its belligerents. Five generations younger than Albertini, four than Renouvin, three than Fischer, two than Schroeder, one than Wilson, Clark is a descendant, he explained, of a refugee from the Irish famine in colonial Australia.[1] Educated in

---

1. *Revolutionary Spring: Fighting for a New World 1848–1849*, London 2023, p. 51. For his early rebellion against the self-serving tropes of official Anglo-Australian

Sydney, he found his way to the Free University in Berlin in the mid-eighties, then to Cambridge, where he wrote a doctorate on nineteenth-century attempts by Protestant missions in Prussia to convert Jews to Christianity, then published a biography of Kaiser Wilhelm II in 2000 and a large general history of Prussia from the seventeenth to the twentieth century, *Iron Kingdom*, in 2006, before producing *The Sleepwalkers* in 2012. Two years later he was appointed Regius Professor of History of the university, and in 2015 knighted for 'services to Anglo-German relations'.

Widespread public acclaim – critical or official – is far from a guarantee of worth. In matters intellectual, frequently the opposite. But not invariably, and this is such a case. Ransacking the dictionary, reviewers reached for every plaudit they could find – 'breathtakingly good', 'easily the best book ever written on the subject', 'monumental', 'superb', 'revolutionary', 'a masterpiece':[2] descriptions none of them unjust, if inevitably less than exhaustive of the object enjoying them. By any measure, *The Sleepwalkers* is a great work of history. What sets it apart within the literature on the First World War that now stretches back for over a hundred years and continues to accumulate with little sign of dwindling are five achievements. First and foremost is the sheer range of its coverage, encompassing in a single volume not only the full Pentarchy of Great Powers which plunged into the war – which was, after all, game too for Fay and Schmitt at the outset of its historiography – together with Serbia, subject to extended scrutiny

---

versions of the First World War, see the interview, published as 'Dieser Krieg hat das ganze Jahrhundert entstellt', *Deutschlandfunk*, 20 January 2014, where he reports that the teacher inculcating his version of these was a follower of Fritz Fischer.

2. Respectively: *London Review of Books*; *Washington Post*; *Boston Globe*; *Guardian*; *New York Times*.

by Albertini, but Clark draws on a much wider body of evidence and argument about its onset than ever before. The condition of that range is a polymathic ease in the languages of Europe beyond the scope of any precursor, yielding a command of sources – primary and secondary – not just in French, German, Italian and Russian, but Serbo-Croatian, Polish and Dutch to boot.

Married to depth of scholarship is pace of narrative. The interactive complexity of Europe's descent into war, involving rival states all prey to internal divisions as they lurched towards the battlefield, has tended to render a clear account of it formally intractable. Clark handles the problem with brio, to such effect that the book was from the start a best-seller. At the same time, cross-cutting the story is an analytic of power and rule that, as Clark would have it, set the parameters for the political actors of the period. Narration and reflection, often at variance with each other in writing about the past, find an ingenious resolution in the structure of the book. The first hundred pages consider the contrast between the two states whose antagonism detonated the war, Serbia and Austro-Hungary, followed by a hundred and fifty on the surrounding polarization of Europe into rival armed camps, the divisions within each of the regimes that came to belong to the two blocs, and the way these forces escalated tensions in the Balkans, before the book reverts to the assassination of the heir to the Habsburg Empire in Sarajevo that set off the crisis of July 1914, and the countdown to the Great War. The movement of the book from the diachronic to the synchronic, and back to the diachronic again, is executed with confident literary skill. Last but not least, a notable feature of *The Sleepwalkers* is the equity of its judgments across a field where so many of even the best scholars have been unable to detach themselves from the passions of the countries where they were formed, or the convictions of the powers superintending them. Distance of geography and of generation from the scene of the disaster has obviously played a role in Clark's freedom from these weaknesses, permitting for the first time a level-headed treatment, critical without saving clauses or special pleading, of all the European powers that took to arms in 1914. Each emerges in a new light from his account.

Serbia and the Habsburg Empire

The most arresting single novelty of *The Sleepwalkers* comes in its opening chapter, devoted to Serbia, regularly marginalized or ignored in much of the literature on the origins of the First World War. Here it receives an extended socio-political account from the overthrow of the Obrenović dynasty in 1903 to the eve of the conflict in 1914, throwing into relief the character of its peasant society, the popular legends of its past, the dominance of the Radical Party in its parliamentary system, the countervailing influence of the Army in its national life, and the expansionist dynamic of the country, powered by both of these forces. Such, Clark shows, was the background to the foundation in 1911 of Union or Death, the conspiratorial network of the 'Black Hand', spanning military and civilian recruits and blurring the boundaries between official and unofficial activities in Serbia, whose most effective leader was the regicide officer 'Apis'. It was in this milieu that a trio of Bosnian boys was trained and armed in Belgrade, and assured clandestine passage across the frontier to Sarajevo for the assassination of the Archduke Franz Ferdinand. The Serbian government was aware of their movement – its premier, the Radical veteran Nikola Pašić, noted the news over a month before the killings occurred, connecting it with the name of a well-known operative of the Black

Hand.[3] Though Pašić and Apis were enemies in domestic politics, they shared the irredentist goal of a Greater Serbia, and there was as yet no open conflict between the two. It was under Pašić, later responsible for his judicial murder, that Apis was appointed director of military intelligence with responsibility for monitoring the country's borders.

Across these lay to the north and the west the Habsburg domains, dubbed Musil-style by Clark – on his own showing, not so appositely – 'the Empire without Qualities'. Though not as minimized as Serbia in standard accounts of the origins of the Great War, the Dual Monarchy would be generally misrepresented by them as a backward, disorganized and incompetent laggard in the comity of major European powers. The reality, Clark contends, was otherwise. True, the *Ausgleich* of 1867 had split the empire into two separate realms, each possessing its own executive, legislature and judiciary, with little political contact between the two, each dominated by an ethnic group which was numerically the largest, but still a minority of the population in its territory. In the Hungarian parliament a highly restrictive suffrage ensured effortless Magyar control over Croats, Romanians and lesser breeds. In the Austrian, after 1906 elected by universal male suffrage, every significant nationality – Czechs, Poles, Italians, Ruthenians and others, along with Austrians themselves – was represented, disputes between them paralyzing proceedings. To that extent, political life was dysfunctional. But above the juridical sundering and ethnic quarrels of the Habsburg lands, the state was held quite firmly together by three unitary pillars under the direct control of the ruling dynasty, the army, treasury and diplomacy,

---

3. For Pašić's role, see *The Sleepwalkers*, London 2012, pp. 53–8 ff.; henceforward *TS*.

whose ministers of war, finance and foreign affairs were appointed by the emperor and vested with pan-territorial powers. It was the first two of these institutions at the top of the system which ensured order and progress within it.

On both scores, Clark argues, the late record of the Dual Monarchy was quite impressive. Unlike Tsarist Russia, it was a *Rechtsstaat* that offered civic freedoms and predictable justice to its subjects; peace and quiet without revolutionary upheavals or violent disorder; not to speak of a famous flowering of cultural life. Economically and educationally, far from bringing up the rear of the Pentarchy, it was in some surprising respects in the vanguard of the time, posting one of the fastest growth rates in Europe and higher enrolment in elementary schools than France or Germany, let alone Italy or Russia. Heavy industry was booming, agricultural exports rising, the railway network expanding. Even in Bosnia – long administered, if only recently annexed, by it – Habsburg rule had brought investment, urbanization and a certain measure of modernity.[4] Unrest in different degrees among allogenous nationalities there was, across the empire. But Bosnia aside, where there were as yet no elections, the development of what was becoming the normal spectrum of political parties in Western Europe – a conservative right, a liberal centre, a social-democratic left – acted as a stay against radicalization of breakaway nationalism, since it divided rather than incentivized ethnic groups: intransigent secessionism still looked relatively weak. But regionally, the Habsburg Empire was on the defensive rather than offensive. In 1908 it had annexed Bosnia to secure the province against any knock-on effect of the Young Turk revolution, only to find itself an impotent witness in the First Balkan War of the end of Ottoman power in

---

4. *TS*, pp. 69–75.

Europe, and in the Second a doubling of the size of Serbia – whose expansionists liked to picture the country as a dagger thrust into the belly of Austro-Hungary – together with the defection of Romania from nominal alliance with the Central Powers. In the wake of these setbacks, mounting fears and fancies gripped Vienna, personified in the antithetical figures of the (temperamentally) languid Berchtold, in charge of foreign policy, and the (perpetually) fire-breathing Conrad von Hötzendorf of the army, now united in a resolve to meet any new threat with force.

The Other Belligerents

At sixty pages apiece, Serbia and Austro-Hungary receive more detailed and consolidated scrutiny than any of the other belligerents, none of whom earn comparable treatment of their internal politics. In the years before the Great War the roles of France, Germany, Russia and England are viewed essentially through the prism of their foreign policies, broken up into smaller segments distributed across successive chapters – an asymmetry no doubt due in part to requirements of setting the stage for the main action, perhaps in part too as better covered in the existing literature. The second part of the book opens with the birth of the Franco-Russian alliance in the early 1890s; the origins of the Entente Cordiale of 1904 between France and Britain; the contrasting position of Germany as a belated entrant into the imperial club they formed; the reasons for the hostility its arrival aroused in Britain; and the signature of the Anglo-Russian Convention of 1907 that completed a polarization of the continent into two camps, for Clark a 'great turning point' in Europe.[5] The next chapter looks

---

5. *TS*, pp. 152–9.

at the ways power was less than unified within all the major states of the time, in a vivid survey of the divisions and confusions in the executive of each – random interventions by assorted monarchs, lack of collegiality in cabinets, bureaucratic intrigues, frictions between military and civilian personnel, background noise of rising mass parties and excitable press campaigns. In this unsettled atmosphere, Clark suggests, there came an alteration in the mentality of power-holders and those around them: not so much outright bellicism as a 'deepening readiness for war'.[6]

That outlook was on display as early as 1906, when the first crisis over Morocco put Europe on edge, and still more in the second crisis of 1911, when with its move at Agadir Germany challenged the French takeover of the Sultanate. On each occasion, a peaceful resolution was reached. Within weeks of the second, however, France's example spurred Italy to emulate it with an assault on the Ottoman province of what is now Libya, emboldening in turn a league of four Balkan states backed by Russia to attack what remained of the Turkish empire in Europe. Out of this fracas Serbia emerged the clear winner, and Austria, which had long regarded the Ottoman Empire as a barrier to Russian expansion and as another conservative multinational realm, a buttress to its own power, the pointed loser. With this, *The Sleepwalkers* returns to the scene at which its first part comes to an end, and recounts the execution of the plot to kill the heir to the Habsburg throne in Sarajevo, then in careful detail the international crisis it unleashed, issuing into the First World War. In his conclusion, Clark asks whether this was inevitable, or rather the resultant of a set of contingent factors, first among them the assassination of the Austrian archduke, itself so nearly a fiasco.

---

6. *TS*, p. 237.

The innovations of this construction do not lie simply in the breadth of sources, drawn from all the powers in play, and the balance of attention accorded each of them. They come, more essentially, from a powerful iconoclasm of substantive argument. The received wisdom about the origins of the Great War, as it existed when *The Sleepwalkers* appeared, was the product of a confluence between two distinct bodies of writing about them: the self-justifying traditions of French, English and Italian historiography dating back to the interwar period, but still going strong into this century, and the repentant German historiography of the Cold War era. The first absolved the Entente of any active responsibility for the outbreak of slaughter in 1914, for which the Central Powers were solely or overwhelmingly to blame. The second indicted Germany as not merely the military initiator, but the premeditated political planner of the war. The former school encompassed the vast majority of historians, from the time of Wilson to that of Obama, in the countries that had joined forces to defeat the Central Powers. The latter was born with the work of Fritz Fischer, published in the sixties, and the school to which it gave rise in West Germany. The two bevelled smoothly together to form a consensus uniting what were once the rival blocs of the early twentieth century. The effect of Clark's work is to sweep this away. But it does so without any *vis polemica*, never taking any adversary front of opinion or outlook as a target. Endnote references to writers well known for contrary standpoints are plentiful and always respectful. Beyond the value of collegiality, Clark is demonstrably generous towards others. This softens the form, but scarcely lessens the extent of his break with the orthodoxy of the hour. A reminder of what he has to say about each of the Great Powers is sufficient evidence of that.

France

The polarization of Europe began with the Franco-Russian alliance of 1894, the first openly explicit military pact between two major powers since the Napoleonic Wars. What brought it about? France's historic foe was Britain, with which it continued in post-Napoleonic times to vie for colonial gains. For these it sought an ally, but on discovering that Germany was not a candidate unless Paris accepted Bismarck's sequestration of Alsace-Lorraine as unalterable, France pursued Russia, as it, too, was a long-term rival of Britain for imperial aggrandizement. Detesting the very idea of a republic, the Tsar was at first resistant, but out of fear that London might come to an understanding with Berlin, ultimately accepted an alliance with Paris as a counterweight. Very large infusions of French capital into Russia – loans and investments – would in due course cement the bond between the two countries. With that, the Third Republic acquired a weapon indispensable for victory over Germany in any war to avenge its defeat in 1870 and regain possession of the province of which it had been robbed.

But France was still at loggerheads with Britain, coming close to blows with it over the marshes of southern Sudan in 1898. After being forced into a humiliating retreat by London, its foreign minister of the day, Théophile Delcassé, decided that French imperial interests could only be advanced by securing formal agreement over Africa with Britain. In 1904 he reached the necessary colonial deal: Paris would stop making trouble over London's appropriation of Egypt, traditionally coveted by France, in exchange for London's go-ahead to a takeover of Morocco by Paris. Lubricated by a royal visit to the French capital, the Entente Cordiale was born. France now had two friends at opposite ends of the European chequerboard, though these had yet to become friends themselves.

Moving too quickly to grasp his prey in Morocco – in defiance of an international agreement stipulating that action there should be multilateral – Delcassé fell from office in 1905. But French predation resumed anyway, provoking successive crises with an unconsulted Germany, each time threatening a war in Europe, but ending with the successful subjugation of the Sultanate by France, a triumph for machinations by the Quai d'Orsay, champion of a forward policy in Africa. Regardless of what government was in office, its permanent staff could behave like a law unto itself, controlling a hidden surveillance system that enabled it to wiretap ministers and produce or withhold what diplomatic documents suited it, for blackmail or other purposes. In 1912 this autonomy came to an end with the arrival of a tough politician of the right as prime minister, Raymond Poincaré, a lawyer from Lorraine bent on recovering the provinces taken from France by Germany. Planting close associates in key positions at the Foreign Office, he set about imposing his own preferences on it. Elected president of the republic the following year, he did not relax his grip on foreign policy, where his priorities were to increase the size and arsenal of the army, strengthen France's alliance with Russia, and tighten its entente with Britain.

Within months of assuming the presidency, Poincaré gave a critical new twist to the pact with Russia. By the terms of the military convention between them of 1893, each state was obliged to attack Germany if Germany attacked the other. The document had also contained an article specifying that if any member of the Triple Alliance of the period – Germany, Austro-Hungary or Italy – mobilized its forces, France and Russia would automatically and without needing to consult each other mobilize theirs. But France had at least twice declined to give effect to this provision, and in 1911 had secured its alteration to just such a requirement for Paris and St Petersburg to consult each other if Austria mobilized. On an official visit to Russia in the summer of 1912, however, Poincaré was shown the text of the treaty between Serbia and Bulgaria preparatory to the First Balkan War that was about to be unleashed. There he noted that it contained 'the seeds of a war not only against Turkey but against Austria', and established 'the hegemony of Russia over the two Slav kingdoms'. Whereupon, on returning to Paris, he promised that if Russia intervened against Austria in a Balkan conflict (backed inevitably by Germany), France would not hesitate to fight at its side.[7] A year later French arms and capital were flowing into the Balkans, and Paris had extended compulsory military service from two to three years. Should such a war break out, Poincaré – overriding the plans of his chief of staff to launch an offensive against Germany in the west, let alone through Belgium – banked on the Russian Army, much larger than that of France, to unleash a crushing assault on Germany in the east.

Another state visit to St Petersburg had been arranged for the summer of 1914. Poincaré, accompanied by his prime minister, set off by sea in mid-July more than two weeks after the killings in Sarajevo, as Austria was preparing its ultimatum to Serbia. His friend Maurice Paléologue, whom he had installed as head of the political department at the Quai d'Orsay, was now the French ambassador to Russia. Three days of confidential talks and ceremonial banquets with the Tsar and Sazonov, the Russian foreign minister, followed. Afterwards Poincaré made sure that not a line was recorded of what passed between them, and that a diary of the trip cast no shadow on his statecraft of peace and probity. More disinterested testimony to the occasion, from among others the military attaché at the French

---

7. *TS*, pp. 296–7.

embassy, makes it overwhelmingly probable that just as in the Balkan crisis of the winter of 1912, France had made far less effort to restrain Russia than Germany had Austria, so in July 1914 Poincaré incited rather than dissuaded the Tsar when the prospect of war was canvassed. His last words to Nicholas were to stand firm. When, after his departure, the Emperor of All the Russias reluctantly gave the order for mobilization, and Germany replied with a declaration of war, the reaction of the president of France on arriving home was elation.

Russia

In Russia too the starting point of its trajectory into the twentieth century was colonial, not in Africa but in Asia, where the Tsar's ambition to extend his empire from Siberia into Manchuria set off a war with Japan. There on sea and land Russia suffered a heavy defeat in 1905, leading to near revolution at home, not finally suppressed till 1906. To master the crisis required a reorganization of the imperial government, hitherto an autocracy untempered by any constitution, the Tsar appointing and dismissing ministers to a council lacking even a chairman. Now Sergei Witte, responsible for a decade of economic growth and modernization of the country's infrastructure, was given the office of chairman – prime minister in effect – with the right to choose his cabinet, and produced a constitution with a (narrowly) elective parliament. But disliked by the court, he did not last long. His successor Stolypin, more conservative but no less capable, continued his work of controlled political and economic reform. For both men, as for Finance Minister Kokovtsov, Russian foreign policy had to be reoriented, after its debacle in the Far East, back to Europe.

There Britain, long concerned at the potential military threat of superior Russian troop strength and shorter lines of communication to India, the most valuable of all London's overseas possessions, had been angling for a deal to abate competition between the two empires where they faced each other in Central Asia and the Near East. To these overtures the new 'united government' in St Petersburg became receptive. In 1907 an Anglo-Russia Convention was reached, a warier arrangement than the Entente Cordiale, but one that for Stolypin and like-minded associates reduced the risk of foreign adventures, allowing concentration on the priority of domestic consolidation. The Tsar, however, put out by the novel autonomy of the government from his person, and retaining the power to receive any minister he wished, colluded with the diplomat charged with the Foreign Ministry, Alexander Izvolsky, in an ambitious scheme – unknown to other ministers of contrary direction – for an expansionist bargain with Austria in the Balkans. Russia would consent to Austrian annexation of Bosnia, in exchange for Austrian support of rights of free passage to Russian warships through the Straits from the Black Sea to the Mediterranean. The deal, however, backfired when Austria absorbed Bosnia in 1908 but Russia failed to gain the consent of any other power, let alone the Ottoman Empire itself, to a revision of the regime reached at the Congress of Berlin blocking its goal in the Straits. Whereupon, amid pan-Slav agitation and international uproar, Russia sought to renege on its green light to Vienna on Bosnia, but in 1909 was forced by an ultimatum from Germany to accept Austria's incorporation of the area into the Habsburg Empire – a humiliation bitterly resented by nationalist opinion in Russia, which led to Izvolsky's fall.

His successor was Stolypin's brother-in-law Sergey Sazonov, a junior functionary in the Foreign Ministry when he was put in charge of it in 1910. A year later his patron was assassinated. Lacking much steadiness of direction, Sazonov's principal concern became to recoup Russia's position in the Balkans. Italy's invasion of Libya had encouraged Bulgaria and Serbia to strike their own blow at the Ottoman Empire, creating a league counselled by Russia – to which Montenegro and Greece adhered – to attack it. Should the gains from their joint onslaught give rise to dispute, Russia would be arbiter of them. In the autumn the Balkan League launched its attack. Confounding expectations, it met with such rapid success that within six weeks the Balkans were cleared of Turkish power and Bulgarian forces had reached the last defensive line outside Constantinople. Disconcerted by the speed of the League's victory, and the risk that Bulgaria might deprive Russia of the Ottoman capital that was its own strategic objective, when its two Slav protégés fell over the division of territorial spoils in Macedonia, Russia made no attempt to arbitrate the dispute – in which the terms of the original agreement between Sofia and Belgrade favoured Bulgaria – and no difficulties at the outbreak of a Second Balkan War, in which Serb, Greek, Turkish and (decisively) Romanian troops overwhelmed Bulgaria, depriving it of all its gains in the First War. The net outcome of the fighting was thus not an unqualified success for Russia. Its emissaries in the Balkans, where there was little coordination of policy from St Petersburg, had not followed a uniform line, and Bulgaria – linguistically and geographically closest of the Slav states in the region to Russia – was now politically lost to it. But Russia was now more deeply involved in the Balkans than it had ever been since its setback at the Congress of Berlin in 1878.

At home, on the other hand, its position was now considerably strengthened. Powered by foreign investment, Russia's manufacturing base had grown by leaps and bounds, its grain exports were soaring, its armed forces modernized, its nationalist press baying at full volume. The caution of Witte and Stolypin was no longer in season, revenge for its discomfiture over Bosnia in sight. On the eve of the Second Balkan War, Sazonov could write to Hartwig, the Russian ambassador in Belgrade, an ultra whose status there was often regarded as virtually that of a viceroy, that 'Serbia's promised land lies in the territory of today's Austria-Hungary', adding: 'Time is working for Serbia and for the downfall of her enemies, who already show clear signs of decomposition'.[8] Confidence that the Habsburg Empire was an anachronism doomed by history was by now common among Russian elites, and Paris was aware of this. From its point of view a 'Balkan inception scenario' – as Clark coins it – offered an opportunity to settle accounts with Berlin. 'By the spring of 1914', he remarks, 'the Franco-Russian Alliance had constructed a geopolitical trigger along the Austro-Serbian frontier. They had tied the defence policy of three of the world's greatest powers to the uncertain fortunes of Europe's most violent and unstable region.'[9] When the July crisis came, the high command in St Petersburg, never on the best terms with civilian ministers, was as eager for war as its counterparts in every other major power, but it did not have to strain unnecessarily at the leash. On learning that Austria had issued a declaration of war against Serbia – words that remained empty for another two weeks since its army was not ready for an invasion – the council of ministers, Sazonov in the lead, did not hesitate: Germany was behind Austria's action, and immediate mobilization against it was required. The Tsar consented to give the order, then conscience-stricken, countermanded it: 'I will not be responsible for a monstrous slaughter.' The next day Sazonov prevailed on Nicholas to reverse himself.

---

8. *TS*, pp. 349–50.
9. *TS*, p. 350.

Germany

After his victory over France in 1870, Bismarck consolidated it with a pact between the conservative monarchies of Russia, Germany and Austria, the *Dreikaiserbund* of 1873, whose combined power was designed to ensure a stable European peace. Soon Balkan revolts against Ottoman rule disrupted the scheme, Russian war against Turkey leading to the Congress of Berlin where Bismarck, forced to choose between his allies, opted for Austria at the expense of Russia, and the following year sealed a secret treaty with it obliging each country to aid the other if either were attacked by Russia. That, however, was an eventuality he wanted above all to avoid, renewing the *Dreikaiserbund* in 1881 and 1884, and when it lapsed three years later concluded an – also secret – Reinsurance Treaty with Russia. France, held in check within Europe, he encouraged to expand its colonial empire overseas, the kind of possessions on which he set no great value, regarding them as mostly a waste of money. Yet within imperial Germany, there was an active and organized colonial lobby that regarded them as the natural perquisite of a Great Power, and increasingly pressed for their acquisition. Needing to retain control of the Reichstag, Bismarck could see that colonies were electorally quite popular, so matter-of-factly took part in the Scramble for Africa in the eighties, in 1884 arranging the conference in Berlin which divided up much of the 'Dark Continent' among assorted predators. Germany's entry into the colonial lists, along with its other members, was uncontentious: was any European state in a position to object?

In 1890 the new kaiser, Wilhelm II – he was still in his twenties – dismissed Bismarck. Vested with less power than Nicholas II, though far more than Edward VII or George V, he was the most intelligent and energetic of the monarchs of period, not a high bar to pass, but also the least balanced or secure; incapable of sustained attention, consistent judgment, or any understanding of himself or others; behind a barrage of bluster, he was a jumble of prejudices and phobias, vanities and frivolities, revelling in the limelight. The attention he attracted as a public figure exceeded by a wide margin his political importance, since the constitution Bismarck had conferred on Germany in unifying it, designed for himself rather than for the emperor who appointed him, centralized power in the office of the chancellor – of which there was no equivalent in Russia, or Austro-Hungary – rather than in the title of the emperor. Not that even this office, once Bismarck was gone, enjoyed any plenitude of it, since the structure of the state was federal, its heteroclite units retaining differing rights and legal systems of their own, restricting in particular the taxes the centre could raise, and so the budgets it could afford. Masking this weakness from foreign view was, on the other hand, the sheer growth and wealth of the German economy as a whole, which in the Wilhelmine epoch came to possess the largest GDP and literate population, not to speak of the most advanced scientific and technological establishment, in Europe.

The Iron Chancellor gone, Germany's first diplomatic move after Bismarck's dismissal was to decline to renew the country's Reinsurance Treaty with Russia, a decision taken in 1890 for which not Wilhelm II but the Foreign Office in Berlin was responsible. Two years later came the beginnings of the Franco-Russian Alliance. Germany was now facing the danger Bismarck had always most feared, the possibility of a war on two fronts. Nor were relations with Britain improved when the kaiser congratulated the president of the republic of Transvaal for routing the Jameson raid, a venture for which London denied any responsibility, but which aroused pro-Boer sympathies across Europe. Worse, in a number of British eyes, ensued in 1897–98. In the Reichstag, the chancellor of the period, Bernhard von Bülow, delivered a speech announcing that Germany now sought a 'place in the sun', not at the expense of other Great Powers, but alongside them, as the natural aim of its *Weltpolitik* – left undefined, but generally understood as a codeword for expansion overseas. The following year the Reichstag approved the proposal by Tirpitz, the country's leading naval hawk, for the construction of a major battle fleet, privately motivated to the kaiser as necessary to compete with Britain.

For Clark, these were the clumsy gestures of a belated empire, which had never historically had colonies, and now when it acquired the means of doing so, found to its frustration that most of the Earth had already been taken by the maritime powers of Europe, virtually all of them smaller and weaker than itself. In this as in other arenas, it was a parvenu, liable to gauche blunders raising diplomatic hackles among more seasoned practitioners. In itself, the kaiser's telegram to Kruger was little more than mildly worded gesture politics, and Tirpitz's naval programme too was 'neither an outrageous nor an unwarranted move', given that 'Germans had ample reason to believe they would not be taken seriously till they had acquired a credible naval weapon'.[10] In the event, the *Reichsmarine* never came near competing in number of warships, let alone bases, with the Royal Navy, and by 1913 Tirpitz publicly accepted it could not do so. In both countries, the press magnified the abrasions between the two empires out of all proportion. The 1890s was also a decade, after all, in which the possibility of an Anglo-German alliance was seriously mooted within the British Cabinet.

Matters changed with the emergence of the Entente Cordiale

---

10. *TS*, p. 148.

in 1904. To the Franco-Russian pincers around Germany were now added the risk of a British maritime extension to them, which it became an aim of the Reich's foreign policy to break up. To the south, French penetration of Morocco offered Berlin an opportunity to try to do so. Germany's defence of Moroccan sovereignty against French colonial pretensions, treated by Paris and London as a crude provocation, was legally irreproachable, as Clark points out. But its practical effect consolidated, rather than weakened the Entente Cordiale, whose partners closed ranks around France's actions and rallied Russia and America to their side. On the Reich's eastern flank, Austrian annexation of Bosnia could claim a quasi-legal basis in the provisions of the Congress of Berlin, which had envisaged ultimate conversion of administration into possession of the province, but Germany's ultimatum enforcing it completed Russian hostility to the country that had once been its closest ally. Two years later, the second Morocco crisis triggered by French military pressure on Fez saw another futile attempt by Germany to assert counter-claims of its own, ratcheting up tensions in Europe for what in the end were paltry gains elsewhere in Africa. On the other hand, in the Balkan wars which followed, out of which Austria emerged strategically the great loser, Germany was a moderating force: 'Berlin was far more restrained in its advice to Vienna than Paris was in its communications with St Petersburg.'[11]

What of its role in the final crisis unchained at Sarajevo? In the winter of 1912, as fighting still raged in the Balkans, the kaiser summoned an emergency meeting of the country's military leaders to his palace, at which he declared that Austria must stand firm against Serbia, Germany support Austria if attacked by Russia, throw most

---

11. *TS*, p. 334.

of its forces against France, torpedo British troop ships, step up submarine production, and ensure the press 'prepare the popularity of a war against Russia'. Chief of Staff Moltke concurred that war was unavoidable and the sooner it came the better. Was this proof of a premeditated plan to engulf Europe in hostilities? Hardly. The kaiser's outburst was a response to a warning by Grey that if a European war started in the Balkans, its consequences would be unpredictable – that is, pretty clearly, Britain might join France and Russia against the Central Powers. Wilhelm sounded off, as he often did, Moltke repeated a refrain common in the top brass of both armed camps in Europe, Bethmann Hollweg – chancellor of the realm – learnt of the conclave only later, and nothing more was heard of it. When in July 1914 an emissary from Vienna arrived to report Austria's determination to attack Serbia after the assassinations in Sarajevo, the kaiser – in the absence of Bethmann Hollweg, and this time without even consulting his military chiefs – issued his unconditional approval of such retribution, what became known after the war as his famous 'blank cheque'. But no sooner did the news come that Britain was attempting mediation than he changed his tune, and once he learnt of the Serbian reply to Austria's ultimatum, rejoiced that peace was now secure. In all, a typical performance: apocalyptic bluster, heedless commitment, hasty beating of retreat, overexcited relief, none of it determinant of actions decided by the chancellor, Foreign Office and General Staff. It was news of Russian mobilization that induced Germany's declaration of war, given the Franco-Russian alliance issued against France as well as Russia, and the apolitical rigidity of Germany's military leadership – its blind adherence to the Schlieffen Plan – that propelled the invasion of Belgium as the best pathway into France, which brought Britain into the war.

Britain

The starting point of its foreign policy too was a set of imperial concerns. Offshore to Europe, confident of its maritime supremacy, it had long been traditional for Britain to keep a 'free hand' among the Great Powers by avoidance of formal alliance with any of them, while expanding its empire overseas. In southern Africa, however, the Boer War had delivered a shock, initial military defeats and later guerrilla resistance bringing home to London the weakness of its army and the isolation of its position in Europe, where sympathies were overwhelmingly pro-Boer. Allies were clearly needed, as they had not been since Napoleon, and when Salisbury retired in 1902, the Conservative government that succeeded his long-running regime lost no time in seeking them. In 1902 it signed a treaty with Japan designed to restrain Russia in the Far East, and in 1904 a pact with France to restrain it from causing trouble in Egypt in exchange for its freedom to take hold of Morocco. In early 1906, a general election put the Liberals in power. The party was more divided than the Conservatives – there had been sharp differences over the Boer War – since it contained a substantial Radical wing suspicious of foreign entanglements, as well as a group firmly committed to the defence and growth of the British Empire. Royal and Conservative fears were allayed when leaders of the latter acquired control of the Foreign Office, War Office and Exchequer in the new government. There would be bipartisan continuity in the diplomatic conduct of the country.

The new Liberal government was immediately confronted with the first Moroccan crisis. It was in no position to question the legitimacy of France's bid for another colony, having approved it in advance. Nor was its new foreign secretary, Sir Edward Grey, scion of the most powerful Whig family in the history of the party, in any mood to do so, closing ranks with Paris against Berlin's challenge to its right to reduce the local sultan to a pawn, as London had the khedive in Egypt. Secret military talks with France, hidden from the Cabinet, discussed joint operations against Germany if war should be required, amid what Clark terms 'astonishing' levels of aggressive reaction within the Foreign Office – which Grey would occupy for the next nine years – a record unique on the continent, making him 'without doubt the most powerful foreign minister of pre-war Europe'.[12] Enjoying a reputation in the political class and the public as devoid of ambition, the soul of decency and honour, he nevertheless possessed – so Clark – a healthy appetite for power and notable skill at surreptitious manoeuvres, as well as strong convictions on the way that peace, as he saw it, could best be kept and the empire defended. Vigilance against German presumption was needed for both. By the summer of 1906 this had been seen off over Morocco, but phobic views of Berlin remained pronounced in the officials around him – nowhere more stridently expressed than in the memorandum of January 1907 circulated by Eyre Crowe, a functionary in its Western department, which Clark – the only occasion when *The Sleepwalkers* departs from measured treatment of all its dramatis personae – subjects to a blistering critique.[13]

Grey, who found Crowe's document 'valuable', himself had wider concerns, which he achieved six months later. On taking office, he had written of his determination to 'see Russia re-established in the councils of Europe, and I hope on better terms than she has been yet'.[14] Like his predecessor Lansdowne, he saw the entente he inherited with

---

12. *TS*, p. 200.
13. *TS*, pp. 162–4.
14. *TS*, p. 140.

France as a stepping stone to the same kind of understanding with Russia, neutralizing the threat it represented to Britain's imperial holdings in Asia, as the former had in Africa. In August 1907 a satisfactory convention with St Petersburg was reached, explicitly concerned with the three regions where the rival interests of the respective empires abutted on each other: Persia, Afghanistan and Tibet. As with France, Grey was careful not to proceed from this arrangement to a formal alliance with Russia – the claim to a free hand still mattered – but within a few years was writing and speaking in confidence of the 'Triple Entente', as a counter to the Triple Alliance composed of Germany, Austro-Hungary and Italy, while his officials did so more freely. The polarization of Europe into two blocs had been completed, though Italy would in due course defect from one camp to the other.

France and Russia were military allies, declared as such. Britain was not one, but when its mettle as a geopolitical partner was tested in the second Morocco crisis of 1911, it passed with flying colours. German attempts to hinder the further consolidation of France's grip on Morocco, naturally resisted by Paris, were met with a threat from London exceeding any pronouncement by its partner across the channel whose actions had provoked the crisis. Without informing the Cabinet, Grey conferred with Asquith and Lloyd George – respectively now prime minister and chancellor of the Exchequer – over a speech for Lloyd George to deliver at Mansion House, in which he announced that if 'the place and prestige' of Britain 'among the Great Powers of the world' were sacrificed to peace – the reference to Morocco, not spelt out, was clear – such a surrender would amount to 'an intolerable humiliation for a great nation like ours to endure'. In effect, this was the first public threat of war by one major power to another in Europe since 1870, all the more striking for the fact that, as Clark puts it, 'to a greater extent than either of the two quarrelling parties, Britain was willing to consider the possibility of a drastic escalation'.[15] Germany settled meekly enough some months later.

When Italy, seeing how easily France had seized Morocco, decided to follow suit by taking Libya for itself, on the pretext that Italians were not being properly treated by the Ottoman authorities there, Grey offered an 'astonishingly favourable' green light to Rome's conquest of the province, telling its ambassador in London that if maltreatment of its nationals forced Italy to intervene, he would tell Constantinople that 'the Turkish government could not expect anything else', and instructed the Foreign Office that Britain must do nothing to obstruct Italian designs.[16] The integrity of the Ottoman Empire, which had once been a traditional British concern, no longer applied. The Balkan wars triggered by Italy's attack on it, drawing Russia ever deeper into the regional hinterland of Constantinople, led to Britain hosting a conference on the fate of Albania, by which time Grey could hint that Russian hopes of a change in the Straits might be accommodated too.[17] Whatever misgivings he might feel about the escalation of disputes in the Balkans, Britain's dependence on its alliance with Russia meant that it could not afford to antagonize it there.

When the final crisis of 1914 erupted, the news from Sarajevo came as a remote distraction to the British Cabinet and political class as a whole, preoccupied above all by Ireland, where the prospect of Home Rule had already led to quasi-mutiny in the army at Curragh, and threatened to see Conservative connivance

---

15. *TS*, pp. 210–11.
16. *TS*, pp. 245–6.
17. Once the First World War had broken out, he agreed to hand over Constantinople itself, 'the greatest strategic prize' of the conflict, to Russia.

at civil war. But it could not have been a surprise to Grey, for as we have seen, he had predicted just the sequence of events that would lead to European war when the Balkan conflicts were unleashed in the winter of 1912[18] – in words that so panicked Wilhelm II that he called his emergency 'council of war' to discuss how to react to them. Grey thus perceived, as clearly as Poincaré and perhaps even before him, the Balkan inception scenario as Clark describes it. Unlike Poincaré, he did not incite or welcome it. But nor did he take any action to resist it, since to do so risked the goodwill of his partners in the undeclared Triple Entente. But once Russian mobilization had set the ball rolling towards the European war he had foreseen, he made sure that the Cabinet would fall into line behind St Petersburg and Paris by threatening to resign if it did not. The German invasion of Belgium swayed colleagues who might otherwise have resisted, though taken as no more than a convenient pretext by others who sided with Grey anyway. But as Keith Wilson showed, the decisive factor in Britain's plunge into the war was Liberal fear that if the party were to split, a coalition government with the Conservatives would inevitably ensue, and fight Germany anyway. As duly occurred two years later.

To lay out in this fashion Clark's treatment of the record of each of the major actors in twenty years that ended in 1914 is to do violence to the form of *The Sleepwalkers*, and its purpose, which is to trace the continuous web of interactions between them whose upshot culminated in the First World War – not a balance sheet of the performance of any given state, but an exposition of the dynamic of a plurality of rival autonomous, potentially antagonistic, power centres. In doing this, it brings home the extent of the challenge

---

18. See p. 158 above.

the book represented to what was by then generally taken to be an established consensus about the war, and explains why the all but unanimous public success of the book was one thing, scholarly reception of it, much more mixed, another. The consensus which by and large had held for half a century rested on two beliefs: the natural assumption of the victor states that, though its cost was high, their cause was just, and the belated conversion of the leading defeated power to acceptance that it had provoked the war, and deserved to be held responsible for it. Without directly engaging with either, Clark effectively did away with both. Since many reputations had been built around work presuming or illustrating them, vehement reactions were only to be expected.

The most vocal came from Germany, where Fischer's indictment of the Second Reich as the architect of disaster in 1914 had not only formed two generations of historians but also became a virtual cornerstone of the identity of the *Bundesrepublik*, as an epitome of Western democracy which had made a clean break with the darkest chapters of the country's past. Less overtly national and political, reception in the Anglosphere was more concerned to defend the liberal decency and integrity of the Entente that won the war, rather than dwell only on Germany's bid for world domination, undeniable enough. But the presence of a number of leading German historians, by descent or expatriation, in Britain and the United States ensured an intellectual overlap between the two areas of response. In the *Bundesrepublik*, hostility to *The Sleepwalkers* was orchestrated principally by the country's most widely read cultural-political weekly, *Die Zeit*, where the editor responsible for coverage of history, Volker Ullrich, led the attack with successive broadsides, supported by fire from the *Frankfurter Allgemeine Zeitung* and elsewhere, mustering a battery of historians of left-liberal persuasion

– Heinrich Winkler and Hans-Ulrich Wehler the most prominent – against the book.[19] Ignoring the findings of Fritz Fischer, Clark had whitewashed Germany's guilt for the First World War, producing a narrative that, however well written and seemingly well documented, was a selective regression behind Fischer, catering to conservative longings for an apologia of the country's imperial past, which alone could explain the extraordinary sales of the book in Germany. In an essay of reply, Clark did not have much difficulty dealing with these charges. In the Anglosphere, alongside overwhelmingly favourable press coverage came a number of more careful, but still markedly critical responses to the book by historians – among them Hew Strachan, Keith Neilson, Stephen Schuker, Gordon Martel – committed to conventional opinion of the origins of the First World War.[20] Taking these as normal differences of professional opinion, without tendentious political imputation, Clark had no comparable reason to react to them.

In general, however heated or hostile were overall verdicts on the book, few were short of at least some legitimate observations about it. Two of these warrant mention. Amid the repeated complaints of his German critics that Clark had ignored the historiographic revolution

---

19. See the hostile notices in *Die Zeit*, Volker Ullrich, 'Zündschnur und Pulverfass', 12 September 2013 and '1914: Nun schlitten sie wieder', 16 January 2014; John Röhl, 'Erster Weltkrieg: Jetzt gilt es loszuschlagen!', 22 May 2014; and Heinrich August Winkler, 'Weltkrieg: und erlöse uns von der Kriegsschuld', 31 July 2014; as well as Lothar Machtan, 'Over-sophisticated – Anmerkungen zu Christopher Clarks Bestseller', *Sehepunkte*, 15 January 2014, and Hans-Ulrich Wehler, 'Beginn einer neuen Epoche Weltkriegsgeschichte', *Frankfurter Allgemeine Zeitung*, 7 May 2014.

20. Respectively, *International Affairs*, March 2014 (Strachan); *European History Quarterly*, July 2014 (Neilson); *New Criterion*, January 2015 (Schuker); *American Historical Review*, June 2015 (Martel).

accomplished by Fischer, Wehler noted, accurately enough, that he had not accorded the German political landscape the same scale of coverage as that of Serbia (or Austro-Hungary). That, however, was not just a function of the reality that these were so much less known or discussed in much of the standard literature on the war, but also of the fact that Clark had already devoted an entire book to the political career of the last kaiser and its institutional and social setting in the Second Reich, with plenty of references to Fischer's ideas about these.[21] As to Serbia, *The Sleepwalkers* would be the object of numerous Serb attacks, culminating in a bulky philippic against Habsburg misrule in which Clark figures as a perpetual Aunt Sally, assailed for ignorant misrepresentation of Apis, the Bosnian boys and much else. The title of the work – *Folly and Malice* – speaks for itself; though in this case too, amid a mass of disobliging aspersions, ordinary empirical correction of details, to which any work of scholarship is liable, especially one dealing with a clandestine conspiracy, can surely be found.[22] If national passions have clearly sharpened such German and Serbian reactions to *The Sleepwalkers*, other kinds of reservation will no doubt emerge as time goes on. So far, however, beyond the admiration for manifest accomplishments, or the objection to specific arguments, that it has attracted, it is fair to say that the book has not received the considered analytic assessment that it deserves.

---

21. *Kaiser Wilhelm II: A Life in Power*, London 2000; a portrait of remarkable moral-psychological balance and political insight.

22. John Zametica, *Folly and Malice: The Habsburg Empire, the Balkans and the Start of World War One*, London 2017; the author was a spokesman for the breakaway Serb Republic in Bosnia, and testified for Radovan Karadžić at his trial in the Hague; see Mark Cornwall's review of his book in the *Times Literary Supplement*, 3 April 2018.

Where to Begin?

There, like many of even the finest works of history, *The Sleepwalkers* is subject to certain limitations. The most significant of these raise questions of construction rather than of postulation, two of them involving omission, one semi-commission. All three derive from the standpoint that Clark adopted in writing the book, and made it the tour de force it became. In his introduction, he explains that its focus would be on *how* the First World War came about, rather than *why* it did so. The latter issue, he suggested, tended to lead historians to look for 'remote and categorical' causes of an essentially abstract character – alliance systems, arms race, high finance, nationalism, codes of honour, imperialism – that bore little relation to the actual promptings of those who took the decisions that led to war in 1914.[23] To understand these, it was necessary rather to follow the key actors and events of the set of states that became belligerents, at close heuristic range. The product of that option is deeply impressive: in its own terms, it could not be bettered. But those terms left a question open: what was the appropriate starting point for the story it unfolded? The centenary of the war saw the publication of more than one book recounting, in not dissimilar style, just the last month before its outbreak. Clark's history is not so point-blank as that. But in beginning chronologically with the Franco-Russian Alliance of the 1890s, after a page or so of retrospect going back to the Franco-Prussian War of 1870, it pays an analytic price.

Perhaps nowhere more visibly than in the regional setting with which it opens, where chapters on Serbia and Austro-Hungary supply the book's *coup d'éclat*. But innovative and gripping as each of them

---

23. *TS*, p. xxvii.

is, neither is really framed in the way it might have been, and should be, as part of a longer history of south-eastern Europe, once the French Revolution had broken out and expanded into the conquests of Napoleon. At the Congress of Vienna the victors over Napoleon restored the dynasties he had displaced, and imposed a Great Power system on Europe designed to repress any new attempts at revolution, and any resumption of wars among themselves that might risk them – a pact of monarchical solidarity that came to be called the Council of Europe. The pentarchy composing it consisted of Britain, Russia, Austria, Prussia and France. Excluded from the discussions at Vienna and the arrangements that followed from it was the Ottoman Empire, as a Muslim power which had not participated in the struggle against Napoleon, camped on the continent since the fifteenth century, ruling a population of Christians.

In the eighteenth century, two European empires had expanded at its expense – Austria advancing south towards the Danube into the Balkans, and Russia taking Crimea and Podolia around the Black Sea. Ideological allies after 1815, in south-eastern Europe they were also geopolitical rivals. Austria had a longer land frontier and shared ethnic communities with the Ottoman realm; Russia shared the religion of most of the Christian subjects of the sultan, and belonged to the same language family as about half of them. Initially, both regarded nationalism as a pernicious legacy of the French Revolution, capable of stirring up further trouble against the reigning dynastic order in Europe, but quite soon their attitude to its emergence as a popular force in the Balkans started to differ: Austria fearing that its spread, inspired by the example of fellow Slavs across the border, threatened the security of its own empire, Russia realizing that appeals to faith and/or kinship could serve it as a lever for a power of its own in the peninsula. The two empires thus soon diverged in their attitude to the sultanate. For Vienna it was an ideal state with which to share a frontier, no longer a threat, but a partner in hostility to ethnic unrest, and so 'the best of neighbours', whereas for St Petersburg it became a decaying enemy suppressing co-religionists, whose territory could be further reduced if favourable opportunities created by them arose. Twice they did, and each time a Russo-Turkish war ensued: in 1828, after the Greek revolution against Ottoman rule, and in 1877 after Serb and Bulgar revolts against the Ottomans. Both times, pressure from Austria supported by Britain and France prevented Russia from reaping the full fruits of its victory.

Not that Russia ever welcomed national revolutions as such – Alexander I had been as alarmed as Metternich by the Greek revolt when it broke out, and Alexander III was furious with the insolence of Bulgarian attempts to act like a sovereign state. When a much stronger and more advanced movement in Hungary threatened the Habsburg Empire itself, Nicholas I did not hesitate to dispatch an army in 1849 to crush it. Whether Schwarzenberg, the strongman of the Austrian absolutism that Russian intervention had saved, subsequently said – or whether the dictum was merely attributed to him – 'we shall astonish the world with our ingratitude', hardly matters, since Austrian conduct during the Crimean conflict that started four years later with an Ottoman declaration of war on Russia, backed by expeditionary forces from France and Britain, lived up to it. Ignoring the demonstration of monarchical solidarity to which it owed its survival, without actually attacking Russia the Habsburg Empire occupied the principalities whose territory now form part of Romania, pinning down tsarist armies in Galicia that were needed to defend Crimea, ensuring Russia's defeat in the first war between the Great Powers since 1815. Its golden rule broken, the Vienna system was finished. France, then Prussia, were soon attacking Austria, then France and Prussia were at war. For twenty years thereafter Bismarck's diplomacy, operating as a one-man surrogate for the Council of Europe of old, kept the Great Powers at peace. But the Balkans remained beyond even his powers of regulation, though he attempted to apply them. For political purposes it was, as it had been from the beginning, a free-fire zone within Europe, which would bring the truce between the Great Powers sworn at Vienna to its apocalyptic ending a century later in Sarajevo.

Gaps and Absences

It was the historian Edward Ingram who, some twenty years ago, pinpointed the Balkans as a structural gap in the order established at Vienna, and traced its consequences: the export of a bellicism banned in the core of the system to a periphery left outside it, where its writ never ran, and the violence this fomented, erupting in successive interactions between popular turbulence below and imperial predation from above, and ricocheting to devastating effect back into the core: first at mid-century in the Crimean War, and ultimately in the Great War.[24] Ingram was a historian of the British Empire in Persia and India, not of Europe, so the absence of his work on Clark's horizon is no reproach. What it underscores, however, is the cost of starting a modern history of the origins of the Great War too late, severed from the legacy of the Restoration, and why and where this broke down. This was not Clark's concern when he wrote *The Sleepwalkers*, so is not in itself a fault. But it points to what could be one. His gaze is

---

24. See his landmark essay, 'Bellicism as Boomerang: The Eastern Question during the Vienna System', in Peter Krüger and Paul Schroeder (eds), '*The Transformation of European Politics, 1763–1848*': *Episode or Model in Modern History?*, Münster 2002, pp. 205–25.

oriented more to the possible parallels to the events of 1914 lying in the future – that is, our present – than to the sources of these in a past remoter than his optic extends. In the former, his analogies can strain: Serbia described in the jargon of the State Department as 'a rogue state', the assassins of Sarajevo projected as forerunners of postmodern terrorism, Prime Minister Pašić embellished as 'a statesman of unparalleled skill at the head of a mass party'.[25] In the latter, his accuracy can lapse: depicting Metternich as at heart a flexible British-style Whig, who accepted the creation of a Greek nation-state forged in revolution, even writing that 'conflicts and crises on the southeastern periphery, where the Ottoman Empire abutted Christian Europe were nothing new', but 'the European system had always accommodated them without endangering the peace of Europe as a whole'.[26] Ingram would have lifted an ironic eyebrow.

If the historical continuity of the Balkan gap is missing, even denied, in *The Sleepwalkers*, its omission is related to what might appear another and larger absence, even if this is never complete. In scanting the abstractions too often pursued by historians as causes of the First World War, Clark's initial list of examples is 'imperialism, nationalism, armaments, alliances, high finance, ideas of national honour, the mechanics of mobilization', in that order. These can 'bring a certain analytical clarity', Clark writes, but their effect is to reduce political actors to mere involuntary executants of such remote forces. The war, however, was a consequence of 'decisions made by political actors with conscious objectives', based on the best information each had to hand. 'Nationalism, armaments, alliances and finances were all part of the story,' he goes on to observe, 'but

---

25. *TS*, pp. xxv–xxvi, 59.
26. *Revolutionary Spring*, pp. 250–2; *TS*, p. 242.

they can be made to carry real explanatory weight only if they can be seen to have shaped the decisions that – in combination – made war break out'. The two passages occur within a few lines of each other.[27] Is it significant, or merely inadvertent, that imperialism, which heads the first – essentially dismissive – list, disappears from the second – conditionally permissive – one? *Lapsus calami* or decision to delete? The evidence in the work that follows is mixed.

The term 'imperialism' is certainly far from being any keynote or leitmotif of the book. But nor is it particularly scouted. One reason for the ambiguity of its showings in the tale is probably its indeterminacy – too many dissonant meanings of imperialism, with different origins, for it to have any single, generally accepted definition; to which can be added its use as a pejorative jeer-word flung at Marxism as the purveyor of an exploded theory of it, calculated to deter any serious historian from adopting the term. In reality, as so often, such prejudice is the fruit of ignorance. For Marx, as for most of his contemporaries, the meaning of the word 'imperialism' – it was how the term first gained currency – was the vainglorious self-promotion of Louis Bonaparte to the title of emperor, in imitation of his uncle, and no more. It was later attached to the wave of new colonial annexations that European states competed to acquire in the last quarter of the nineteenth century, which prompted Hobson to develop the first serious theory of imperialism. It was on this work that Lenin largely built his own account of it, which appeared during the First World War itself, and has since been widely misread. This is in part because the brochure, as he called it, that bears the title *Imperialism*, composed in 1916, was designed for publication in Russia, where it would have to pass the tsarist censorship, so nowhere does it even mention the First World

---

27. *TS*, p. xxvii.

War that occasioned it, about which Lenin could only write elsewhere with freedom in neutral Switzerland.[28] As he explained when it was published in St Petersburg after the fall of Tsarism:

> This pamphlet was written with an eye to the tsarist censorship. Hence, I was not only forced to confine myself strictly to an exclusively theoretical, specifically economic analysis of facts, but to formulate the few necessary observations on politics with extreme caution, by hints, in an allegorical language – in that accursed Aesopian language – to which tsarism compelled all revolutionaries to have recourse whenever they took up the pen to write a 'legal' work. It is painful, in these days of liberty, to re-read the passages of the pamphlet which have been distorted, cramped, compressed in an iron vice on account of the censor

– a caveat typically ignored in later commentary on the text in the West, where attention has since focused overwhelmingly on the argument of the censor-curtailed brochure, which would take competition between big trusts powered by finance capital for monopoly control over outlying markets and raw materials as the driver of imperialist expansion, unaware that this was not the capstone of Lenin's case, set out in his political interventions of the time.

In these, he made it clear that it was not finance capital as such, a relatively recent phenomenon, which had ignited the war, but a deeper structural feature of capitalism, long preceding the emergence of trusts, which converted economic competition between firms into military conflicts between states. That was *uneven development* – Lenin's own specific, original contribution to an understanding of the imperialism of his time. If – he wrote – 'uneven development and

---

28. Lenin, 'Preface to the French and German Editions', *Collected Works*, Vol. 22, Moscow 1964, p. 189.

wretched conditions of the masses are the fundamental and inevitable conditions and constitute premises of this mode of production',[29] the contemporary world had seen a dramatic intensification of this process. 'On the whole capitalism is growing far more rapidly than before', but 'this growth is becoming more and more uneven'.[30] It was therefore an error to believe that 'the domination of finance capital *lessens* the unevenness and contradictions inherent in the world economy, whereas in reality it *increases* them'.[31] After 1871, 'Germany grew strong three or four times faster than England or France; Japan about ten times faster than Russia. There is and can be no other way of testing the real strength of a capitalist state than that of war.' For 'under capitalism, the even economic growth of individual enterprises, or individual states, is impossible. There is nothing else that periodically restores the disturbed equilibrium than crises in industry and wars in politics.'[32]

New Imperialism

In Europe, Germany had within a few decades overtaken Britain as the leading industrial power, but its share of the planet outside Europe was a pittance compared with the empire Britain possessed, less than a tenth of it. How else was the disparity to be corrected than on the battlefield? To call for a United States of Europe, as if there could be any concord between the rival powers of the day, as some well-

---

29. 'Imperialism, the Highest Stage of Capitalism (A Popular Outline)', Ibid., p. 241.
30. Ibid., p. 300.
31. Ibid., p. 272.
32. 'On the Slogan for a United States of Europe', *Collected Works*, Vol. 21, Moscow 1964, p. 341.

meaning socialists were doing, was utopian. 'Uneven economic and political development is an absolute law of capitalism.'[33] Few historical generalizations are exceptionless, and Lenin was wrong to think that the geopolitical logic of uneven development was inevitably war. Britain could cede its global primacy to the United States without resort to arms, as Britain never had the slightest intention of doing to Germany. But within the Europe of the belle époque, which was Lenin's concern at the time, the rule he spelt out held good.

It did so, however, for a reason that escaped his theory, which the other major thinker to develop an original vision of imperialism during the Great War understood. For Schumpeter, imperialism had little or nothing to do with capitalism. Marxist attempts to maintain the contrary were aberrations: most businessmen abhorred war as a disturbance to trade. Imperialism was an ancient phenomenon that had long preceded capitalism, as the first agrarian civilizations, all of them generating a class of warriors, attested.[34] Sociologically, modern imperialism was the product of an atavistic inheritance from the age of absolutism, which bred aristocratic landowners moved by values of honour and fame, for whom warfare was a vocation. This was a class that did not quit the political stage when society ceased to be feudal, but continued to form a vital component of the governing order under capitalism, as a stratum accoutered with culture and accustomed to rule in ways that financiers and manufacturers were not. 'Whoever seeks to understand Europe must not overlook that even today its life, its ideology, its politics are greatly under

---

33. Ibid., p. 342.

34. As Lenin was well aware: 'Colonial policy and imperialism existed before the latest stage of capitalism, and even before capitalism. Rome, founded on slavery, pursued a colonial policy and practised imperialism.' *Collected Works*, Vol. 22, p. 260.

the influence' of a 'war-oriented nobility' of pre-capitalist stamp, for 'while the bourgeoisie can assert its interests everywhere, it "rules" only in exceptional circumstances, and then only briefly'.[35] Export monopolies might benefit from imperialist aggression, but they could not of themselves propel it, whereas along with glory, land had always been a basic value of the aristocratic outlook, so enlargement of territory a natural objective. This was a theory of imperialism, like Lenin's, composed during the First World War, and it too was unable – in Schumpeter's case, precluded by a university post as well as government censorship – to mention it, publishable only in 1919 when it was over.[36] Its sweeping generalizations and psychologistic tack – Assyrian, Persian, Egyptian, Roman, French, Prussian, Russian autocracies cast, if with some differences, into the

---

35. Joseph Schumpeter, *Imperialism and Social Classes*, New York 1955, p. 92. Though in translation the title of his essay has acquired a singular, its German original was plural – 'Zur Soziologie der Imperialismen' – allowing, if not proceeding, to a taxonomy of its subject.

36. The inspiration behind Schumpeter's essay was naturally quite distinct from Lenin's. An Austrian patriot, he bridled at German attempts to subordinate its ally during the war, and by 1917 was hoping for a separate peaceful way out of it, in memoranda designed for the emperor and his court, to be put into practice by a 'grand seigneur' supported by the whole 'higher nobility' of the empire: see *Aufsätze zur Wirtschaftspolitik*, Tübingen 1985, pp. 269–71, and the comments of Richard Swedberg in, *Joseph A. Schumpeter: His Life and Work*, Cambridge 1991, pp. 46–64, much the best biography, and the pioneering research of Ulrich Hedtke, architect of the Schumpeter Archive available at schumpeter.info, and author of successive essays on his findings. It is striking how unaware Schumpeter seems to have been, at the time he was writing it, of the contradiction between his sociology of imperialism, treated as an aristocratic atavism, and the remedy he proposed for it, entrusting command of the state to a grandee from the Austrian nobility conceived in the image of conservative British rulers who had successfully constructed a 'Tory democracy' in which the masses knew their place. He would subsequently generalize this ascription to the argument that it was aristocratic political leadership alone which assured stability to capitalist democracy.

same hamper – would limit its influence even among followers of Schumpeter. The contemporary range of his theory was also overly eurocentric, ignoring the American imperialism of McKinley, TR, Taft and Wilson, in a country without any counterpart to the anciens régimes of the Old World.[37] Yet given that the struggle of 1914–18 was essentially a struggle within Europe, Schumpeter's account cast a light on the Great War ironically complementary to that of Lenin. Together, they make a peculiarly apposite combination for understanding its genesis, though of course – neither was more than a brief sketch – not an adequately documented or complete one.

In the first half of the nineteenth century, the pentarchy of powers that emerged from the Congress of Vienna were all imperial constructions in name and deed, with the exception of Prussia; three of them extending their extra-European possessions without disturbing the peace of Europe by friction between them. In the last quarter of the century, this changed with the advent of what historians have called the New Imperialism – a concerted surge of expansion, in which all the major (and many minor) powers of Europe competed for penetration and seizure of as much of the territory of the earth as they could reach and control. Behind this wave of appropriation lay the impact of two technological developments: the spread of railways, dramatically reducing the time required to cover long distances, and the invention of telegraphy, magically accelerating communications across them. Vast spaces, hitherto typically an encumbrance if not an outright hindrance to the building of an effective apparatus of rule, now became for the first time not only administratively manageable,

---

37. In later years at Harvard, he would revise his verdict on the military-aristocratic atavism of imperialism, observing that there was no essential difference between American 'ethical' and German 'national' imperialism.

but potentially invaluable sources of power projection, as the cases of America and Russia demonstrated.[38] Out of this alteration, the ideology of *Weltpolitik* – first publicly articulated by von Bülow in the Reichstag in 1897, but an outlook shared by all the leading states of the time – arose: the idea that the twentieth century would belong to those states that could secure large portions of the Earth's surface for themselves, and them alone. The dynamic impact of this doctrine within Europe, and the practices that followed from it, were vividly perceived by Paul Schroeder.[39] In *The Sleepwalkers* it is by and large missing. Clark does remark, at the very end of his book that 'the crisis that brought war in 1914 was the fruit of a shared political culture', though without explaining what this might be – and promptly adding: 'But the crisis was also multi-polar and genuinely interactive', the conjunction making clear where the emphasis should fall.[40]

Inordinate Empire

The way in which the fates of the periphery within and without Europe were intimately connected is graphically illustrated by the Balkans. In 1878 Britain, which had intervened to prevent larger Russian gains than the detachment of Serbia and Bulgaria from the

---

38. For this change, see in particular the writing of Richard Langhorne, *The Collapse of the Concert of Europe: International Politics 1890–1914*, London 1981; *The Coming of Globalization: Its Evolution and Contemporary Consequences*, London-New York 2005; and most recently '1914: Anniversary of an Accident or a Design?', *European Review of International Studies*, Summer 2015, pp. 5–18.

39. See his long essay 'International Politics, Peace and War: 1815–1914' in T. C. W. Blanning (ed.), *The Nineteenth Century*, Oxford 2000, at pp. 188–200.

40. *TS*, p. 561. What Clark has in mind by a 'shared political culture' here is probably less the general mind-set of *Weltpolitik* than a cult of masculinity common to the decision-making elites of the period, for which see his reflections on pp. 358–61.

Ottoman Empire, was awarded Cyprus in compensation, and four years later took Egypt, for which France gained compensation in Tunisia. This was followed by a generalized scramble for Africa, Britain and France taking the lion's share, but Belgium and Germany sizeable chunks too, culminating in the seizure of Morocco by France, triggering the annexation of Libya by Italy, which in turn ricocheted back into the Balkan Wars that cleared Macedonia, Thrace and Albania of Ottoman rule, setting the stage for 1914. Elsewhere, the United States was seizing Hawaii, Puerto Rico and the Philippines, Japan taking Taiwan and Korea, and occupying southern Manchuria. Between 1876 and 1914, Lenin would point out, the total area of the world controlled by the six leading colonial powers increased by over 50 per cent, without including Russia's conquests in Central Asia, most of them carried out in the 1860s and early 1870s. In percentage terms, the biggest gains were achieved by France, whose colonial territory multiplied tenfold. But absolutely, it was still no match for the British Empire, over a century older, three times larger in size, seven times in population, proportionately comparable to the Spanish empire of the early sixteenth century as 'inordinate' within the set of powers comprising the imperial state-system of the time[41] – though not structurally by reason of its singularity among its peers as an insular sea-power, whose maritime supremacy was global, terrestrial power relatively more provincial.

The difference between the two was plain from the time of the Congress of Vienna, when the Cabinet in London stipulated that Britain would play its part in the negotiations between the members of the Quadruple Alliance that had defeated Napoleon only on condition its command of the seas was not subject to discussion.

---

41. Perry Anderson, *Lineages of the Absolutist State*, London 2013, pp. 60–1.

Land could be parcelled out as the victors wished, the oceans were for England alone. When in due course *Weltpolitik* became the wisdom of the age, Britain was no slouch in the press for territory – the only colonial power to fight full modern wars to victory from one end of Africa to the other, the Sudan to the Transvaal. The ruler responsible for these, Lord Salisbury, was as sceptical of the value of colonies as Bismarck, and generally more ironical; yet under him the empire swelled as it had not done since the elder Pitt. Grey, an ardent supporter of Kitchener's expedition to Khartoum and Milner's bid to crush 'Kruger's wretched regime', was made of different stuff. Thrilled at the news of fighting against the Boers, he felt a 'stirring all down the backbone', as if in a 'war for freedom' more uplifting than lesser duties on the Northwest frontier or the Nile 'one had no right to be staying and talking', rather than fighting in person;[42] backing Kitchener's concentration camps for the enemy when these were required. On taking office, he was the first foreign minister in Europe proud to have long called himself, explicitly, an 'imperialist' (naturally, a liberal one). He had never set foot in Europe; the only language he knew was English. The one time he had ever left the country at all was to tour the West Indies, on an official mission sent by Chamberlain to the Caribbean wing of the empire. But he knew what the subcontinental wing meant to his class – 'The pride of England would be broken if India were lost' – and built his diplomacy around the priority to keep it. Clark is mistaken to suggest that 'he appears to have cared little for the British Empire'.[43]

---

42. T. G. Otte, *Statesman of Europe*, London 2020, p. 155.
43. *TS*, p. 201. Down to the end, Grey was monitoring operations at the Simla Conference by the Raj (where Hardinge, at the outset his closest confidante in the FO, was by then viceroy) to circumvent Russia and bamboozle China in Tibet. There, in the words of its leading historian, British manoeuvres 'ended in

In the disproportion between the huge size of Britain's accumulated possessions and mastery of the seas that secured it, and the superior efficiency, technology, growth, and military prowess of Germany, lay – as not a few contemporaries, without understanding the idea or knowing the term, sensed – the most explosive charge of uneven development in Europe. But it was not a tension that simply and straightforwardly led to a world war. For that outcome to occur, a further kind of uneven development had to be at work. The most advanced economy and army in the continent had to be tied to the most anomalous polity among the Great Powers. Clark makes a persuasive case for Habsburg success in modernizing its administration, its industry and agriculture, its educational and medical level, even much of its electoral system in the last decades of its existence. Yet he underplays, nevertheless, what had become by the early twentieth century the insuperable abnormality and latent fragility of a purely dynastic structure composed of a plurality of nationalities, lacking any one of them numerically dominant enough to hold it together as a political or social system. It was that last peculiarity which set the Austro-Hungarian Empire apart from the Russian – or even the Ottoman, once severance of its Balkan and Arab provinces had converted it into Turkey.

The historian who saw this most clearly, and wrote about it most eloquently, was Laurence Lafore, not a reference for *The Sleepwalkers*. Everywhere else in Europe, states could by 1914 appeal to nationalism as a basis for popular identification or support. Even where monarchies of the most conservative stripe remained

---

a charade', whose long-term effects – the McMahon Line, battleground in the Sino-Indian War of 1962, still in dispute today, was a byproduct – could only be described as 'something of a disaster': Alastair Lamb, *The McMahon Line: A Study in the Relations between India China and Tibet 1904–1914*, Vol. II, London 1966, pp. 519, 589.

intact, the nation-state had become a signature of modernity. The Habsburg state alone could make no such appeal, and to boot was vulnerable not only to restive nationalities within its borders, but to the intrusive actions of lesser states sharing – or claiming – an ethnic identity with them. 'While Great Powers might be excused for decorous meddling in the affairs of small ones, Austro-Hungary was by 1914 unique in being a Great Power in whose affairs small ones meddled. The [International] System had no procedure for handling such a situation,' wrote Lafore.[44] Finally, the Habsburg elites took matters into their own hands in a last desperate bid to solve it. Treaty-bound to help it, Germany – traditionally unfamiliar and impatient with quarrels in the backward Balkans – was blind to the probable consequences of doing so; Russia, France and England no less, in their reactions to the condensation of imperialist contradictions in south-eastern Europe, as modern and pre-modern forms and forces fused after Sarajevo. Uneven development had released a chain-reaction beyond any collective control.

Somnambulists?

If the legacy of the Balkan gap at the Congress of Vienna, and the dual *Sprengstoff* laid by the fuse of uneven development in the system of empires to which it gave rise, are missing in *The Sleepwalkers*, they are not at variance with it. Matters are somewhat different with the third criticism that can be made of Clark's version of the origins of the First World War. That bears on two interrelated features of his account: its title, and its conclusion. Were the politicians and generals who

---

44. *The Long Fuse: An Interpretation of the Origins of World War I*, Philadelphia 1965, p. 57.

led their countries into the abyss so many somnambulists, unaware of what they were doing? Could the abyss have been avoided? The title of the book failed to persuade a good number of historians, some unsympathetic to Clark's case, others outspoken admirers of it. Hew Strachan, a temperate adherent to Entente orthodoxy, commented: 'To call the principal actors "sleepwalkers" is to suggest that they were unaware of what they were doing, had little conception of war and its dangers, and were not seized of the seriousness of what they were about. The bitter irony is that they knew enough about all these things but, although awake to them, could still not control them.'[45] Gordon Martel, a mordant critic of the book, went further. The title was 'one of the many contradictions at the heart of Clark's book. The image of sleepwalkers, lacking in control, unaware of what they were doing, conflicts with his premise that the key decision-makers "walked toward danger in watchful, calculated steps", that they made their decisions "with conscious objectives". In his determination to absolve Germany and Austria of responsibility Clark reverts to a view popularized by the revisionists of the 1920s. His views would not be out of place in *Die Kriegsschuldfrage* and would have been applauded by Max Montgelas and his fellow editors.'[46] From the opposite camp, Thomas Laqueur too – for whom *The Sleepwalkers* was 'not only the best book on the origins of the First World War I know, but a brilliant and intellectually bracing model for writing history more generally' – demurred at the idea the actors in the story could be regarded as sleepwalkers 'blind to the horrors they were about to bring into the world'.[47] There Clark was wrong on a question that mattered: page

---

45. 'The Origins of the First World War', *International Affairs*, March 2014, p. 435.

46. *American Historical Review*, June 2015, p. 953.

47. 'Some Damn Foolish Thing', *London Review of Books*, 5 December 2013.

after page of his own narrative demonstrated the contrary. It would be Paul Schroeder, finally, who delivered the most telling judgment on the metaphor. He agreed that none of the key decision makers were deliberate warmongers. But the image of blind somnambulists was misleading. Sleepwalking is unconscious behaviour – 'that of a person who wakes up at night to find himself out in the street, not knowing how he had got out of bed or why. That was certainly not how actors played the international game before World War I.'[48]

Clark's reply to these objections has been twofold. He had never said the decision makers of 1914 acted unconsciously. 'On the contrary, they were all constantly scheming and calculating, plotting virtual futures and measuring them against each other.' He had called them sleepwalkers not because they were actually asleep or unconscious, but because he was struck by 'the narrowness of their vision'. It was true that 'the title makes it easy to parody the book, on the basis of a willful misunderstanding of the metaphor'.[49] But – second defence – political leaders in Europe had not made that mistake. *Bundespresident* Frank-Walter Steinmeier, 'a keen reader of history', had cited it as a lesson in the need for caution and circumspection in international relations, as had Helmut Schmidt. In France, François Hollande and Emmanuel Macron had both made the same use of it. Likewise in Greece Yanis Varoufakis. 'These were readings of the book's argument I could live with, as they referenced the complexity of the aetiology advanced in it.'[50] Do these rejoinders settle the matter? Certainly Clark's explanation of what he meant by his title is close to Schroeder's correction of it, without its edge or its amplitude. Still, the

---

48. See below, p. 353.
49. 'Brexiteers, Revisionists and Sleepwalkers', in *Prisoners of Time*, London, 2021, p. 215.
50. 'Brexiteers, Revisionists and Sleepwalkers', pp. 222–3.

question remains whether a metaphor without elucidation or warrant in the text, that is easy to misrepresent, was the best choice for a title of the book. Appeal to its use by politicians, inherently attracted to soundbites, is no vindication of it.

The more serious difficulty lies in the suggestion at the beginning and end of the book which is substantive rather than metaphorical. *The Sleepwalkers*, Clark declares, is 'concerned less with why the war happened than how it happened'. The first approach has a distorting effect, because it 'creates the illusion of a steadily building causal pressure', reducing political actors to mere vectors of forces beyond their control. The second, by contrast, in looking closely at the 'sequences of interactions' between 'decision makers' that generated given outcomes is necessarily 'saturated with agency'. Taking the decision makers as agents allows 'the *why* questions, as it were, to grow naturally out of the *how* questions, rather than the other way round'.[51] In common usage, an agent is typically accompanied by a particular adjective – we speak of a 'free agent': free to choose between alternatives. So it is natural that starting with an emphasis on agency, Clark ends with a stress on contingency – a perspective inspired, he says elsewhere, by Holger Afflerbach: the sense that events did not have to happen as they did, since if other decisions that were possible had been taken in 1914, the war could have been avoided. 'I have tried to remain alert to the fact that the people, events and forces described in this book carried in them the seeds of other, perhaps less terrible futures.'[52]

---

51. *TS*, pp. xxvii–xxviii.
52. *TS*, p. xxix.

Contingency and Origins

How persuasive is this way of framing the book? For the most part, Clark is careful not to commit himself categorically to the thesis that the First World War could well not have happened.[53] He speaks simply of 'the merit of opening the story to an element of contingency', without specifying what, or how large or small, that element might be. But the implication is clear that it is likely to be considerable. For why otherwise would Clark find an insistence on it 'hugely inspiring'?[54] But convincing? *The Sleepwalkers* doesn't put the question to the test. Within the flow of its narrative, the issue as such never arises. But its course points in another direction. It is enough to pose a few counterfactual queries to see this is so. In that age, could the social order of Europe have shed its elites, their habits and outlooks – all that is embodied in Arno Mayer's 'persistence of the old regime'? The Great Powers have renounced imperial objectives? Diplomats forsworn military alliances? Economic development become even? Overseas possessions been equally distributed?

Of course not, a reply might go, but why should that have led to a European war which no power deliberately sought, all had reason

---

53. There is one exception, which slips through in a subordinate clause, offset by the main clause that follows it: 'Important as it is to understand that this war might easily not have happened and why, this insight needs to be balanced with an appreciation of why and how it did in fact happen': *TS*, p. 362. The verb 'understand' asserts, unambiguously, that it was something of a fluke, but the demonstrative adjective 'this' before the war allows for the uncontroversial interpretation that it was just chance – that Princip, who did not even look to aim at the archduke, hit rather than missed him – which detonated the Great War *that summer*, without lessening the odds that an inter-imperialist war was all but certain to break out in short order anyway.

54. *Prisoners of Time*, p. 219.

to fear, and hitherto had been successfully avoided? The answer to which is no mystery. For present purposes, it can be resumed in three stark facts of the antebellum years: the fiasco of successive conclaves to promote peace; the conviction expressed, often quite early by politicians in every leading country, that war was inevitable, and by their generals that the sooner it came, the better; and finally, and most decisively, the accelerating tempo and escalating sequence of international crises that either threatened or delivered wars in the last eight years of peace. As to the first, the utter failure of the two Hague Peace Conferences, the first (1899) called by the Russian Tsar, the second (1907) by the US president, to achieve any common agreement, speaks for itself. As to the second, in 1908 the politician widely held the most devoted of his peers to peace, Sir Edward Grey, could tell an intimate that any nation, if it was strong, sought a war every forty years or so. 'It was so with us between forty and fifty years after the Crimean War, and it was so with Russia; and it was so with the United States nearly forty years after her Civil War.'[55] So too it was likely to be with Germany, nearly four decades after the Franco-Prussian War. Across the water, there were abundant examples – Bethmann Hollweg, Poincaré and Sazonov among them – of a not very different fatalism about the inevitability of a major war in Europe, while in the high command of every major army candid declarations of a positive will for war, fought at a favourable moment, could be found in pronouncements by Joffre, Moltke, (Henry) Wilson, Hötzendorf, Sukhomlinov; all predicting victory, without specifying within what timespan. As to the third, after contemplating war over Morocco in 1906, Britain menaced it in 1911, Germany threatened to attack Russia

---

55. Written in 1908. See above Keith Wilson, *The Policy of the Entente*, cited at p. 158.

over Bosnia in 1909, France struck Morocco in 1911, Italy invaded Libya in 1911, Russia fomented two Balkan wars in 1912–13, Austria declared war on Serbia in 1914. In less than a decade after the archduke was buried, every member of what was once the Pentarchy had gone to or over the brink of hostilities. The First World War, Keith Wilson observed, struck Europe because 'no Great Power, no regime, no body of ministers, was prepared to curb its imperial inclinations, tendencies or pretensions'.[56] Had Princip missed in Sarajevo, would Serbia have ceased to aim at a break-up of the Habsburg Empire, or Austro-Hungary at a breakdown of Serbia, or Russia at retribution against Austria? Would Germany have abandoned *Weltpolitik*, France hope of avenging Alsace-Lorraine, England command of the seas? To imagine this set of states anticipating the League of Nations without its failures, or the European Union without its wars, are not credible counterfactuals. If not in 1914, sooner rather than later a Great War was bound to happen.

That Clark could not affirm but float the idea that it was in some way aleatory follows from the priority of 'how' over 'why' in his tracking of its origins. The enormous gain that choice yields in *The Sleepwalkers* is plain: in detail and complexity, no other account of the path to the First World War comes near it. But, undeniably, it involves a cost when it comes to the *origins* of the war — not the same thing. Sticking so close to the actions of individuals, and the train of events which ensued from them, risks what might be called the 'illusion of immediacy'. That is: since given agents often have a choice of alternatives before them, their decisions look contingent — they could have acted otherwise. Historically, there are cases where this holds good. But the First World War is not one of them. Tacitly, Clark's

---

56. *Problems and Possibilities*, Stroud 2003, p. 203.

way of contrasting the 'how' to the 'why' of it, immediate agency versus remote causality, counterposes the freedom of an existential contingency to the force of an historical necessity. These, however, are not incompatible. Actors can choose freely within the terms of reference in which they move, without being aware of what governs these.

Clark, as widely remarked, writes with the narrative and stylistic skills of an accomplished novelist. Perhaps ironically, however, it was a novelist who could have provided him with a better defence of his title, though it would have required a modification of his preface. Hermann Broch's trilogy of 1931–32 was also called *The Sleepwalkers*, but the meaning of his title was not the same. Tracing the lives of three very different individuals from the dusk of Bismarck's rule to the last year of the First World War, each of whose stories is accorded a literary form of its own, Broch produced an uncanny premonition of Nazism shortly before it came to power. His three characters were sleepwalkers because, living out their private or semi-public dramas, none of them knew of the future towards which they were blindly moving. Conscious motives and actions of every sort are given full play; so too the supervenient direction of a world of which unawares they were agents, in the needed other sense of the word.

2. 1848–49

A decade later *Revolutionary Spring*, Clark's history of the upheavals of 1848–49, shares many of the most memorable qualities of *The Sleepwalkers*, but it also brings others that come as a surprise. Like its predecessor, it delivers a riveting literary narrative, studded with striking conceptual insights. It too is informed by strong personal feeling, kept under tight control. But the emotion differs, as does what comes of it. *The Sleepwalkers* was not explicitly, but plainly moved by revulsion at the catastrophe of the First World War and distaste for the exegetics of its victors: revolt at what happened, and the ways it is still justified. By contrast, *Revolutionary Spring* shows a warm sympathy for those who rose up against their rulers at mid-century, and admiration of the causes for which they fought: solidarity with suffering and courage. One book is a critical history from above, dealing with the elites who decided the fates of those they governed; the other essentially a history from below, focusing on rebels against the fates assigned to them. The subject matter of the two books yields also a difference of scale. The first deals just with the six belligerents of 1914. The second covers the continent, larger and smaller countries alike, from Denmark to Sicily, Ireland to Poland, a task requiring even wider command of the languages of Europe. Its dedication is a passage from the Kalevala, the folk epic of Finland, in the original; its sources include texts in Magyar, Romanian, Turkish. An increase in the scale of research and composition follows.

Visual gifts and cultural range are among other attractions of the work. '*Revolutionary Spring* brims with poetry, novels, memoirs and paintings', noted Alexander Zevin in the *New York Times*. 'Clark is drawn to color, sound and dress. There must be more hats per capita here than in any other account of 1848 – from brushed bourgeois top hats to Phrygian caps with tricolor cockades and the black Calabrian hats with long red feathers favored by student rebels.'[57] Lynn Hunt, writing in the *New York Review of Books*, remarked that in remaining 'purposefully focused on the details' of his story, 'they come to life in his writing, which is simultaneously absorbing and propulsive,

---

57. 'The Only Revolutions That Matter', *New York Times*, 13 June 2023.

not unlike a novel by Charles Dickens or Victor Hugo'.[58] Poets – Herwegh and Petőfi – are actors in the drama; Heine a witness to its prelude, a poem by Brecht epigraph to its conclusion.

The book falls into four parts: Europe prior to the revolutions of 1848; the character and course of the revolutions themselves; the counter-revolutions which put an end to them; and the consequences of these upheavals. The change of register compared with *The Sleepwalkers* takes a graphic turn from the start, pre-revolutionary Europe opening with a chapter on the 'social question': comprising a detailed ethnography of class divisions in the 1830s, dwelling on the material conditions in which the poor and precarious lived in the countryside or in towns, and ending with the jacquerie of Ukrainian peasants against Polish landowners who were themselves fighting against the Austrian state in the three-sided Galician explosion of 1846. There follows a chapter looking at the 'amorphous ideological formations' of the period, which opens with a wonderful section on the audacity of proto-feminist thinkers of the time – Claire Démar, Suzanne Voilquin, Jeanne Deroin, Flora Tristan.[59] It then proceeds to the ideas of liberals, radicals and conservatives; admixtures to them of religiosity or patriotism; (principally) metaphorical and (far less frequently) literal denunciations of slavery. In all, a tohubohu of conceptions with few clear boundaries between them.

Next comes the July Revolution of 1830 in Paris, sparked by bourgeois protests – lawyers and journalists prominent in these – against Charles X's suspension of the constitution, and fought to victory by workers on the barricades. What it yielded was an Orleanist monarchy and

---

58. 'The Orphan among Revolutions', *New York Review of Books*, 5 October 2023.

59. *Revolutionary Spring: Fighting for a New World 1848–1849*, London 2023, pp. 104–9. Henceforward *RS*.

narrowly censitary assembly, embodying the interests of a moderate *juste milieu* which in 1832 and 1834 crushed workers in revolt against their lack of gains from the change. In the wake of these events a 'far left', structurally weak but increasingly radical – personified in figures like Buonarroti, Blanqui or Büchner – took shape in Europe. In Italy, Mazzini emerged as a propagandist of genius, committed to conspiratorial violence but not to social revolution; in Germany, Robert Blum as a capable republican worker-orator; in Hungary Kossuth as a fiery journalist. Presiding over the societies in which they became active were various complacent brands of oligarchic or autocratic repression, the differing worlds of Guizot, Metternich or Pio Nono, none of them affording space for any popular initiative. In one urban centre after another, discontent gradually built up.

Upheavals

In 1848 the bill came due, with a chain of volcanic eruptions across Europe, beginning not in Paris but in Palermo. There in January notices announced the imminence of a rising against the Bourbon monarchy in Naples, in the hope that one would materialize. Curious to see if anything did, crowds gathered in various locations and fighting broke out against a regime detested by Sicilian notables and paupers alike. When royal reinforcements sent by sea failed to regain control of the island, while liberal and radical pressures mounted on the mainland too, at the end of the month Ferdinand II hastened to promise a constitution.[60] In Paris, Clark shows, fellow spirits reported the news. But the uprising that broke out there on February 22, when a liberal banquet to press the case for electoral reform was

---

60. *RS*, pp. 265–78.

banned, required no encouragement from abroad. Crowds expecting a festive occasion rioted at its prohibition, panicky troops fired into them, and when bourgeois National Guards started to fraternize with an enraged *menu peuple*, Guizot resigned, Louis Philippe fled the country and the second French Republic was declared. As in 1830, in three days it was all over. The impact in Austria, Hungary, Prussia and Lombardy was immediate. After a day of demonstrations and fighting in Vienna, Metternich decamped to the safety of London on 13 March Reformers were in charge of a Magyar administration by 17 March. Fierce battles in the streets of Berlin – ten times the number of casualties in Vienna – forced the Prussian king to withdraw his army from the city on 19 March. An urban insurrection had driven Austrian troops out of Milan by 27 March.[61] Lesser towns in Germany and Italy were engulfed in similar scenes. By June revolution had reached Bucharest. If England remained untouched, Clark argues that was in part because the early emergence of Chartism allowed its traditional rulers time to introduce measures to damp down social unrest, but also and more significantly because by 1848 they had constructed the densest police network in Europe for the suppression of sedition; while in Spain the regime of Narváez quickly stamped out the first flickers of protest in Madrid.[62]

What did the upheavals of 1848 achieve? They formed governments, without much or any prior experience in them. They elected parliaments, if only in France by universal male suffrage: 'ponderous bodies' concerned with their own dignity, short of either revolutionary charisma or traditional splendour. More durably, they proclaimed an assortment of new constitutions, the Danish charter

---

61. *RS*, pp. 295–331.
62. *RS*, pp. 336–42.

still extant today. Emancipation? 'The task of our time' according to Heine, already in the 1820s. But though slavery was formally abolished by the Second Republic, nowhere in the Caribbean or other colonies was it actually extinguished. Women? For all the contributions of distinguished women to the new scene, patriarchy remained immovable. Jews did obtain civil rights; in Wallachia the local Roma were freed in law, but ended up still slaves. But between these variously oppressed groups, there was no fusion of stirrings for liberation.

After describing the rise of these revolutions and their proximate effects, Clark divides their downfall into two phases, 'entropy' and 'counter-revolution' – the first, political loss of momentum; the second, destruction by armed force. Already by April, the tide was turning against the left in France, as elections to the National Guard and the National Assembly showed. The same drift was visible in Berlin. In Vienna it was reversed, popular pressure prompting the court to withdraw from the city – if to its advantage, the pluralist composition of the Habsburg Empire giving it room to regroup in friendlier provincial settings for a comeback, with a freedom of action which other *anciens régimes* did not enjoy. In Baden, meanwhile, an attempt at republican insurrection came to grief in the countryside, making clear how disconnected were urban radicals from the peasantry everywhere. National impulses, capable of initially strengthening the revolutionary cause, also ultimately damaged it, since while they could mobilize loosely defined forces of progress, they could also rapidly divide them, dynasties playing on tensions between ethnic groups in Habsburg lands, in Schleswig-Holstein or Pomerania, even on sub-national frictions in Italy. Nationalism, in Clark's judgment 'the most dispersed, emotionally intense and contagious experience of the revolutions', easily became a danger to them – he compares it to the effect of heroin on an addict, producing 'states of unforgettable elation and an amazing readiness to risk everything', but also destroying fellowship among the oppressed and handing their oppressors opportunities to pit them against each other.[63]

'Entropy' ends with an account of the June days in Paris: a popular rising against the Assembly's decision to close the National Workshops set up in March to provide employment for the jobless and destitute, crushed with ferocious military violence by a veteran of colonial repression in Algeria. Though the Mobile Guards firing across the barricades were recruited from much the same artisan strata as the insurgents on the other side of them, Clark vindicates Marx's view that what the savagery of the showdown spelt was the end of a myth, 'the dream of a united revolutionary front under the banner of "universal suffrage" ', which could only be sustained by bracketing the social demands that had brought the revolution to power. 'The triumph of liberty, property and order was the triumph of one force over another. The rhetorical fireworks of Lamartine had metamorphosed into the actual cannonades of June.'[64]

Counter-revolutions

The revolutions of 1848 had begun in the kingdom of Naples. The counter-revolutions which would end them started there too. In mid-May, crowds still pressing for constitutional reform in the capital were mown down by Swiss Guards, martial law was declared, a general crackdown on dissent ensued, and by September Sicily

---

63. *RS*, pp. 540–8.
64. *RS*, pp. 564–5.

had been reconquered by Bourbon troops. The ease and efficiency of this liquidation of the revolution in Southern Italy had – unlike its pioneering revolution – a wide impact in Europe, emboldening those who detested the regime changes of the spring but had feared to oppose them openly. In Prague, the Bohemian revolution fell to the troops of Prince Windischgrätz in June. Lombardy followed in July, Radetzky routing the Piedmontese army which the patriots in Milan had summoned to their aid and retaking the city in August. Further east, the Croat nobleman Jelačić led a Habsburg-loyal army against the Hungarians in September, while Ottoman and Russian interventions – the first at the behest of the second, which then took over – knocked out the Wallachian revolution. In Vienna – where, as in Paris, protests against the cutting of emergency public expenditure by a conservative ministry had led to a bloody clash in August – power passed in October to a radical coalition of workers and students, swept away at the end of the month by Windischgrätz: Blum was executed, and the young Franz Joseph installed as Habsburg Emperor. In December France enacted its own, suitably electoral, version of a European scenario, with the overwhelming victory of Louis Napoleon at the polls for president of the Republic. For the peasantry, the middle class and much of the working class who rallied to him, his name was the promise of a return to the order, and an intimation of the glory of the first consul and his future.

Not all was over yet, however. In contraflow to the dominant direction of the continent, came a second – now better organized, less liberal – revolutionary spell in areas not yet subject to the mailed fist of a newly energized conservatism. North of the counter-revolution in Naples, Pio Nono had been obliged to temporize with liberal opinion by allowing a couple of advisory assemblies under a law-and-order ministry. In October, his hated minister of the interior was assassinated to popular rejoicing, at which the pope fled his possessions in central Italy. Universal male suffrage was introduced, elections held, and in February 1849 a Roman Republic declared. Mazzini arrived from London, Garibaldi from Montevideo. Taxation was lowered, the death penalty abolished, and competent administration begun. In southern Germany, when the Frankfurt assembly – elected indirectly from assorted princely states and dominated by a liberal-conservative majority – failed to achieve national unity by securing acceptance either of an imperial constitution by the various states of the country, or an imperial crown by the king of Prussia, it opened the way for radicals to launch an insurrection and declare a republic in Baden in May 1849. In Hungary, once the Austrian army reconquered Vienna, it soon took Budapest too, forcing the Magyar assembly east to Debrecen. There in April 1849 it declared Hungarian independence, without specifying what form the future Magyar state would take. By June, a Hungarian army of 170,000 mustered by Kossuth had recovered much of the old kingdom.

In each of these cases, the second flare-up of revolution was snuffed out by foreign intervention. A French army dispatched by Louis Napoleon bombarded Rome into submission. Prussian troops finished off the republic proclaimed in Baden. In Hungary, after Franz Joseph begged Nicholas I on his knees to rescue the House of Habsburg, a Russian force of 200,000 joined Austrian and Croat forces to overpower the Honvéd, the Magyar revolutionary army, which capitulated in August. By the autumn Mazzini, Garibaldi and Kossuth, along with a multitude of other fighters, were in exile: most of them permanently. Though national aims and ideals were prominent, however ambiguously, in the revolutions of 1848–49, internationalist engagements had been a notable strand in them, too.⁶⁵ But as Clark remarks, geopolitics was a terrain on which revolutionaries were no match for the forces of reaction, inherently stronger since they were entrenched in the military bastions of the state system, with their own, superior versions of international collaboration.⁶⁶ Louis Napoleon complied with the suppression of Hungary by Nicholas I in exchange for a free hand to seize Rome. Nicholas answered Franz Joseph's appeal to help Austria crush the Magyars for fear that Hungary might spread its contagion to Poland. Palmerston connived at Russia's invasion of Hungary to ensure Austria's survival as an ally for Britain. Russia and Austria exercised joint pressure on Turkey to hand over the fighters who had found refuge there.

The victory of European counter-revolution was not just material: it also brought with it, Clark contends, a lasting change in the ideological atmosphere of the continent, the migration of doctrines according primacy in politics to force from their origins on the left to thinkers of the right. It was a former Jacobin, Luigi Angeloni Frusinate, a close friend of Buonarroti, who pioneered this outlook with a book *On Force in Political Affairs* in 1826, and it would be developed not only by Marx and Engels, but more famously announced by Bismarck, and popularized as a general theory by the publicist Ludwig von Rochau in his *Grundsätze der Realpolitik* of 1853. These were different versions of realism – Marx giving primacy

---

65. Symbolized by the Polish general Józef Bem, a veteran of the Napoleonic era, now a commander in the defence of Vienna, then for the Hungarians in Transylvania, finally Ottoman governor of Aleppo: *RS*, pp. 684–5.
66. 'Perhaps the single most dangerous feature of nationalism was that it lured revolutionaries onto terrain where they were destined never to find a firm footing, the terrain of geopolitics, on which they would always be outgunned by the powers of the old regime' – the counter-revolutionaries were 'much better' at 'collaborating internationally than their opponents': *RS*, pp. 12, 549.

to economic forces, Bismarck to military strength, Rochau more concerned with changes in the cultural sphere.[67] But in common was a pragmatics of power within and between states, at the opposite pole to the starry-eyed idealism that had inspired so many revolutionaries in 1848. In the finale of his narrative Clark takes moving leave of these, reporting the number of those certainly or probably killed, describing the last rites of the executed, the psychic dislocation of survivors,[68] the varying fate of exiles.

Asymmetry

The controlled strength of feeling in *Revolutionary Spring* does not exclude but prompts depth of thinking about its subject. Clark's reflections on revolution and counter-revolution are typically fresh and original. Was the extreme deprivation and misery depicted in his panorama of the social question prior to the revolutions of 1848, a precipitant of their outbreak? Were the riots they occasioned a sign it was coming? No: 'there was no direct causal nexus' between popular distress and political upheaval, though 'fear of subaltern violence shaped the unfolding of revolution throughout its course. It was not an exogenous factor, pressing on the revolution from the outside, it was part of the revolution itself.'[69] This wasn't the only fear afoot in these years, which also saw plots by a small far left to overthrow the established order by insurrection, ventures doomed to failure that landed the culprits in jail or exile. Had these become a bygone

---

67. *RS*, pp. 679–80.

68. Poignantly captured by Jókai in his novel *Political Fashions* (1861) in the figure of Petőfi, imagined as surviving rather than being killed in 1849: *RS*, pp. 695–7.

69. *RS*, pp. 89, 92.

irrelevance when the big popular explosion of 1848 occurred? Far from it, Clark suggests, for the spectre of a Blanquist *coup de main* distracted the attention of the authorities in Paris from the real task at hand, to adjust their forms of control to changing conditions: the effect was to make them 'spend the last eighteen years preparing for the wrong revolution'.[70] What erupted instead was an inchoate revolt, 'anchored not in seditious conspiracy, but in the waning of respect and trust' for the regime, and the emergence of the right of assembly as a cause capable of temporarily uniting 'heterogeneous disaffected elements'. Therein was a lesson for a wider aetiology of revolutions. In one of his most pregnant observations, Clark writes,

> The accumulation of pressures around the suffrage question draws our attention to a plane of causation that is sometimes lost from view when we think of revolutions as the consequence of remote causes (economic cycles, the distillation and refinement of ideas) and proximate events (the appearance of a poster announcing an insurrection, the accidental discharge of a bullet, a massacre that transforms the emotional chemistry of a city). Between the remote and the proximate is an intermediate plane of causation: the accumulation of political tension, the hardening of language, the collapse of consensus and the exhaustion of compromise, the emergence of tripwire issues – a political dynamic that lives neither in years nor in hours, but in months and weeks.[71]

Since the revolutions of 1848 were unpremeditated, the measures they passed or decisions they took after the event largely improvised.[72] In

---

70. *RS*, p. 293.
71. *RS*, p. 294. 'Between the remote and the proximate, there is an intermediate plane of causation': an apposite description of the analytic fourth chapter of *The Sleepwalkers*.
72. The one exception, Clark notes, came in Wallachia, where alone the

diametric contrast, the counter-revolutions that levelled them were highly planned, the fruit of careful calculation and disciplined timing: operations ordered by rulers or their ministers, and executed by military commanders, they exemplified political intentionality as its bluntest. The sympathy of Clark's narrative of the revolutions does not extend, naturally, to the repressions which delivered their quietus. But he recounts them without any open resort to a vocabulary of antagonism, in a tone as even as his discussion of the limitations of the revolutions themselves. The difference in his attitude to the two camps finds expression rather in an asymmetry in his treatment of the actors in each. *Revolutionary Spring* contains many a lively and perceptive portrait of those on the rebellious side of the conflicts that divided European politics in the years after the defeat of Napoleon – Buonarroti and Blanqui, Voilquin and Belgioioso, Lamennais and Lamartine, Mazzini and Cattaneo, Széchenyi and Kossuth, Hecker and Blum, among others. On the other side, two of the statesmen overthrown in 1848 are accorded full portraits, Guizot and Metternich. Set against his family background and Protestant affiliation, Guizot's character, outlook and gifts are captured lucidly enough; whereas Metternich is wildly miscast as inwardly a reform-willing tolerant English Whig who took the Greek Revolution in good part.[73] Yet neither played any significant role in the events of 1848–49, which drove them off the stage. Matters are quite different with the architects of counter-revolution, who acted decisively in them. We are told little or nothing about Schwarzenberg, though he appears during the suppression of the Galician revolt in 1846, is on the scene during the

---

revolutionaries designed their takeover of power in advance, and uniquely, too, enacted a modicum of land reform: *RS*, pp. 374–7, 513–16.

73. *RS*, pp. 236–8, 250.

revolution in Palermo in 1848, is with Radetzky in the reduction of Milan, with Windischgrätz in the recapture of Vienna and installation of Franz Joseph on the throne; then as prime minister, orchestrated the military defeat of the Hungarian Revolution by Russia, presided over the reconstruction of the Habsburg state in Austria, and its check to Prussia in Germany. Likewise, Windischgrätz and Radetzky are names rather than persons. So too Oudinot who destroyed the Roman Republic for Louis Napoleon; of whom Clark offers no telling sketch, any more than of a largely absent Nicholas I.

Concentration on the elites who made the decisions that set Europe alight in 1914 was not a failing of *The Sleepwalkers*. The masses of the continent were not involved: a virtually undiluted history from above was faithful to a quest for the origins of the war. The revolutions of 1848–89 were a conflict of an altogether different type, not between elites but between elites and those they ruled, inviting a history from below – but one that could not historically yet be wholly such. Is the relative disproportion in its coverage of the two sides in the civil wars of that biennium a failing of *Revolutionary Spring*? Not really. Further enlarged, an already massive work could have become unmanageable. Undeniably, though, both of Clark's books pay a price for what they bracket. In *The Sleepwalkers*, absent was the pressure of the New Imperialism behind the accelerating toboggan of the European elites to war. In *Revolutionary Spring*, it is the grid of the Vienna system lying beneath the landscape of the social question, the blurring of ideas, the constriction of regimes, of that time – in a word that stands for an era, one that is missing in the book, the Restoration. Avoided perhaps by Clark as too brusque and simple-minded a label for the period, it is one that nevertheless conveys, however telegraphically, the real bent of the system against which rebellion eventually came, and was checked. The order constructed by the pentarchy of victorious powers in 1815, and christened by its architects – Alexander I, Metternich, Castlereagh, Hardenberg and Talleyrand – 'the public law of Europe', was designed to stamp out the embers of the French Revolution and the image of the usurper who had threatened the stability of every throne in Europe. As bulwarks against any renewed disorder of the kind these had brought, it comprised two variants of conservative monarchy, autocratic absolutism – in different forms, Russia, Austria, Prussia – and oligarchic constitutionalism, Britain and less securely France. Common to both was devotion to the principles of hierarchy, property, and legitimacy, invigilated wherever necessary with violence. The joint hegemons of the system, as Paul Schroeder observed, were the two great empires at opposite poles of it, Russia and Britain, respectively the dominant powers of Europe on land and sea. It is scarcely an accident, though it is not registered by Clark, that both were proof against the contagion of 1848, which unfolded precisely across Napoleonic Europe, whose memory the Vienna system was designed to obliterate. Geopolitically, the upheavals of that year were like a posthumous revenge for the exile of St Helena.

Liberals in Government

By definition, of course, liberals were constitutionally minded. But there, everything depended on what kind of constitution they favoured – what powers an assembly possessed, on what suffrage it was based. With the consent of the victorious powers, Louis XVIII granted France a Charter, whose suspension by Charles X provoked his overthrow, yielding in the July Monarchy a suffrage that was somewhat less narrow, an assembly with considerably greater rights, and from start to end of the regime ministries for the country's most distinguished liberal thinker – Guizot's ascent culminating in the office of prime minister, until he was overthrown by just the kind of popular tumult that had put him into the seats of power in 1830. Did his career place him categorically beyond the Vienna system, or quite comfortably within it? Clark supplies a typically wide-ranging and generally fair survey of liberal thinkers and their concerns, political and economic, in the Restoration era – drawing on examples from Spain, France, Italy, Germany, Britain, if without bringing home the originality and systematicity of the leading school of the time, the French *doctrinaires*, or the degree of their political rejection of the French Revolution. But how does he judge their performance as actors in the events of the time?

On the one hand, his verdict on their roles in 1830 and in 1848 is objectively stringent. In both cases, French liberals initiated and led protests against what they attacked as abuses of the Charter – in the first its suspension, in the second refusal to concede its improvement – which aroused a popular clamour that overturned the regime responsible for these denials of liberty. Each time the liberals whom the revolutions put into power promptly crushed those who got them there. 'The blood of the people has flowed, as it did in July [1830], but this time, the generous blood will not be betrayed,' wrote *La Réforme* in February 1848; as in June it punctually would be.[74] The story was not different elsewhere in Europe.

> The more frightened the liberals became of the left, the more they themselves gravitated towards the forces of order. Wherever liberals were in government, they subjected democratic political clubs, public meetings and demonstrations to police surveillance and rigorous countermeasures, while at the same time turning a blind eye to right-wing attacks on the legitimacy of the revolution. Within the

---

74. *RS*, p. 293.

> revolutionary assemblies, the liberals tended increasingly to vote together with their former conservative enemies, against the deputies of the moderate and radical left . . . Satisfaction and a sense of liberal accomplishment were certainly part of the motivational mix, but a deeper and more important driver of liberal behaviour was the fear of further instability. From the summer of 1848, liberals adopted an increasingly schematic and apocalyptic view of political and social conflict. They saw themselves locked in a zero-sum conflict with an enemy that represented the absolute negation of the bourgeois social order.[75]

That judgment comes in the course of Clark's account of the counter-revolutions of 1848–49. Yet when he arrives at the upshot of those years, the tenor of his story changes. For what were the after-effects of its 'revolutionary spring' in Europe? There could be no reversion, he argues, to the *status quo ante*. The events of 1848 had modernized politics, with the introduction of constitutions, elections, parties of a kind that had not existed previously and were here to stay, these becoming the standard equipment of every contemporary democracy. In the aftermath of the revolutions, what would emerge most influentially from them were flexible coalitions of a liberal-conservative stamp, born of a rapprochement between newly moderate former revolutionaries and now more pragmatic traditional elites, which marginalized old left and old right alike. These were governments that modernized their societies with new industries and infrastructures, above all railways. Committed to investment and development, they improved the administrations they headed and transformed the cities they ruled. Regimes with a less heavy hand than in the past, they relied on public relations more than censorship. What they stood for was a post-revolutionary settlement that went beyond

---

75. *RS*, pp. 648–9.

simple prophylaxis against any recurrence of upheavals from below. For the political peace at which they aimed was not just a benefaction that needed to be bought by prosperity and progress. If anything, it was rather the other way round, civil peace seen as a condition of the values of progress and prosperity.[76]

Peel is for Clark the politician who anticipated this pattern, a conservative who could alter his outlook when circumstances required it, and become a capable, efficient reformer. It was men like him – Cavour in Italy, Manteuffel in Prussia, Bach in Austria, together with lesser-known figures, including many an ex-*quarante-huitard* police official, their careers exemplifying a 'mass mobility across the political spectrum' – who left their mark on the subsequent epoch. Their flexibility was not an entirely new phenomenon. Already in the pre-revolutionary years, there were politicians who offered variants of it: the 'moderate turn in Italian liberalism' inspired by the ideas of Gioberti, the prudent sensibility of Guizot's France, the authoritarian liberalism of Narváez in Spain. Even if its 'charisma would be tarnished' in 1848 'we should not underestimate the futurity of this kind of limited politics'. For across a common ground where 'disparate elements of a political nation defined by wealth and education could join hands', it was an outlook which 'prefigured the reformist centrism that would dominate the political life of most European states after the mid-century revolution'.[77]

---

76. *RS*, pp. 709–14.
77. *RS*, pp. 240–8.

Lessons

Does that mean the revolutions were a failure, as most historians have judged them, a turning point for Europe that didn't turn? For Clark, such a conclusion would be a category mistake, like asking whether a flood or a hurricane is a success or a failure. Like historical forces of nature, revolutions are objective events that have no aims. Revolutionaries do, but no revolution has ever delivered what they set out to achieve. Nevertheless, revolutions are 'deeply consequential'.[78] People are not the same afterwards, as Bismarck knew, and said of himself. It is natural to wonder whether things could have gone better, if they had acted differently, and in this work, unlike *The Sleepwalkers*, Clark supplies five specific counterfactual scenarios for a preferable outcome – if liberals had been more open to radical politics; if radicals could have agreed on a persuasive social programme; if nationalist entanglements had been avoided; if liberals and radicals had insisted from the start on control of armies; if all monarchs had shown the wisdom of Dutch and Danish kings in presiding over a peaceful transition to responsible parliaments.[79] But, in this too unlike *The Sleepwalkers*, his new book contains no real appeal to contingency. Understandably, the notion that counter-revolution might not have prevailed, or been supernumerary, is never entertained as a serious hypothesis. Rather, the emphasis falls on lessons of the experience of 1848 for the present.

These take two forms, one directly political, the other more analogical. The first offers a prescription, with a qualification. Its major premise runs like this:

---

78. *RS*, pp. 744–6.
79. *RS*, p. 750.

At a time when 'liberalism', shorn of its charisma and emptied of its history, is equated on the left with colonial violence, plutocracy and market-driven economics, and on the right with leftist fads and social licence, it is worth remembering what a rich, diverse, risky and vibrant thing liberalism was. The liberal vision of a metapolitics focused on the discursive mediation of interests is as indispensable now as it was then.[80]

Qualifier:

But liberals were also a constellation of interest groups. The radicals were right to denounce their blind spots and the inconsistencies born of self-interest; radical arguments for democracy and social justice were a crucial corrective to liberal elitism. The radicals were the first to see who was in danger of being left behind by a politics focused on parliaments and constitutions; they were the first to see how extreme inequality would corrode the fabric of a political order that failed to integrate the poorer social strata.[81]

Conclusion:

The failure of liberals and radicals to listen to each other was one of the central impediments to a deeper political transformation. When liberals denounced democrats as 'communists' and radicals ridiculed 'parlia-parlia-parlia-parliaments' of the liberals, they enacted one of the central tragedies of 1848. On the other hand, neither radicals nor liberals (with some virtuous exceptions) managed to make much sense of the intractable problems of rural society, a category encompassing the great majority of Europeans. This was a glaring omission, for which they would pay dearly.[82]

---

80. *RS*, p. 749.
81. *RS*, pp. 749–50.
82. *RS*, p. 750.

Prescription:

> How should we optimize the functionality of liberal institutions while accommodating the demand for social justice, or for the profound – and potentially unpopular – changes to meet the challenge of climate change?[83]

At various points in the book, Clark suggests a name for that needed combination. In the autumn of 1848 the 'motley crowd' of students, lawyers, journalists, radical artisans and insurgent proletarians who held brief power in Vienna 'contained the seeds of a new kind of left-wing politics, in which social and political demands would flow into a coherent platform, the politics that would later be called social democracy'.[84] Just as in the Roman Republic a year later, the programme of its triumvirs – Mazzini the theorist – proclaimed that there would be 'no war of classes, no hostility to existing wealth, no wanton or unjust violation of the rights of property', simply 'a constant disposition to ameliorate the material condition of the classes least favoured by fortune'.[85]

Clark's *placet*:

> The left was already on the path away from the romantic revolutionism of the 1840s towards a democratic republicanism focused on the social well-being of citizens. The spectre of 'communism' that haunted middle-class liberals and conservatives became a way of not seeing or understanding what the radicals

---

83. *RS*, p. 749.
84. *RS*, p. 614.
85. *RS*, pp. 658–9.

were actually asking for. The second-wave radicals were precisely not 'communists'; they were the ancestors of today's social democrats.[86]

Too much should not be made of these elisions of period and category, signals of Clark's social sensibility more than of ideological allegiance. His location is rather to be sought in that eloquent, if never dominant, line of liberalism that was open to the challenge of socialism, and sought an approximation or fusion with it, in some cases a subsumption, one that descends from Mill to Russell and Dewey, later to Bobbio, Habermas and Rawls – philosophers all – with fewer outliers in sociology or history, Clark a distinguished exception. It is a tradition that has always been liable to possible strain at the join between the two impulses in its make-up. Perhaps particularly so where history, refractory to conceptual abstractions, impinges on it. By immersing it for the first time in the full flux of a vast revolutionary – and counter-revolutionary – drama, Clark has greatly enriched its dual vision. But the characteristic strain is still there, visible in the construct of a 'post-revolutionary synthesis' in the 1850s presented as the impressive achievement of a moderate liberalism – an administrative modernization of Europe bringing a new prosperity and peace to its citizens, in its way comparable to the rising living standards and welfare systems of the post-war order set in place in the 1950s.[87] For Clark the true legacy of 1848 was the European 'revolution in government' that presided over these advances.[88]

---

86. *RS*, p. 659.
87. *RS*, pp. 746, 709–41.
88. *RS*, p. 4.

Liberalism in Power

There is an obvious difficulty, however, in attributing the kind of progress he extols in the post-revolutionary years – economic, technical, urban, mediatic – to the revolutions that were crushed in 1849. For the same kind of improvements arrived in the same years, in still larger measure, in Britain and the United States without any revolution. What they essentially recorded was the progress of capitalism, a reality that for most purposes *Revolutionary Spring* – where the term rarely occurs – ignores. That its advance in the Anglo-Saxon world was well ahead of anything to be found in continental Europe is a reminder of the political differences that separated these societies from those that underwent the upheavals of 1848. They had undergone their own revolutions much earlier, and more successfully, in 1648–49/1688–89 and in 1775–83 – the latter in some respects an extension of the former. In both cases, these were transformations of the state whose condition was the weakness or absence of a feudal countryside which enabled a capitalist class, rural and urban, to secure stable power: in Marxist terms, bourgeois revolutions accomplished without significant threat from below. In France that threat materialized in Year II of the First Republic, traumatizing the property-holding classes across Europe – the Napoleonic regime which followed repressing the Jacobin side of the Revolution, but transponding the dynamic it unleashed into wars of expansion menacing thrones from Portugal to Poland.

Victory over Napoleon restored the Bourbon monarchy as a linchpin of the Vienna system, against whose Orleanist version the uprising of 1848 broke out. The urban structure and population of Paris were no longer, however, those of 1789: six decades later, industries in the city had grown, lower classes were larger, socialist ideas were in circulation. There was now a tangible proletarian threat, not just to the aristocratic order reinstalled at Vienna, but to central bourgeois interests and values too. If we ask why the revolutions of 1848–49 were all extinguished so swiftly and ruthlessly, Clark supplies the answer vividly and comprehensively at the level of intermediate causation he identifies in his account of how they originated: showing how the old order regrouped, why it could coordinate across borders so much better, what popular anchorage it could rely on, where its decisive advantage in armed force lay, which ethnic and social divisions it could exploit among its adversaries. But in the same way that there was a level of causation, just as real and as powerful, above the plane of immediate actors and events on which he concentrated in *The Sleepwalkers*, so in the drama depicted in *Revolutionary Spring* there was such a plane too: the overarching fact on which Lukács, in particular, insisted, that by 1848 the European bourgeoisie had lost its innocence. It knew the dangers to it of popular mobilizations, and in the company of traditional privilege and power was quick to throttle them. Too *plumpes Denken* for Clark?

In contending that the revolutions were in any case not failures, his emphasis falls on the conservation and development of their achievements, despite their apparent defeat. Not that he embellishes unduly the post-revolutionary synthesis he discerns in the 1850s. He makes clear its costs. Delaying 'the arrival of universal suffrage in Europe for half a century or more', and narrowing 'the band-width of socialist dissent', this was a synthesis founded on 'the continuing political exclusion of the popular classes whose courage and violence had made the revolutions possible and on the marginalization of the democratic politics that spoke in their name'.[89] But since there were now constitutions, parliaments and parties, not to speak of more efficient bureaucracies and faster growth, all was not lost. These were pointers to the future and the kind of democracy we enjoy today, called 'liberal' not by accident. For liberalism in this vision is the bridge across epochs from the time of Cavour to that of Biden; its metapolitics – the 'discursive mediation of different interests' – the abiding principle of a responsible collective life, which failed in 1848 because moderates and radicals would not listen to each other. Clark doesn't consistently defend it, granting the force of Marx's mockery of the dream of political harmony between classes in the revolution, but nor does he ever criticize the notion of a 'metapolitics' as he defines it, which might seem first cousin to Habermas's 'ideal speech situation'. So too, it might be asked, is it possible to speak of liberalism today without mention of the prefix defining the format of its hold on the world across the past four decades? For that matter, and more germanely as within Clark's own remit, without consideration of the First World War, fought in this country in the name of liberal civilization by a liberal government? Consummation of the moderate progressivism of the previous half century?

Victory in Defeat?

In his introduction to *Revolutionary Spring*, Clark speaks of the mistake that posterity made in supposing that the continental experience of 1848 was a failure, among whose remote consequences would be the advent of Fascism in Italy, Nazism in Germany and the Bonapartism of De Gaulle in France. The reality was rather that 'the

---

89. *RS*, p. 747.

1848 revolutions were *not* in fact a failure: in many countries they produced swift and lasting constitutional change'.[90] The breadth and depth of the alterations in government its upheavals triggered have transformed Europe for the better. The revolutions might in the short run have brought defeat to the activists who fought for them. But 'their momentum communicated itself like a seismic wave to European administrations, changing structures and ideas, bringing new priorities into government or reorganizing old ones, reframing political debates'.[91]

Biographically, the introduction to *Revolutionary Spring* hints at what may be the sources of the extent of this conviction. It is true, Clark tells us, that the narrative of these upheavals 'lacks a moment of redemptive closure', and 'it was precisely the stigma of failure that put me off the 1848 revolutions when I first encountered them at school'. Now that he understands their complexity better, however, he can appreciate the contribution that both those with whom he sympathizes and those with whom he does not made to their paradoxical success. The demands of one side, admired by many historians, have 'entered the repertoire of modern liberal democracy'. Yet, he continues, 'while I share this affinity for newspaper-reading, coffee-drinking liberals and radicals, it seems to me that an account that views events only from an insurgent or liberal standpoint will miss an essential part of the drama and meaning of these revolutions. They were a complex encounter between old and new powers, in which the old ones did as much to shape the shorter- and longer-term outcomes of the revolutions

---

90. RS, pp. 2, 4.
91. 'Why Should We Think about the Revolutions of 1848 Now?', *London Review of Books*, 7 March 2019.

as the new.'[92] The equation is not demonstrated in his book, which says little about those who manned the counter-revolution and not a great deal about the regimes it established or restored. What its postulation under the rubric of a joint success, however, perhaps suggests is the function of what might in this version of their upshot, with a touch of irony be called the 'redemptive opening' of the revolutions to a better future extending all the way to the present. The role played by contingency in *The Sleepwalkers*, where its effect is to occlude the logic of empires, is not reiterated in *Revolutionary Spring*. But in the saving grace with which its narrative ends a structural equivalent might be detected. This time, the effect is one not of occlusion, but consolation. The magnitude of authorial investment – intellectual and emotional – in the drama of 1848–49, yielding so mighty and passionate a monument of scholarship, taking a decade or more to produce, could seem ill rewarded were its tale to end on a lowering note, the need for a sanguine conclusion compositionally overwhelming. Something like that, at least, may account for the disjuncture between stark evidence of defeat and hidden signs, all the same, of victory.[93]

---

92. *RS*, p. 8; the old themselves were changed in doing so, as Bismarck conceded in his memoirs.

93. Historians have noticed this. Lynn Hunt: 'Clark wants to counter negative views by emphasizing the many beneficial outcomes of the insurrections, but like others who have tried to put a more positive spin on the events of those years, he faces a daunting task.' Alexander Zevin: 'The sense of failure that hovers around 1848 cannot be dispelled by counting the rail lines laid down in its aftermath.'

Prognosis

Revolutionary Spring ends, however, not on a note of solace, but with a thought-provoking parallel exempt from any. The risings of 1848 broke out before political or social ideas had acquired systematic demarcation into adjacent or antithetical doctrines, separating right, centre and left. These crystallized afterwards, generating relatively hard-and-fast political divisions and institutionalized parties corresponding to them of a new kind, which proved long-lasting features of high modernity. Today, however, are we not coming out of these, in a reverse movement taking us into an ideological landscape which is becoming as amorphously mixed and confused as that of the 1830s, even if doctrines of old still litter it as so many fossils? Such a meltdown of past certainties, and resultant criss-crossing of once polarized slogans and war cries, is not Clark's conjecture alone. Roberto Schwarz has recently given it expressive form, without converting impressions into axioms, in his tragicomedy on the fall of Dilma in Brazil.[94] Clark illustrates his proposal by pointing to movements like Trump rallies, Occupy Wall Street, QAnon in America, *gilets jaunes* in France, *Querdenker* in Germany, the Freedom Convoy in Canada, and it would be easy to add more. In general, he adds, 'heightened ambient awareness of precarity and the preoccupation with waning social cohesion recall the grim diagnoses of the 1840s'.[95]

The historical parallel is certainly suggestive. How far is it persuasive? At the socio-political level, the mutability Clark indicates

---

[94] *Rainha Lira*, for which see Mario Sergio Conti's discussion, 'A Brazilian Comico-Tragedy', *New Left Review* 136, July–August 2022, pp. 41–52.

[95] *RS*, p. 754.

is clearly – some would say spectacularly – on display in the switching of electoral constituencies, workers now voting in large numbers for parties regarded as on the right, the well-off and well-educated in large numbers for parties categorized as on the left; changes quantified and theorized by Thomas Piketty among others. In such swapping of once traditional affiliations, ideologemes of the hour can migrate from one camp to another with startling ease, confirming Clark's reading of the times. But such quicksilver shifts, and dissolution of familiar doxa, are confined to the plane of domestic politics. On the international plane, fixity and uniformity are perhaps more widespread and pronounced – at least in Europe – than ever before, as tropes of the New Cold War fill out and harden into a near unanimous *Weltanschauung*.

More openly topical-political in his references and concerns than most historians, Clark has been prone to contemporary analogies that risk misfiring into anachronism: not a few in *The Sleepwalkers* – the inability of Austria to secure Entente sympathy for action against Serbia, likened to Security Council failure to serve sanctions on Syria; the troika's diktats that stifled the troubles of the euro, inspiration for how the Great War could have been avoided;[96] and they recur in *Revolutionary Spring* – Blum, as it were, a forecast of Hartz or Scholz; the pantomime on Capitol Hill in January 2021, akin to the invasion of the National Assembly in May 1848.[97] But these are throwaway lines, that can be discarded. Parallels between the 1830s/40s and the last couple of decades, argued and illustrated with care, are another matter, and if not incontestable, are to be respected. They imply no conformism; rather the contrary. After invoking the 'fissured, multifarious' quality of politics in 1848 – anxieties about inequality,

---

96. *TS*, pp. 555, 559.
97. *RS*, p. 552.

domestic tumults entangled with foreign affairs, irruptions of violence, utopia and spirituality, lack of any definite sense of the future — here is how Clark ends his great, debatable work: 'If a revolution is coming (and we seem very far removed from a *non-revolutionary* solution to the "polycrisis" we currently face), it may look something like 1848: poorly planned, dispersed, patchy and bristling with contradictions.'[98] There are worse prognoses of what could be in store.

---

98. *RS*, p. 754. Italics in the original.

6

PAUL SCHROEDER

In December 2020, the greatest American historian of his generation died in Pennsylvania. A solitary obituary, concentrating on his family life, appeared in the small town in Illinois where he had taught for thirty-four years, in a newspaper with a circulation of about 25,000, which had recently filed for bankruptcy. Some months later, a short notice of his death, and appreciation of his person and work, written by a former pupil teaching in West Virginia, who herself died soon afterwards, appeared in a newsletter of the American Historical Association. Since then H-Diplo has published a forum on Schroeder – dominated by political scientists rather than historians. For all practical purposes, in the country of which he was so particular a product, his passing was ignored by the discipline to which he devoted his life.

The contrast between Schroeder's stature as a thinker and a scholar and the silence at his departure was no doubt due in part to the unusual pattern of his output. Across sixty years, he published just five books, one of them seemingly detached from the rest of his writing, another a collection put together for him by colleagues, while in the same decades he produced over eighty scholarly articles, in two dozen journals of five countries and in some thirty-six different books assembled by others: essays rightly described by friends as 'a ceaseless explosion of ideas – brilliant, original, forcefully and carefully argued' contravening 'the superstitions of the profession, the flood of conventional knowledge' which 'the surrounding sources of information have spread like a sterile sort of gloss over contemporary historical thought'.[1] The scattering of so many lights over such a wide, yet often relatively arcane, expanse of publication contributed, of course, to obscuring them from public attention.

Beginnings

Certainly, too, the mutism at his death was also in part due to the modesty typical of Schroeder's background and personality. Son of a Lutheran minister in Cleveland, the third of eight children, he was a product of the Midwest, where he spent his whole professional career, far from the academic peaks of the East and West Coasts connected to the hubs of power in Washington and of communications in New York. Inheriting his father's faith, he was educated at a Lutheran university in Kansas, in training for a ministry. In his youth he served as a pastor, a calling to which he kept till he was twenty-seven, when he decided his talents were better suited to history. While still in charge of a congregation, he completed an MA about American relations with Japan on the eve of the Pacific War. So independent was it of views of the subject then current

---

1. Paul W. Schroeder, *Systems, Stability and Statecraft: Essays on the International History of Modern Europe*, David Wetzel, Robert Jervis and Jack Levy (eds), New York 2004, pp. 1–2; henceforward *Systems*.

that the chair of his committee assailed it with outraged vehemence, only agreeing to pass the thesis, given the level of research it contained, on condition it was lodged in the university library with his condemnation of it. Undeterred, Schroeder submitted it to the American Historical Association for its annual Beveridge Prize, unaware that this was for the best postgraduate, not undergraduate, dissertation of the year. Nevertheless he won the award. Two years later, after Schroeder's postgraduate study under John Rath at the University of Texas, it was published by Cornell in 1958 as *The Axis Alliance and Japanese–American Relations, 1941*.

Like the thesis on which it was based, the book was prompted by Schroeder's dissatisfaction with both of what were then the major opposing American interpretations of the outbreak of the Pacific War: that it was the inevitable product of Japan's aggressive expansionism in East Asia, entry into Indochina following its conquests in China, or that it was the intentional product of Roosevelt and his circle, spurred by Tokyo's announcement of an Axis Pact with Berlin and Rome in the summer of 1941. Schroeder rejected the former and dismissed the latter. In a careful analysis of successive stages in Japanese–American diplomacy from February to November 1941, he showed that after Hitler attacked Russia – with which Japan had a signed a neutrality pact – and the US declared a trade embargo on Japan, Washington secured effective agreement to two of its three main demands on Tokyo: that Japan put the – anyway largely nominal – Axis Pact into abeyance and exit from southern Vietnam, leaving unsatisfied only the demand that it withdraw from China. Instead of sealing the extent of this victory, however, the US re-escalated the issue of the Axis Pact, insisting on its public repudiation plus a pull-out from China, while refusing any summit between the two countries. 'Japan was clearly asking for less, and the United States demanding more, in November than in May.'² The result was to back Tokyo into a corner, and trigger a war that could have been avoided had the US decided to deal with the threat from Germany first, shortening the Second World War by defeating Hitler before forcing Japan to withdraw from China. Schroeder's judgment was unequivocal: 'American policy from the end of July to December was a grave mistake.'³ Not an insatiable Japanese militarism but the liberal moralism of a self-righteous American public, unwilling to compromise its principles in pursuit of a reasonable peace, was to blame for the war in the Pacific. The young Schroeder's case, 'deliberately and excellently controversial' as one admirer described it, met with a generally respectful reception among the specialists who reviewed it, where its judgment was taken as echoing Kennan's critical verdict on American diplomacy in general. Striking, certainly, in the work of one who had been a pastor when developing the plain-spoken realist standpoint of the book.

By the time it appeared in 1958, Schroeder had become assistant – later associate – professor at Concordia Senior College, a Lutheran

---

2. *The Axis Alliance and Japanese–American Relations*, p. 173. The top US commanders dissented from the line taken by the administration, believing that 'it was unnecessary, and probably even harmful, for the United States to insist on an immediate evacuation from China': pp. 178–9, as, too, did the American ambassador in Tokyo, Joseph Grew.

3. 'On the verge of a major diplomatic victory, the United States abandoned its original goals and concentrated on a third, the liberation of China. This last aim was not in accord with American strategic interests, was not a limited objective, and most important, was completely incapable of being achieved by peaceful means and doubtful of attainment even by war': *The Axis Alliance and Japanese–American Relations*, pp. 202, 203.

campus in Indiana, and changed his field of study to Austrian diplomatic history of the early nineteenth century, focussing at Rath's suggestion on Metternich's role in the years following the Congress of Vienna, research which took him with a Fulbright to the Austrian capital. Its fruit was his second book, *Metternich's Diplomacy at Its Zenith, 1820–1823*, which came out in 1962. Just as he had sensed there was something amiss, without at first knowing exactly what it was, in the contending accounts of the origins of the Pacific War, so he started his research on Metternich believing that the standard modern account of his statesmanship, Heinrich von Srbik's portrait of an enlightened conservative, averse to autocracy but devoted to monarchy, was essentially accurate, if insufficiently documented and perhaps over-systematic. It was only when he began to study the sequels to the Congress of Vienna at Troppau, Laibach and Verona that he concluded Srbik's interpretation was untenable.

In the aftermath of the settlement at Vienna, Metternich had indeed displayed diplomatic talents of a high order, perhaps even genius, and notched up a series of striking successes in suppressing revolutionary movements and preserving Austrian hegemony in Italy, feats comparable in the nineteenth century only to those of Bismarck. But contrary to Srbik – and today even more pointedly, his current hagiographer Wolfram Siemann – Metternich was not a 'constructive European statesman' with a long-range vision of the continent, but a repressive Austrian diplomat given to short-range manoeuvres and expedients, who was neither basically constructive, nor particularly European, nor genuinely conservative. From Scandinavia to the Low Countries to the Mediterranean, Metternich's aim was not to make things happen, but to stop them happening; his understanding of unrest in Spain was sterile and superficial; even in Britain, he thought civil liberties and parliamentary rule an invitation to revolution. He was certainly European, in a sense that Palmerston or Clemenceau were not. But the European society to which he was attached was that of a narrow aristocratic class, beyond which lay the dangerous abyss of a middle-class world. He valued the unity of the pentarchy of powers that had brought Napoleon down, but not to the point that he was ever willing to sacrifice the interests of Austria to any higher principle, as Alexander I had been those of Russia, and was quite prepared to split England and France away from the trio of Eastern monarchies when his goals required it. Nor, most fundamentally, was he a conservative statesman of Burkean stamp, as Srbik had presented him. The absolutism he defended might once have had a certain grandeur and fitness, but by his time it was becoming an anachronism, which he was incapable of acknowledging. Where a liberal was one who welcomed change and sought to promote it, a conservative accepted change, but sought to restrain and guide it – a stance not to be confused with that of either a 'stand-patter' who wished to preserve everything as it was, or a 'reactionary' who wanted to restore an order already past. In these years, Metternich's policy was occasionally one of reaction, usually one of standstill, and 'seldom if ever' one of conservation. What he stood for was not *Erhaltung*, but *Beharren*.[4]

Tacitly expressed in this taxonomy was Schroeder's own credo. In apportioning blame for the breakdown of relations between Japan and America, he had taken an early distance from liberalism. In his verdict on Metternich he made clear what he understood by conservatism. Like its predecessor, this book too was well received in the profession and earned him another rung in his career, an appointment within a year of its appearance to a position in what would become his permanent academic home, the history department of the University

---

4. *Metternich's Diplomacy at Its Zenith, 1820–1823*, Austin 1962, pp. 240–58.

of Illinois at Urbana-Champaign; a big campus in the Midwest which he preferred to offers from either coast as closer to family and friends, with a good scholarly reputation. A question that was obviously raised by his portrait of Metternich was whether just four years in a career spanning half a century was enough on which to pronounce a categorical judgment of him as a ruler, and Schroeder at first intended a sequel on his performance in the 1830s. But becoming bored with the subject, he changed direction to study Austria's role in the Crimean War after Metternich had fallen from power. As he did so, his focus inevitably widened, since this was a European conflict involving in one way or another all the major powers of the continent, of which he devoted principal, though not exclusive, attention to two.

Austria, Great Britain and the Crimean War would become the hinge of Schroeder's oeuvre as a whole. Structurally and chronologically, it both looks back at the epoch and continent that forms the object of his magnum opus to come, *The Transformation of European Politics 1763–1848*, and forward to the writing which followed that on the slope descending to the First World War. The two powers singled out in its title played, in Schroeder's reckoning, antithetical roles in what was to be the fatal breakdown of the Concert of Europe designed at the Congress of Vienna, which had kept the peace of the Old World for nearly forty years. When hostilities between Russia and Turkey, backed by England and France, loomed in 1853, Austria – taxed in much of the literature on the Crimean War with oscillating feebly or opportunistically between the two sides to it – had actually sought, wisely and courageously under the leadership of its foreign minister Buol and over domestic opposition, to preserve the Concert according to its rules by 'grouping' Russia in a common negotiation of the European powers with Turkey. When Ottoman, Tsarist, British and French intransigence foiled Vienna's attempts to avoid war, Austria dislodged Russia from its occupation of the principalities – today's Romania and Moldova – where Turkey was technically suzerain, but remained neutral in the war waged in Crimea, and ultimately mediated its end with the Treaty of Paris. Britain, by contrast, not only heedless of the ideals of the Concert, but brutal and treacherous in its conduct towards Austria, led the way in the attack on Russia, and under the warmongering leadership of Palmerston sought to expand the fighting from Crimea to the Baltic, with the aim of dismembering the Russian Empire itself. Schroeder's depiction of the destructive role of the Whig ministry in the war, fruit of an ostensibly liberal ideology tainted with Austrophobic prejudice, is scathing.[5]

Viewed in its own terms, *Austria, Great Britain and the Crimean War* was a powerful and original work of history. The terms, however, were self-limiting. The book says virtually nothing about the origins of the war, very little about either the Ottoman role or the French part in the conflict, does not try to reconstruct Russia's course in it, and – perhaps within its remit most critically – misconstrues the priorities of British strategy, which had far more to do with an economic, political and military calculus of imperial interests in Asia than with notionally liberal ideals.[6] The book's emphasis, as its preface explains, falls elsewhere: not on motivations but on outcomes. Shattering the Concert, the Crimean War benefitted none of the parties to it. Russia, weakened by its defeat, was humiliated by forcible disarmament

---

5. *Austria, Great Britain and the Crimean War: The Destruction of the European Concert*, Ithaca–London 1972, pp. 416–22: henceforward *AGBCW*.

6. Many years later, Schroeder would concede the Ottoman Empire touched off the fighting with a preemptive blow against Russia, while Britain waged a preventive war to stave off tsarist threats to India: see 'The Transformation of European Politics: Some Reflections', in Wolfram Pyta (ed.), *Das europäische Mächtekonzert*, Cologne 2009, p. 35.

in the Black Sea. Austria, which saved Russia from worse injury in the Treaty of Paris, was rewarded with bitter resentment for its ingratitude in failing to reciprocate the military help the Tsar had given it in crushing the Hungarian revolution in 1849, and a payback of neutrality from Russia when France attacked it in Italy. In turn the hubris of French victory in Lombardy pitched Louis Napoleon into disaster in Lorraine. England found a unified Germany, to which it had looked forward as a liberal partner to check an autocratic Austria, to be neither liberal nor a partner under Bismarck, but a military-industrial rival to its pre-eminence – Prussia, the one power to stay out of the Crimean imbroglio, the only real gainer from it. For Schroeder, the original Concert had always depended on a set of smaller Italian and German states in Central Europe, organized under Austrian hegemony, functioning as buffers between the constitutional states of Western Europe and the absolutist monarchies of Eastern Europe. By the 1870s these buffers were gone, and Bismarck's revival of a Concert system under his own management, adroit as it was, predictably proved a harsher and more brittle set of arrangements, which could not outlast him.

Framing this work was a set of striking propositions which revealed for the first time another side of Schroeder's mind. Most historians – the overwhelming majority – are ill at ease with anything to do with theory. Conceptualization, in any sharp or far-reaching sense, is foreign to them. *Austria, Great Britain and the Crimean War*, by contrast, is filled with a series of mordant analytic formulations, often of a pointedly original kind, a trait that would distinguish his writing thereafter. Among other dicta, it was here that Schroeder launched what would become one of his best-known arguments, that the 'balance of power' – a *passe-partout* of much diplomatic history – was an overrated, too often empty phrase. Though it could sometimes serve to prevent empire or hegemony of one state over others, it was not a key to international peace, for it could equally generate wars, as it frequently had in the eighteenth century. It was easier, in fact, to argue that various sorts of hegemony – from that of Austria in Italy, or the Holy Alliance in Poland, to that of the United States in North America – had more often resulted in peace than the balance of power had done.[7] The British assault on Russia in the 1850s was not to be upheld in its name.

Nor was the lesser perpetration of violence in defence of its interests by Austria than by Russia to be attributed to a higher code of conduct. 'Virtue in international affairs is almost always the daughter of fear or necessity', which does not make vices virtues.[8] What counts in relations between states are not the intentions of those who rule them, but the results of their actions, which they rarely can calculate. For peculiar to international politics is a combination of high rationality and purposefulness of means, with great uncertainty and unpredictability of outcomes. Here little or no relationship holds between power and responsibility, problems and resources, merits and rewards, crimes and punishments: 'Lazarus or Croesus, the wisest actors can play Rosencranz and Guildenstern, the stupidest Hamlet.' Statesmen were often no more responsible for the success of their policies than farmers for that of their crops.[9] Understanding such outcomes required the right starting point, which was not unit-analysis of any given state or its decisions, but system-analysis of the ensemble of powers in motion, and the upshot of the interactions between them; and when judging these, recognition that in international politics genuine values – such

---

7. *AGBCW*, pp. 401–4.
8. *AGBCW*, p. 412.
9. *AGBCW*, pp. xiv–xvi.

as peace, progress and justice – were not concordant, but opposed to each other. 'A call for peace with progress and justice is a demand for sunshine with rain and snow.'[10]

'Transformation'

It would be twenty years before Schroeder's next book appeared. Commissioned by Oxford University Press in 1980 as a prequel to the best-known volume in its series on modern Europe, A. J. P. Taylor's *Struggle for the Mastery of Europe*, published in 1954, *The Transformation of European Politics 1763–1848* met with universal acclaim. This was a 'great book', wrote Tim Blanning, combining magisterial narration, analytic brilliance and eloquent exposition, 'a landmark in the historiography of modern Europe'; or in Hamish Scott's words, there was 'immeasurable benefit' to be derived from this 'splendid' study, 'one of the very rare works which can be said to transform its subject' which would 'never look the same again'.[11] Starting at the conclusion of the Seven Years' War and ending at the outbreak of the Springtime of the Peoples, Schroeder had coverd the international scene between these dates in eight hundred pages of unfailing erudition, gift for analytic synthesis and grasp of detail, delivered with trademark trenchancy.

Transformation opens with a preface that is a manifesto for the field it would renew, what was once diplomatic, redefined as international, history: a difference that in Schroeder's scholarship

---

10. *AGBCW*, p. 428.
11. Blanning: 'Paul W. Schroeder's Concert of Europe', and Scott: 'Paul W. Schroeder's International System: The View from Vienna', *International History Review*, November 1994, pp. 714, 680.

was more than terminological, denoting not just a wider substantive focus, but a structural alteration, taking as its object not binary or other relations between singular states, but the system of interactions in which all states pursue their goals. The decisive paragraph reads,

> This book aims, among other things, to offer a concrete refutation of the view, not uncommon in recent decades, that so-called diplomatic history is superficial event-history, meaningless if not attached to the real forces shaping history and society and forming only a small part of them, the kind of history which, pursued for its own sake, gets nowhere and misses the forest for the trees. It will try, by detailed historical exposition rather than theoretical argument, to meet the view of Marxists that international history without a Marxist perspective misses the roots of international politics lying in socio-economic conditions, class structures and relations of production, of *Annales* historians that it misses the essential framework of history, the deeper structures and conjunctures of serial and total history, of *Gesellschaftsgeschichte* that it misses the driving force of modern history, the transformations wrought by industrialization and modernization. I do not doubt that traditional diplomatic history often misses the forest for the trees. I am convinced, however, that Marxists usually miss the forest for the roots; that *Annalistes*, if they pay any attention to international history at all, miss the forest for the total global landscape; and that the *Gesellscaftsgeschichtler* miss the forest for the lumber industry.

Against these misdirections Schroeder set out the path he would take: 'to see and understand the forest of international politics as a professional forester would do, with knowledge of and respect for scientific forestry as an autonomous discipline, closely related to others and drawing on them, but also possessing its own rules and system'. That meant taking as central questions what makes forests grow and die, what different forms and structures they assume, how these may gradually change over time, and not least 'what is required to prevent forests from giving way to desert'. In short, he ended, 'international history must be done systematically and ecologically, and must be done as international history, not primarily as a branch of or contribution to anything else'.[12]

Out of this methodological manifesto came the central claim that forms the theme of Schroeder's book, that the system of international politics underwent an epochal change in the second decade of the nineteenth century. The history it recounts is divided into three periods. In the eighteenth century, the foreign policy of European states was driven by balance-of-power principles which were believed to favour peace by ensuring that no overmighty state arose to threaten the security and independence of others, but in practice created continual instability and conflict, triggering one ruthless war after another. When the most destructive of these, the Seven Years' War, came to an end, it was widely thought that an exhausted calm would follow. Instead the three great Eastern monarchies, Russia, Prussia and Austria, fell upon Poland, slicing most of it up between them in 1772, and six years later the revolt of American settlers against the British monarchy detonated an Atlantic war pitting France, Spain and the Netherlands against Britain. Before it was over, Austria and Prussia were at blows over succession to the throne of Bavaria, and well before it started Russia had attacked the Ottoman Empire in the longest and bloodiest war of the period, beginning in 1768 and ending with Russian control of Crimea. *Raison d'état* dictated all these conflicts, which were close to a zero-sum game in which – so Schroeder – 'the motive and rule of all action was to advance the

---

12. *The Transformation of European Politics 1763–1848*, Oxford 1992, pp ix–x; henceforward *TEP*.

interests of the state – meaning first of all its power, security and wealth, but also, almost equally, its monarch's honour and prestige and rank among other princes'.[13]

The French Revolution of 1789, often presented as an upheaval inaugurating a new epoch, did not significantly alter this pattern, the war waged against it three years later by Prussia and Austria, each seeking territorial gains at the expense of France, belonging to the traditional repertoire of the major powers of the period. The revolution in France was a 'contingent event', a rupture at unit level which could have been avoided, as revolutions were elsewhere on the continent. At system level, by contrast, wars were structural and inevitable. Two years earlier, a further wave of them was set off with the attack launched by Turkey on Russia in 1787, Austria participating against Turkey before joining in the attack on France. Thereafter, a virtually unbroken sequence of 'great systemic wars' swept across Europe for another twenty-three years.

In the course of these, developments in France would intensify international conflicts in two ways, taking their underlying logic to extremities never known before, without changing them systemically: firstly, by introducing the *levée en masse* to mobilize armies of a far more formidable sort than in the past, and secondly, by injecting a new ideological spirit into the confrontation between states. Out of these innovations came the rise to power of Napoleon: an adventurer distinguished from the hereditary rulers whose company he would eventually join less by his military or administrative gifts, than by a complete lack of scruples or restraints in the pursuit of 'power after power', in Hobbes's expression, to no other end than acquire insatiably more of it. Schroeder tracks his successive campaigns from early triumph

---

13. *TEP*, p. 8.

in Italy to final disasters in Russia, then Germany, with pithy assurance. His imperial rule modernized France and adjacent lands where it enjoyed a passive consent, but was everywhere ruthlessly exploitative and indifferent to human life, ultimately digging its own grave.

The one lasting benefit Napoleon conferred to the continent he despoiled was to convince the allies who brought him down that they must abandon the power-political free-for-all he had exploited and they had themselves traditionally practised. They had instead to construct a new international order antithetical in character, based on cooperation between the major monarchies of Europe rather than competition between them, in the service of a durable peace. This they achieved at the Congress of Vienna. There, the settlement devised by the statesmen of the Quadruple Alliance that had defeated France, Alexander I, Metternich, Castlereagh, and Hardenberg, with some assistance from Talleyrand as a transfuge from Napoleon's regime, was designed to spare the Old World henceforward from the two great scourges of recent memory, revolution and war. That meant jettisoning balance-of-power doctrines that had proved so destructive, in favour of the novel, very different principle of a 'political equilibrium', which Schroeder defined as 'a Europe of independent sovereign states, equal in rights, status and security, if vastly unequal in power, responsibility and influence, protected by a balance between power on the one hand and rights, law, morality and consensus on the other'.[14]

On this basis, the settlement reached at Vienna had four components. The purpose of alliances would no longer – as in the past – be capability-aggregation with a view to war, but mutual restraint to maintain peace. The victors would receive territorial satisfaction for

---

14. *TEP*, p. 504.

the sacrifices they had made in a common cause, but these would be moderate and equitable by the standards of the age: Russia regaining most of Poland; Austria accorded hegemony in central Europe with control of northern Italy and leadership of the confederation of states created in Germany; Prussia rewarded with an extension to the Rhineland; Britain left in possession of Dutch and French colonies in the tropics. In France, the Bourbon monarchy was restored within the borders of 1790, and an indemnity on the country imposed. Informing all these arrangements was the principle of legitimacy enunciated by Talleyrand at the Congress – the long-standing rights of hereditary rulers to their lands and sovereignty over them, understood as the public law of Europe – and the kind of moral and legal equilibrium it required and propagated: 'a balance of satisfactions, a balance of rights and obligations and a balance of performance and payoffs, rather than a balance of power'.[15] The guarantor of those would be the pentarchy of Great Powers formed with the readmission of France to their ranks at the Congress of Aix in 1818.

These states were not all of the same weight. The two flanking powers of Russia and Britain, without rival respectively on land and sea, shared hegemony within the system. Between the five powers frictions were not uncommon, but for two generations they were contained by the common purpose of the Concert of Europe they composed, to prevent war and suppress revolution. In their eyes, these dangers were interconnected. But they were not, Schroeder suggests, of equal moment. 'European leaders were not driven to seek lasting peace because they feared revolution. They did so because they feared war, had learned that war *was* revolution, and wanted no

---

15. 'The Nineteenth-Century System: Balance of Power or Political Equilibrium?', *Review of International Studies*, April 1989, p. 143.

more of it.'[16] The result was an alteration of collective mentalities so deep that the term in the New Testament for repentance – '*metanoia*, a turning around of the mind' – could be used to capture it. The long-term consequences of this change, Schroeder argued, were enormous. They amounted to the very opposite of a restoration, as the Vienna settlement was too often characterized then and later. This was a revolution historically more momentous than the Industrial or the French revolutions.[17] An index of its effect across the nineteenth century was a drop in European deaths on the battlefields of the nineteenth century to a seventh of the levels preceding it.

The epic twenty-six years from the French Revolution to the Congress of Vienna are given five hundred pages in *Transformation*, the subdued thirty-three that succeeded them, three hundred – less coverage for lesser events, yet affording similar instruction. When signs of renewed disturbance threatened the post-war peace, the architects of Vienna, though differing at times on tactics, proved sure-handed in dealing with them. In 1819 Metternich had little difficulty quelling student and literary unrest in Germany with the Carlsbad Decrees, Liverpool and Castlereagh in gagging critical reaction to Peterloo. When liberal revolutions broke out in Spain and Naples in 1820, Austrian troops restored order in southern Italy, and three years later a French expeditionary force put paid to impractical attempts to create a premature constitutionalism in Spain. None of these troubles enjoyed significant popular support, for it was a period when the masses shared the outlook of their rulers, wanting peace

---

16. 'Did the Vienna System Rest on a Balance of Power?', *American Historical Review*, June 1992, p. 700. 'It is wrong to suppose that the fear of popular revolution or the popular pressures created by French revolutionary ideas or Napoleonic reforms motivated them to construct a more peaceful international system.'

17. *TEP*, p. viii.

and order rather than political experiments. That was not so when Greeks rose against Turkish rule in 1821, when the peasantry of the Peloponnese exploded in a social and religious rebellion against their Muslim masters and neighbours, and nationalist agitators appealed to the Tsar for help against Ottoman power in Orthodox solidarity. But loyal to the principles of the Concert, Alexander I refused to take Russian imperial advantage of the uprising, denouncing it as a menace to the peace of Europe confected by revolutionary conspirators in Paris. When the Greek movement persisted, arousing philhellene sympathies across Europe, his successor Nicholas I reached an agreement with London and Paris (Vienna remaining pro-Turkish throughout) on a prophylactic intervention to prevent complete Ottoman victory; which, after escalating into a Russo-Turkish war, ended with the creation by the three European powers of a formally independent Greek state, a protectorate of the Concert administered by a Bavarian prince – revolution averted and the peace of Europe preserved.

The strength of the new international order was revealed by the outcome of the next challenge to it, when in 1830 the Bourbon legitimist Charles X was overthrown in France, the Dutch monarchy was evicted in Belgium, and a Polish rising against Russian rule proclaimed a provisional government – all three events blows to the compact of Vienna. Each was resolved in turn without significant damage to the Concert. In France, power was transferred virtually overnight to the Orleanist branch of the Bourbons in the person of Louis Philippe, and in good time proletarian protest and republican dissent were swept up. In Belgium, great power differences over the country's future were smoothed away by the induction of another German prince as monarch of a neutral state, guaranteed by the Concert. In Poland, Russian troops crushed Polish resistance without much demur in the pentarchy. The order of Vienna had shown itself flexible enough to accommodate change, even where initiated under doubtful auspices (fighting in the streets of Paris, machine-breaking and looting in Brussels), recuperating the better side of the revolts where these were compatible with it, perforce accepting a heavier hand where they were not. Politically, Europe was now more clearly divided than it had once been, between liberal-constitutional governments in the West and absolutist monarchies in the East. But pragmatically, the unity of the Concert was for the most part unimpaired.

The short shocks to it of 1830–32 soon absorbed by the Vienna system, the 1840s were internationally speaking a largely uneventful decade, its calm ruffled only by petty Anglo-French disputes over Spain, a small set-to in Switzerland, and the suppression of passing trouble in Cracow by the Eastern monarchies. Closing it came the much larger drama of 1848, with revolutions against the established order sweeping like wildfire across the continent, in France, Germany, Italy, Austria, Hungary, Poland, the Principalities. These were possible, Schroeder argues, just because the political order created by the victors over Napoleon was never the counter-revolutionary system of repression and reaction caricatured by its critics. Enjoying widespread popular consent, it had no need for tyranny. Its governments might be conservative, but they were also 'legalistic and peaceful, restrained by treaties and the rules of the essentially cooperative and consensual games they had learned to play. They were inhibited from using force against their peoples or each other.' Radicals expected them to remain 'passive targets of their attacks', and when they rose up against their rulers, they gave way 'almost without a fight'. If they soon recovered and the revolutions petered out without achieving any of their ends, that was in part because, beyond the succession of so many, at times interconnected, national upheavals, the international system in which every state was embedded remained intact. No wars broke out between them; no treaties were scrapped; no frontiers were changed: an 'astounding' outcome, proof that 'as a way of preserving a political balance in Europe', allowing different actors to pursue their ends without violent collisions, 'the 1815 system was in 1848 still as necessary and effective as it had ever been'.[18] True, it could not and did not last forever, and worse was to follow it. The last words of *Transformation* read: 'The light that began to shine in international politics in 1815 was brief, fitful and wintry. It would be followed by a long twilight, and an even longer, bitterly cold night. Let there be no mistake, however, 1815 was not a false dawn. It marked a new day, and it helps to make other new days thinkable.'[19]

How to take the measure of *Transformation*? A masterpiece of architectonic narrative, it is difficult to think of any comparable work since. At the time, Schroeder tipped his hat to Taylor's history of the next fifty years of European diplomacy, but a subsequent devastating essay on the latter would make it clear how little the two books actually had in common.[20] Certainly, no other work of history comes near the power of its demonstration of the political reality and autonomy of international systems. What of its own politics? *Transformation* is plainly the product of a conservative mind. How far did that shape its achievement? At the margins, it undoubtedly affected Schroeder's judgment of selected persons and nations. Within the pentarchy whose story is essentially that of the book, the two powers which already had centre stage in his work on the Crimean War, Austria and England, stand out: Austria as the fulcrum of the Concert created

---

18. *TEP*, pp. 799–801.
19. *TEP*, p. 804.
20. Dissected as a *locus classicus* of vacant balance of power truisms: 'A.J.P. Taylor's International System', *International History Review*, March 2001, pp. 2–27.

with the defeat of Napoleon, against whom it had fought longer than any other country, and which depended more than any other on the Concert for its status and survival as a Great Power; England, as the paymaster of the coalition against Napoleon, and the steadiest of the original powers at Vienna, if becoming over time the least constructive of them.

Taxed with too favourable a view of Austria's role in the international politics of the time, Metternich featuring as the 'flawed hero' of the tale, Schroeder would reply that such a criticism was in error. Austria was not better than the other Great Powers, it was simply different – a *Hausmacht* owing its lands less to conquest than others, more to tradition, marriage and compromise, whose ethnic heterogeneity and strategic proximity to a much larger, more militarized Russia forced it to seek security in concertation rather than conflict. As to its rulers, not Metternich, mostly a 'clever but shallow diplomat', but Leopold II, 'a great statesman' who anticipated the design of the Concert of Europe before it became possible, was the true hero of his book.[21] Along with Castlereagh, an 'uncommon fund of good sense' whose appointment as foreign secretary in 1812 was as providential for Britain and Europe as that of Churchill in 1941. The same could not be said of Canning, 'a vain, ambitious schoolboy who never quite grew up', or Palmerston, a demagogic opportunist successful only so long as the Concert, which he manipulated and undermined, persisted.[22] Britain's part in crafting the system of Vienna was central, but in keeping it in good shape after Castlereagh was gone, not infrequently erratic to minimal.

---

21. *TEP*, p. 88; 'Balance of Power and Political Equilibrium: A Response', *International History Review*, November 1994, p. 747.

22. *TEP*, pp. 458, 361, 755–6.

Still, in the struggle against Napoleon special allowances had to be made for it. Wars in the name of honour might belong to the pernicious balance-of-power politics of the eighteenth century, but Britain's decision to declare war on France in 1803 'because it could not stand being further challenged and humiliated by Bonaparte' was justified, even if Napoleon himself did not want war, since British honour was at stake. The bombardment of Copenhagen, sinking the Danish fleet without provocation or warning in 1807? 'Desperate expedients are understandable in desperate times.' War with America in 1812? 'American historians have made little of the paradox that the infant democratic republic should have entered this titanic world struggle on the side of one of modern history's worst tyrants.' Why did it do so? Can it have been that 'Jefferson and Madison shared Napoleon's visceral hatred of Great Britain'?[23]

That last phrase might seem to invite a *tu quoque*, given the depiction of Napoleon by Schroeder himself. A critic of American moralism in his first book, in *Transformation* he gives free rein to what could be thought close to it. As a ruler Napoleon did not *go* wrong: 'his whole character and career were fundamentally wrong'. Starting out as a ruthless military dictator in France, he was an utterly lawless adventurer, respecting no promise, scruple or convention in his lust for glory, empty of any end beyond it. Seething with rage and frustration at Britain, unable to think of what to do with Austria or Prussia after defeating them, since they were too large and too far from France to be annexed, grabbing Spain with an odious combination of force, treachery and swindle, invading Russia with less rational purpose than Hitler, Bonaparte was a corsair, a condottiere and a capo mafioso,

---

23. *TEP*, pp. 243–5, 329, 400.

whose foreign policy amounted to a criminal enterprise.[24] At home, an initially enlightened despotism became steadily less enlightened and more despotic. Abroad, his empire was a structural impossibility, a 'vast experiment in colonialism within Europe', founded on military conquest, extortion of plunder and conscription of cannon fodder, which even if accompanied, as colonies typically are, with a certain measure of modernization, could never have lasted.

Undeniably, much in Schroeder's portrait of Napoleon is incisive and accurate. But signs of a loss of balance are also plain. Characterization of his empire as a colonial system within Europe overlooks the obvious difference that it lacked the racial hierarchy inseparable from colonialism, making Schroeder's analogy of it with Hitler's conquests more polemical than historical. If a comparison were sought, the Roman empire after Caracalla, involving no ethnic distinction among citizens, would be closer. So too, heaping of multiple titles of obloquy on Napoleon is self-defeating. Historically, a corsair, a condottiere and a mafioso belong to different cultures and epochs – stringing such disparate figures into a single stock malefactor points to the weakness at the centre of Schroeder's commination. For in a full-dress essay on his target published during the composition of *Transformation*, he pressed home his charge of Napoleon's criminality in ways that undo it. It was not a moral, but a political judgment, he maintained: a classification that was not concerned with specific actions or episodes in Napoleon's career – rulers like Frederick II or Catherine II had committed equivalents – but rather with the reality that he alone systematically, deliberately violated international law,

---

24. *TEP*, pp. 230, 348–9, 343, 396–7; 'arguably the greatest corsair, condottiere and capo mafioso in history': 'Napoleon's Foreign Policy: A Criminal Enterprise', *Journal of Military History*, April 1990, p. 160.

cynically aware that he was doing so, while invoking it to condemn others. For historians to cover the enormity of this record with euphemisms, or to suggest that at some stage he just lost his way, was 'to deny his demonic dimension', making him less great and less interesting than he was. 'This is to diminish Napoleon. Let him be Lucifer, not Samson.'[25]

That, however, was for Schroeder to have his cake and eat it. The distinction between political and moral judgments that warrants the label 'criminality' rests on the claim that Napoleon trampled on international law, but as Schroeder himself at one point confesses, and then forgets, *nullum crimen sine lege*. He may have been unfamiliar with John Austin's critique of the very idea of international law, demonstrating that it was no more than 'opinion', unsupported by any authority giving it the force of meaningful legislation. But that by the twentieth century it was a term to which all states would pay lip service, and if possessed of any power flout as they pleased, he could not have been unaware. As for the eighteenth and early nineteenth century, the locution did not yet even exist as a common currency. Unwritten conventions governing relations between states of course there were, and Napoleon certainly defied these. But Schroeder misread his violations of them as the psychic pathology of an individual, when what they actually reflected was a much more significant collective change. Napoleon's disregard of any limits in his exercise of power, rightly emphasized by Schroeder, was the product of a revolt, in which he was far from alone, against the limits of the world in which he made his way. In international politics, these were

---

25. 'Napoleon's Foreign Policy: A Criminal Enterprise', pp. 148–50, 159–60. The implications of the fact that after defeating and holding him, the Allies never put Napoleon on trial, rendering Schroeder's verdict an incongruous anachronism, do not seem to have struck him.

the traditions of royal solidarity: monarchs did not devour monarchs. Hereditary rulers might constantly be attacking one another, with the intention of seizing territory or population or other forms of wealth from them, but there was a built-in limit to their aggressions: straightforward geopolitical regicide – destroying a reigning dynasty, abolishing an entire state – lay beyond it.

In Schroeder's period, the one apparent exception proved the rule. Poland could be partitioned without scandal – 'it was an example of system-conforming behaviour'[26] – because it was de facto a nobiliary republic, whose monarchs were merely elective. Lacking any hereditary legitimacy, they could be disposed of without much fuss. The houses of Wittelsbach or Savoy, Orange or Wettin could not be given the same treatment by their peers. These were rules for which Napoleon had not the slightest respect, treating thrones across Europe as so many baubles to be distributed to his kin or liegemen. So though he awarded himself imperial rank and proliferated titles in his entourage, every monarchy had reason to fear him, and he no reason to see in their inherited rights any necessary limit to his own power.

That explosive *décalage* derived, naturally, from the French Revolution that was Napoleon's political birthplace, however much he later sought to efface it, and the springboard of his career. Schroeder makes no secret of his lack of sympathy with it. The French Revolution was not just a contingent event at the lower unit-level of the international system, it was a 'disastrous failure' – producing not liberty, equality and fraternity, but 'chaos, civil war, and rule by force and terror', discrediting revolution and democracy for two generations to come, and discouraging 'the very idea of political reform and popular participation in politics of any kind'. True, the

---

26. *TEP*, p. 18.

seed of the democratic ideal survived, and later democracies were 'to some extent' indebted to the Revolution. But if so, hardly the French themselves. By the time of the July monarchy, Schroeder could write of the 'immaturity and unrealism of the French body politic'. For, 'as almost always in history, the French government needed to be wiser, less selfish and short-sighted than its people, and found it hard to meet the need'. Such Rhadamanthine judgments, as Derek Beales would call them, say more about Schroeder's sensibility than their object. But they offer a backdrop for considering what he has to say about the time when the French Revolution and its Napoleonic outcome had become anathema in polite society. Though here he mentions political ideas, it is fair to say they play curiously little role in his narrative. *Transformation* is marked by the paradoxical absence, given Schroeder's unusual early grounding in the classical canon of philosophy, of any of the leading thinkers of its age.[27] The lacuna can be regarded as more than incidental, since one of its effects is an uncritical treatment of the *pièce de resistance* of the ideology of the Restoration, the notion of 'legitimacy', which in *Transformation* is divested of its actual meaning as the sanctity of all inherited property and privilege, to be wrapped in the loftier toga of Metternich's favourite trope, 'the public law of Europe', as if such a thing existed, other than as a licence for the pentarchy to act as it pleased.

The grandeur of Schroeder's representation of the peace of Vienna after the wreckage of so many wars tearing Europe apart – spelling out

---

27. As noticed by Beales, in a vivid and otherwise very admiring review of the book: 'given that a change of attitudes is central to his story, it is strange that he does not devote a single line to contemporary theorists. Hume, Rousseau, Saint-Pierre, Kant, Bentham, Hegel, Maistre are not in the index'. *English Historical Review*, April 1996, p. 396.

with compelling precision and detail, over such a wide expanse of time and space, why it was an epochal turning point, generating a hitherto unknown sort of international system – is incontestable. There is no question that the transformation of direction and scale which he describes occurred. What powered the change, and what its effects were, are another matter. For Schroeder the driving force behind the arrangements of Vienna was fear of reversion to the kind of conflicts that had raged between states since the late eighteenth century. War was the great engine of destruction threatening European society. Among its byproducts was revolution, against which society must defend itself too. But within the pentarchy war was the overarching dread. It is striking, however, how little evidence Schroeder offers for this claim. Not a single quotation, from any of the principal actors at Vienna, or those advising or assisting them, is mustered to support it. Whereas statements illustrating the contrary, that the overriding fear of the pentarchs and their company was revolution, litter the documents of the time.

There was a simple reason why. Four monarchies decided the fate, and settled the map, of Europe. After conquering Napoleon together, they became satisfied powers, each awarding themselves, by mutual agreement, substantial enhancements of the territory and population they controlled, while doling out minor portions to lesser states. France alone, as befitted the loser on the field, was reduced in size, but compensated with admission in due course to their number as again a fellow monarchy, and soon with acquisition of what would become a very large colony across the water in the Mediterranean. That the arrogation of such determining prerogatives to the pentarchy alone, proclaiming a clear-cut division between Great Powers and smaller fry, made a mockery of the notion that the settlement of 1815 guaranteed a Europe of states that were 'equal in rights', is obvious.

Before the Congress of Vienna was even over, Friedrich Gentz, its secretary and author of its Final Declaration, the one original mind to grace it, could write with candour of its work: 'The grand phrases of "reconstruction of social order", "regeneration of the political system of Europe", "a lasting peace founded on a just division of strength" were uttered to tranquillize the people, and to give an air of dignity and grandeur to this grand assembly; but the real purpose of the Congress was to divide among the conquerors the spoils taken from the vanquished.'[28]

That was a simplification, but it expressed a central truth. Once they had settled the main business of the Congress, over which the distribution of territory had occasioned brief tensions and *pro forma* threats between the states running it, fear of wars between them subsided to vanishing point, so remote was such a possibility. Fear of revolution, by contrast, haunted them for a generation. In 1815 the aim of the Allies was for Wellington 'to put an end to the French Revolution'.[29] For Castlereagh, the priority of Allied diplomacy must be 'to inspire the states of Europe with a sense of the dangers they have surmounted by their union', and 'make them feel that the existing concert was their only perfect security against the revolutionary embers more or less existing in every state of Europe'.[30] Five years later, for Metternich the Concert faced 'indescribable calamities to society' if the 'moral gangrene' of the middle classes with their talk of 'constitutions' and 'reform' was not

---

28. Written on 12 February and 5 July 1815: see *Memoirs of Prince Metternich*, Vol. II, London 1881, p. 553; *Dépêches inédites du Chevalier de Gentz aux Hospodars de Valachie*, Vol. 1, Paris 1876, pp. 153, 156.

29. Wellington to Castlereagh, 11 August 1815: see Mark Jarrett, *The Congress of Vienna and Its Legacy: War and Great Diplomacy after Napoleon*, London–New York 2013, pp. 165, 428.

30. Carsten Holbraad, *The Concert of Europe*, London 1970, p. 19.

checked.[31] Another two years on, and Alexander I was declaring at the Congress of Verona: 'The sole aim of the Alliance is that for which it was formed: to combat revolution.'[32] For Castlereagh, the Greek revolt was 'a branch of that organized spirit of insurrection which is systematically propagating itself throughout Europe', while 'Turkey, with all its barbarisms, constitutes in the system of Europe what may be regarded as a necessary evil'.[33]

These are not sentiments generally discoverable in *Transformation*, where they would jar with the lenitive image of a Restoration enjoying such wide consent that little repression was ever needed to enforce it. When popular discontent does surface, the general tenor of Schroeder's report of it is a reproachful regret rather than any hostile alarm. Ferdinand VII, though 'not highly endowed with intellect and character', wanted to heal Spain's wounds, the constitution of the liberals who revolted against him was impractical, and French intervention to suppress them a political and military success. The spread of their utopian notions to Naples was unfortunate, Austrian intervention to restore order may have been unedifying, but its leadership in Italy was indispensable. The excesses of the Greek rising, ignited by conspiracies and accidents, provoked those of Turkish retaliation.[34] There is far more critical treatment of episodes like these in Mark Jarrett's subsequent work on the Concert system.[35]

---

31. Metternich, *Memoirs*, Vol. III, London 1881, pp. 464–5.
32. Alexander I to the Comte de la Ferronays, 27 October 1822, cited in Jarrett, *The Congress of Vienna*, p. 207.
33. Castlereagh to the Tsar, 16 July 1821: Jarrett, *The Congress of Vienna*, pp. 297, 469.
34. *TEP*, pp. 607–8, 627, 613–14, 615, 617.
35. Jarrett's study is now much the best close-up narrative of these years of the Restoration.

Schroeder was by his own description a conservative historian; yet he was a deeply principled and humane one. What accounts for the dismissive – at times seemingly callous – note of his comments on successive outbreaks of opposition to the order of Vienna, or his contention that this was so mild that revolutions against it eventually became easy?[36] Certainly, one explanation lies in his conceptual architecture. Such upheavals were, like the French Revolution whose inspiration lay behind all of them, unit-level events, below the plumb line of systemic significance that was the focus of *Transformation*, and as such necessarily of secondary moment. So he could write coolly, not just of the way the pentarchy stopped the dangers to it in Greece with a tame foreign monarchy, and raised no objection to French colonial seizure of Algeria, as events with a higher-level functionality. For all its costs to Paris, 'France's hold on Algeria and Britain's toleration of it were useful to the international system'. Otto's government in Athens was 'an unsatisfactory outcome in various ways', since it was German and Catholic in a Hellene and Orthodox society, burdened with foreign debt – but 'from the international vantage point, it had its advantages'. For 'Algeria and Greece are further instances of how the Vienna system', after all,

---

36. Prompting Blanning to wonder politely how 'Polish exiles in Paris or Italian revolutionaries rotting in Austrian prisons would have reacted to the news that "it was relatively easy and safe to promote revolution" in Europe after 1815': 'Paul W. Schroeder's Concert of Europe', p. 711. Without withdrawing this claim, Schroeder would later admit that Poland represented a major problem that the Vienna Settlement failed to solve, the nationalities question, while pointing out that Ireland was another, even more glaring case of the same, whose 'conflicts and tragedies' in some ways even exceeded those of Poland – in Ireland even his hero Castlereagh was a hardliner in repression – yet no one included them in the litany of complaints against the Settlement: 'The Transformation of European Politics: Some Reflections', p. 28.

'worked to manage crises, preserve peace, and maintain a balance of satisfaction among major actors'.[37]

That, Schroeder had early insisted, was what counted: internationally, order comes before justice, and to ask for both at once is to expect sunshine in a snowstorm. 'No international order can be expected of itself to promote a better, more just society, or judged primarily on how well it does so', he repeated in *Transformation*. 'To expect it to do so is not only to ignore the necessary, inescapable priority of the pursuit of order over justice in international affairs, but to demand of an international order what it cannot deliver and what would ruin it for its other central purposes if it tried'.[38] Such an axiom leaves unanswered, however, the question: what then of justice at unit level? Does it, too, necessarily come after order, as established? Logically speaking, order may indeed precede justice. But does that mean, politically speaking, that international order is within its rights in overriding any domestic justice? Are roots irrelevant to the forest that grows from them? That Schroeder was aware of the problem, and could not bring himself to deny any answer to it is tacitly acknowledged by him, in the same breath as he extols the examples of Greece and Algeria, when he goes on to admit that the revolutions of 1830 'revealed the deep divergence between peasant and worker concepts of liberty'.[39] By the time he reaches the revolutions of 1848, at the very end of the book, there comes the decisive retrospective correction of the way the Vienna system is portrayed at the incipit of his account of it. After hailing, once again, 'the different international politics' and 'more stable, peaceful era' it made possible, he continues:

---

37. *TEP*, p. 710.
38. *TEP*, pp. 576, 577.
39. *TEP*, p. 711.

It could not last forever, and did not. The elites which supported it and profited from it were too narrow in their outlook and limited in their social base. The system they set up, despite its undeniable improvements over previous systems, contained a number of unjust and unworkable features. The capacity of this system for absorbing and facilitating change and meeting new problems and challenges, though far greater than previous ones, was limited at the outset and stunted in important ways later on. Above all, the international order established in 1815 was too closely linked in the public mind, justly or unjustly, with a domestic political and social order already past its peak when the system was created, certain to be superseded or overthrown, and widely perceived as oppressive and stifling.[40]

As a concluding verdict, this is not so far from Adam Zamoyski's punning dictum that the effect of Vienna was an 'Arrest of Europe', alienating educated people everywhere. That Schroeder could so readily, without changing gear, alter the gist of his own portrayal of the settlement of 1815 speaks to an important truth about it. His factual exposition of the Concert of Europe as an epoch-making transformation of the international system remains a theoretical and historical landmark. His political evaluation of it was more contestable, and even in his own writing ultimately somewhat variable. The difference between the two leaves the design of his structural achievement untouched. Distinct from it, however, was a limit in the design itself. There the most important criticism of *Transformation* would lie. A decade after its appearance, a collection of twenty-two essays on Schroeder's arguments and their implications for the diplomatic history of Europe from the early seventeenth to the turn of the twenty-first century was published in Germany.[41] Among a

---

40. *TEP*, pp. 802–3.
41. Peter Krüger and Paul Schroeder, *'The Transformation of European Politics, 1763–1848': Episode or Model in Modern History?*, Münster 2002.

distinguished array of responses to the book, one in particular stood out. Its author was Edward Ingram, historian of the British Empire in India and the Middle East.[42]

In his contribution, he pointed out that the Vienna system had always been structurally flawed by its omission of the Ottoman Empire from the Concert of Europe, excluded because it was not Christian, although it covered the whole south-east quadrant of the continent. The settlement between the Great Powers reached at Vienna had rested on a clear-cut demarcation between Europe, where a lasting peace between them would prevail, and the rest of the world, where colonial wars and conquests could proceed unchecked, on the understanding that these would not extend to armed conflict between rival colonizers themselves. For this division to hold good, however, there had to be an unambiguous boundary closing the core off from the periphery of the system, and agreed regulation of actions in the periphery. The territory of the sultanate, stretching from Europe into Asia and Africa, negated both requirements. The result was that the bellicism which Vienna banished from the core, instead of finding a harmless outlet in remote lands overseas, ricocheted back into it from the Balkan gap in the system, first with the Greek revolt, then via the Principalities into the Crimean War, eventually blowing up the peace of Europe at Sarajevo.

Responding to his critics at the end of the collection, Schroeder had no real comeback to this one.[43] For, undeniably, *Transformation*

---

42. 'Bellicism as Boomerang: The Eastern Question during the Vienna System', in ibid., pp. 207–25. Ingram was born in India, trained in Oxford, taught in Canada, and died in New Zealand. His contribution to rethinking the general history of Europe has already been noted: p. 213 above.

43. Conceding that Ingram's critique was a fundamental challenge to his account of the Vienna system, and showed great insight, he confined himself to

had failed to register the enormous consequences of the Balkan gap in the international system of 1815. To this day, no detailed study exists of the way in which the door of the Concert was shut to the Sublime Porte at Vienna. Schroeder can hardly be blamed for his lack of attention to that, Ottoman archives anyway being inaccessible to him. But what is clear is that in the eyes of the pentarchs, the sultanate was a legitimate monarchy whose rights over its lands and its subjects were to be respected like those of any other dynastic realm, even if its faith was alien and its methods barbarous. Uniquely among extra-European states, indeed, for over a century it had enjoyed normal diplomatic relations with the major powers of Europe. Yet if any form of rule could be described as colonial in character within Europe, it was not Napoleonic but Ottoman, even if its structure of domination was not racial but religious, generating national movements – often inspired by the French Revolution – against it of an intensity and duration exceeding anything elsewhere in Europe, including those against Napoleon's empire.

This, as indicated by his reaction to the Greek revolt, was not a landscape where Schroeder felt at home; nor, of course, on the Turkish side of it either. What he could see, and engaged with, were the knock-on effects for the Concert of trouble in the Balkans and

---

observing that Ingram antedated the deliberate export by Europe of bellicism to the periphery, which had developed only after the Concert system had declined in the late nineteenth century: 'Epilogue: Transformation or Evolution – Linear or Catastrophic', in ibid., pp. 330–1. Some years later, he would qualify this claim, remarking that while it was true European imperialism and bellicism, which had been rampant in the eighteenth century, were 'in remission' between 1815 and the mid 1850s, this applied only to eastward expansion. For westward it was indeed being 'diverted' – by proxy across the Atlantic to North America, where in this era the United States became 'the most bellicose, aggressive and imperialist state in the world': 'The Transformations of European Politics: Some Reflections', pp. 30–1.

in the Near East – the sultan's summons of an Egyptian army to crush the revolt in the Peloponnese precipitating the ambitions of Mehmet Ali, his nominal *locum* in Cairo, to take over the Ottoman Empire, or failing that to subtract the Levant from it. Twice, the ensuing conflicts triggered the sharpest conflicts within the Concert of the 1830s and 1840s, pitting France against Britain and Russia, each time involving blatant violations of the Concert's prohibition (*apud* Schroeder) of the humiliation of one member by another.[44] On the third occasion, when a minor dispute between France and Russia over clerical precedence in the Levant escalated into outright war within the Concert, Ingram pointed out that it was the Porte that took the initiative in setting the Crimean conflict alight, rather than any of the European participants. The peace of Vienna 'collapsed when the natives crashed the party at the colonials' club'.[45] It is noticeable that at no point in all these imbroglios does Schroeder extend to the Ottoman state and its rulers the kind of fine-grained calculus of diplomatic motive and manoeuvre accorded the European players in them. Turkey remains an opaque residual in his narrative, which escapes its systemic logic.[46]

How far do such limitations affect the magnitude of *The Transformation of European Politics*? In the end, very little. Schroeder was confident enough of what he had produced to disclaim any pretention to the visual beauty of landscape painting, the smooth polish of a massive sculpture, the imposing boldness of an architectural design. 'The only way I know how to do history resembles working in

---

44. For a scathing account of this record, see Korina Kagan, 'The Myth of the European Concert: The Realist-Internationalist Debate and Great Power Behaviour in the Eastern Question, 1821–1841', *Security Studies*, Winter 1997/1998, pp. 1–57.

45. 'Bellicism as Boomerang', p. 225.

46. 'In a sense it was too un-European and unmodern to collapse even after military defeat': *TEP*, p. 659.

wrought iron.' That involved 'gathering and combining an intractable mass of raw materials', and 'beating them into the shape one feels ought to emerge'. But though the end product might not be beautiful, possibly even graceful, 'wrought iron has one virtue: if made well, it can bear considerable weight'.[47] No better case for the strength of the book could be made. Yet if an alternative image of how it might be assessed were needed, painting could supply one. *Transformation* could be compared to the representation of an epic scene – or even a miracle? – by an Old Master, whose composition is near perfect, if its coloration more uneven, some figures given too dark, others too light a tone, and the picture missing a panel on the right; yet withal a work of such grandeur that its flaws do not seriously diminish it.

Towards the First World War

Schroeder was in his mid-sixties when *Transformation* came out. It was his last completed work. A decade later, it was at the initiative of three friends that a collection of magnificent essays covering the full range of his different interests appeared under the rubric of *Systems, Stability and Statecraft*. He had always been a prolific article writer, and produced about half of his output in this form after the publication of his magnum opus. Of these, perhaps a third were substantial *postillas* or sidebars to it, in which he either modified or extended its arguments. Among the former was a self-correction that the *Transformation* of its title was 'not a revolution like the French one or others' that created 'a fundamentally different set of norms, rules and institutions', more closely resembling 'an evolution than a revolution – though not restoration or reaction';

---

47. *TEP*, p. xiii.

rather than marking any simple break with the eighteenth century, it owed important roots to its predecessor, on which it built.[48] Among the latter probably the most important was his major essay, appearing first in Germany and then in America, on 'The Life and Death of a Long Peace: Austro-German-Russian Relations 1763–1914'.[49] Another set of texts was the fruit of a long-standing engagement with international relations theory, which he took much more seriously than most historians have done, out of a natural affinity for its theoretical bent. There, in his view, at fault was the dogma of the balance of power as a universal leitmotif of interstate relations, an assumption admittedly shared in their own less articulate idiom by most historians, but taken to a logical extreme in the 'neorealism' associated with Kenneth Waltz, the dominant school in American IR at the time. Contradicting Waltz was the weight of evidence of the past, which showed – as Schroeder illustrated at length – that not balancing against the most powerful state of the hour, but band-wagoning with it, was the most common response to the emergence of any would-be or actual hegemon.[50] Nor could states be treated as so many equivalent agents, distinguished from each other only by virtue of the size of the assets – territory, population etc. – allowing them to enforce their will on others. A functional differentiation was inherent in any international order, where intermediary states,

---

48. For example, 'there was more of Pitt's 1805 policy in Castlereagh's of 1812–15 than I formerly recognized': 'The Transformation of European Politics: Some Reflections', in Pyta, *Das europäische Mächtekonzert*, pp. 25–6.

49. Originally appearing in Ulrich Lappenküper et al. (eds), *Masse und Macht im 19. und 20. Jahrhundert*, Munich 2003, republished in Raimo Väyrynen (ed.), *The Waning of Major War: Theories and Debates*, London 2006, pp. 33–63.

50. Case set out in 'Historical Reality vs Neo-Realist Theory', *International Security*, Summer 1994, pp. 108–48, his first and longest intervention in this field, in which he also held that a hegemony could be so benign or unassailable that it warranted neither deliberate challenge nor anxious adhesion.

not just Great Powers, often played a vital role. After subsequent altercation with defenders of neorealism, Schroeder would express regret that he had wasted so much time and energy engaging with it. But political theory mattered greatly to him, and he returned to the topic again repeatedly.[51] While always noting the difference between political scientists and historians, he also emphasized that each could learn from the other, the former the need for detailed empirical controls, the latter the value of conceptually informed systematic enquiry. In one of his last and most important contributions to these debates, he developed his critique of neorealist attachment to the balance of power further, adding to the list of strategies at variance with it 'grouping' as advocated by Metternich and 'transcending' as pursued in various ecumenical schemes of the early modern period, and increasingly in the contemporary world. Schroeder himself, he admitted, had 'for a fairly long time' been a realist historian, 'in the unreflecting, untheoretical manner of most historians', and had only gradually become convinced that realist assumptions about the inexorable pressures of power and competition were 'penultimate truths', liable to obscure the ultimate truth that international politics was better conceived as a quest for order and peace, in which considerable historical advances had been made. That did not mean realism should be discarded, but its proper role was

---

51. *Seriatim*: 'History and International Relations Theory: Not Use or Abuse, but Fit or Misfit', *International Security*, Summer 1997, pp. 64–74; 'International History: Why Historians Do It Differently than Political Scientists', Colin and Miriam Elman (eds), *Bridges and Boundaries: Historians, Political Scientists, and the Study of International Relations*, Cambridge, Mass. 2001, pp. 403–16; 'Why Realism Does Not Work Well for International History', John Vasquez and Colin Elman (eds), *Realism and the Balancing of Power: A New Debate*, Upper Saddle River 2003, pp. 114–27; 'Not Even for the Seventeenth and Eighteenth Centuries: Power and Order in the Early Modern Era', Ernest May, Richard Rosecrance, and Zara Steiner (eds), *History and Neorealism*, Cambridge 2010, pp. 78–102.

as a *Grenzbegriff* like human mortality, a conceptual boundary rather than a constitutive structure of human action in history. Understood in that way, an irenic coexistence between political scientists and historians was eminently possible.[52]

The major part of Schroeder's work after *Transformation*, however, lay in two other areas where it took a radically new direction, if in each case with a telling antecedent in his earlier work. The first of these was the issue of the genesis of the First World War. There already in 1972, after completing his book on the Crimean War, he produced a remarkable essay in response to one by Joachim Remak, who had argued that in its origins the Great War was a Third Balkan War between Austro-Hungary and Serbia, triggered by the contingent event of the assassinations in Sarajevo.[53] Not wrong in itself, Schroeder contended, this account overlooked the systemic crisis engulfing all the main states in Europe by the outbreak of the war. For war itself was a normal phenomenon of international relations, as well attested by history, and the real question was not why peace had collapsed in 1914 but why it had taken so long to do so. The answer to that lay in the stabilizing role that Austria had played in the Concert of Powers after 1815, and the reasons why it became destructive a century later. So long as Bismarck held power in Germany, and – aware of the critical importance to it of the survival of Austria – managed the Concert, a European peace was preserved. Once he was gone, only Britain could have assumed the same role. But its priority was the preservation of

---

52. 'Why Realism Does Not Work Well for International History', pp 123–6.
53. 'World War I as Galloping Gertie: A Reply to Joachim Remak', *Journal of Modern History*, September 1972, pp. 319–45, in response to Joachim Remak, '1914: The Third Balkan War – Origins Reconsidered', *Journal of Modern History*, September 1971, pp. 353–66, preceded by 'The Healthy Invalid: How Doomed the Habsburg Empire?', *Journal of Modern History*, June 1969, pp. 127–43.

the British Empire, for which it required understandings with its main rivals in overseas expansion, France and Russia.

Once these were secured, the trio of Entente powers effectively ran the international system, leaving Germany, bent on developing a *Weltpolitik* for itself too, isolated on the continent, its only ally Austro-Hungary, the weakest of the big powers. Regarded by all the others as the 'sick man of Europe' destined to break up, threatened by the debacle of the Ottoman state in the Balkan Wars that doubled the size of Serbia, and viewed by Russia as the principal obstruction to it in the Balkans, in desperation Vienna lashed out against Belgrade after the Habsburg heir was shot in Bosnia. In doing so it precipitated the disaster of a general war which only Britain was really in a position to avert, had it been willing to act in the spirit of Castlereagh or Aberdeen. But it had long become indifferent to the fate of Austria, and was not more responsible for the cataclysm of 1914 than the other powers, all driven by egoism and myopia in a system from which the ethos of mutual restraint actuating the Concert of old had vanished. In an important essay published three years later, Schroeder refined the regional side of this analysis, arguing that in the summer of 1913 the critical upshot of the second round of the Balkan wars was the emergence of Romania, whose intervention as the leading state in the area determined its outcome, and empowered by victory, its defection from the alliance that had previously tied it to Austria and Germany. Completing Habsburg isolation in the region, the loss of Romania was a more decisive blow to Vienna than even the murders in Sarajevo.[54]

---

54. 'Romania and the Great Powers before 1914', *Revue Roumaine d'Histoire*, 1975, I, pp. 39–53; a text followed the next year by an essay on British policies, or lack of them, towards Central and Eastern Europe from the nineteenth century to the Second World War: 'Munich and the British Tradition', *Historical Journal*,

Some thirty years later, Schroeder returned to the genesis of the Great War in two essays at the end of the century which he wrote in fairly quick succession, though published four years apart, and a third which came out a bit later. Like much of Schroeder's writing after *Transformation*, these were texts commissioned by others for collections they put together, a form to which Schroeder perhaps adapted too readily, at the expense of consolidating his ideas in books bearing his name, especially in the case of his work on the origins of the First World War. The first was a chapter on international politics from 1815 to 1914 in *The Nineteenth Century*, edited by Tim Blanning, which came out in 2000: the longest single text he published after *Transformation*, of which he had envisaged a sequel at the time, to which this came closest. After rehearsing the general themes of his account of Concert coordination for peace at system level and the Crimean War which brought it to an end – now tempered with the concession that a 'Metternich system' of domestic repression at unit level had come into being alongside it, and helped to discredit it – he developed a critical outline of the Bismarckian system which had succeeded it. After the Prussian victory over Austria in 1866, Bismarck could and should have stopped with the creation of the North German Federation, preserving the independence of the South German states that were so important as an intermediary stabilizing factor in Europe. But in following his triumph over Austria with a victory over France in 1870–71 that absorbed these realms into the unified German Empire, he founded a state sure to unsettle Europe as too large and powerful for its neighbours. To keep the peace

---

1976, I, pp. 233–43. Taken as a trio with 'Galloping Gertie', the sequence raises the possibility that after his study of the Crimean conflict, Schroeder might have considered the idea of writing on the run-up to the Great War, had not Oxford commissioned the history that became *Transformation* in 1980.

thereafter, he had to resort to a series of expedients for controlling the result — initially monarchical solidarity, ultimately diplomatic brokerage — that ended less by balancing antagonisms between the powers than by creating antagonisms to balance them, which could not outlast him. No comparable master of statecraft succeeded him.

Instead, what ensued after 1890 was an acceleration of the rivalries outside Europe that had always coexisted with concertation inside it, but with the arrival of the New Imperialism of the late nineteenth century increasingly overpowered the latter. New technologies of conquest, new zones of predation, and new entrants into global competition — Germany; Japan; Italy; King Leopold; the US with its Monroe Doctrine the most unvarnished of all — escalated the scramble for colonies and spheres of influence among these and other powers. Fashoda, the Boer War, the Russo-Japanese conflict were so many turning points. Intensified rivalries outside Europe inevitably inflamed tensions within it, hardening alliances between states into antagonistic blocs for the aggregation of capabilities against each other, and militarizing diplomacy between them. In the general pursuit of *Weltpolitik*, Germany was — if not in words, in practice — the most cautious of the Great Powers. But, given its geographical position in the centre of Europe and its provincial traditions, it was in any case bound to be a loser. That was not necessarily fatal to it. But for Austria, which could not even muster a *Weltpolitik*, the change in the tenor of European politics spelt disaster. Its last attempt at a pact with Russia disintegrated over Bosnia; Germany was humiliated over Morocco; Italy fought to seize Libya from Turkey; the Balkan states waged war against the Ottomans and amongst themselves; Serb officers detonated the attentat in Sarajevo. Throughout the July crisis that ensued, 'the Central Powers held the initiative, other powers reacting to it; they started the war'. But 'who started' and 'what caused' the war were not the same. Austro-German aggression was not its cause, since all the powers were playing by more or less the same rules, and now lack of them in a spirit of *va banque*. The deeper answer lay in the long-term failure of European governments to do what was necessary to keep the peace and avoid doing what was likely to destroy it. None of the powers desired a general war, but 'the fund of assurances and mutual restraints' which replaced the Vienna system had run out.[55]

By the time this chapter in *The Nineteenth Century* was published, Schroeder had produced a fuller and sharper critique of standard explanations of the outbreak of the First World War. Originally designed for a volume on counterfactuals in history edited by three colleagues at the University of Ohio, *The Unmaking of the West*, from which a reader's report excluded it, his contribution appeared instead in *Systems, Stability and Statecraft*.[56] Rejecting once again the notion that the Great War was a contingent event that might well not have taken place, this time Schroeder developed a sustained argument for what kinds of counterfactuals were licit or illicit as historical hypotheses. Unacceptable were the imaginings of 'virtual' history. Acceptable were suppositions embedded in 'both the actual experience of historical actors and in those constructions or reconstructions of history constantly made not only by historians but also everyone who reflects on the past'.[57] Familiar arguments that the First World War could have been avoided if Austria and Germany had only enacted

---

55. 'International Politics, Peace and War', T.C.W. Blanning (ed.), *The Nineteenth Century*, Oxford 2000, pp. 206–9.

56. Philip Tetlock, Richard Ned Lebow and Geoffrey Parker (eds), *Unmaking the West: 'What-If?' Scenarios That Rewrite History*, Ann Arbor 2006.

57. 'Embedded Counterfactuals and World War I as an Unavoidable War', *Systems, Stability and Statecraft*, p. 159.

progressive, liberal reforms that would have yielded a moderate foreign policy rather than reckless military aggression were without foundation. Austria had passed a good many such reforms, and both countries pursued more prudent and moderate external policies prior to 1914 than their foes in the Entente: nothing to compare with the pattern of British or French aggressions in Africa and Asia, or Russian in the Middle and Far East. Nor could Germany, as often argued, have just relied on its industrial lead to achieve a peaceful ascendancy in Europe, since Russia, with over twice its population, had an economy that was growing faster. Still less could the Dual Alliance count on geography as a path to primacy in Europe, since as the Central Powers they lay exposed to land attack from more than one direction, as the Entente trio did not. Strategically, centrality was not an asset but a handicap.

The reality was that both powers were caught in an international system that had from 1815 onwards consisted of two games – one in Europe, where so long as the Concert born in Vienna held good, cooperation prevailed over competition between the powers; the other overseas, where competition proceeded unchecked, but staying clear of conflict. After 1870, however, that changed. An increasingly ruthless imperialism overseas gradually infected metropolitan diplomacy in Europe itself, and with it an unbridled *Realpolitik* of opposite blocs released from Bismarckian constraints. Yet it was not so much the double game, or the rise of the New Imperialism itself, so much as a set of common assumptions born from them – that is, the emergent political culture of the time – which were determinant of the First World War. Objectively, geopolitical options other than the general slide to catastrophe in 1914 were still available. Past experience offered many an example of the dangers of war if a declining state like Austria felt its status as a Great Power was at risk, as in 1859 and 1866, and a repertoire of the remedies to protect peace in cases of danger, which had proved their worth in Poland, the Ottoman Empire, the Low Countries. Yet in an 'astonishing departure from tradition', faced with the manifest danger of a European War, the time-tested ways of avoiding it were ignored by all parties.[58] Serious collective action had become impossible for the Great Powers to imagine. The common stamp of their responses to the crisis in July was inaction.

So it was that Austria, the state which had historically depended most for its own security on the Concert of Europe, in a last despairing throw broke most definitively with it, like 'the blinded Samson pulling down the pillars of the temple'. So too Russia, in the name of such shibboleths as honour, prestige and Slavdom, signed its own death warrant in 1914. 'The tragedy of its origins', concluded Schroeder, 'thus connects with the tragedy of the war itself, in its hyperbolic protraction and destruction, evoking, like Shakespeare's *Romeo and Juliet*, the verdict: "All are punished."'[59]

His final published essay on the First World War drew a clear distinction between its 'immediate' and its 'general' causes. The first lay in the crisis of July 1914 itself, where the reigning view was that Austria unleashed the conflict with its ultimatum to Serbia. With that Schroeder agreed. The second stretched back to changes in the international system in the preceding quarter of a century, with the arrival of the new phase and form of imperialism that went under the name of *Weltpolitik*, but could better be dubbed with the Spanish adage 'Stealing horses to great applause', which the text took for its title. That had got under way with the Berlin Conference of 1885, which legalized the theft of African territory as part of international

---

58. *Systems*, p. 188.
59. Ibid., p. 191.

law, and soon extended across Asia, borne by the 'virtually universal triumph of the belief that the survival and prosperity of European states in the twentieth century would depend on their success in world policy, i.e. imperialism'.[60] By 1898 a sea change had occurred, as successive initiatives and conflicts overseas – the British conquest of Sudan, the crisis over Fashoda, the passage of the German naval bill, the Second Boer War, the escalation of European rivalries in China that would precipitate the Boxer Uprising, the Spanish-American and Russo-Japanese wars – ricocheted back on relations between metropolitan states within Europe itself.

Alone of the Great Powers in lacking overseas colonies, the Dual Monarchy took part only in the expedition to crush the Boxers. In the Balkans, it faced a long-standing rival in Russia, yet when Tsarism came close to breakdown from internal revolts after its defeat by Japan, neither Austria nor Germany attempted to take advantage of its weakness, and by abstaining from any preemptive attack on Russia, saved it from destruction. Taking office in Vienna as foreign minister in 1906, the conservative statesman Aehrenthal was a Russophile of Bismarckian outlook, who in 1907 negotiated an agreement with Izvolsky, his opposite number in St Petersburg, allowing Austria to annex Bosnia – which it had administered for two decades under nominal Ottoman suzerainty – in exchange for greater Russian rights in the Straits. In Schroeder's view, this was an arrangement in keeping with the traditions of the Concert of Europe as recast by Bismarck. But when France and England, which had their own ambitions for the Straits, baulked at it and Russia reneged on it,

---

60. 'Stealing Horses to Great Applause: Austria-Hungary's Decision in 1914 in Systemic Perspective', in Holger Afflerbach and David Stevenson (eds), *An Improbable War: The Outbreak of World War I and European Political Culture before 1914*, New York–Oxford 2007, p. 29.

Austria proceeded anyway with the annexation of Bosnia, which at the Congress of Berlin had been envisaged by all parties as the eventual outcome of the administration awarded it by them. Russia refused to accept Austria's move, but when Germany threatened it with an ultimatum, it had to back down, furious at its humiliation. Aehrenthal had made 'the last serious attempt' to revive the previous ethos of European politics, but his initiative 'not merely failed miserably but confirmed and accelerated the trend it was meant to reverse'.[61] The second Moroccan crisis, the invasion of Libya, two Balkan wars and the killings in Sarajevo followed in quick succession.

So by the time the last occurred, Austria no longer had any policy towards the other Great Powers, where the others all had such policies: France, Russia and England were resolved to quash German *Weltpolitik* as a threat to them, Russia to eliminate Austro-Hungary as a Great Power *tout court*. Austria for its part had given up the effort to return its sphere in Europe to at least Bismarckian rules – not ideal ones, certainly, as the 'half piracy, half legality' of its action in Bosnia showed, but far better than what replaced them. It had learnt the system was rigged against it, and was 'bound to conclude that it must do something drastic' to change what was threatening to strangle it. 'Not every reckless gamble is irrational; it may be rational to choose one form of death over another.' Austria committed suicide not out of fear of death, but of the hangman. 'The hangman was not a particular enemy power, but the international system.'[62]

Schroeder's final published commentary on 1914 contrasted 'two master narratives' on the origins of the First World War, the 'majority' opinion that it was the product of Germany's drive for

---

61. Ibid., p. 40.
62. Ibid.

world domination, in tandem with Austria's bid to crush Serbia, and the 'minority' view that it was the outcome of a universal indifference to the rules of an international system accepted as a civil association. He declared his allegiance to the last. An association of this kind was to be conceived along Oakeshottian lines, for which prudence was the great virtue and recklessness the cardinal sin. Judged by that metric, if a rank order of subjective blame were to be constructed (in an objective analysis of the causes of the war this was, of course, a subaltern enterprise), Serbia would unquestionably come first, followed by Russia, then Germany, then Austria (but only since 1912); followed by France ('harder to appraise') and Britain ('indifference' or 'inaction'? – yet its naval talks with Russia were 'playing with fire in a room of high explosives'). As for later belligerents, Italy was the most cynically reckless of all in its contempt for the norms of civil association, while the United States was historically quite ignorant of them. None had paid the slightest heed to Butterfield's warning that 'an international order is not a thing bestowed on us by nature, but is a matter of refined thought, careful contrivance and elaborate artifice. At best, it is a precarious thing, and though it seems so abstract it requires the same kind of loyalty, the same constant attention, that people give to their country or to other, private causes which only the international order enables them to follow.'[63]

In scale and detail, Schroeder's corpus on the origins of the First World War does not compare with *Transformation*. Composed of discrete essays, whose themes overlap with one another, it lacks the

---

63. 'Reflections on System, System Effects, and Nineteenth-Century International Politics' in James W. Davis (ed.), *Psychology, Strategy and Conflict*, London 2013, pp. 168–78. Citation: Herbert Butterfield and Martin Wight (eds), *Diplomatic Investigations: Essays in the Theory of International Politics*, London 1966, p. 147.

architectural unity and sustained narrativity of his *chef d'oeuvre*. But intellectually it is arguably more original, representing in two ways a sharper challenge to received historical opinion. The first of these was political. When *Transformation* appeared, the Vienna system had for a good while already been rehabilitated as the benevolent guarantor of an orderly peace in Europe. Schroeder's exposition of its virtues surpassed any other in precision and eloquence, but in substance was not new. What was completely original was the contrast he drew, not just with the Napoleonic era to which it put an end, but the eighteenth-century style of international politics out of which the First Empire had grown; and the claim that the Congress of Vienna wrought a revolution more momentous than the arrival of British industry or the overthrow of the French monarchy in the same period.

But that could still be described as a redescription more than a disruption of what was hitherto believed. Schroeder's work on the First World War, on the other hand, was a frontal challenge to conventional explanations of it as the product of an aggressive German militarism and will to domination – the version of events propagated by the victors of 1918 that was becoming canonical not just in the Anglosphere, but in Germany itself, at the time he first started writing about them. In the last few years, there has been a displacement of historiographic focus from the role of the Second Reich to that of the other Great Powers in the crisis of July 1914. But, if less narrow in geopolitical space, it has often been even narrower in historical time, with an increasing number of studies devoted simply to the sequence of events in the month that led to the outbreak of the war. There too Schroeder broke with prevailing fashion, posing a theoretical challenge with his insistence that neither concentration on a single state nor on the final countdown to hostilities could yield a satisfactory explanation of the war. Neither 'Who started it?' nor

'How did it start?' was the most meaningful question to ask. Only 'What caused the disaster?' permitted a real answer, which had to start some way back, and not be national, but systemic in form.

That, Schroeder provided with typical verve and acumen in successive essays outlining the sharpest account we possess of the fatal dynamics that led to the Great War. Just as *Transformation* was powered by the contrast he drew between the Concert system and the predatory anarchy that preceded it, so was his depiction of the subsequent international disorder by the break it made with the Vienna system. Not a complete break, since the Concert lingered on as a notional ideal to which lip service was paid, and practice sporadically conformed, but essentially replaced by a game of power-political *Realpolitik*, controlled at first under Bismarck, then increasingly unbound. Schroeder had glimpsed this process early on in his career, but when he addressed the epoch directly in this phase of his writing, he deepened his analysis of the period enormously by integrating into it for the first time the imperialist fixations of the age, as ultimately the dominant force in the system. That in turn allowed him to return to the monarchy that had been his primary European field of interest from the start, Austria, and to show that what was by then the least considered of the Great Powers proved in the end to be the most decisive for the continent's 'descent into the maelstrom', as a structural victim of the system that ended in revolt against it. He was the designated scholar for the fatality of that denouement.

Like every intellectual achievement, even the finest, Schroeder's had in this field its limitations too. Fundamentally, the division he made between unit and system levels that informed all his work was too rigid, and could not really be sustained even when he first made it in his Crimean book. For there on his own showing domestic politics had a crucial, shaping impact on British foreign policy, popular

Russophobia fostering the demagogic Whiggery of Palmerston's drive to war that he so detested, the key resultant of an international crisis unleashed by dispute over the Holy Places in the Near East. By the end of *Transformation*, he could concede that the social basis of the Vienna system in the aristocratic elites of Europe was too narrow for it to last, but without drawing the logical conclusion that his inaugural postulate, that a forest could be studied without heed to its roots, was untenable.[64] What else were such roots, in the time he declined to call a Restoration, but those of class – the privileged landlords and officers who had prevailed over Napoleon, but were still obsessed with the dangers of revolution, far more than of war?

Gliding across them so easily could be done without serious damage to an account of international politics in the epoch of Castlereagh and Metternich, as noted above. In that of Moltke and Curzon, much less. Schroeder noted the rise of mass politics, role of the press, modern technologies of destruction in post-Concert Europe, but in assigning final responsibility for the outbreak of the First World War to the political culture of the newly imperialized international system of the age, he left it too socially unrooted. There was still, of course, anxiety at trouble from the dispossessed among the possessor classes

---

64. That there may have been an underlying political reason for the sharpness of the division he made between unit and system levels is suggested by a late confession: 'Worst of all, one of the most powerful and beneficial aspects of the developments which have transformed Western, and to a great extent world society since 1815, i.e. the rise and spread of liberal democracy, the politicization of the masses, and the increasing need for governments to legitimate themselves through constitutional processes of election, may work in an important way against a learning process promoting systematic thinking in international politics.' For 'even in mature liberal representative democracies', the short-term political rewards of appealing to a mass electorate with facile catchwords and slogans were overwhelming. See 'The Transformation of Political Thinking, 1787–1848', in Jack Snyder and Robert Jervis (eds), *Coping with Complexity in the International System*, Boulder 1993, p. 68.

of the time, but true fear of revolution had by the closing years of the century largely disappeared, except in Russia, and with it earlier inhibitions about war. Above, the ruling order had in composition become somewhat more dilute, but in outlook was not much changed. Below, the ruled remained largely powerless. Politically, however, nationalism was a more powerful passion than socialism, affecting elites and masses alike; the latter all too susceptible to it, the former well able to steer it. The bellicism that Ingram thought the Concert of Europe exported to the extra-European world, and flowed back into it through the Balkan gap, was now coursing continent-wide through the traditional caste in power, as Schumpeter understood.

In characterizing the international system of the time, Schroeder identified its key change as a reversion to balance-of-power politics of an eighteenth-century kind, now garbed in the post-Concert language of *Realpolitik*, a term coined in the aftermath of the failure of the revolutions of 1848. The first was an English invention, the second German. In 2001 he devoted one of his most authoritative essays to a demolition of A. J. P. Taylor's deployment of the balance of power as the leitmotif of his *Struggle for the Mastery of Europe*, showing how empty a phrase it was, capable of defining anything and its opposite. Less all-purpose, the notion of *Realpolitik* was more ominous, or at least had become so by the time Europe was sinking towards the Great War. Originally, in the fifties, Schroeder had counterposed realism to moralism in international politics, deploring the latter, and at the turn of the eighties argued that it was futile to try to expunge *Realpolitik* from them, as this would amount to attempting to eliminate international politics as such. The realities of power were inherent in them and had to be accepted. A politician like Gladstone, continually invoking morality and the rule of law as the principle of his foreign policy, was himself a practitioner of *Realpolitik*, as his appropriation of Egypt and much else showed. There was a connexion between the two, but whereas morality should proceed out of *Realpolitik*, transcending it in Hegelian fashion, in Gladstone it was the opposite: his '*Realpolitik* emerged out of his morality', understandably bringing on him charges of hypocrisy that could not be laid against Bismarck, his customary foil.[65] By the time Schroeder was writing about the New Imperialism, the term *Realpolitik* had acquired an unequivocally negative connotation for him, as not so much an outlook taking a measured account of the realities of power that could scarcely be wished away, but rather the pursuit of selfish aims incompatible with the common interests of other states, without prudent scruple or restraint – just what *metanoia* had overcome in the pentarchy of old.

Did such a disposition govern the conduct of all the powers – if not invariably, persistently – in the period leading to 1914? In Austria, only post-Bosnia. Britain? Schroeder's criticism of its long indifference to the fate of Austria is stinging, holding it largely responsible for the final isolation of Vienna, and seeing it as part of a general pattern in British foreign policy, extending from Palmerston to Chamberlain: London protesting its concern for the balance of power in continental Europe, without doing much or anything about it, while its actual imperative was always the growth or protection of its vast overseas empire – the motive that determined its pacts with France and Russia, rather than fear of Germany. As for Germany, it was not the overweening bully and aggressor of caricature, but much of the time rather cautious and moderate, as its position forced it to be. Or so a reader of Schroeder's

---

65. 'Gladstone as Bismarck', *Canadian Journal of History*, 2, 1980, p. 195; *Systems*, p. 119; an essay prompted by Mack Smith's dictum that 'Gladstone was more like Bismarck than Gladstone'.

major essays on the origins of the First World War would think. But there, very unusually for him, he was not consistent. For in a review of Niall Ferguson's *Pity of War*, contemporary with 'Embedded Counterfactuals', he argued that it was wrong to think that had Britain not entered the war, it could have survived a quick German victory over France and Russia with its empire intact, and a Europe less shatter-prone to Communism and Nazism. To the contrary, 'sensible Britons could see that the *consequences* of German victory would be Napoleonic', and 'tragic as World War I and its outcomes were, a German victory would have been worse'.[66]

In 1971, Schroeder opened his sequence of essays on the First World War with a judgment on Fischer's work about Germany. Though many of his formulations were open to challenge, most of what he said about its foreign policy was true. After 1890 'Germany did pursue world power', in a bid that had 'deep roots' in the domestic structures of the country. His error was to believe that this was the '*causa causans*, the central driving force behind the war'. That it was not, for two reasons. Fischer had not considered the foreign policies of the other Great Powers, nor understood that there was no single cause for the war: it was overdetermined by a multiplicity of intertwining causes within the international system of the time. Crucially, among them was the breakdown of the system itself. That was the meaning of the title of his essay, an image borrowed from Hexter, which referred to the way that 'the very devices built into a system to keep it stable and operative under stress' could, once they were 'subjected to intolerable pressures, generate forces of their own which cause the system to destroy itself'. There were, of course, contingent events which started the war in 1914, but that did not mean

---

66. 'World War I: A Tragedy, Not a Pity', *Historian*, Fall 2000, pp. 125, 127.

the war itself was an accident, or that had Europe escaped it then, 'it could have continued to avoid disaster indefinitely'. The repeated crises that had preceded 1914 were the sign of 'a general systemic crisis, an approaching breakdown'. The relevant question to ask of the time was not 'Why War?', but 'Why Not War?' For once the Concert of Powers created at Vienna was gone, and no comparable system replaced it, interstate relations could not but revert to its natural state before 1815. 'War was still the *ultima ratio regum*. World War I was a normal development in international relations; events had been building towards it for a long time.'[67]

Ferguson's book on the war had many attractive virtues: well written and clearly argued, it was full of local insights and brought a particular analytic strength to the fiscal dimensions of military competition and wartime resource management race. But his central argument was an aberration: England had made a fatal error in misreading German aims as Napoleonic in character, requiring its entry into the war, prolonging it at enormous cost to itself and every power in Europe, leaving the United States the only winner of the war. Had England stayed out of the war, Germany would have inflicted a swift defeat on France and Russia, as it had France in 1870, leading to a continental order dominated by Germany much as the EU would become three-quarters of a century later – sparing Europe the horrors of Nazism and Stalinism, and allowing Britain to rule the waves peaceably, along with much of the planet, for a good while longer. Schroeder rejected this notion. Such a counterfactual was entirely artificial and untenable. What it ignored was that 'regardless of German aims, which quickly became fairly Napoleonic, sensible Britons could see that the *consequences* of German victory would be Napoleonic', requiring as

---

67. 'World War I as Galloping Gertie', pp. 319–22.

in the past the British Empire to resist them.[68] There was no chance that they would have resembled the harmonious, prospering Europe of Maastricht. Military victory rarely breeds moderation, and the kind of peace a triumphant Germany might have imposed on Europe could be seen at Brest-Litovsk, with the further scourge of mounting anti-Semitism unleashed by the future wider Reich and its satellites in Eastern Europe. The British Empire could never have survived as a thriving concern alongside such a German Empire, which itself would have been faced with a 'revisionist Russia and France; an opportunist Italy; a chaotic, quarrelsome Eastern and South-Eastern Europe; and a resentful Austro-Hungary'.[69] The controlling fact was that Imperial Germany was 'too strong and centrally located to be an ordinary, safe, Great Power, but never populous, large or powerful enough to impose its rule on all the others'. The war and what came of it were tragic, but had Germany won, the result would have been yet more catastrophic.

This was a powerful rejoinder to Ferguson, characteristic of Schroeder's ability, unique among his peers, to weld incisive intellectual judgment and a wide-ranging grasp of international history into compact shape,[70] yielding much the best assessment of *The Pity of War* in just three pages of a learned journal. On a number

---

68. 'World War I: A Tragedy, Not a Pity', p. 125.

69. Ibid., p. 126.

70. An example critical of Ferguson *en passant*: 'Neither an initial advantage in economic resources nor greater "killing efficiency" have normally been decisive in nineteenth- or twentieth-century warfare – otherwise the Confederate States of America would have swiftly lost the Civil War, Germany and Japan would have been quickly defeated in World War II, and the Third Reich would have destroyed the Soviet Union in 1941. Ferguson's evidence really helps explain what everyone knows happened: the two factors largely negated each other, a remarkable German war effort served to avert defeat, but it never quite overcame the Allies' material advantage': *World War I: A Tragedy, Not a Pity*, p. 125.

of major issues, he was unquestionably right. A Great War could not have been avoided, as Ferguson claimed, in the Europe of that period. The notion that had it ended with a quick German victory, the outcome would have been a European Union *ante diem* was an anachronistic fantasy. Even had, Britain abstaining, Germany rolled up Russia and France in relatively short order, it lacked the demographic, economic and cultural-political weight to dominate the whole continent. Thus far, Schroeder was on firm ground. But in underwriting the standard British phobia that the Second Reich posed a threat of 'Napoleonic' dimensions to Europe, he strayed from it and was inconsistent. Napoleon was a threat to all the monarchies of his time as a product of the French Revolution, carrier *malgré lui* of a universal ideology which he curbed, but could never entirely suppress; in the eyes of many, a magnetic statesman at home, and a military genius abroad. Wilhelmine Germany might boast of technological and industrial prowess. But it was not the product of any political transformation of continental resonance. It lacked any ideology of international moment. It did not possess any political or military personality remotely comparable to Napoleon. Nor, decisively, did it nurture unlimited aims of expansion like his. Schroeder's suggestion, that it did, with its – tell-tale – misfit adverbial qualification ('fairly Napoleonic'), is contradicted by everything else he wrote about Imperial Germany, which stressed its combination of bluster in words and moderation in deeds. Having rightly pointed out in the past that if it was bent on world power at all costs, it could have attacked Russia in 1905, 1908–9, even 1911, with far greater chances of success than in 1914, he conceded even now that the motivation of its plunge into the Great War was more defensive, fear of growing Russian strength, than aggressive. That once fighting had started, Germany contemplated annexations was true, but not peculiar to it. All its enemies did the same. None more single-mindedly than Italy (which would not have fought the Central Powers if Britain had not entered the war and covered its coastlines), among whose explicit conditions for joining the war were acquisitions in Dalmatia, the Dodecanese and Africa; while the Entente powers all awarded themselves generous slices of land in advance of victory.

What accounts for Schroeder's departure here from the tenor of the rest of his writing on the First World War, all of which resists identification of any single power as *the* malefactor of the conflict? Only a surmise is possible. But it looks as if, on this one rare occasion, he allowed himself the kind of historical anachronism he otherwise abhorred, and under the influence of emotions that the struggle against Napoleon had aroused in him, was swayed by conventional British apologetics of the hour into projecting onto Germany the shadow of France a century earlier. According to this doxa Britain had to enter the war, as it had always done when faced with the menace of any too expansionist power in Europe, for at stake was the fate of liberty and equity on the continent, not to speak of its own possessions beyond it. The cost in human lives, on which Schroeder understandably dwelt in his indictment of Napoleon, he did not compute in the Great War: about ten times the number of deaths, in a fifth of the time of killing.

Worth it, as patriotic Anglophone historians and others still maintain? Schroeder did not, saying simply that the end result would have been still worse had Germany prevailed. Even with a quick victory, Britain aloof? Millions of lives would have been saved. Britain could never have stayed apart, would have been his reply: it had to intervene. But though he was not wrong in thinking that, the reasons that he implied for its doing so – the need to uphold British 'traditions' and defend the safety of the realm – were at variance with his own convictions, and with the truth. In keeping with the same logic, he would later explain that the most dangerous myth generated by the First World War was not the legend of 'war guilt' branded by the Allies into Germany at Versailles but the 'war-innocence lie' flung back at the Allies by German rejection of Versailles. As if the first was not the architect of the second; nor the protraction of a hyperbolic war (Schroeder's own terms) to be held a progenitor of what followed it – Fascism, Stalinism, Nazism and a second, still more savage round of the same.

Missing in the snapshot he took to counter Ferguson is something that Schroeder's account of the descent towards the First World War, without question the most profound and acute body of writing on it that we possess, nevertheless lacked: a cogent explanation of why the international system created at Vienna in 1815 was eventually consumed in the European conflagration it set out to prevent. The answer lies in a misjudgment of the order of its concerns. For Schroeder, the statesmen of Vienna thought European society needed to prevent revolutions in order to avoid wars. In reality it was the other way round: for the Pentarchs, Europe needed to avoid wars in order to prevent revolutions. So when after 1848–49 the spectre of revolutions faded, its brief revenant exorcized in 1871, war resumed what he rightly called its normal position in international affairs (normal that is, in societies as elite-encrusted and class-divided as those of most recorded history), becoming in the natural course of events, once again, *ultima ratio regum*.

A New World Order?

Continuous chronologically and thematically with the history traced in *Transformation*, Schroeder's bloc of texts on the eventual 'sickening of the peace' that the Vienna system had given Europe, and the reasons it perished in the flames of 1914, was a historical enterprise of the same calibre and order, if not the same scale: the major product of his retirement. But in the same years, he was deeply preoccupied with his own time, about which he developed two distinctive, interconnected lines of argument that can be regarded as a single body of writing, returning to questions that had originally started him as a historian. The first sign of this emergent focus came in a piece he published in early 1985, in which he maintained that the current international system was, 'from the crucial standpoint of avoiding major and general wars, far superior to any in the history of international politics'.[71] Far from sickening, since its inception in 1945, it had grown stronger over time, West and East alike making or accepting massive adjustments – the decolonization of the Third World, defection of Yugoslavia and China as Soviet allies, decline of the appeal of communism, weakening of American hegemony in the Western hemisphere. Great Powers no longer fought wars for decisive victory in them. States which had once typically been made by war, now understood that trade, industry and technology yielded greater gains than could be won on the battlefield. This was not cause for any simple optimism: conflicts galore could be found in the contemporary world, not a few of them violent, and deadly nuclear dangers remained. But it was reason to reject any crippling pessimism about the future.

Fortuitously, the article was well timed: within a few weeks of its appearance, Gorbachev had become leader of the Soviet Union. A decade later, when Schroeder returned to the same issues in 1994, the Cold War had ended, the USSR disappeared, and Bush senior

---

71. 'Does Murphy's Law Apply to History?', *Wilson Quarterly*, Winter 1985, p. 87.

proclaimed a New World Order. After his expedition in the Gulf, that slogan had fallen out of favour, but as a conceptual shorthand for the post–Cold War scene, he argued it had historical justification. What did it designate? The New World Order could be defined as 'an international system in which the United States and like-minded friends and allies act, preferably under the aegis of the United Nations, to preserve or establish peace by upholding international law and order against aggressors, law-breakers and oppressors'.[72] There was overwhelming historical evidence that a system of this kind had emerged over the past half century, one shaped not by the classic weapons of police or military force – deterrence and compellence – but by the peaceful means of 'association-exclusion': voluntary associations like the European Community or NATO for those who wished to share the rules they represented and the benefits they brought, and sanctions for those who defied or broke such rules. Compellence, of course, was not to be abandoned altogether: it could play a 'contributing' role in the New World Order. But only association-exclusion could achieve a durable settlement of long-standing conflicts such as that between Israel and the Palestinians. What could not was resort to external force by Great Powers to intervene in civil wars or ethnic conflicts, or to overthrow oppressive governments. Neither the strife in Bosnia nor the tyranny in Iraq were amenable to any lasting solution by coercion of this kind, from which no constructive learning process, that took time, was likely to emerge. Did Americans themselves have the patience needed for such learning? They had shown it in the past, and needed to acquire it once again.

Three years later, defending the importance of the kind of

---

[72]. 'The New World Order: A Historical Perspective', *Washington Quarterly*, New Year 1994, p. 26.

scholarship he had classically practised, Schroeder felt he could write: 'The Vienna era pointed towards a future that is now being realized.' What it had 'dimly foreshadowed' was now flowering. The startling cluster of political changes that had occurred in the eighties – the fall of authoritarian regimes in the Soviet Union, Eastern Europe and South Africa, coming on top of earlier developments in the Mediterranean, Latin America and East Asia, showed 'what trends and principles are winning'. Too cautious about the prospects for rapid progress, he had himself not expected such welcome improvements in the system of the world. In many states the road to a stable liberal democracy and economic prosperity was no doubt still long and rocky, and holdouts of tyranny and ethnic cruelty in areas like Iraq and onetime Yugoslavia showed that old-fashioned power politics was not quite extinct. But it was heartening that they no longer determined Western reactions to the third effort to create a liberal democracy in Russia, after the failures of 1905 and 1917. Rather, there was a unanimous desire to help Russia towards political liberty and a market economy. The same could be said of humanitarian intervention in the Balkans. 'It is time for historians to recognize that the age of classic international politics, governed by the structural determinants of anarchy, self-help and balance of power, is over.'[73]

On much the same note, a text the following year argued that centuries of struggle with the intractable problem of reconciling a general peace with a diversity of independent states, far from being futile or self-defeating, had led to an exponential increase in peaceful transactions across the borders of states, and to an international order

---

73. 'Does the History of International Politics Go Anywhere?', in David Wetzel and Theodore S. Hamerow (eds), *International Politics and German History: The Past Informs the Present*, Westport 1997, pp. 27, 28, 33; *Systems*, pp. 277, 279, 284.

that offered a tangible prospect for managing the conflict between the two. International politics was not condemned to a perpetual game of competitive power-politics. It was 'firmly on the list of great constructive achievements, such as capitalism or organized religion, which also have their dark side', to which realism was blind, as 'liberal institutionalism' – with which he sided – was not. Of course, there was no guarantee that even the new and better system of today would ensure a durable peace: if it gave reason for hope, it was of 'a sober, disenchanted kind, free of utopian expectations', right or left. Three such expectations posed special dangers: utopias of peace through power (realism), peace through law (legalism) and peace through justice (moralism). Missing from each was the vital element of politics proper, which alone could harmonize the conflicting rights and claims of international life.[74]

Drafted in 1997 and completed in 1999, Schroeder's most far-reaching attempt at a barometer of the time, 'The Cold War and its Ending as "Long-Duration" International History', was published in 2000. The Annales school was no longer supreme even in France. But paradoxically its famous concept of the *longue durée* was applicable in the field which *Annalistes* most despised as mere diplomatic history. From the early seventeenth to the mid twentieth century, Europe had seen the dominance of successive, distinct systems of international relations, of which Schroeder offered an intricate periodization, which three times in four centuries (1618–48, 1787–1815, and 1914–45) had collapsed into hypertrophic wars. After 1945, however, the Cold War represented the gradual emergence of another kind of international politics, not primarily rooted in a drive for empire on either side,

---

74. 'Grounds for Hope or Optimism?', in Roger Kanet (ed.), *Resolving Regional Conflicts*, Urbana-Chicago 1998, pp. 137–8, 151.

nor in a balance of power struggle for security and advantage, nor even a clash of ideologies, though it quickly became all of these. It started with wartime allies intending to 'continue their cooperation and promote general peace and security' without, however, having reached any 'agreement on a concrete, practical definition of peace'.[75] So it took time for competition between them to arrive at an eventual consensus – decades of conflict and a decisive military-political outcome, if with a sense of mutual restraint throughout, until a new definition of peace, and the norms and rules it required, was worked out. The Cold War was a time when the wartime omissions were made good, first in a limited détente, then a somewhat positive one around the Helsinki accords, and finally in a convergence on new principles. Alongside this sequence came the pacification and integration of Western Europe, redefining peace not just as absence of war but as joint economic development for prosperity, democratization, human rights, a market-oriented economy and liberal representative government – forms of progress coinciding with the Cold War, but not a product of it, which promoted détente and came to be adopted as ideals in Eastern Europe and after 1985 by the USSR itself.

Such an interpretation of the present, Schroeder remarked, was only suggestive. On an optimistic reading, it would be the arrival of a new epoch marking not just a temporary and partial breakthrough to world peace, but a permanent achievement, 'like that of manned heavier-than-air flight in 1903'. On a pessimistic reading, it would be one more deceptive renewal leading to another great systemic crisis, which even if it helped avoid further wars, was no proof it could

---

75. 'The Cold War and Its Ending in "Long-Duration" International History', in John Mueller (ed.), *Peace, Prosperity and Politics*, Boulder 2000, p. 273; *Systems*, p. 259.

master new world problems ahead. Were the existing system to fail, the greatest threats to it were likely to come from within, succumbing as its predecessor in Vienna had done to internal decay rather than external assault, some elites or governments trying to exploit it in their own interests, others defecting from or rebelling against it. A particular kind of optimism would be a menace to it in another way – belief that market forces could of themselves solve problems of world order. The market was an indispensable servant, but a bad and perilous master of such an order, one which could not even furnish a decent economic existence to most people on Earth. Economics was a narrower sphere of human activity than politics, and 'a lasting peace can only be one that keeps changing and adapting to new demands for justice'.[76] Only politics was capable of that.

Schroeder's final reflection on these issues came in a paper published by the *Journal of the Society of Christian Ethics* in 2004, with the significant title 'International Order and Its Current Enemies'. The Scriptures spoke far more about peace and justice than about order. But in international affairs, order came before peace or justice: not normatively or even chronologically, but structurally, for 'international peace and justice are unthinkable without international order in the way that liberty is unthinkable without law or good health without a sound physiological system'. The order now prevailing in the world was not primarily based on the threat or exercise of coercion, as always in the past, but voluntary association and – where rejected – exclusion. It had four principal enemies: terrorism, failed states, extreme social inequities and deformities, and the current policies and actions of the US government, 'reflecting the outlook of a large segment of the American people'. Of these, the last was

---

76. *Peace, Prosperity and Politics*, pp. 276, 280; *Systems*, pp. 263, 266.

a greater long-term danger to world peace and justice than either terrorism or rogue states, if less than 'the grave imbalances between various members of the world community, in terms of their wealth, power, security and ability to achieve their minimum goals within the system'. The reality of the US challenge to the emergent world order, in the shape of a war of choice in the Middle East and the doctrine justifying it, was, however, unmistakable, and the danger that Americans could do most about. To acknowledge that the country was on a wrong, dangerous course must mean to hope that it would fail in it – hopefully a moderate failure, allowing the course to be corrected, but one that was bound to involve hurtful losses to fellow countrymen. 'It is easy for me: I am an old man with nothing to lose or gain by speaking openly.'[77] Real courage, commitment and endurance were needed for anyone answerable to an active constituency, and with greater practical responsibility, to do so.

America Abroad

With the new century, the focus of Schroeder's interventions changed. The high value he placed on a new world order, which he had greeted before even the Cold War wound up, did not alter. But his estimate of its immediate prospects did. The result of that alteration was a body of writing that set him apart from any other American historian of his time, less scholarly but not much less significant in its own way than his work on the European past.[78] Two features of it stand out.

---

77. 'International Order and Its Current Enemies', *Journal of the Society of Christian Ethics*, 2, 2004, pp. 194, 198–200.

78. Work now collected in *America's Fatal Leap: 1991–2016*, London–New York 2025.

Schroeder was a historian with a record of more serious engagement with international relations theory than any contemporary. Though highly critical of its neorealist turn, he shared many of its concerns and some of its ideas; and more generally felt an affinity with political science, not infrequently abhorred by historians, among whose thinkers he may have enjoyed closer associates than in his own profession. The cast of his writing on politics owed something to that connexion. At the same time, he had always defined himself as a conservative, and remained one.[79] But there too his outlook was unusual, closer to European than American connotations of the term; in his case, convictions inflected – never ostentatiously, seldom more than glancingly – by his formation as a Lutheran.

As early as 1991 that sensibility was discernible in his reaction to the impending US eviction of Saddam from Kuwait. A 'private citizen', with 'no responsibility for any decision', or 'special audience to address', he had started to write on the morning of 15 January, two days before Operation Desert Storm began, 'partly as catharsis, acquittal of conscience, a symbolic gesture', but mainly 'out of a feeling that not everything has been said' and 'what was omitted needed saying'. The expedition against Iraq was 'a just, unnecessary war'. The world was moving towards a better order, and it was precisely because 'states and peoples, especially in the West, increasingly rely on the undisturbed course of world commerce, no longer desire or believe in military solutions, and want to act in community and by consensus' that led Saddam to think he could get away with his seizure of Kuwait. He had to be stopped. But was war

---

79. He had voted for Dewey in 1948, and been an Eisenhower Republican up to 1964, he later told a correspondent; but in 1980 voted neither for Reagan nor Carter, opting instead for the maverick Independent Republican candidate John Anderson, a congressman from Illinois.

the right way to do so? It would come not only at a high cost in human lives, physical destruction and socio-economic dislocation, but would threaten these very gains themselves. Like it or not, in making war on Iraq, the West risked 'destroying the new, international system in order to save it'. There was a better alternative, to leave Saddam in Kuwait and trap him there with a blockade, cutting Iraq completely off from the rest of the world and denying it any sale of oil, till he was forced to withdraw, utterly discredited and fatally weakened. Were the American people too impatient for such a response? If so, it would 'prove we are unfit for world leadership'. But forty-five years of US presence in Europe, forty in Korea, and thirty-five of backing for Israel had shown that the American public was capable of great patience, and today such fortitude was of special value in what should be 'a disenchanted loyalty, a disillusioned patriotism'.[80]

Amidst the overwhelming bipartisan consensus behind Operation Desert Storm, Schroeder was not quite alone as a conservative critic of the Gulf War. Robert Tucker and David Hendrickson were two others. A decade later, matters were very different. When the World Trade Center and the Pentagon were hit kamikaze-style by planes commandeered by Al Qaeda in September 2001, national reaction brooked no paltering: for such terrorism, punishment must be condign, the evil rooted out in its lair. The US attacked Afghanistan on 7 October, the country – as too the West – solidly behind it. Within a month of the invasion Schroeder published 'The Risks of Victory: An Historian's Provocation', an essay of unique prescience about the decade to come. In it, he argued that if it were true, as now trumpeted, that after 9/11 everything was different, the study

---

80. 'A Just, Unnecessary War: The Flawed American Strategy in the Persian Gulf', *ACDIS Occasional Paper*, March 1991, pp. 1, 4, 11–12.

of history would be redundant. But it was not: neither the essential structure of contemporary international politics nor human nature had changed. The past offered an analogy with the present situation: not Pearl Harbor, so often invoked, but the First World War, which had three instructive lessons for the United States. A Great Power should never give terrorists a war they wanted and it did not; it should always take into account the long-term consequences of its actions for international affairs; and it should reckon not just with the dangers of defeat, but the risks of victory. After spelling out the ways in which the Black Hand in Serbia and the rulers of Austro-Hungary illustrated the first two dangers in 1914, and the reasons why the situation of America in 2001 differed from that of the Habsburg Empire a century earlier, Schroeder moved to the third lesson.

What were the likely consequences of destroying the Taliban regime in Afghanistan? States were not fungible, dispensable or readily replaceable entities, as Austria had thought Serbia would be, and the Entente had treated Austria as if it were. Overthrowing a bad state was no guarantee of creating a good one, as the elimination of the Wilhelmine Empire in 1918, followed fifteen years later by the arrival of Nazism, demonstrated. 'Can we or anyone provide stable government for Afghanistan?' If not, who would be left to deal with the mess that was sure to ensue? Moreover, even in the best case – swift victory, minimal losses, a non-terrorist government in Kabul – where would this leave the United States? Inevitably, it would further enhance the hegemony America enjoyed in the Middle East. But for any hegemony to be stable, it had at least to be perceived as 'natural, invulnerable and tolerable, if not wholly benign', and in this region there was no chance of US hegemony being seen as natural, because it was not. 'The obvious truth is that we do not belong there in the same way as we belong in the Western hemisphere, the Atlantic, central and eastern Europe, and in the Pacific.' A powerful American presence in the region was widely felt to be alien, corrupting and oppressive, and if Americans asked themselves why they should be a target for Al Qaeda, the answer was not far to seek: 'the terrorists attacked us *here* because we are *there*'. Far from hoping to reinforce US hegemony in the Middle East, they should be planning to wind it down. The best start they could make would be to declare decisive victory in Afghanistan quickly, and go home. 9/11 was a tragedy for those killed and those directly affected by it, but it was not a *national* disaster: 'it was a sneak punch for which we were surprisingly unprepared'. Americans had less to fear from the patent fanaticism of terrorists than from their own latent fanaticism, what Kennan had called 'the blind egotism of embattled democracy'.[81]

A year later, after occupying Afghanistan, the United States was preparing to invade Iraq. Six months before it did so, Schroeder published a denunciation of the enterprise in the *American Conservative*, the opening salvo in what would become a dozen eloquent interventions against the war launched in March 2003. The practical hazards of the adventure were quite clear, many widely discussed, even if rarely the unreckoned costs and manifold difficulties of running, rebuilding, democratizing and stabilizing Iraq. These, however, were prudential considerations. More important were the questions of principle at stake. Did Americans have the right to wage a preemptive war against Iraq to overthrow its regime? Could such a war be described as necessary or just? What long-range effects would it have on the international system? His answer was unambiguous. 'A campaign to overthrow Hussein by armed force would be an unjust, aggressive, imperialist war', which, 'even if it succeeded (indeed, perhaps especially if it succeeded), would

---

81. 'The Risks of Victory', *National Interest*, November 2001, pp. 31, 33–4, 36.

have negative, potentially disastrous effects' on American leadership in the world and the prospects for general peace, order, and stability. 'In other words, a preemptive war on Iraq would be not merely foolish and dangerous, but wrong.' Preemptive wars by a state were only justified if it faced a threat to it that was imminent, direct, critical and uncontrollable by any other means. Iraq posed no danger to the US, whereas it was difficult to imagine a more dangerous and illegitimate norm than the US claim to be justified in waging war on a much smaller, weaker state without proof of a threat to itself. To do this was to attack the foundations of the international system itself, which rested on the premise of independent states with equal juridical status and rights, and the growth of associations between them for stable peace and security. An assault on Baghdad would demolish both. Schroeder himself was a conservative 'by every standard save the one-sided American spectrum', who had no sympathy with the view that the US had generally been an imperialist power – its overall record had been more anti-imperialist than the reverse – and was no foe of US hegemony, which had done more good than harm since the Second World War. But the exercise of final authority by one government over a community foreign to it *was* imperialism. Neither terrorism nor nuclear weapons, pretexts for invading Iraq, were new dangers; Europeans had survived the first in the nineteenth and twentieth centuries, and Americans the second during the Cold War. They supplied no basis for a preemptive war, which even where justified often had led to further conflicts. Charles Beard had been wise to warn of such effects. 'If we carry out what we are now planning, regardless of any short-term success we may have, our chickens will ultimately come home to roost.'[82]

---

82. 'Iraq: The Case Against Preemptive War', *American Conservative*, 21 October 2002, pp. 18–20.

By 2004 they were already doing so. The revelations of Abu Ghraib, for which no level of the administration accepted responsibility, were sickening, although they fitted the broader pattern of a 'Gulag Archipelago of detention camps and interrogations centres over the Middle East and Central Asia'. What would it say of the American public, 'or at least a major part of it', if 'this supremely ugly scandal' did not 'at last produce an overdue and overriding sense of revulsion against leaders and a policy that have led their country to this shameful pass?'[83] In considering the choices before the electorate in the autumn, differences in personal qualities and beliefs between Bush and Kerry were not decisive, and their announced programmes and goals in Iraq and beyond were notoriously 'not that far apart'. But a change in the country's foreign policy was needed, and had to be credible. That ruled Bush out. Nations had switched leaders in time of war to their advantage in the past: the elder Pitt or Churchill were examples. No conservative should consider it dishonourable to vote for Kerry now as a necessary evil, while vowing to oust him four years later.[84] Bush was basing his electoral campaign on the war his administration was waging against terror. But Al Qaeda was a criminal band, not a state, and to declare war on it was to dignify it as if it were. Worse, Bin Laden had counted on a counterblow from America to the blow he had inflicted on it, in the hope that this would rally the Muslim world around him, and in elevating its pursuit of him to the status of a full-blown war, America had given him what he wanted. What the US should have done was to declare Al Qaeda a criminal band, against which it would take all necessary measures, but one whose

---

83. 'For Shame', *American Conservative*, 7 June 2004, pp. 7–9.

84. 'Misreading the 9/11 Report', *American Conservative*, 13 September 2004, pp. 7–20.

key enemies were the Muslim governments of the Middle East, who had primary responsibility for dealing with it. Europe, too, closer to the region and more threatened by the band, had an important role to play in combatting it. In America itself, the war on terror was a sham, as everyone knew: for the overwhelming majority of the population what it meant was not sacrifice or mobilization, but tax cuts and a spending spree.[85]

Bush Jr nevertheless re-elected, Schroeder returned to the charge in the mid-terms of 2006. The administration was now banging the drum of the Disastrous Consequences of Failure in Iraq, which the Democrats – Hillary Clinton to the fore – were not rejecting, merely recycling Kerry's Bright Promise of Handling Iraq Better, both parties remaining committed to the idea of winning the war. The American public had a deep-rooted resistance to admitting failure in foreign policy, but that was what was now urgently needed, and historical experience had repeatedly shown that to do so could bring unexpected benefits. In Korea, in Vietnam, on Russia, on China, the US had repeatedly proclaimed goals that were not achievable at any acceptable cost and risk. In each case, a highly favourable outcome had nevertheless ensued, not essentially due to American power or skill, but to international conditions not under American control. The reason lay in the fact that successive opponents who could not be defeated by military force were neither as powerful nor as stable, nor as aggressive or united, as the US had supposed, whereas the West was more suited to wage a contest over what kind of government, society, economy and politics was best at peaceful coexistence. The same logic applied to terrorists, as it also did to Iraq today. The

---

85. 'The War Bin Laden Wanted', *American Conservative*, 25 October 2004, pp. 114–19.

invasion of Iraq was a bid for informal empire which had failed. That meant a 'disimperialism' was required, whose goal should be to withdraw US forces from the country, scrap plans for a vast embassy in Baghdad, review US bases in the region with local governments with a view to reducing them, abandon the aim of democratizing the Middle East, and call an international conference to discuss how to deal with a now inevitable civil war in Iraq. All that should be done from strength not weakness, protecting the vital interests of America and maintaining its necessary leadership, to lay the basis for useful relations with countries of its former or would-be empire, as others had done. However feasible or thinkable, such a policy would not be implemented by either the current administration, or any future administration or electorate, since – 'an elephant in the room I have carefully avoided hitherto' – the US had forfeited control of its policy in the region to Israel and the Arab-Israeli conflicts related to it, and no party or public was going to take steps to regain it.[86]

The following year, a long two-part article concluded Schroeder's series in the *American Conservative*, though not on US foreign policy under Bush. The retired general put in charge in 2003 of the reconstruction of Iraq, Jay Garner, had urged prompt withdrawal of US troops and letting Iraqis sort out the situation after the invasion themselves. The proposal was logical, but it meant giving up the American dream of moulding the Middle East in the image of the US, and Iraq into the central base for American hegemony over it. Iraq was being destroyed as a state and a functioning society; and leaving aside the human tragedy involved in that, no stable Middle East was conceivable with Iraq as a 'political, social, religious, ethnic and economic black hole' in it. The notion of creating an independent,

---

86. 'Liberating Ourselves', *American Conservative*, 9 October 2006, p. 15.

liberal-constitutional democratic Iraq that was also an American satellite had always been a grotesque self-contradiction. It had taken a thousand years of often incredibly violent and twisted history to produce such democracies in the West. 'Yet we proposed to bring about this transformation in Iraq through one short easy war. What were we thinking?' The US was Western, Christian, strongly pro-Israel, imperialist, individualist and materialist, as well as capitalist, rich and extremely powerful. These were basic characteristics it was not going to change, and many it should not, but they disqualified it from promoting democracy in the Middle East, whose central problems were internal to it, which the US could not resolve and would continue after an American exit from it. For the United States to believe itself capable of offering an answer to them was comparable to an Ottoman sultan proposing that he be invited to arbitrate the religious disputes of sixteenth-century Europe.[87]

Americans now thought the war in Iraq had gone wrong, rather than that it was wrong, amid Micawberish schemes for a 'surge' from figures like Petraeus, or for remaining disguised as leaving, from Senators Clinton or Biden. A genuine US withdrawal from Iraq would not be easy or risk-free, or of itself solve the problems of Iraq or the region. But without one, there was no solution. All-out civil war could well break out in Iraq, threatening its neighours and the whole Middle East. Would that encourage a common battle against Islamic radicalism? A conference of all states concerned at such a prospect could help to avert it. The US itself had lost the credibility to call such a gathering. But if it had given real, verifiable evidence of its intention to withdraw, it could participate in one, defending its legitimate interests in the region, and helped by others to do so,

---

87. 'Open Fire', *American Conservative*, 24 September 2007, pp. 10–14.

simply as a power too big to fail altogether without endangering the stability of the international system as a whole, on which in the last resort the welfare of every state depended. Such a strategy was perfectly feasible, but it had to be conceded that it was not realistic. Setting aside the limitations of the country's national leadership, and the attitude of its two major parties, the American public itself had endorsed and participated in the madness of the war on Iraq. Its current disappointment with it was superficial, lacking any sense of its cost for Iraqis, for future generations in America, or for those who had served in it. This was not, Schroeder wrote, 'a verdict delivered from above by a dispassionate observer convinced that he has all the answers. It is a painful, disillusioned reflection from someone long convinced that the American public was by and large growing up and changing for the better also in international politics, who now, near the end of his career and life, grows less confident of that maturity.'[88]

His last word on the war came the following spring, five years to the month after it had begun, published in the *American Interest*, a journal founded by Francis Fukuyama and Walter Russell Mead. The Bush administration maintained that the US was now defeating the insurgency in Iraq, and by winning the war was enabling the country to thrive as a friendly independent state, freeing America to turn to other concerns. That the insurgents were in the process of being defeated might be 'true after a fashion'. Success against the insurgency, however, did not mean victory in the larger war. Most insurgencies fail, either dying out on their own or crushed by superior military force. But there was little prospect of any long-term stabilization of Iraq. How then could America overcome 'the disastrous heritage of five years of scandal, crime, humiliation and destruction in Iraq, and

---

88. 'Fire Fight', *American Conservative*, 8 October 2007, p. 21.

the legacy of neglect of Palestinians and other issues', and 'restore our blackened reputation in the world'? Only if the country took a momentary tactical success in Iraq as reason for a retreat without further loss could any real victory later be possible, after an American adventure of 'ghastly inevitability', that had been 'half tragedy, half-farce, and all folly'.[89]

These were Schroeder's final words on the US in Iraq, in the closing months of the Bush administration. But two years earlier he had published in the same journal the most powerfully composed of all the historical analogies he had drawn with it. 'Mirror, Mirror on the War' is a comparison of the performance of the US military and political elites over Abu Ghraib with French conduct in the Dreyfus Affair. There were obviously fundamental differences, not least in scale, between the two. But in one particular there was an uncanny resemblance, if with a nuance *in parvo*. That was in what each told one about 'the essential human qualities of the actors involved and the societies in which they live'. In France, the story of Dreyfus is well known. A captain in the army of Jewish origin, wrongly charged with treasonous sale of secrets to the German embassy, Dreyfus was convicted and sentenced to life imprisonment on Devil's Island off French Guyana. When the head of counter-intelligence detected the real traitor, the culprit was cleared in a couple of days, while a subordinate forged documents to further incriminate Dreyfus, whose conviction was confirmed. Amid growing public uproar, the forger committed suicide, leaving a note claiming he had acted on orders to save the honour of the army, Dreyfus was recalled and his sentence quashed. The affair had lasted five years, dividing the country, because the High Command refused

---

89. 'Leave or Lose', *American Interest*, 1 March 2008.

to acknowledge that its court martial had delivered a verdict in error, though eventually its long-time chief of staff, who had championed the belief that Dreyfus was guilty, resigned when his innocence was proved and withdrew into private life. With this single belated exception, the military – and a good part of the political – elite of France had for Schroeder crossed the line between a mistake and a crime, not only breaking the law to protect its reputation, but negating the rule of law by consciously arrogating to itself the right to do so. Dreyfusards exaggerated the significance of the affair as a threat to the Republic, which was never in danger. France, after all, could then be described (a major change of opinion for Schroeder) as 'freer and more democratic than any other major European state'. But in showing that 'too many Frenchmen in high places were willing to ignore evidence, bend facts and accept or do what they knew at bottom was wrong', it did reveal 'a serious intellectual and moral deficit in integrity' in French public life of the period.[90]

Critics of Abu Ghraib and US interrogation centres could also exaggerate their enormity, viewed comparatively. But that did not alter the fact that, like the Iraq War itself, they, too, were a blunder that became a crime, the elite in charge of the centres denying any responsibility for the practices to which they led, and proceeding to the same tactics of cover-up to which the top brass and their allies in parliament had resorted in France. America 'got itself into a tragic mess by a roughly similar process with a roughly similar underlying cause: a national deficit in intellectual and moral integrity' – one with which a majority of Americans collaborated. A founding principle of the Third Republic was equality before the law, which the actions of the High Command undermined. No domestic law was broken in Iraq,

---

90. 'Mirror, Mirror on the War', *American Interest*, 2006, pp. 41–53.

but for sixty years the United States had based its world leadership on the principle that in international relations states should be treated as equals, according to rules applicable to all. It did not always act on that principle, and sometimes violated it, but never repudiated and often benefited from it. But the Bush administration's practices of preventive war and indefinite preventive detention undermined the principle, 'claiming in effect a higher law for the United States and negating any general rule of law in the international arena'. Nor had the administration encountered any significant opposition to its stance. 'Put bluntly, most Americans still seem to believe that anything done at home or abroad to make them safe from terrorists is fine regardless of legal niceties.' The war itself would not necessarily lead to disaster. 'The United States has throughout its history enjoyed an extraordinary margin for error in international affairs and probably still has enough to handle this one.'[91] A common muddling-through outcome was quite possible. Why then bring in all this history?

The Dreyfus affair had ended as well as it did because it occurred during the best years of the Third Republic, when relative prosperity and an improved international position 'helped make a surface resolution possible'. But that was all it was. It did not answer the underlying question the affair had posed, whether the Republic would remain true to its ideals. After the Great War had drained France's reserves of energy and civic unity, and Germany overwhelmed it in 1940, the country's highest values became saving the government's authority and the army's honour, at the cost of civil and political liberties and the fate of the nation's Jews. Therewith the Vichy regime wrote 'the last tragic and shameful chapter of the Dreyfus Affair'. After the war De Gaulle wrote of its leaders, overgenerously

---

91. Ibid.

but with deep insight, that they had thought too much of Frenchmen and too little of France. 'Too little that is, about what France really stood for.' That was a tragedy Americans should ponder. It was easier to be hopeful about America's chances of escaping its current debacle relatively unscathed than about its longer-range future. Christ's saying in Luke stood as a warning: 'If they do this when the wood is green, what will happen when it is dry?'[92]

Throughout, from the Gulf War to the Surge, Schroeder's punctual political interventions in these years were informed by his historical scholarship in a way without counterpart in the commentary on current events elsewhere in the profession. They were written for a broad public. But he did not fail to extend the same political stance to a more general comparative perspective, characteristically placing the war on Iraq in a theoretical framework informed by his command of modern history. The concluding essay of *Systems, Stability and Statecraft*, 'The Mirage of Empire and the Promise of Hegemony', written a few days before US troops reached Baghdad, conjoined just this trio of concerns. The fate of that collection must have been a disappointment to him: intellectually the most brilliant production that ever appeared under his name, ranging over the full arc of his many gifts and interests, its reception was close to zero — just one notice, a little over a page in length, though warm and discerning, was all.[93] Three years later Schroeder developed that final essay into a richer and fuller version, over double the length, with a significant alteration of its title: 'From Hegemony to Empire: The Fatal Leap'.[94]

---

92. Ibid.

93. By Lothar Höbelt of Vienna, terming Schroeder 'probably the foremost expert on the history of international politics in the world'; *International History Review*, June 2006, pp. 402–4.

94. In I. William Zartman (ed.), *Imbalance of Power: US Hegemony and*

By now it was clear that the War on Terror and the invasion of Iraq had proved a fiasco, and Obama was president. Schroeder judged his administration unlikely to continue this failed venture, although also unlikely to 'acknowledge failure and abandon the venture', rather than simply redirecting US goals and strategies. What the attack on Iraq had amounted to was a US bid for empire, instead of hegemony. The two were conceptually and practically quite distinct, even if the boundaries between them could at times be blurred. Empire was the imperative control, formal or informal, of one power over other communities, where hegemony was the leadership of one state acknowledged by others without negating their independence, and typically conferring benefits if also some constraints on them. The first was incompatible with the modern international system; the second was not. Hegemonies were often tempted to become empires, and could yield to the temptation; but they could equally resist it. Since the sixteenth century, Europe had known a succession of hegemonic rulers who had overreached themselves, attempting to build empires – Charles V, Philip II, Ferdinand II, Louis XIV, Charles XII, as in more recent times Napoleon, Hitler and Stalin, each accorded a pithy description. None of their would-be empires had lasted. By contrast, rulers or states that declined this path – Richelieu, Leopold I, Fleury, Bismarck – had not come to grief in the same way. In recent times, the most obvious and impressive example was the US option for hegemony rather than empire in the West after the Second World War.

There was no basis to the claim by apologists for the Bush Doctrine that the world had changed so much after 9/11 that the distinction between these two contrasted forms of power ceased

---

International Order, Boulder–London 2009, pp. 61–87.

to hold. The opposite was the case. Conditions had changed, but in such a way as to render impossible emulation even of those empires of the past which had been successful for a time. British conquest and occupation of Egypt in the nineteenth century, which had lasted down to and beyond the First World War, showed all the reasons why America could not hope to repeat the experience in the same region in the twenty-first century. The country was still mired in Iraq. Could it change course constructively? Britain pursued a selfish policy of defending and expanding its empire against Napoleon until continual setbacks on the continent taught it that victory could only be achieved by leadership of a consensual coalition making common cause against him. Had the US applied that lesson in 2003, by rallying a broad and willing coalition to isolate and deter Saddam rather than seeking to invade and topple him, it would have acted as a responsible hegemon. At this late hour, could it recover such a position? It was impossible to say; in pessimistic moments, he thought it might now be too fatally compromised; in more optimistic moods, he felt there was a reasonable chance of rehabilitation. All that was clear was that 'sane hegemonic leadership in the international community' was the only viable road to follow.

Published in expanded form after Bush had left the White House, Schroeder's argument belonged to the time of Bush's tenure of it, during which the text originated, adjusted six years later to a more sceptical tone about his homeland.[95] Under Obama, perhaps out of

---

95. The first sentence of the original version read: 'No one can doubt that the United States is currently the leading power in the world, and few at least in the United States would disagree that it needs to exercise world leadership in some fashion.' In the revised version, this became: 'Most people consider the United States the leading power in the world, and most of its citizens believe it should exercise

relief, perhaps exhaustion, he wrote no more about contemporary US foreign policy. Instead, in his one address about America's role in the world, he sought to situate its first 175 years within the larger history of the West, not in a particularly flattering light.[96] The country had won independence and expanded its territory with no more than a mediocre military performance, and had never defeated a major external enemy, save Japan, without powerful allies. The condition of its rise was the creation in Europe of the international system that came into being after Napoleon, when the Pax Britannica brought stability and free trade to much of the world outside Europe, from which American commerce and diplomacy benefited; while the Vienna settlement brought peace to Europe itself, above all its Eastern wing where the three great military monarchies of Russia, Austria and Prussia avoided major war between themselves, with two brief exceptions, for a century and a half. This in a period when the United States, without ever facing a serious foreign threat, 'carried out an unprecedentedly rapid and extensive course of territorial expansion, marked by aggressive war, treaty violations, ethnic cleansing, coercive diplomacy and widespread organized and spontaneous violence'. In effect, 'an important reason for America's easy and inexpensive success at territorial expansion despite the attendant illegality and violence was the restrained, law-abiding character of European international politics'. Geopolitically, rough-house American success was a function of peace-abiding European progress. In that sense

---

world leadership.' In the same paragraph, 'The current pursuit of American empire is undermining the chances for a useful, benign American hegemony', became 'has already undermined' the 'possibility of a useful American hegemony'.

96. 'Europe's Progress, and America's Success, 1760–1850', in Frederick Schneid (ed.), *The Projection and Limitations of Imperial Powers, 1618–1850*, Leiden 2012, pp. 170–95.

the US was for most of its history, diplomatically speaking, a rentier state – that is, one 'living off and profiting from the capital accrued from the struggles and achievements of others', confident that the contribution of its values, ideals and example to the general welfare of the world justified it in doing so.[97] There was nothing unusual or shocking about that. But Americans should be aware that the age of their earlier good fortune was over. The tide that carried the nation so irresistibly forward to greatness had long been ebbing, and could now be running in the opposite direction.

Last Thoughts

In the spring of 2010 Schroeder gave the substance of this essay as a talk at UCLA and the following day came for supper, together with some other friends, a convivial evening in the course of which the First World War came up. About that, it was clear we disagreed. He told us he had written a review of Niall Ferguson's *Pity of War*, which I looked up after he went back to Illinois, and dropped him a note about, attaching a notice of the book I had written taking a different view, to which he wrote a lively reply. Thereafter we corresponded at irregular intervals about his ideas, from our contrasted standpoints; he as a Burkean conservative, I an unreconstructed Jacobin. When I remarked to him that I was struck by the greater affinity of his outlook with the so-called English School of international relations than with any American trend, he readily agreed, stipulating only that Michael Oakeshott had also been very important to him:

---

97. 'Europe's Progress and America's Success', pp. 190, 195.

I am usually labelled by others, especially realist IR theorists, as a liberal internationalist. (Others say I'm a Hegelian.) I would deny it, though not vigorously, because I agree with both and with constructivists on many points and in many conclusions we currently draw, but basically I do not have a liberal bone in my body (as you have noticed from our discussions) while appreciating the invaluable contribution a sane liberalism makes to human development and progress. What I think I am is an old-fashioned Burkean conservative – presently especially in the USA an endangered species on which the so-called conservatives have declared open warfare and are waging a war of extinction. This means that if I had to name a school I belong to, it would be precisely the English school – Bull, Martin Wight, Adam Watson, Herbert Butterfield, M. S. Anderson and others.[98]

In the spring of 2016, I asked him if he would be willing to entertain the idea of an interview covering his formation, career and work, intended to 'explain to readers at large the background to your practice and proposals as a historian, starting with your first book and extending beyond *Systems, Stability, and Statecraft* to your subsequent writing, on the Iraq War and other topics.' Offering to send him a brief sketch of the kind of questions I had in mind, I noted that there were certainly others more suitable, and better qualified than myself for the task, and if the idea were in principle acceptable to him and they were available, I would be more than pleased. He replied that he would consider the proposal, 'a welcome bolt from the blue in the midst of a torrent of unpleasant junk in this crazy and interminable election season', but without any commitment to it.[99] His personal feelings about being interviewed were like those of Andrei Gromyko, he said, who told an enquiring journalist he wasn't interested in himself. I sent him a list of possible topics and questions,

---

98. 22 August 2015.
99. 28 and 29 March 2016.

to which he answered that he was willing to proceed, but needed to know the format of such an interview and its possible publication. It would take a series of sessions, I replied, which might then appear as a book along the lines of one done with Raymond Williams in the 1970s, or more recently Suleiman Mourad, historian of Islam. But that would be for him to decide.

The project would have to wait till the following year, he wrote back, due to family commitments but also to two things on which he had been 'working at a snail's pace more out of a feeling of duty that sane people ought to be saying something when so much craziness is being said and done'. One was 'a long proposal for a relatively short book on the European international system from the late 18c to about 1923, entitled "WWI and the Vienna Settlement: The Last 18c War and the First Modern Peace"', which he had yet to complete but when ready would send me for the interviews. The other was 'a relatively short article on the current political crisis in the USA', entitled 'An Organized Hypocrisy', applying 'to the GOP what Bright, Lloyd George and others said about the 19c Tories'.[100] That was in the process of revision, for a tight deadline. After raising a quizzical eyebrow at the idea of 'Trump and Salisbury as bedfellows', if surely a caricature of what he was going to say, I said I looked forward to the piece, and when it arrived, wrote him a longish, friendly but critical response, suggesting he might be overly alarmist about the Republican Party. Shortly afterwards, the article appeared in the *American Interest*. In it he wrote that the Republican Party, wanting to reduce the Democratic Party 'to a size where it could be drowned in a bathtub', was 'so mired in organized hypocrisy it can only offer fearmongering, bombastic rhetoric, and empty promises'. For their part, 'Democrats ought to

---

100. 8 July 2016.

be sensible enough to know that they need a serious Republican Party as a rival if the American political system is to work over the longer term.' That required them to have three goals in mind. 'The first is to defeat Trump, which seems easy at first blush but may not prove to be so. The second, more difficult, is to wrest control of the Senate and if possible the House from the GOP. The third goal, however, is to help the GOP by means of these defeats to return to its senses and restore it as a normal, sane, reform-minded conservative party.'[101] This was the last text he ever published, and the only one devoted entirely to the domestic politics of his country.

'The election results have been devastating for me,' he confessed the following year. He did not now feel ready for interviews. The same message contained a surprise, casting an unexpected light on possible changes in his outlook. 'I have just read Wolfgang Streeck's *How Will Capitalism End?* Very interesting and impressive, I thought; I suppose you know it. It would be good to talk about it and other related works sometime. I suppose my general reaction is that I agree with his general analysis but remain slightly more optimistic about finding our way through it.'[102] Once back again in the States in 2018, I told him I was retiring from UCLA and asked if the interviews would be possible now. He explained that after his wife sustained a serious injury, they had been obliged to move from Illinois to Pennsylvania, where one of his daughters lived, but a further series of setbacks in the family had prevented him from getting much done. Perhaps he could do them the following year. In June 2019, he wrote me that though frail, medically he had been given a clean bill of health, and they could start by Skype in July. A first biographical session was

---

101. 'An Organized Hypocrisy', *American Interest*, 19 September 2016, pp. 43–4.
102. 6 January 2017.

completed. In August he told me the sleep disorder from which he had been suffering had worsened, but sent me his draft on the First World War, 'now just a supplement to some other things I've published and no longer a book proposal'.[103] Then in October he wrote me that his insomnia had become so severe that he didn't think he could continue. To his regret, 'it looks as if it will not work out'. A year later he died; it was another year before I learnt of his death.

The draft he had sent me was based on an address he gave at High Point University, North Carolina, in February 2015. There, I later learnt, he asked his audience whether it was worth pursuing a final book on the First World War at his advanced age, to which the answer was a unanimous yes. It is the longest text he ever produced on the subject, and corresponds to what may have been a customary form for him. For in November 1988, some two years before submitting *The Transformation of European Politics* to OUP, he wrote to them saying he had completed 'something between a very long, full outline and a draft of the entire book',[104] a description which captures rather accurately 'World War I and the Vienna System: The Last Eighteenth-Century War and the First Modern Peace' as he left it. His intention with it differed somewhat, since it aimed not only to be taken seriously by scholars but to appeal to an educated lay readership. 'My main reason and motive for trying to write the book at this late stage in my life is not the usual academic one. It derives instead from a conviction that certain things on this subject need saying, above all to a wider public and especially in America' – and in 'today's world situation'.[105]

---

103. 23 August 2019.
104. Letter to OUP, 23 November 1988.
105. 'World War I and the Vienna System', pp. 5, 3. Now collected in Paul Schroeder, *Stealing Horses to Great Applause: The Origins of the First World War Reconsidered*, London–New York 2025.

His purpose was simple: if you want to understand how a durable peace can be constructed and sustained, study the Vienna system; if you want to understand how wars can occur and international systems break down, study the First World War. So the text would be comparative: divided into a first half dealing with the former, a second half with the latter.

In resuming his case for the Concert of Europe that maintained peace until the Crimean War, Schroeder introduced a self-criticism. He had overdone his attack on the notion of a balance of power as playing any causal role in peace after Napoleon, in two ways. Some kind of balance between the powers was inherent in any multistate system, since without it, there would be a single power controlling a universal empire. It was also true that he had tended to accept uncritically, if rejecting its current usage, the *Realpolitik* assumption that meaningful power could only be 'hard', that is, dependent on coercion. But there was the 'soft' power of values and traditions, which the Concert had classically deployed too. It was also true that he had not explored with a detail comparable to its rise the reasons for its eventual fall. There the key probably lay in the general tendency of all human institutions to suffer over time from the fatality of entropy.

Turning to the origins of the First World War, Schroeder noted the publication of a range of important bodies of research since he had last written on the question, qualifying the one-sided, if otherwise justified, emphasis by Fischer on Germany's responsibility for its outbreak: works by Stefan Schmidt, Sean McMeekin, Dominic Lieven and others, showing the part that France and Russia had played in it. Most influential of all had been Christopher Clark's best-seller *The Sleepwalkers*, which 'provided the alternative narrative needed', and with whose critique of the paradigm dominant in recent years Schroeder agreed.[106] He himself had consistently argued that the Great War was a 'natural and predictable, though not strictly inevitable, outcome of the international game then being played by almost every power involved, large middle and small'. Until near the end, there had been one exception, Austro-Hungary, mainly because 'its government recognized that it was too threatened externally and challenged internally to compete successfully or even to survive as a great power' in this game, which resembled 'a version of poker that permitted and incentivized players not only to make risky bids for huge prizes, but also to join secretly or openly with as many other players as possible, coordinating their strategies for maximizing their gains and compelling their opponents to accept losses' or be driven out of the game altogether.[107] The mere prospect of such an outcome, giving one side an insurmountable superiority over the other, led with high probability to a general systemic war, which could only be stopped by changing the rules of the game. Only Austria had tried that, over Bosnia, and it had failed. Instead a tide of reckless policies and actions had swept all the Great Powers towards the endgame, in which middle and smaller powers – Italy, Serbia, Bulgaria, Greece, Romania, even the Ottoman Empire – had eagerly joined. The resulting 'collective tide of recklessness swept the European ship of state onto the reef'.[108]

This was Schroeder's interpretation of 1914, not Clark's, but the latter's work portrayed the outbreak of the war in much the

---

106. 'World War I and the Vienna System', p. 23.
107. Ibid., pp. 24–5.
108. Ibid., p. 26.

same way. Where they differed was in their view of the mind-set of the elite that plunged Europe into war. They agreed that none of the key decision-makers were deliberate warmongers, but as noted earlier, the image of blind 'sleepwalkers' was misleading. The more accurate metaphor would be to say they moved towards what was disaster for all of them, in the American phrase 'with eyes wide shut'.[109] Sleepwalking was unconscious behaviour — that of someone waking up at night to find themselves out in the street, not knowing how they had got out of bed or why. That was not how actors played the international game that led to the war. They had behaved in a way familiar to everyone in daily life: acting with eyes wide open and steadily fixed on a goal in highly purposive style, alert to the reactions of others insofar as they might affect that goal, but with eyes firmly closed to the broader consequences of such action for the wider community and general system to which it might belong. This kind of behaviour, Schroeder added, needed no special explanation. It was a normal aspect of individual and collective action encountered in all sorts and arenas of activity — a large part of what we do as human beings, which we can often recognize in ourselves. But it could be guarded against, and under the Vienna system it was. In the descent towards the Great War it was not. No actor in the system gave any thought to what the consequences of the deletion of Austro-Hungary from it were likely to be. Sensing this, Austro-Hungary rebelled against the system, only to bring itself down with the system. Before the war, Russia, Italy, Serbia and Romania had all wanted to destroy it, and during the war France and England fell in with their aims. The result? In 1918 Austro-Hungary received its quietus. The war itself, moreover,

---

109. Ibid., p. 353.

however ruinous it became, was too short for the Allies to learn the lessons the victors had done from the much longer struggle against Napoleon. So Versailles was no Vienna. In the vacuum left by the extinction of the Habsburg Empire, Central and Eastern Europe became the spoils of the foreseeable battle between Germany and Russia to dominate them.[110] So it became, once again, the triggerzone for the next world war.

All this was of urgent relevance today. With the end of the Cold War, an international system like that of Vienna, 'intentionally designed to limit, control, and manage competition and conflict and thereby promote cooperation and overall peace and stability' could have been constructed. Instead a blinkered *Realpolitik* prevailed, 'ignoring the opportunity to expand the European Union to include Russia or form links with it after the downfall of the USSR, in favour of expanding NATO to the borders of a shrunken, chaotic and humiliated Russia, or the decision to invade Iraq'.[111] Worse, there was now an obvious elephant in the room too, 'the war of climate change that the world has long been waging against nature itself'. In that war victory as normally defined was inconceivable: the only tolerable outcome was a stable worldwide truce and coexistence with the forces of nature, impossible without the development of a better, more comprehensive and durable, international system. That was 'a danger and a task that trumped all others'.[112] The challenge it posed was very different from that which faced Europe in 1812, one that was far more complex and demanding, for which no one could suggest the Vienna system as a model or blueprint; and it was a problem that had a special bearing in the US, given 'the

---

110. Ibid., p. 103.
111. Ibid., p. 111.
112. Ibid., pp. 112–13.

exceptionalism so deeply rooted in America's history, institutions and popular culture, especially in its current debased and dangerous form', and 'the extraordinary provincialism, self-preoccupation, and superficiality this entails in world affairs'. Of all major countries in the world, the United States was most in need of confronting the task, yet 'least disposed and equipped by its history, self-image, basic outlook and current political institutions and habits, to do so'.[113]

The singularity of Schroeder as a historian, and a man, lies open on the page in this final text. He had a strong moral sensibility, one that impelled him to intervene publicly on political issues of his time, with the trenchancy and precision of his professional scholarship, in ways that few contemporaries did. He combined a notable sense of responsibility as a citizen with a good sense of humour as a person. He was intellectually very self-confident, but without airs or pretension of any kind: a complete lack of vanity describes his personal style. He shunned all conventional forms of publicity, part of the reason for being so relatively inconspicuous outside the academy. He was a conservative, and remained one to the end, but would prove more humane in outlook than many a self-declared liberal. He was a patriot, if one who became critical of his country; and from the beginning, the opposite of parochial – not just as a Europeanist, but as an observer of the world.

Among historians he was closest in stance to Kennan, who had encouraged him in his youth, and about whom he later wrote appreciatively,[114] though their temperaments were so different: he

---

113. Ibid., p. 114.

114. In a consideration of *The Decline of Bismarck's European Order: Franco-Russian Relations 1875–1890*, published in *Slavic Review*, September 1980, pp. 490–2.

had none of Kennan's self-dramatization, mood-swings or nostalgia, and of course was superior as a scholar. For Kissinger he had little but contempt,[115] and was cool about Ferguson, subsequently Kissinger's apologist. Gaddis, who acclaimed Bush Jr as Prince Hal, he ignored. Among political scientists, he took particular exception to Mearsheimer and in lesser measure to Waltz, as exemplars of the neorealism he disliked, though both were as hostile to US hubris in Iraq and at large as he was himself. These were all writers about the political relations between states. As to the social relations within states, in which international conflict or cooperation was inevitably rooted, Schroeder had much less to say. Out of ideological conservatism or intellectual specialism? At first, no doubt both. But over time, his unswerving decency led him to increasing concern about his own society, and openness to radical questioning of it. In the new century, he could write with admiration of a Marxist study of the origins of the modern state system,[116] while entering entirely pertinent reservations about it, and could consider the notion that capitalism might be nearing its end, without being shocked at the thought.

What set Schroeder finally apart as a scholar, and a mind, was

---

115. 'Can Diplomatic History Guide Foreign Policy?', *International History Review*, May 1996: 'To call Kissinger a fraud because no one could be as profound as he sounds, in person and in print, would be unfair. The gibe is not, however, unfair applied to this book', replete with 'truisms and commonplaces set out in orotund prose', 'assertions and generalizations that sound impressive, but do not withstand critical examination': pp. 358–9.

116. 'Class and the Making of the International System', *European History Quarterly*, Vol. 35, 2005, pp. 119–25, a laudatory review of Benno Teschke's *The Myth of 1648: Class, Geopolitics and the Making of Modern International Relations*, though observing that while both England and France were atypical states in the passage to modernity, in the eighteenth century they pursued common ends in the same international system, rather than representing alternative systems.

the span of his writing across the centuries since the Enlightenment, and the unity of the vision he drew from it. His founding contrast between the eighteenth and nineteenth centuries revolutionized study of the international relations in both, enabling him in due course to link the first systemic war of the twentieth century to the last of the eighteenth, rather than to its predecessor in the nineteenth century, and the order that emerged from the second systemic war of the twentieth century to the peace of the early nineteenth, rather than to the interbellum of the twentieth century; yet ultimately leading him to fear in the emergent conflicts of the twenty-first, a reversion once more to wars of pre-revolutionary stamp. Schroeder abhorred lazy analogies, and the curve of his work eschews them; each connexion was grounded in close attention to the detail of its epochs. In the first decade after the end of the Cold War, his reading of the signs of a new world order was liable to an ingenuous optimism, as he was aware himself. In the second, it was subject to a sharp correction, culminating in something close to, but never quite, despair. It is not difficult to imagine his verdict on the war in Ukraine. His final text makes it clear, nevertheless, that he had not abandoned hope in the *longue durée* – provided there was one.

ACKNOWLEDGEMENTS

For critical comment on one or several of these essays, I would like to thank especially: Holger Afflerbach, Klaus Grosse Kracht, Thomas Meaney, Geoffrey Parker, Anders Stephanson and Françoise Waquet.

For research in the *Bundesarchiv* in Koblenz, and holdings of the universities of Berlin (Humboldt) and Hamburg, I am very grateful to Leona Pröpper; in the Biblioteca Nazionale Braidense of Milan, to Matteo Dapei; and to the help of Michele Salvati and Stefania Grassi with the archives of the *Corriere della Sera*.

For practical or other information about historians discussed in them I am indebted to: John Beeler, Suzanne Belovari, Jakob Borchers, Mark Cornwall, James Davis, Scott McConnell, Gianfranco Finizio, Jonathan Huener, Paul Kennedy, John Mueller, David Murphy, Bernhard Olpen, Frederick Schneid, Hamish Scott, Edward Spiers, Cathryn Steele, David Wetzel and William Zartman.

INDEX

Entries for six historians who are the focus of this book appear in bold

Academy of Social and Moral Sciences, 44
Acheson, Dean, 129
Aehrenthal, Alois von, 30, 77, 308–9
Afflerbach, Holger, 228, 308
Alatri, Paolo, 70, 72
Albertini, Alberto, 50, 53, 69, 72, 73, 90
Albertini, Leonardo, 86–7
Albertini, Luigi, xi–xiv, 49–90, 98, 130, 136–7, 181–3
Alexander I, 212, 246, 268, 277, 280, 291
Alexander III, 212
Ali, Mehmet, 296–7
Al Qaeda, 330, 332, 334
Allain, Jean-Claude, 98
Alvaro, Corrado, 50, 54–55

American Historical Association, 7, 263, 265
American Interest (journal), 338, 348
American Political Science Association, 126–7
American Conservative (journal), 332, 336
Anderson, John, 329
Angeloni, Francesco, 241
Annales school, 38–40, 39n56, 274
Apis (Dimitrijević, Dragutin), 184–5
Appuhn, Charles, 21
Aron, Raymond, 39
Asendorf, Manfred, 105, 123, 133
Asquith, Herbert Henry, 13, 163, 170, 174, 204
Aulard, Alphonse, 8, 46

INDEX

Austrian Orange Book, 79
Atkin, Nicholas, viii–ix

Bach, Alexander von, 249
Badel, Laurence, 20, 34
Balfour, Arthur, 152
Barié, Ottavio, 53, 72, 88
Barker, Ernest, 126
Barnes, Harry Elmer, 23, 24
Barraclough, Geoffrey, 14
Basch, Victor, 15
Bathurst, Lilias Margaret, Countess, 163
Beales, Derek, 288
Beard, Charles, 333
Becker, Annette, 10
Becker, Jacques, 10
Beer, Samuel, 128
Belgioioso, Cristina Trivulzio di, 244, 280
Benda, Julien, 26
Bentham, Jeremy, 288
Berchtold, Leopold Graf von, 187
Bem, Józef, 241n65
Bethmann Hollweg, August von, 106–7
Bethmann Hollweg, Theobald von, 13, 94, 101–2, 106–7, 107, 123, 132, 201, 230
Bibliothèque et Musée de la guerre (BMG), 8, 11, 20
Biddiss, Michael, viii–ix

Biden, Joseph, 256, 337
Bin Laden, Osama, 334
Bismarck, Otto von, 18, 31, 41, 91–2, 102, 108, 116, 153, 168, 172, 190, 197–8, 212–3, 223, 241–2, 250, 267, 271, 292, 300–2, 306, 308, 309, 312, 315, 343
Black Hand, 184–5, 331
Blanning, Tim, 273, 292, 302, 305
Blanqui, Louis Auguste, 235, 244
Bloch, Camille, 26
Bloch, Marc, 38–9
Blum, Robert, 235, 239, 244, 260
Bobbio, Norberto, 253
Boers, 151, 176–7, 198, 223
Bolsheviks, 59, 64, 119
Bombosch, Wolfgang, 133
Bonomi, Ivanoe, 66
Bormann, Martin, 117
Bosworth, Richard, 53, 60
Botzenhart, Erich, 102, 124
Bourdieu, Pierre, 45
Brandt, Willy, 99
Braudel, Fernand, 38–40, 39, 45, 109
Bridge, Roy, 166
Bright, John, 348
British Gazette, 173–4
British Journal of International Studies, 150
Broch, Hermann, 232
Brunner, Otto, 134

Büchner, Georg, 235
Bullen, Roger, 166, 166n36
Bullock, Alan, 85,
Bülow, Bernhard von, 77, 198–9, 221
Bund Oberland, 101, 112, 133
Buonarroti, Philippe, 235, 241, 244
Bush, George H. W., 323
Bush, George W., 334–5, 341, 344, 356
Butterfield, Herbert, 310

Cadorna, Luigi, 61–3
Caillaux, Joseph, 19
Calvin, John, 103
Cambridge University, 45, 181–2
Campbell, Alec, 140n3
Campbell-Bannerman, Henry, 164
Carnegie Endowment for International Peace, 11, 26, 29
Cartel des Gauches, 16, 19
Carter, Jimmy, 329
Cassirer, Ernst, 125
Castlereagh, Robert Steward, Viscount, 167, 172, 246, 277, 279, 283–4, 290–1, 292, 301
Catherine II, 285–6
Cattaneo, Carlo, 244
Cavour, Camillo Benso, Count of, 51, 52, 249, 256
Cecil, Gwendolen, 178
Chabod, Federico, 39

Chamberlain, Joseph, Lord, 153, 223, 315
Chandler, Raymond, 149
Charlemagne, Emperor, 116
Charles V, 343
Charles X, 234, 280
Charles XII, 343
Chatelet, François, 39
Christian-Democratic Party, 99–100, 130, 131
Churchill, Winston, 14, 145, 173–4, 174n41, 283, 334
Clark, Christopher, xiv–xvi, 181–261, 351–2
Claudel, Paul, 30
Clay, Lucius, 127, 129
Clemenceau, Georges, 13, 28n45, 267–8
Clinton, Hillary, 335, 337
Colarizi, Simona, 68, 72
Committee of Imperial Defence, 164
Conservative Party, 91–2, 164, 202, 205–6
Conti, Mario Sergio, 259
Conze, Werner, 134
Coolidge, Calvin, 1–2
Cornelissen, Christoph, 133
Cornell University, 128, 265
Cornwall, Mark, 209
Corriere della Sera (newspaper), 49–50, 52, 53n6, 54–5n9, 58, 61, 63, 67–73, 77, 87–8

Council of Europe, 211–3
Council of Foreign Ministers, 129
Craig, Gordon, 128
Crédit Lyonnais, 19
Crispi, Francesco, 51–2
Croly, Herbert, 11
Crowe, Eyre, 146–7, 149, 153, 203
Cru, Norton, 29
Curato, Federico, 59
Curzon, George, 163, 165, 180, 313

Daily Mail, 50–1
Daily Telegraph, 163
D'Annunzio, Gabriele, 54–5, 57–8, 64, 70
Davis, James W., 310
De Gaulle, Charles, 36–7, 43–4, 257, 341
Dehio, Ludwig, 93, 97
Delcassé, Théophile, 18, 190, 191
Démar, Claire, 234
Demartial, Georges, 14–7, 33
Democratic Party, 348
Depretis, Agostino, 51–2
Deroin, Jeanne, 234
Der Spiegel (journal), 130
Deuxième Bureau, 20
Dewey, John, 253, 329
Diaz, Armando, 63
Dickens, Charles, 233–4
Di Felice, Renzo, 65

Die Welt (newspaper), 104
Die Zeit (newspaper), 104, 207–8
Dönitz, Karl, 36
Dreyfus, Alfred, 15, 45–6, 339–41
Duggan, Christopher, 56
Duke University, 128
Dulles, John Foster, 129
Durkheim, Émile, 23
Duroselle, Jean-Baptiste, 38, 44–5, 47

École des Sciences Politiques, 39
École Pratique des Hautes Etudes, 39
Éditions Rieder, 25
Edward VII, 197–8
Einaudi, Luigi, 54, 71
Eisenhower, Dwight, 129, 329
Elman, Colin, 300
Elman, Miriam, 300
Epstein, Klaus, 97
Erdmann, Karl-Dietrich, 122
Erhard, Ludwig, 130
European Defence Community, 129
European Union, 124, 231, 317, 319, 354

Fabre-Luce, Alfred, 17–20, 32–3,
Facta, Luigi, 66
Fascist Party, 66–7, 69, 257, 321
Fay, Sidney Bradshaw, xiv, 2–5,

INDEX 365

10–1, 21, 24–5, 27–8, 98, 136, 182–3
Febvre, Lucien, 38–40
Ferdinand II, 235, 343
Ferdinand VII, 291
Ferguson, Niall, 177, 316–7, 318, 321, 346, 355–6
Finizio, Giancarlo, 63, 75
Fischer, Fritz, xii–xiv, 91–138, 161–2, 181, 189, 207–9, 316, 351
Fitzgerald, Ella, 149
Flandin, Pierre-Étienne, 38
Fleury, André-Hercule, Cardinal de, 343
Fleutot, François Marin, 38
Ford Foundation, 39
Franco, Francisco, 43
Frank, Robert, 34, 37
Frank, Walter, 102–3, 107–8, 110, 113, 117, 124
Frankfurter Allgemeine Zeitung (newspaper), 104, 207–8
Frankfurter Rundschau (newspaper), 104
Franz Ferdinand, Archduke of Austria, viii, 3–4, 77, 100n17, 184
Franz Joseph I, of Austria, 239, 240–1, 244–5
Frederick II, 31, 285–6
Freedom Convoy, 259
Free France, 43–4
Free University of Berlin, 181–2

Friedrich, Carl, 127, 128
Fukuyama, Francis, 338
Futurists, 56

Gaddis, John Lewis, 356
Garbe, Daniel, 33
Garibaldi, Giuseppe, 51–2, 240
Garner, Jay, 336
Geiss, Imanuel, 105, 130, 132
Gentz, Friedrich, 172, 289–90
George V, 28, 197–8
Gérin, René, 16, 33
Gerstenmeier, Eugen, 130
Gestapo, 34, 38
Gide, Charles, 14, 30
Gioberti, Vincenzo, 249
Giolitti, Giovanni, 52–5n9, 57–60, 63, 65–6, 68
Girardet, Raoul, 46n68
Gladstone, William, 164, 314–5
Goede, Arnt, 124, 125
Goerdeler, Carl Friedrich, 100n18
Goethe, Johann Wolfgang von, 125
Goethe Institute, 99
Gooch, John, 62
Gorbachev, Mikhail, 322–3
Government Affairs Institute (GAI), 126, 126n53, 127, 128, 128n56, 129
Grenville, John (Guhrauer, Hans), 140, 178
Grew, Joseph, 266

Grey, Sir Edward, 6–7, 80–2, 86, 143, 146, 151–7, 159, 162, 170, 174, 175–8, 202–6, 223, 230
Gromyko, Andrei, 347
Grosse Kracht, Klaus, 100, 103–6, 112, 121, 131,132, 135
Guerrini, Irene, 62
Guieu, Jean-Michael, 40
Guiso, Andrea, 63
Guizot, François, 235–6, 244, 246–7, 249
Gwynne, H. A., 163, 174

Habermas, Jürgen, 99, 253, 256
Haldane, J. B. S., 174
Halder, Franz, 118
Hamburg University, 102, 110, 115, 122, 124–5
Hamerow, Theodore, 324
Hamilton, Lord George 180
Hankey, Maurice, 164
Hardenberg, Karl August von, 246, 277
Harding, Warren, 1–2
Hardinge, Charles, 146, 165, 273
Harjes, Kirsten, 93
Harmsworth, Arthur (Lord Northcliffe), 50, 53
Harmsworth, Harold, 53
Hartwig, Nicholas, 195–6
Hartz, Peter, 260
Harvard University, 2, 127, 128, 220

Havas news agency, 33
H-Diplo, 263
Hecker, Friedrich, 244
Hedtke, Ulrich, 219
Hegel, Georg Wilhelm Friedrich, 125, 288, 315
Heiber, Helmut, 112–3
Heidelberg University, 134
Heller, Hans-Joachim, 176
Hendrickson, David, 330
Herwegh, Georg, 233–4
High Point University, 350
Hinsley, Harry, 151, 162
Hitler, Adolf, xiii, 32, 36, 38, 42–4, 95–7, 100n18, 102–3, 106, 108, 113, 115–6, 118–9, 125, 162, 265–6, 284–5, 343
Hobbes, Thomas, 276
Höbelt, Lothar, 342
Hobson, John A., 215
Holborn, Hajo, 128
Holbraad, Carsten, 290
Hollande, François, 227
Honnorat, André, 8, 21
Honvéd, 240
Hoover, Herbert, 1–2
Hopper, Edward, 149
Hötzendorff, Franz Conrad von, 230
House, Edward M, 'Colonel', 11
Hugo, Victor, 233–4
Humboldt University, 2, 122

Hume, David, 288
Hunt, Lynn, 233–4, 258
Hussein, Saddam, 329–30, 332

Ingram, Edward, 213, 295–6, 297, 314
Ingram, Norman, 16
International History Review (journal), 155–6,
Ipsen, Hans-Peter, 124
Irish Nationalists, 144
Isaac, Jules, 22–6, 28–9, 31–4, 93, 136
Isis Press, 173
Izvolsky, Alexander, 30, 194

Jarrett, Mark, 290, 291
Jaurès, Jean, 15, 23, 25, 30
Jelačić, Josip, Count, 239
Jervis, Robert, 264, 313
Jessen, Ralph, 132
Joffre, Joseph, 230
Johns Hopkins University, 128
Jókai, Mór, 242
Joll, James, 136, 144
Journal of Contemporary History, 111–2
Journal of Modern History, 6
Journal of the Society of Christian Ethics, 321
Jouvenel, Bertrand de, 39

Kagan, Korina, 297
Kanet, Roger, 325
Kant, Immanuel, 288
Karadžić, Radovan, 209
Kaspi, André, 26, 32
Kaufmann, Thomas, 123
Keble College, 140
Kellerhof, Sven Felix, 104
Kennan, George, ix, 266, 332, 355
Kennedy, Paul, 149, 151, 159–60, 163
Kerry, John, 334, 335
Kiesinger, Kurt, 100
Kipling, Rudyard, 163
Kissinger, Henry, 355–6,
Kitchener, Herbert, 176–7
Kokovtsov, Vladimir, 193
Kossuth, Lajos, 235, 240, 244
Krüger, Peter, 199, 223

Labour Party, 14, 126, 175
Lafore, Laurence, 224–5
Lamennais, Félicité de, 244
Lamb, Alastair, 223–4
Langdon, John, viii–ix
Langer, William, 128
Lansdowne, Henry Charles, Marquess of, 143, 151, 164, 203–4
Lappenküper, Ulrich, 299
Laqueur, Thomas, 226
La Réforme (newspaper), 247

Laval, Pierre, 35
Lavisse, Ernest, 15, 46
League of Nations, 1–2, 33, 231
Lebow, Ned, 305
Leeds University, 140, 149, 172
Lenin, Vladimir, 215–16, 218–20, 218, 222
Leopold II, King of Belgium, 14, 283, 304, 343
Levy, Jack, 264
L'Esprit International (journal), 11
l'Humanité (newspaper), 15
Liberal Party, xiii, 51, 148, 152, 164, 202, 246–9, 254–6
Licata, Glauco, 53, 72
Lichnowsky, Karl Max, Prince, 158
Lieven, Dominic, 351
Ligue des Droits de L'Homme, 14–16, 19, 32
Litchfield, Edward, 126–7, 129, 129n59
Lloyd George, David, 13, 30, 139–40, 163–4, 204, 348
Louis Philippe I, 236, 280
Louis XIV, 343
Louis XVIII, 246
Luftwaffe, 108
Luigi, Einaudi, 69
Lukács, Georg, 255
Luther, Martin, 103
Lycée Louis-le-Grand, 8
Lyttleton, Adrian, 60, 70

Machtan, Lothar, 208
Mack Smith, Dennis, 58, 315
Macron, Emmanuel, 227
Magrini, Luciano, 75, 82
Magyars, 241
Maistre, Joseph de 288
Mann, Michael, 40
Manteuffel, Hasso von, 249
Marley, Charles, 173
Martel, Gordon, viii–ix, 208, 226
Marx, Karl, 215, 238, 241–2, 256
Massey, Isabella, 76, 79, 86
Mathiez, Albert, 46
Matteotti, Giacomo, 71–2
Matthew, H. C. G., 177
May, Ernest, 300
Mayer, Arno, 229
Mazzini, Giuseppe, 51, 59, 235, 240, 244, 252
McKinley, William, 220
McMeekin, Sean, 351
Mead, Walter Russell, 338
Mearsheimer, John, 356
Meinecke, Friedrich, 93
Melograni, Piero, 68
Metternich, Klemens, von, 116, 167, 172, 212, 214, 235–6, 244, 246, 267–9, 277, 279, 283, 288, 290–1, 300, 302, 313
Mill, John Stuart, 253
Milner, Alfred, 223
Ministry of Education, 115–6

INDEX 369

Mobile Guards, 238
Moltke, Helmuth von, 86, 95, 201, 230, 313
Mombauer, Annika, viii–ix, 94n5
Mommsen, Wolfgang, 97
Monger, David, 151
Montgelas, Maximilian von, 226
Monzali, Luciano, 70
Morel, Edmund, 13–4
Morgenthau, Hans, 128
Morning Post, 163, 173, 174
Mourad, Suleiman, 347–8
Mueller, John, 326
Mussolini, Benito, xii, 38, 66–7, 69–73, 70n28, 88, 89, 119

Napoleon I, 6, 116, 125, 142, 166, 202, 211, 222, 244, 255, 268, 276–7, 279n16, 281–7, 289, 296, 311, 313, 317–20, 343–5, 351, 353
Napoleon III, 166, 167–8, 215, 239–41, 245, 271
Narváez, Pánfilo de, 236, 249
National Bloc, 66, 68
National Foundation of Political Sciences, 44
National Guard, 236–7
National Liberals, 91–2
Navy League, 5
Nazi Party (NSDAP), 93, 100–1, 104, 106–11, 112, 115–16, 123n47, 124, 126, 132–3, 134, 136, 232, 257, 316–7, 321, 331
Neilson, Keith, 178–80, 208
Neumann, Franz, 128
New Republic (journal), 11
Newton, Douglas, 177
New York Review of Books, 233–4
New York Times, 233
Nicholas I, 167, 193, 196, 212, 245, 280
Nicholas II, 13, 18, 30, 197–8, 240–1
Nicolovius, Georg Heinrich, 106–7,
Nitti, Francesco Saverio, 65, 67
Nizan, Paul, 25
Nora, Pierre, 45–7
Norddeutscher Rundfunk (broadcaster), 133
North Atlantic Treaty Organization, 323, 354
North German Federation, 302
Notre Dame University, 128–30

Oakeshott, Michael, 346–7
Obama, Barack, 189, 344–5
Oelke, Harry, 123
Office of Strategic Services (OSS), 7
Olpen, Bernhard, 105–6, 109, 112, 133
Oncken, Johann Gerhard, 133
Orlando, Vittorio, 13, 62, 65, 89

370   INDEX

Otte, Thomas, 147, 159, 178
Oxford University, xiii, 5, 6n8, 91, 126, 136, 140, 149, 175, 295, 302–4

Paddock, Troy, viii–ix
Paléologue, Maurice, 26, 78–80, 192
Palmerston, Viscount, 162, 241, 267–8, 270, 283, 312–3, 315
Panofsky, Erwin, 125
Parker, Geoffrey, 305
Pašić, Nikola, 184–5, 214
Peel, Sir Robert, 249
Péguy, Charles, 23–5, 30
Pentagon, 129n59, 330
Pentarchy, 167, 186, 321
Pericles, 113
Pétain, Philippe, xi, 33, 35–6, 43–4
Petőfi, Sándor, 233–4
Petraeus, David, 337
Petzold, Stephan, 110–2, 132
Philip II, 343
Piketty, Thomas, 260
Pio Nono, 235, 239–40
Pitt, William, Earl of Chatham, 334
Pleyer, Kleo, 108, 112–3, 112–4, 116–7, 124
Pluviano, Marco, 62
Poincaré, Raymond, xi, 6–7n10, 13, 16, 18, 20–2, 26–8, 30, 32, 41, 79, 80, 191–3, 230
Prague University, 112

Princeton University, 128
Progressive Party, 91–2
Pyta, Wolfram, 270, 299

Radetzky, Johann, Graf von, 239, 244–5
Radical Party, 56–7, 143–5, 148–9, 184, 202, 281
Raffalovitch, Arthur, 21n34
Ranke Society, 124
Rath, John, 265, 267
Rawls, John, 253
Reagan, Ronald, 329
Red Army, 36
Reichsmarine, 199
Reichstag, 92, 197–9, 221
Rein, Adolf, 108, 112, 114–6, 118, 124–6
Remak, Joachim, 301
Renouvin, Jacques, 37–8
Renouvin, Michel, 38,
Renouvin, Pierre, x–xi, xiv, 1–47, 93, 98–9, 137, 181
Republican Party (US), 1, 348, 349
Resistance (French), 33–4, 36–8
Revue des deux mondes, 11, 22
Revue Historique, 28–9, 34, 46
Ribbentrop, Joachim von, 100
Richelieu, Cardinal, 31, 343
Ritter, Gerhard, 93, 97, 98, 100, 100n18, 122, 132–3n62
Robbins, Keith, 151

Rochau, Ludwig von, 241–2
Rockefeller Foundation, 39
Röhl, John, 100
Rolland, Romain, 25
Rommel, Erwin, 118–9
Roosevelt, Theodore, 41, 220, 265
Rosebery, Archibald Primrose, Earl of, 176n44
Rosenberg, Alfred, 117n38
Rosencrance, Richard, 300
Rousseau, Frédéric, 29
Rousseau, Jean-Jacques, 288
Rousseff, Dilma, 259
Royal Navy, 143, 199
Russell, Bertrand, 253
Russian Army, 192

Sabrow, Martin, 132
Saint Pierre, Charles-Irénée Castel, Abbé de, 288
Salandra, Antonio, 13, 55–8, 60–2, 67
Salisbury, Robert, Marquess of, 41, 146, 152–3, 168–9, 173, 177–8, 202, 223
San Giuliano, Antonio, Marchese di, 82, 83
Sanderson, Claire, 40
Sazonov, Sergei, 13, 78, 86, 192, 194–6, 230
Schieder, Theodor, 134
Schmidt, Helmut, 99, 227

Schmidt, Stefan, 351
Schmitt, Bernadotte Everly, xiv, 2, 4–7, 9, 11–2, 23–5, 98, 136–7, 182–3
Scholz, Olaf, 260
Schorske, Carl, 128
Schneid, Frederick, 342
Schroeder, Paul, xiv–xvi, 181, 221, 227, 263–357
Schuker, Stephen, 208
Schumpeter, Joseph, 218–20, 314
Schwarz, Roberto, 259
Sciences Po, 46
Scott, Hamish, 273
Scott, Sally, 164
Security Council, 260
Seeberg, Erich, 101, 103, 106–7, 123, 133
Seeley, John Robert, 115
Seignobos, Charles, 14
Seton-Watson, Christopher, 51, 67, 70
Shakespeare, William, 307
Shotwell, James, 11, 29
Siegel, Mona, 93
Siegfried, André, 44
Siemann, Wolfram, 267
Sixth Army, 118
Smith, Jean Edward, 129
Snyder, Jack, 313
Socialist Party, 52, 56, 66

372 INDEX

Société d'histoire de la guerre (SHG), 8
Sonnino, Sidney, 57, 60
Sorbonne, xi, 2, 8, 21, 32, 38–9, 47
Souvarine, Boris, 21
Spranger, Eduard, 133
Srbik, Heinrich von, 267
Stalin, Joseph, 114, 129, 343
Stanford University, 128
State Department, 7
Steding, Christoph, 107–8, 133
Steinberg, Jonathan, 97
Steiner, Zara, 146–8, 151, 159, 163, 300
Steinmeier, Frank-Walter, 227
Stevenson, David, 308
Stolypin, Pyotr, 194–6
Strachan, Hew, 208
Strandmann, Hartmut Pogge von, 105, 132
Streeck, Wolfgang, 349
Sturmabteilung (SA), 104, 124, 134
Süddeutsche Zeitung (newspaper), 104
Sukhomlinov, Vladimir, 230
Swedberg, Richard, 219
Swiss Guards, 238–9
Széchenyi, István, Count, 244

Taft, William Howard, 220
Taliban, 331
Talleyrand, Charles Maurice de, 246, 277–8
Tatum, Art, 149

Taylor. A. J. P., 91, 92, 98, 135, 139–40, 273, 282, 314
Teschke, Benno, 356
Thompson, Mark, 60
Thucydides, 2
Thuillier, Guy, 33
The Times, 49, 163
Touraine, Alain, 39
Tournès, Ludovic, 40
Tristan, Flora, 234
Tronchet, Guillaume, 8
Truman, Harry S., 129
Trump, Donald, 259, 349
Tucker, Robert, 330

UCLA, 128, 349
Ullrich, Volker, 104, 207–8
Union of Democratic Control, 14
University of Aberystwyth, 110
University of Bayreuth, 105
University of Berlin, 101, 117
University of Chicago, 2
University of Erlangen, 106
University of Illinois, 268–9
University of Konigsberg, 113
University of Ohio, 305
University of Texas, 265
University of Virginia, 128
US Army, 102
Uttenruthia Verband, 106

Vaillant-Couturier, Paul, 13
Varoufakis, Yanis, 227
Vasquez, John, 300
Väyrynen, Raimo, 299
Victor Emmanuel III, 55
Viviani, René, 79, 80
Voilquin, Suzanne, 234, 244

Walther, Rudolf, 104
Waltz, Kenneth, 299, 356
War Office, 202
Washington Quarterly, 322–3
Wehler, Hans-Ulrich, 207–9
Wehrmacht, 101, 118
Wellington, Arthur, Duke of, 290
Wetzel, David 264, 324
White Book (German government), 22, 79
Wight, Martin, 310
Wilhelm II, 13, 21, 32, 95, 176–7, 181–2, 197, 201, 206
Williams, Raymond, 347–8
Wilson, Harold, 174
Wilson, Sir Henry, 230
Wilson, Keith, xiii–xiv, 139–80, 206, 231,
Wilson, Woodrow, 1–2, 11, 64, 89, 164, 220
Windischgrätz, Alfred, Prince, 239, 244–5
Winkler, Heinrich, 207–8
Witte, Sergei, 193, 195–6
Wright, Quincy, 128

Yale University, 128
Yellow Book (French government), 15, 17, 22, 79

Zametica, John, 209
Zamoyski, Adam, 294
Zartman, I. William, 342
Zechlin, Egmont, 122
Zevin, Alexander, 233, 258–9